Land Resource Economics and Sustainable Development

Land Resource Economics and Sustainable Development presents a pragmatic approach to the issues of land use and sustainable development. Breaking away from the narrow focus of most economics texts on resources, this unique book encompasses current political and ecological concerns, but at the same time provides readers with the essential economic tools for rationally discussing land-use conflicts.

In combining economics with ecology, the book is able to address a wide range of resource issues that have not been discussed in other economics texts. These include soil erosion, wetlands preservation, global climatic change, urban/rural conflict, urban land use, range management, forest management, and management of public land for multiple use. The broad scope and practical perspective of this text make it useful to students, interdisciplinary researchers, and professional economists and managers working in the fields of economic development, the environment, agriculture, and forestry.

G. Cornelis van Kooten is a professor in the departments of Agricultural Economics and Forest Resources Management at the University of British Columbia.

G. Cornelis van Kooten

Land Resource Economics and
Sustainable Development:
Economic Policies and the
Common Good

UBCPress / Vancouver

ISBN 0-7748-0445-9

Canadian Cataloguing in Publication Data

Van Kooten, G.C. (Gerrit C.)
   Land resource economics and sustainable development

   Includes bibliographical references and index.

   ISBN 0-7748-0445-9
1. Sustainable development.   2. Land use – Economic aspects.   3. Economic
policy.   I. Title.

HD75.6.V36 1993   333.715   C93-091228-4

UBC Press gratefully acknowledges the ongoing support to its publishing program
from the Canada Council, the Province of British Columbia Cultural Services
Branch, and the Department of Communications of the Government of Canada.

UBC Press
University of British Columbia
6344 Memorial Rd
Vancouver, BC V6T 1Z2
(604) 822-3259
Fax: (604) 822-6083

Contents

Preface

This book evolved out of my own research in agriculture and forestry
and out of courses in land economics that I taught at the Universities
of Saskatchewan and British Columbia over a period of ten years. In
general, the students in land economics at these schools differed in
their academic backgrounds and in their living environments; yet, the
tools that are used to examine land-use conflicts are similar. Students
in British Columbia tend to be more sensitive to land use in an urban
setting (e.g., the need for open space and denser settlement), but they
are also interested in water and air quality, biodiversity and old-growth
forests, scenic amenities, and so on. While Saskatchewan students are
more interested in land use issues related to agriculture, they are obviously not insensitive to a beautiful landscape, opportunities for recreational activities, or the need for wildlife habitat. Therefore, the
methodology presented in this book is useful to both types of students,
since it is appropriate for analyzing many problems related to multiple
land use and land-use conflicts.

The tools of economics, as employed in this text, provide a useful
means for talking about real world problems. In particular, they provide a functional starting point for *rationally* discussing land-use conflicts. Certainly, economics does *not* lend support to any one viewpoint
in matters dealing with land use, environment, and sustainable development. Economics provides a perspective on multiple land use and
land-use conflicts that is helpful in resolving the debate between environmentalists and developers, assuming that a compromise is desired.
As opposed to the rhetoric and populist arguments one usually finds in
the media concerning land-use issues, economics provides a rational
and focused approach to solving problems. Surprisingly to some, it can
lend support to the arguments of environmentalists in many situ-

ations, although some of those in the environmental movement are among the first to reject economic arguments. Economics also provides a clearer understanding of why differences exist and, thus, how they might be resolved.

Although much of the focus in this book is on practical issues, a certain amount of theory cannot be avoided. The theory is necessary because some of the methods for resolving land-use conflicts require that individuals understand the reasons why such and such a measure is used. Therefore, it presumes that individuals have some familiarity with economics, although those with no such background will still find many parts of the book valuable. The attempt throughout the book will be to provide examples of how economics deals with various topics related to land economics.

Acknowledgments

A deep debt of gratitude is owed a number of individuals, without whom many of the ideas in this text would not be possible. The intellectual origin of this book owes much to the literature and approach used to solve land-use problems at Oregon State University during the 1970s. I am indebted to Ward Weisensel, who made a significant contribution to the chapter on soil depletion; Jack Knetsch, who opened my mind to the problems of nonmarket measurement (Chapter 7); Fred Obermiller for his help with the chapter on range management, especially the grazing fee isssue; Richard Porter for comments on chapters 13, 15, and 17; Steve Clark and Anthony Scott for their contributions to my thinking on sustainable development; Chris Gaston, Gregg Delcourt, Patrick Kinyua, Rob Flick, and many other students, who have read earlier drafts of chapters in the book and made comments that helped to improve them; Kathy Shynkaryk, Retha Gerstmar, and Mabel Yee, who helped in many ways at the ground level of manuscript preparation; Surendra Kulshrethstha, with whom I have debated the role of secondary benefits; David Haley and Jeanette Leitch, who contributed to my understanding of forest tenure arrangements in British Columbia; and Louise Arthur, who has been a teacher, colleague and friend. There have been others as well, too numerous to recount. To all of these, I wish to express my thanks. The large number of errors of omission and commission that remain should not be attributed to any of these individuals. I also wish to thank my daughter, Charissa, for her contribution to many of the figures in the text. The Canadian Social Sciences and Humanities Research Council provided financial support for much of the writing pertaining to soil conservation and preservation of undeveloped agricultural land. Finally, I am grateful to the Forest Economics and Policy Analysis Research Unit at the University of British Columbia and its director, Ilan Vertinsky, for support and encouragement.

Land Resource Economics and Sustainable Development

1
Introduction

Readers may well wonder what the subject of land economics is about. In particular, what entails land? For the purposes of this book, land is defined as any resource that cannot be moved from its current site. At least, it cannot be moved without incurring a prohibitive cost that may be infinite. Thus, land resources include agricultural land, forestland, residential, commercial, and industrial land, recreational land, bodies of water such as lakes and rivers, the waste receptor capacity of land (e.g., garbage dumps, hazardous waste sites), and historical sites and national monuments (e.g., Great Wall of China). Given such a list, it is also important to note that land resources include all the activities that occur on land, namely, forestry, mining, hunting, hiking, fishing, and so on. As Nigel Richardson notes, 'the concept of land involves the entire ecosystem, the *natural order* which embraces water, air and living things' (1989:4).

This text seeks to provide an introduction to issues of land use and the economic tools that can be used to resolve land-use conflicts. In particular, tools of economic analysis are used to address allocation of land among alternative uses in such a way that the welfare of society is enhanced. Thus, the focus is on what is best for society and not what is best for an individual, a particular group of individuals, or a particular constituency (e.g., loggers or environmentalists). What this text seeks to provide is a balanced and just approach to decision-making concerning allocation of land resources.

Historical Perspective on Land Economics
It is useful to begin our examination of land economics by considering its intellectual genealogy and the underlying philosophies that affect society's view of land resources. It is the philosophical roots that are

important to an adequate understanding of land economics. There are basically three lines of descent.

(1) The first line of descent is the *classical line*. Classical economics originates with Adam Smith's *The Wealth of Nations*. Other figures in the classical line of descent include Robert Malthus, whose idea about the diminishing welfare of a nation stemmed from increasing natural resource scarcity; David Ricardo, who is well known for his concept of land rent (discussed in Chapter 2); and the great synthesizer of classical thought, John Stuart Mill. These early classical economists were concerned primarily with land and population – whether or not population would outstrip the capacity of land to support it. The system of thought that they developed was based on deductive, logical systems derived from specific ends and factual premises. It is non-normative in its predictions to the largest extent possible. Classical systems are elegantly precise in statement but are generally static, relying, even in their discussion of dynamics, on mechanical and reversible systems. The line of descent followed through the marginal economists (Jevons, Walras, and so on), Alfred Marshall, the new classical economists of Great Britain and the United States, the Keynesians, and, finally, the new welfare economists. This line of descent is, essentially, mainstream economics.

(2) The second line of descent, the *positivist line*, originates in the British, Bacon/Pearsonian positivism of the natural sciences and in statistics. Methodologically, it is empirical, inductive, and non-normative. In its purest form, it is not based on theory nor is there an attempt to set ultimate or absolute standards. The best known positivist was George F. Warren, the Cornell horticulturist, who was influenced by the positivism of the agricultural and natural sciences. He was not influenced by other schools, and he sought to geographically locate the lines of transition between classes of lands suitable for various kinds and intensities of farming. He looked at rural land use simply by focusing on the comparative profitability of real world farms; he went to farms, studied their characteristics, and tried to relate these to profitability. His student, A.B. Lewis, developed a program of land utilization research and applied inductive techniques to land classification. Like Warren, he sought to find the underlying characteristics of land productivity.

(3) Perhaps the most important line of descent is the *institutional line*. It is important simply because it has, since the 1950s and until recently, been neglected in land economics, despite the fact that land economics had its beginnings in institutionalism. This line of descent has its economic origin in the German Historical School of Economics and its

philosophical origin with John Dewey. While empirical and inductive in nature, institutionalists are less empirical than are positivists, and they have a normative bent to their prescriptions. Institutionalists are characterized (a) by the inclusion of a broader array of variables than is the case with the other lines of descent, (b) by a more inclusive definition of the relevant economic variables, and (c) are more willing to incorporate in their analytical systems whatever factual data appear necessary to understand and to resolve real world problems.

The two primary figures in this line of descent are R.T. Ely (who studied in Germany during the late 1800s and thus was influenced by the German Historical School of Economics) and John R. Commons. Ely joined Commons at the University of Wisconsin to form the Institutional or Wisconsin School of Economics. This school of economics was concerned with property and contract in the economic process and their application to land and industrial organizations, especially monopolies and public utilities. Around 1920, this school originated the study of *land economics*. The distinguishing characteristic of land economics was its orientation towards defining and solving real world problems. While the early problems that were examined by this school dealt with land tenure in farming (and farm management in general), research soon focused on problems dealing with forestland cutovers, and, during the 1930s, when land prices were depressed and agriculture in general was experiencing difficulties, it focused on solving problems by defining alternatives to existing institutions. Some of the things that they looked at were community planning, rural zoning, adult education, and credit reform.

The importance of land economics was apparent in two important pieces of legislation that were passed in the United States in the mid-1930s. The first of these was the Taylor Grazing Act of 1934. This act dealt with the problem of open access resources, a problem that exists today in areas such as the fishery. The Taylor Act basically put an end to the era of open, unregulated grazing on public lands. The second important piece of legislation was the Flood Control Act of 1936 that, as it turns out, was the precursor of cost-benefit analysis. The reason for this is that the act stated that, federal participation in flood control could be obtained, 'if the benefits to whomsoever they may accrue are in excess of the estimated costs' (Castle et al. 1981:425). Cost-benefit analysis is the subject of Chapter 5.

It was also during the 1930s that the various lines of descent began to merge. Land economists became more aware of statistical techniques.

They also became aware of neoclassical economic theory and, particularly, the new welfare economics. After the Second World War, the field of concern broadened to include not only grazing, flood control, and forest cutovers, but also issues concerning the rural/urban fringe, regional planning, rural-based recreation, renewable ocean resources, and renewable resources in general. It was also after the Second World War that land economics became indistinguishable from natural resource economics, as the natural resource economists in economics departments began to interact and, in general, to influence natural resources in agricultural sciences. Indeed, natural resource economics is often considered to be simply a branch of neoclassical economics. The early institutional journal *Land Economics* is now indistinguishable from most other neoclassical economics journals, and institutional economists must now turn to the *Journal of Economic Issues* in order to monitor developments in institutional economics. Thus, while institutional economics can no longer be uniquely identified with land economics, it has not disappeared entirely.

Conflict in Land Economics

It appears that land economics is simply a subset of the larger natural resource economics as indicated in Figure 1.1. However, as the discussion in the preceding section indicates, it is not at all clear that such a distinction can be made. Based on the writings of economists such as Nicholas Georgescu-Roegen, Philip Mirowski, Warren Samuels, and Herman Daly as well as a great deal of literature in biology, ecology, and even physics, it is not at all clear that land economics is a proper subset of natural resource economics, which, in turn, is a subset of either the larger fields of agricultural economics or neoclassical economics.

Neoclassical economics tends to treat natural resources the same way that it treats capital. The production function is written as $Y = F(K,L)$, where Y represents output, K represents capital, L is labour, and F is the production function. In some cases, this might be true. For example, if trees could be grown on the same land without a deterioration in the quality of that land over time as a result of tree growth and forest harvest operations, then investment in trees could be considered the same as investment in any other capital good. But the opposite is true, forest growth and harvest operations will eventually cause a deterioration in site quality that cannot be entirely prevented through, nor overcome by, technological change. The ecodiversity of old-growth forests is replaced by the mundanity of plantation forests.

Figure 1.1

Schematic of intellectual family of land economics: Perception #1

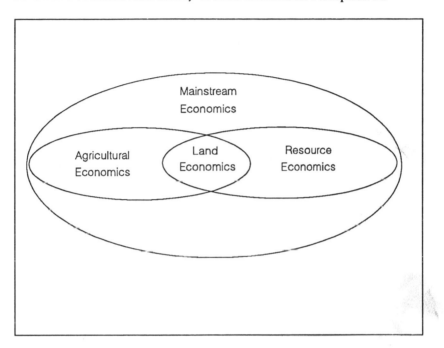

One limitation of neoclassical economics is that it has trouble dealing with environmental issues. As the aforementioned commentators have noted, environmental issues often deal with irreversibility, but neoclassical models are founded on mechanical analogies of reversible systems. The problem of irreversibilities is also present in land issues (viz., urbanization), although modern neoclassical economists (neo-Marshallians) might argue that irreversibility is a problem of investment and time. For example, *given sufficient time*, urban land can always revert back to rural land. But this argument skirts the issue by failing to appropriately account for reality.

Finally, there is the underlying conflict arising from the historical, philosophical roots of land economics. Land economics is rooted in institutional economics and has its origins with the German Historical School. (The same is perhaps true of agricultural economics and some aspects of natural resource economics, such as environmental economics.) Thus, institutional economists look at culture as an important factor in determining policies and appropriate economic solutions in particular situations. Neoclassical economists, on the other hand, tend to downplay cultural, institutional, religious, and other factors, including them in the ceteris paribus (everything else held constant) assumption. Thus, the schematic presented in Figure 1.1 no longer holds. There are no neat subsets, and the subject of land economics intersects disciplines such as natural resource economics, institutional economics, and neoclassical economics but is not wholly encompassed by any one of these (Figure 1.2). Land economics takes into account urban and community planning, geography, sociology, biology, ecology, pedology, law, philosophy, mathematics, physics, and almost any other discipline that is somehow related to land and the environment. Perhaps this is why, as discussed in Chapter 8, land economics may be evolving into what is increasingly being referred to as 'ecological economics.'

Figure 1.2

Schematic of intellectual family of land economics: Perception #2

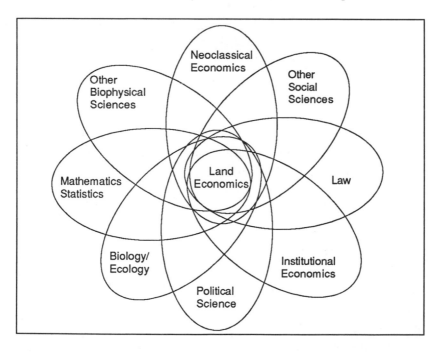

The purpose of this book is not to attempt to coalesce all the different views of land, resource, and environmental economics but to present a neoclassical view of land economics that is sprinkled with some institutional thought. The traditional economics view is primary, because it offers a unified and rational approach to the evaluation and identification of solutions to problems of land-use conflict. However, this is not to suggest that other approaches are not useful, only that such approaches tend to be ad hoc, with little or no consistency in methods for analyzing natural resource issues. For additional discussion and alternative views of the issues discussed in each chapter, the reader is directed towards the section References and Suggested Readings found at the end of the book.

Plan of the Book

The book is divided into six sections. The first section comprises chapters 2 through 4; it focuses on theoretical aspects and seeks to develop a background for subsequent discussion. Chapter 2 is concerned with defining rent, while Chapter 3 focuses on welfare measurement. The concept of externality – benefits and costs imposed on others – is discussed in Chapter 4. Externality is important for evaluating land use in the rural/urban fringe, determining policy to alleviate agricultural land degradation, preservation of agricultural lands and wild lands, and designing solutions to global warming. Theoretical elements are also found in the other sections, because, for historical reasons, certain theoretical developments occurred in response to particular issues. Therefore, these developments are best examined in the problem context in which they occur.

Project evaluation and economic development are examined in Part Two (chapters 5, 6, and 7). Chapter 5 discusses cost-benefit analysis as a tool for evaluating natural resource development in the context of other methods of evaluation; cost-benefit analysis focuses only on economic efficiency. In Chapter 6, a particular aspect of project evaluation is considered, namely, regional development. The main tool of regional development is input-output analysis, and this methodological tool is described in detail. Finally, Chapter 7 is important for the non-economist as well as for the economist, as it deals with the measurement of commodities (goods and services) for which markets do not exist. Nonmarket commodities are things such as preservation and recreation, hunting, viewing, and other values that are often considered to be non-economic items by non-economists. Economists seek to provide monetary measures of changes in air quality, species numbers, recreational opportunities, watershed function, wilderness preservation, and so on. Both the importance and methodology for doing so are provided in this chapter.

The extension of economic tools into sustainable development and land use is found in Part Three (chapters 8, 9, and 10). In Chapter 8, the concept of sustainable development is defined and compared with traditional concepts in economics, namely, those of conservation and a safe minimum standard of conservation. Further, the idea of coevolutionary development and the possibility of future resource scarcity are discussed, as is the economics of delaying irreversible development of land. Global warming is a problem related to market failure and land use but also to global politics. It is the topic of Chapter 9. However, the purpose in Chapter 9 will only be to introduce the reader to the issues and the contribution that economics has to make to the climate change debate. The effect of global warming on Canada will also be examined. The economics of soil conservation is examined in Chapter 10; in particular, is agriculture sustainable in the face of soil erosion?

The focus of Part Four is on the role of government in managing and controlling private land-use decisions. Chapter 11 is concerned with land-use planning and control, primarily in an urban setting, although issues of agricultural land preservation and conflicts along the urban/rural fringe are also examined. Rural land use and preservation of wild lands are covered in Chapter 12. Included in that chapter is a discussion of the distorting effect that government programs have on agricultural land use; current policies appear to be leading to land use that is not sustainable over time. This theme is expanded upon in Chapter 13, where government policies relating to irrigation and wetlands are examined. Government policies in these areas have resulted in regional development but also in a misallocation of land resources.

Part Five deals with public land use. Given the preponderance of public ownership of land in Canada, it is appropriate to consider whether this type of land use is economically efficient. While some of the traditional topics of forest and range economics are discussed (e.g., optimal harvest of timber), the primary focus is on conflicting land uses. Chapters 14 and 15 provide the technical and economic background for public forest and range resources, respectively, while Chapter 16 concentrates on land-use conflicts and their resolution in a way that maximizes the overall welfare of society. In this case, the conflict involves not only ranchers that use public range and timber interests but also recreationists, preservationists, and other users of public lands. Methods for resolving these conflicts are examined, as is the history of public land management in the United States and Canada.

The text concludes with Part Six (Chapter 17), a discussion of ethical concerns. Economics can only provide insights and potential solutions to the ecological problem, but ultimate responsibility for implementing solutions and bringing about needed changes to the ways society organizes its economic activities rests with individuals and the governments that represent them. This, in turn, depends upon the ethical foundation of society and the individuals within it. Economic science is itself grounded in a particular philosophy, and this determines its ethical stand with regard to the environment. Ethics is important to an understanding of how society views both the environment and the proposed solutions to the ecological problem.

Part One:
Theoretical Considerations

Introduction to Part One

Certain techniques of economics have found acceptance in society, because they provide a reasoned approach to decision-making. One of these techniques is welfare measurement or applied welfare economics. This refers to the measurement of costs and benefits accruing to various citizens. The point of welfare measurement is to determine if certain public policies (decisions) provide a net benefit to society and to determine who are the benefactors and the beneficiaries of particular policies. Obviously, policies that do not yield a net benefit to society as a whole should not be pursued, unless there is a sound reason to proceed regardless. Such a reason might be a desire to redistribute income towards a certain group or for purposes of community stability. Whatever this reason, by first providing the welfare calculations, the argument is focused on the reason for ignoring the principle of maximizing net income (viz., net domestic product). Economic theory is important because it provides a framework for the proper measurement of economic welfare.

Welfare measurement consists of a proper concept of the rent accruing to a resource, which is the topic of Chapter 2. It also consists of proper measures of welfare for consumers and producers; providing such measures is the topic of Chapter 3.

Finally, property rights are an important component of any economics system and of welfare measurement. They are particularly important when it comes to land use and other resource issues, such as environmental degradation. The role of property rights and the motivation for government intervention in land and resource markets is the topic of Chapter 4.

Each of the subjects covered in these chapters is an important building block for analyzing issues to be discussed in later sections. Therefore, the reader is encouraged not only to understand the analyses presented but, more importantly, to consider what implication these theoretical concepts have for real world problems.

2
The Concept of Rent: Is Land Unique?

The concept of rent is closely associated with land, and, originally, it was not used in conjunction with any other resource. Rent can be thought of in a number of different ways, and the modern, neoclassical view of rent is somewhat different than the classical view. What is common to all theories about rent is that the government can, in principle, tax away the rent (the excess) without affecting output decisions.

The way contemporary economists view rent can be discussed with the aid of Figure 2.1. The average variable cost (AVC) of producing output q initially declines, but, due to diminishing returns, it eventually must rise. Indeed, unless diminishing returns are present in production, it is not possible to talk about rent. Average total cost (ATC) is the sum of average fixed costs (AFC) and average variable costs. Assuming perfect competition, and if the price of q is p_0, the firm will produce at a level of output where price equals marginal cost (MC), output q_0. At q_0, there are no rents and the entrepreneur covers only his or her variable costs. If output price falls below p_0, the firm will shut down. If price is above p_0, then the firm earns some return over and above variable costs that can then be used to offset fixed costs. This return is referred to as *quasi-rent.*

If the price of output is p_1, the entrepreneur earns enough to cover both variable and fixed costs of production. Included in the fixed costs is a return to capital and entrepreneurship. Now, if price rises above p_1, say to p_2, the entrepreneur will earn a pure profit given by area p_2abe – an area also referred to as pure rent or simply rent, although this terminology increases confusion, as is indicated below. The total area p_2acd is quasi-rent, and it constitutes a return to fixed factors of production. Of course, the pure profit will be bid away in due course as a result of competition. This will be true even if the market for q has some barriers

Figure 2.1

Modern view of rent

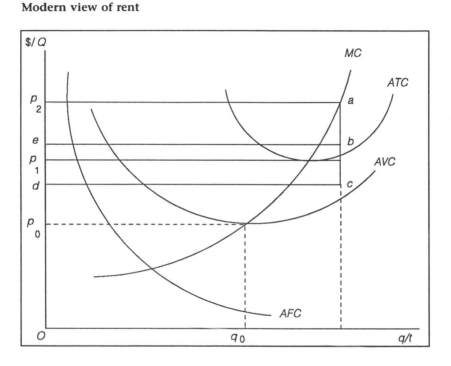

to entry; only the time required to bid away the pure profit will take longer than in the absence of entry barriers.

It is important to notice that the term quasi-rent, as used in the context of Figure 2.1, applies to any fixed factor of production, not just land. Indeed, it is implicitly assumed that land is no different than any other factor of production; it can be increased over time and, hence, is not considered to be fixed in absolute terms.

This is the view of rent that originates with the marginalist school of economics that appeared in the latter half of the 1800s. However, it is not the concept of rent advocated by the classical economists David Ricardo and John Stuart Mill, or by Karl Marx and by the great neoclassical economist Alfred Marshall, all of whom considered rent to be associated only with land. Indeed, to distinguish between land rent and rent as a return to any capital good, Marshall uses the term 'quasi-rent' (as used here) to refer to the latter, reserving the term 'rent' for use with land. The original conceptions of land rent are considered in the following sections and this concept is then expanded to other natural resources.

The Concept of Land Rent

It has already been noted that rent only exists if there exist diminishing returns to production. This is certainly true for land, since it is not possible to satisfy all of the world's food needs from a given area (or single acre) of agricultural land, regardless of the amounts of other inputs employed. The concept of rent is inextricably associated with land, since there is a finite limit to the amount of land that is available to a region, country, or the world, despite, for example, the engineering feats of the Dutch in taking land from the North Sea.

Ricardo observed that land varied in quality and that expending the same amount of effort and expense on two fields of equal size resulted in a different yield due to inherent differences in the qualities of the land – qualities that were original and indestructible. For Ricardo, these qualitative differences were due to differences in soil fertility. The price that the output fetched had to cover the costs of producing that output on the poorest quality land, otherwise no output would be forthcoming from that land. Naturally, land of better quality earned more than the cost required to produce that output, and this 'excess' or difference between the value of output on poor versus good land is called rent.

Consider the following example. Two fields lie in close proximity to one another, but field A is naturally more fertile than is field B because it has more humus or is less stony. Suppose the farmer expends the same amount of effort or expense (i.e., seed, chemicals, machine time, and so on) on the two fields. Despite experiencing the same climate, field B averages 30 bushels (bu) of wheat per acre (ac) over a period of 15 years, while A grows an average of 35 bu/ac. If both fields are 200 ac in size, and assuming the price of wheat is $3/bu, the return of field A exceeds that of field B by an average of $3,000 per year. Since the farmer apparently finds it worthwhile to continue producing on B, it is possible for the government to tax away the $3,000 annual rent on field A without affecting the farmer's input decisions.

This concept of rent is illustrated with the aid of Figure 2.2, where *AC* represents average cost and *MC* represents marginal cost. However, there are several important differences between the notion of (Ricardian) rent presented in the preceding paragraph and that presented in Figure 2.2. First, the rent on field A must be determined from the marginal field C and not from field B, since B also earns rent but C does not. Second, Ricardo did not consider changes in the organization of production, additional effort, or additional outlays on inputs as prices rose. That is, he ignored movement along the marginal cost curve. Such adjustments

Figure 2.2

Concept of land rent: Three different fields

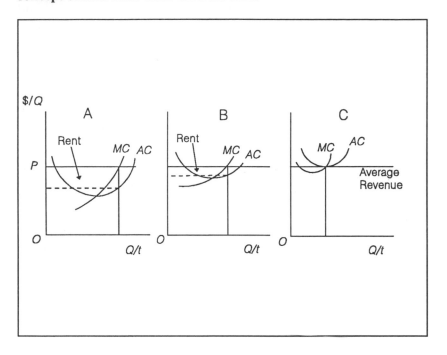

accounted for another component of rent, as discussed below in connection with Marx.

It was Ricardo's contention that, as the price of output rises due to increases in population, for example, less and less fertile (i.e., increasingly marginal) land would be brought into production. An economy will continually expand its agricultural production onto marginal land – land that could not be profitably cultivated at a lower price. However, with an increase in price, production can earn enough to cover all expenses, including an adequate return on capital used in production. When marginal land is brought into production, this implies that the owner of better land (more fertile land or land situated in a location with better climate) will earn a *differential rent*.

Von Thünen Rent: Location Theory
The Ricardian concept of rent can, perhaps, be best explained through the use of Johan von Thünen's critique. Von Thünen argued that rent was a function of location and not of land fertility or climate. In the

early to mid-1800s, von Thünen published a book on land use entitled *The Isolated State*. He considered land quality in the isolated state to be uniform, which contradicted Ricardo's notion that land quality varied, with rent accruing to land of better quality. Rather than focusing on the agricultural production capability of land, von Thünen considered rent differentials to arise from transfer costs (e.g., transportation costs).

In Figure 2.3, a single city-state is assumed to be surrounded by land of uniform quality. Differing land uses form in concentric rings about the city, as is indicated in the top portion of the diagram. Land nearest the city is used for growing vegetables, dairying, and grains. Next is a ring of forestland followed, respectively, by pasture land and hunting areas (which are the farthest from the centre). The reason for this pattern lies with rent differentials that arise from transfer costs, as illustrated in the bottom portion of the diagram.

If vegetables are grown next to the city, there is, essentially, no transfer cost associated with marketing them. Thus, the farmer located nearest the city can earn a rent given by OR_A on the vertical axis in the bottom half of the diagram. For farmers located at a greater distance from market, a transfer cost is incurred, and this reduces the rent that they earn. However, they continue to earn a normal profit in addition to any rent they may obtain. As the distance to market increases, the rent accruing to land use A declines, as indicated by the rent-distance-to-market function for land use A. The same is true for the other land uses. For these land uses, the rent would be lower if the activity were to take place at the market, that is, next to the city. Of course, that is why land uses A are undertaken, as opposed to forestry and so on, nearest the city.

The rent-distance functions for different land uses decline at different rates, because costs of production and transfer costs differ for alternative land uses. At the point labelled 1, the rent-distance function for land use A intersects that of B from above. Thus, beyond distance D_A, the return to land use B is greater than the return to land use A, if production and transfer costs are taken into account. Therefore, for distances from market up to OD_A, land use A will dominate; for distances from market between OD_A and OD_B, land use B will dominate; and so forth for land uses C, D, and any others. The change in land use occurs at the intensive margin – the margin of land-use transfer. The extensive margins occur where the rent-distance functions intersect the horizontal axis. The result of landowners pursuing land uses that result in maximiz-

Figure 2.3

Von Thünen rent model

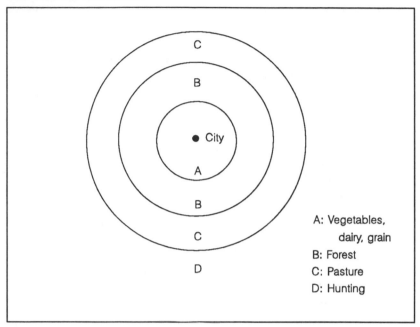

A: Vegetables, dairy, grain
B: Forest
C: Pasture
D: Hunting

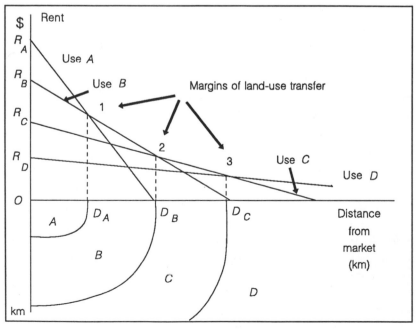

ing rent is concentric rings, as indicated in the top portion of Figure 2.3.

Notice that farmers located near the city earn the highest rents, and those living farther from the city will earn lesser rents – even where land is employed in the same uses. In this case, it is location and not land quality that determines the rent; transfer cost is the key to rent differentials. Again, it would be possible for the authority to tax away the rent without changing the land-use pattern. The von Thünen model has been used by economists to estimate benefits of recreational activities (Chapter 7) and to study spatially separated markets. It has been used to explain urban development (Chapter 10) and location decisions by pulp and paper mills in the southern U.S. Indeed, the model forms the basis of location theory used by geographers and economists alike.

The Ricardian concept of rent is similar to that illustrated in Figure 2.3, except that location is only one of the many factors that could give rise to rent. While von Thünen focused on location with respect to market and Ricardo focused on soil fertility, factors such as number of growing degree days, days without frost, distance to water or rail transportation, depth of topsoil and subsoil, slope of the land, direction of slope, and a large number of other factors determine rents available from land. It is the combination of all of these factors that determine land rent, and, in terms of Figure 2.3, all of these factors should be included on the abscissa.

Differential and Absolute Rent

Karl Marx agreed with Ricardo's concept of rent in principle, although he pointed out that Ricardo had missed an important component of rent. Marx observed that even the owner of marginal land could charge a fee (e.g., crop share) to someone who would be willing to grow crops on the land. This led Marx to distinguish between *differential* rent and *absolute* rent. Differential rent referred to rent as conceived by Ricardo, although Marx expanded on this concept. Absolute rent referred to the rent an owner could charge even on land that experienced no differential rent. Absolute rent can be thought of as *scarcity rent*. This is the rent that results when price is greater than marginal cost; it comes about whenever the supply of a resource is limited, as is the case for land and other natural resources. This is illustrated in Figure 2.4, where the flow of services from land (Q) is restricted to an amount Q^0 by physical limits to the availability of land; the distinction between differential and scarcity rent is as indicated.

Absolute rent was ignored by Ricardo, because it did not fit into his overall system. In particular, Ricardo's theory was a labour theory of value: an object has value only because it embodies labour. The fact that land could have value without embodying labour, which is the essential point of Marx's absolute land rent, did not fit into the Ricardian theory; hence, Ricardo did not allow for absolute rent.

Marx also took the concept of differential rent one step further. He distinguished two types of differential rent. First, as the price of agricultural output rises, production will expand onto marginal land, and, thus, land of better quality will earn rent (or higher rent). This concept is identical to the Ricardian conception of rent as discussed above and is referred to as rent accruing at the extensive margin.

However, a second form of differential rent might also result when output prices rise. Farmers will put more effort (labour, fertilizer, etc.) into producing crops on land that is not marginal. As a result of the higher price, these efforts will yield additional rent in the same way as indicated in figures 2.1 and 2.2. If land is the only factor of production taken to be fixed, *and if production is characterized by diminishing returns*, then an increase in price will result in a movement upwards along the marginal cost curve, with a subsequent increase in returns over variable costs of production, that is, rent. Such rent accrues at the intensive margin of production.

The second concept of differential rent is important because, in Marx's view, as soon as the second form of differential rent comes into force, it is the better soils that regulate the price of production. Then the worst soil, that which forms the basis of differential rent of the former type, can even yield a rent. Further, while differential rent does not affect the price of output, the same is not true of absolute rent. Indeed, any increase in absolute rent will result in a direct increase in price.

Other Conceptions of Land Rent
Although John Stuart Mill contributed nothing new to the concept of land rent, it should be pointed out that he agreed with Ricardo's position and defended the Ricardian conception of land rent against attacks by others. In particular, the American economist Henry Carey argued that, as agricultural output prices rose, agriculture expanded onto land that was of better rather than of poorer quality. This observation was based on the American experience of western expansion, which, in some cases, was onto better quality land. However, recalling von Thünen, the expansion was actually onto marginal land, albeit of higher fertility, since it was, at least in the first instance, further away from market.

Figure 2.4

Differential and scarcity rents

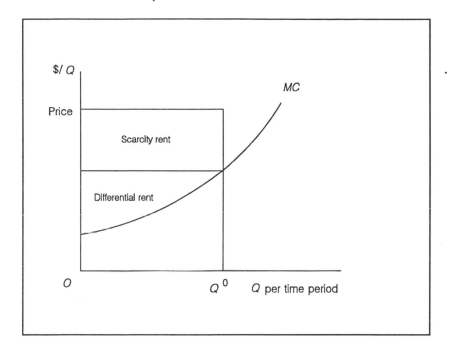

Indeed, von Thünen's arguments about land rent themselves constituted an attack on Ricardo's concept of land rent, since Ricardo was, essentially, interested in land fertility and not location.

Finally, the American economist Henry George contributed to the literature on land rent by arguing: (1) private ownership of land is inherently monopolistic, (2) rent is economic surplus not generated by entrepreneurship, and, therefore, (3) land should be owned by the public, or, if privately held, the surplus should be taxed away. George advocated a single tax of land rent, believing that rising prices for agricultural outputs would drive up rents so that, by capturing those rents, all future government programs could be funded from this tax. This 'single tax' fitted George's overall political philosophy. He considered land to have a peculiar characteristic in the socioeconomic system, he focused on land tenure institutions, and, finally, he was concerned about the equity and efficiency issues inherent in the private capture of land rents.[1]

The marginal economists of the late nineteenth century argued that the essential categories of inputs into production were simply capital and labour, ignoring land as a separate category of production. In this framework, rent on agricultural land is simply the price of the service of soil fertility. There is nothing unique about land that required separate categorization, since the appropriate concept of rent is that embodied in Figure 2.1. As already noted, Marshall was well aware of the writings of the marginalist school, and, since he felt uncomfortable with the separation of factors of production in a way that neglected land, he referred to rent as conceived in Figure 2.1 as quasi-rent. Thereby, he reserved the term 'rent' to mean land rent in the original, Ricardian sense.

There was one item that still concerned the marginalists – the absolute fixity of land. Although later marginalists were to deny that land cannot be produced, that it is not absolutely fixed, Walras, for one, did not go this far. With absolute fixity, however, rents on land would rise over time as agricultural output prices rose. This led Walras to argue for the nationalization of land and, in its absence, for a tax on rents.

Opportunity Cost
Land can generate returns in more than one use. The use that generates the greatest net return or rent is the most efficient use, while the rent that can be earned on the land in its next best alternative use is its *opportunity cost*.

Land Rents and Soil Depletion
Concern about future agricultural productivity and soil depletion has resulted in a vast literature pertaining to soil degradation (Chapter 12). In this section, a particular aspect of that problem, namely, rent and taxation in the context of soil depletion is examined. It is possible to define land rent net of soil depletion. Depletion constitutes the sale of the substance of the resource, and the corresponding payment is not income but a transfer, comparable to the sale of title to land itself. Therefore, to properly analyze land rent – that income which can be taxed away without affecting output decisions – one must examine four economic aspects or characteristics of land or soil.

Perdurable Matrix (Flow Resource)
This is a *pure flow* resource with a non-critical zone. It is determined by location, climate, subsoil, drainage, inexhaustible nutrients, macro-relief, and so on. Under ordinary circumstances, the pure flow is enduring, permanent, or nonperishable; but it can be affected by human actions

such as strip mining, flooding due to construction of reservoirs, paving, and so on. It is indestructible due to neglect or abuse incident to farm operations. The question is: What contribution does this matrix make to land rent? What is the implication for taxation?

To understand this characteristic and its relationship to rent, consider two examples pertaining to location and fertility, respectively. Two farmers have identical costs, yields, crops, macro-relief, and so on but are located at different distances from the grain elevator. Jones trucks grain 5 miles to the elevator, while Smith trucks it 50 miles. Suppose each gets $4/bu at the elevator. Subtracting transportation costs, the farm gate prices for Jones and Smith are $3.97/bu and $3.78/bu, respectively. Smith receives $0.19/bu less than Jones. Since Smith stays in business (i.e., earns a normal profit), Jones must earn an economic rent of $0.19/bu. The $0.19/bu can be taxed away without affecting Jones's decision regarding what to produce and how to produce it – the tax does not affect resource allocation.

Next, consider the case where Smith and Jones have identical farms next to each other, but Smith's soil is more saline than is that of Jones. Hence, Jones's yield is greater by 5 bu/ac. Since Smith stays in business, the economic rent per acre which can be taken from Jones by taxation is 5 multiplied by the farm gate price; if that price is $3.90/bu, the rent accruing to Jones is $19.50/ac. If land markets function perfectly, and there is evidence to the contrary, then Jones's land is also worth more than is that of Smith by $19.50/$i$ per acre, where i is the real interest rate.

Subject to the ceteris paribus assumption, other factors, such as macro-relief, have a similar impact. This notion of rent, then, is differential rent.

Conservable Flow (Flow with Critical Zone)

The *conservable flow* element of virgin soil fertility is that which takes some pain to keep in the original state but is worth that pain, because it is less than the cost of replacement and less than the present value of future income. It is economical to take pains to conserve this component of the land matrix, because it is expected to yield future incomes the present value of which exceeds the present value of the conservation costs. Examples of conservable flow elements of the soil are humus and thin topsoil. Conservation in this case is effort devoted to reducing the loss of the virgin flow resources that may, but need not, be deteriorated by use. Thus, liquidation of a conservable flow component of the soil is considered to be an 'irreversible' loss, not because the soil cannot be rebuilt, but because it cannot be rebuilt without costing more than it would have cost to simply conserve the virgin soil.

For illustrative purposes, let us compare the conservable flow component of soil with a human-made structure. Structures deteriorate over time; soils deteriorate with use. That is, nature undermines the work of human beings in the former case, while humans undermine the work of nature in the latter. Maintenance is humankind's struggle against nature and time, but conservation is our struggle against use and ourselves. While time destroys structures, it works towards soil conservation as it lets nature work to restore the status quo that existed before the land was put to the plough. In terms of its economic implications, assets undergo time depreciation and we permit depreciation allowances in the tax system. But land does not, as a rule, undergo time depreciation. It is an infinite flow resource unlike any other asset that has a finite flow, although there are some characteristics of land that are finite, as is shown below. Mason Gaffney (1965) puts it as follows: 'If old soil is to be replaced by new, it is almost always done by mending the old, not scraping it off and beginning fresh. Obsolete structures, on the other hand, can rarely be mingled with new ones. They are torn down and the ground cleared for a new start.'

Now consider the rent attributable to this characteristic of the soil. The net rent is equal to the net income (including, as a cost, the normal rate of return) due to conservable flow elements of the soil minus conservation costs. This is the value that can be taxed away without affecting production decisions.

Finally, tenure arrangements or cyclical circumstances (e.g., high land prices followed by low agricultural prices and high interest rates) permit individuals to hold tenure over land, with little equity in soils that have a high proportion of conservable flow elements. This poses the danger of liquidation, followed by abandonment to creditors, landlords, or taxing agencies. An example of this occurred in the United States, where, as the pioneers moved west, they found agricultural land consisting largely of conservable flow elements – high grasses embedded in shallow soils and a region with little rainfall. Excess grazing due to lack of property rights or ownership of the resource destroyed the range. Although the range can be brought back to its original productivity, studies show that it can be done only at considerable expense, with benefit-cost ratios below 1.0 (i.e., costs exceed revenues). After the land was destroyed, private individuals were uninterested in ownership so that much land in the western U.S. is now managed by the Bureau of Land Management (BLM) and the U.S. Forest Service (see Part Five).

Revolving Fund (Stock Resource)

That element of virgin soil fertility that is not economical to conserve but is economical to replace or renew with materials imported from off-site is referred to as the *revolving fund*. It is a stock resource much like inventory. Examples of the revolving fund component are nutrients, such as nitrogen and phosphorous, that can be replaced by fertilizer, and, in some cases, moisture that can be replaced by irrigation water. Revolving fund components leave the soil and become embodied in crops and livestock.

The income imputed to the revolving fund is not a part of rent. Rather, it is a return to an improvement to the site, analogous to the return on capital tied up in storing grain. After initial depletion of the virgin material, each decision to reinvest is independent and requires its own incentives. It represents a sacrifice of human alternatives – an opportunity cost.

Expendable Surplus (Finite Fund)

The *expendable surplus* is similar to the perdurable matrix except that the former is infinite, while the latter is finite. The expendable surplus is often very large, and, hence, its emplaced value (nonuse value) is low and hardly perceptible.

The liquidation value of these elements exceeds their emplaced value (or is expected to in the foreseeable future). Further, they are not economical to replace when they are expended. In the case of the perdurable matrix, the resource fund is infinite and all income accruing to it is rent. However, when the fund is finite, a depletion charge is to be subtracted from the imputed income. Rent is equal to the imputed income minus the depletion charge.

Consider, as an example, excess topsoil of 250 centimetres (cm) such as can occur in the Palouse region of western Idaho and eastern Washington. The excess topsoil can be considered excess conservable flow. Now consider exploitation of this excess topsoil by sod farming. Every year 5 cm of topsoil are removed with the grass sod. It is not until after 50 years that all of the excess topsoil has been depleted. It is at that time that the topsoil must be considered to be like conservable flow, and steps must be taken to ensure that further soil loss either does not occur or occurs at a rate that does not affect the future availability of the resource.[2]

Returning to the sod farming example, the amount of surplus used this year has no effect on the amount available next year. Removing sod this year strips 5 cm of the excess (surplus) topsoil from the 250 cm excess base, but it is still possible to strip away 5 cm next year. It is not until the fiftieth year of sod farming that the expendable surplus is finally depleted (exhausted). Then the land can no longer be used for sod farming but, under our assumptions, is still usable for crop production. Therefore, the 5 cm stripped away this year has no effect until the fiftieth year. Only in the fiftieth year is the expendable surplus liquidated. What is the liquidation value in the fiftieth year? It is the value of 5 cm of excess topsoil at that time. The appropriate depletion charge today is the contribution of the 5 cm of topsoil to the liquidation value discounted to the present. Suppose liquidation value of 5 cm of topsoil is $1,000 (the return in a given year over opportunity cost). Then the current year depletion charge is equal to

$$1,000/(1+i)^{50},$$

where i is the interest rate. The depletion charge next year is $1,000/(1+i)^{49}$, and so on for following years. The depletion charge is very small early on but increases each year as the expendable surplus becomes fully depleted.

The amount of income that can be taxed away is equal to the income from the expendable surplus minus the depletion charge. The implication of this analysis is that oil fields and mines are able to bear much higher taxes than is currently believed, because depletion occurs at some date in the future and not next year, as is often presumed in methods for calculating depletion charges.

Summary
The foregoing discussion is summarized in Table 2.1. In the analysis, land values were attributed to soil characteristics. However, the characteristics found in the *perdurable matrix* include elements that have nothing to do with the soil per se. They include location, climate, macrorelief, and so on. The one thing that prevents us from valuing land according to physical attributes or things such as agricultural productivity is the other uses of land and externalities. Land values *cannot* be

related to soil characteristics except in very rare circumstances. One purpose of the remainder of this book is to indicate what factors do affect land values and, thereby, land use.

Table 2.1. **Rent from various components of soil**

Perdurable matrix	Net income from this source is *all* rent.
Conservable flow	Rent = Income - Conservation Costs
Revolving fund	Income is a return similar to any return on capital investment. NO RENT
Expendable surplus	$Rent_t = Income_t - Depletion\ Charge_t$

Economists are interested in identifying the best use of land – the use that maximizes the return (or rent) to the land. The economist refers to this simply as the use (or mix of uses) of land which maximizes society's welfare. In the next chapter, tools for measuring welfare are examined.

3
The Theory of Welfare Measurement

In this chapter, the theory of welfare measurement is examined from the viewpoint of developing usable measures of changes in consumer and producer welfares resulting from government decisions with respect to public and private land use and from public investments in the natural resource sectors. The measures considered here are important for social cost-benefit analysis, which is used to analyze the economic efficiency aspects of such decisions. (Chapter 5 describes the methodology of cost-benefit analysis as it relates to water resource projects, although the general method can be used to evaluate other land and resource investments or policies as well.) It is important to recognize that cost-benefit analysis does not deal solely with financial measures of viability, but that it also considers such things as preservation values, scenic values, hunting and hiking values, costs of water and air pollution, and so on. Measurement of these values is difficult because markets are not always available for commodities such as clean air; this is why these types of values are referred to as nonmarket values. While measurement of nonmarket values is the subject of Chapter 7, the theoretical measures developed in this chapter are the foundation for measuring them in practice. This chapter begins by considering welfare measures for consumers, followed by those for producers. The final section brings the measures together.

Measures of Changes in the Welfare of Consumers

Three theoretical measures of consumer welfare are generally employed in economics. These are consumer surplus (CS), compensating variation (CV), and equivalent variation (EV). Each of these measures is discussed in the following sections, and problems concerning their use are highlighted.

The Notion of Consumer Surplus

The concept of consumer surplus was first introduced by the French engineer Dupuit in 1833. Consumer surplus is used to measure the welfare that consumers get when they purchase goods and services. The general concept is well known to economists and is simply the difference between an individual's marginal willingness to pay and the market price. The marginal willingness-to-pay curve is simply the individual's *Marshallian* or *ordinary* demand curve, which is derived from that person's utility function and budget constraint along with market prices, as is shown below. If the price of a commodity is given by P_0 in Figure 3.1, then the consumer surplus is given by the area denoted by a. The consumer surplus is determined as follows. The consumer will purchase q_0 units of the commodity at a price P_0. The value which the consumer attaches to an amount q_0 of the commodity is given by area $(a + b + c)$ – the area under the demand curve. (The demand function can, therefore, be thought of as marginal benefit function.) Since he or she must sacrifice an amount equal to area $(b + c)$ to purchase the commodity, the consumer gains area a – the consumer surplus.

Figure 3.1

Notion of consumer surplus

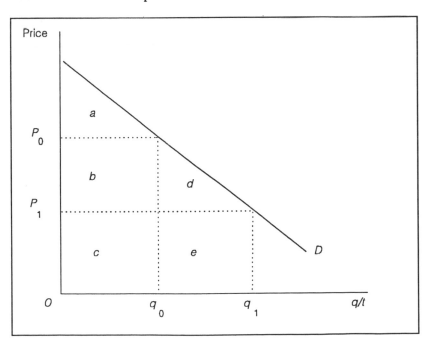

In applied welfare economics, we are generally not interested in total consumer surplus but, rather, in the change in CS that an action (e.g., an agricultural program, a change in land use or the building of a dam) may bring about. Suppose, for example, that a policy results in a change in price from P_0 to P_1 in Figure 3.1. Initially, the consumer purchased q_0 units, but, given price P_1, q_1 units of the commodity are purchased. Prior to the reduction in price, the consumer surplus was given by area *a*. After the price is reduced, the consumers can purchase the same quantity (q_0) as previously, but they pay less for it. Therefore, they gain area *b*, which is the difference between the amount they paid for quantity q_0 when the price was P_0 and the amount they paid for the same quantity at the lower price P_1. However, by increasing purchases of the commodity from q_0 to q_1, the consumer only pays an amount given by area *e*, but he or she places a greater *value* on the additional purchases – a value given by area ($d + e$). Therefore, by increasing purchases from q_0 to q_1, the consumer gains a surplus given by area *d*. Thus, the *change* in CS due to a reduction in the price of the commodity is given by area ($b + d$). Total CS from purchasing q_1 units of the commodity at a price of P_1 is given by area ($a + b + d$).

Now consider what happens when a government policy results in a change in the income received by a consumer. In Figure 3.2, it is assumed that income falls. For a normal good, this will cause the demand schedule to shift to the left from $D(m_0)$ to $D(m_1)$, where m_0 and m_1 are the initial and final levels of income, respectively. At fixed price P_0, the change in CS is given by

$$\Delta CS = \text{area } [a - (a + b)] = -\text{area } b.$$

As a result of the income change, less of the commodity is purchased (q_1 instead of q_0) and *CS* falls from area ($a + b$) to area *a*. Hence, the loss in *CS* is given by area *b*.

Since the purpose of the consumer surplus measure of welfare change is to provide a monetary measure of the change in welfare of consumers due to a change in a government policy, one must ask whether CS is the best measure of welfare in the case of income change. It is not! The best measure of the change in consumer welfare is not area *b* but simply the difference in income; $m_1 - m_0$. Only in some circumstances are the two measures equivalent. This indicates that CS is only an approximate measure, and, indeed, it is not the only measure of consumer welfare available to us. In some cases, it is not even possible to derive measures of either the direct change in income or consumer surplus. It is in these cases that the other measures, namely, compensating variation and equivalent variation, are important.

Figure 3.2

Consumer surplus and a decrease in income

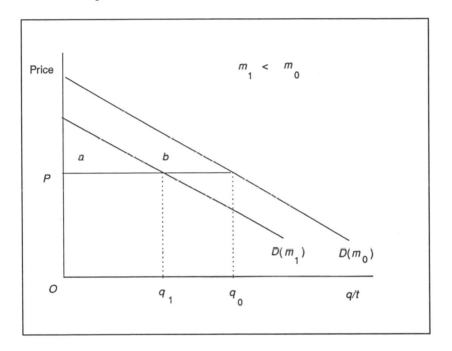

Ordinary versus Compensated Demands

Before proceeding to the CV and EV measures of consumer welfare, it is important for us to distinguish between Marshallian (ordinary) and *Hicksian (compensated)* demand functions. This is done with the aid of Figure 3.3. In this figure, it is assumed that the consumer allocates his or her budget between two goods, q and G. Good q is the one of interest, and commodity G may be considered to constitute all other goods and services available to the consumer. The price of G is assumed to remain fixed throughout the analysis, so its price is set at 1.0. That is, if q constitutes only a small portion of one's budget, then G can be thought of as income and the numeraire, or a type of measuring stick.

The upper portion of Figure 3.3 illustrates the case in which a consumer maximizes utility subject to a budget constraint. It is assumed that the consumer initially faces a price of P_0 for q (recall that the price of *G* is 1) and that he or she has a fixed budget of m_0. The size of the budget and the price of *q* determine the location of the budget constraint and its slope, respectively. If the entire budget is spent on commodity *G*, then m_0 units of *G* can be purchased (point *A*); if the entire budget is spent on *q*, then m_0/P_0 units of *q* can be purchased (point *B*). The slope of the budget line is given by the negative of the price ratio or $-P_0$. (The price ratio is obtained as the negative of the 'rise' divided by the 'run': $-m_0/m_0/P_0 = -P_0$.) In equilibrium, the consumer attains the indifference curve (utility level) U_0 at point O in the upper portion of the diagram. He or she consumes q_0 units of *q*. The combination (q_0, P_0) constitutes a common point on *both* the Marshallian and Hicksian demand curves in the lower portion of the diagram.

Figure 3.3

Derivation of Marshallian and Hicksian demand functions

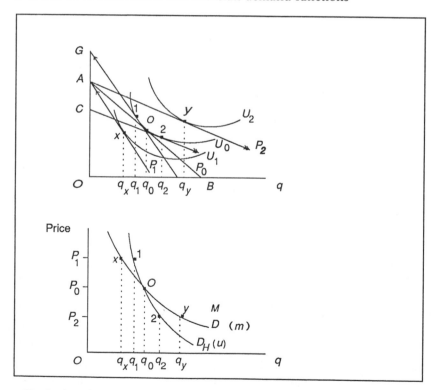

To derive the ordinary or Marshallian demand function for *q*, we hold the budget amount m_0 fixed and change the price of *q*. At the higher price P_1 ($P_1 > P_0$), the budget line is steeper and the consumer adjusts purchases of G and q to achieve a new equilibrium at the lower utility level U_1 (point x). He or she now consumes q_x units of q. The combination (q_x, P_1) constitutes a second point on the ordinary demand function. A third point on the demand function is found by reducing the price of q from P_0 to P_2 ($P_2 < P_0$). The budget constraint pivots out, as is shown in the upper portion of the diagram (the slope of the budget line is less steep), and the consumer adjusts purchases of G and q according to his or her personal preferences. A new equilibrium is established at point y, with utility level U_2 and q_y units of q purchased. The combination (q_y, P_2) constitutes a point on the ordinary demand function, as is shown in the lower portion of the diagram. By connecting the points x, 0 and y in the lower half of the diagram, the Marshallian or ordinary demand function is drawn. It is labelled $D_M(m)$ to indicate that it is the Marshallian or ordinary demand function and that it depends upon the level of income or budget m.

More correctly, the ordinary demand function is written as: $D_M(P_q; m, P_G)$. That is, changes in the price of q constitute movements along the ordinary demand function, while the function will shift whenever the budget level (m) changes. It will also shift whenever the price of G (other goods and services) is altered.

To derive the compensated or Hicksian demand function for q, we hold utility at a constant level, say U_0, but continue to alter the price of q. In order to compensate the individual so that he or she is able to maintain the original utility level U_0, we must either give the individual additional income or take some away. That is, in this case, rather than allowing utility to change (as in the derivation of the ordinary demand function), we allow income to change as needed to maintain the original level of welfare or utility. That is why we use the term 'compensated' – individuals are compensated to keep utility at a given level. The fact that individuals are 'compensated' to remain at U_0 says something about property rights – it assumes that the individual has a right to U_0 and nothing else.

At the higher price P_1 ($P_1 > P_0$), the budget line is steeper. The budget line is shifted to the right (income or compensation is provided to the consumer), so that the individual can attain the original level of utility (U_0).[1] This is what compensation is all about. The consumer faces a new price regime and adjusts purchases of G and q to achieve a new equilibrium at point 1 on U_0. He or she now consumes q_1 units of q. The combination (q_1, P_1) constitutes an additional point on the compensated demand function (in addition to point (q_0, P_0)). A third point on the compensated demand function is found by reducing the price to P_2 (P_2 < P_0). The slope of the budget line in the upper portion of the diagram is less steep, and income must now be taken away from the consumer in order to get him or her back to the original indifference curve. The amount that needs to be taken away is given by the distance AC on the vertical axis (since income is measured in units of G). Again the individual adjusts purchases of G and q, because the price ratio facing him or her has changed. A new equilibrium is established at point 2, with the original utility level U_0, but q_2 units of q are purchased. The combination (q_2, P_2) constitutes another point on the compensated demand function, as is shown in the lower portion of the diagram. By connecting points 1, 0, and 2 in the lower half of the diagram, the Hicksian or compensated demand function is drawn. It is labelled $D_H(U)$ to indicate that it is the Hicksian or compensated demand function, and that it depends upon the level of utility.

The correct form of the compensated demand function is: $D_H(P_q; U, P_G)$. Again, changes in P_q will cause one to move along the demand curve, but changes in P_G will cause the compensated demand function to shift. Finally, the compensated demand function will shift whenever the *target* utility level (U) is adjusted.

Notice that the slope of the compensated demand function is steeper than that of the ordinary demand function. Also, the functions always intersect at the point that they have in common, namely, the original or some target situation. This is important in the analysis that follows, because whether the original or target situation is used says something about the property rights to which an individual is entitled. Further, the Marshallian demand function for a market commodity can be estimated from actual data, because it is a function of own price, prices of substitutes and complements (other goods), and income, all of which are observable. Hicksian demands are a function of, among other things, utility levels that are unobservable – viz., $D_H(P_q; U, P_G)$. Hence, they cannot be estimated from observed market data. Nonetheless, they are useful for estimation of consumer welfare in cases where goods or services are not traded in markets.

From a mathematical point of view, the ordinary and compensating demand curves are analogous. The ordinary demand function is found by *maximizing* an individual's utility subject to the budget constraint. Upon doing so, one derives the ordinary demands as a function of prices and income. This is called the *primal* problem. The *dual* problem is then to *minimize* the budget subject to maintaining a certain level of utility (or minimize the cost of attaining a particular indifference curve). In this way, one derives the compensated demands as a function of prices and utility.

Compensating and Equivalent Variations

Earlier we considered consumer surplus as a measure of the welfare change of a consumer. However, as we indicated, consumer surplus is not a true measure of welfare change. It can be shown that CS may, in some situations, be an ambiguous measure of changes in consumer welfare; but it is also not a true measure of welfare. In this section, we define the correct theoretical measures of welfare change, namely, compensating variation (CV) and equivalent variation (EV).

Suppose that there are two commodities G and q, as before. Again, G is chosen to be the numeraire good so that changes in welfare can be measured in its terms. Now consider an increase in the price of q from P_0 to P_1. We then define the compensating variation of the price increase as the amount of money – measured in terms of G – required to compensate the individual for the higher price of q so that the individual is able to maintain the initial level of utility. The situation is depicted in Figure 3.4.

In Figure 3.4, the price increase in q causes the consumer to purchase commodity bundle Q_1 on U_1 rather than bundle Q_0 on U_0. By drawing a line parallel to the new price ratio tangent to U_0, in the same way that we did when we derived the compensating demand curve, it is possible to measure the CV of the price increase on the vertical axis as the distance $m_0 - m_1$.

The equivalent variation of an increase in the price of q is the amount of money (or G) that would have to be taken away from the consumer to provide him/her with a utility level of U_1 at the original set of prices. (Notice that this is different from the case of CV, in which we focus upon the original utility level (U_0) and the new set of prices.) In Figure 3.4, the EV of an increase in price of q is measured by $m_0 - m_2$.

If, instead, the price of q had declined, we could simply switch the labels on the price ratios and the indifference curves in Figure 3.4. As the reader can verify, the compensating variation is then given by $m_2 - m_0$, and the equivalent variation is given by $m_1 - m_0$. Thus,

$$CV \text{ of a price increase } = - EV \text{ of a price decrease}$$
$$EV \text{ of a price increase } = - CV \text{ of a price decrease.}$$

This illustrates that *CV* and *EV* are defined with respect to a reference utility level or reference set of *property rights*. *CV* is defined with respect to the original or currently existing property rights (original indifference curve), while *EV* is defined with respect to a proposed set of property rights (the new indifference curve). This idea of associating property rights with the concepts of CV and EV is particularly important when it comes to valuing goods and services that are not traded in the marketplace.

Figure 3.4

Compensating and equivalent variation for a price increase

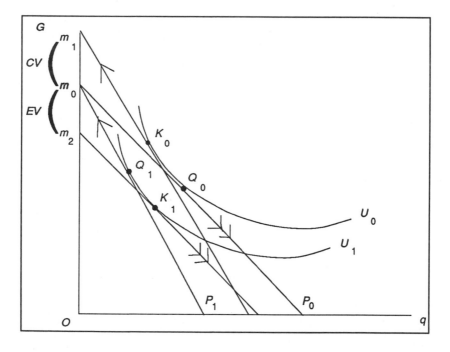

Thus, in Figure 3.5, the compensating variation of an increase in the price of q is equal to the area under the Hicksian demand curve (between the two prices P_0 and P_1) for the original utility level. That is, CV is the area under the Hicksian demand curve that is labelled with U_0, indicating that the compensated demand function is fixed upon the original indifference curve. Likewise, the equivalent variation of an increase in the price of q is equal to the area under the compensated demand curve for the final utility level (again between the two prices). Again, whether one considers the compensating or ordinary demand function, it can be viewed as a marginal benefit curve, with the area under it constituting a measure of benefit.

Figure 3.5

Relationship among compensating and equivalent variations and consumer surplus

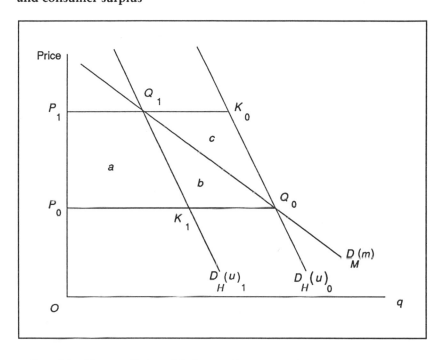

Consider Figures 3.4 and 3.5 in order to clarify this further. In Figure 3.4, the movement along U_0 from Q_0 to K_0 represents the substitution effect of a price change, while the movement from K_0 to Q_1 represents the income effect. Therefore, the change in prices with utility held constant (i.e., the movement from Q_0 to K_0 in Figure 3.4) can be represented as a movement along the compensated demand curve from Q_0 to K_0 in Figure 3.5. The area under this compensated demand (U_0 held constant) between P_0 and P_1 measures the compensating variation of the increase in the price of q; the CV measure ($m_0 - m_1$) in Figure 3.4 is equal to area ($a + b + c$) in Figure 3.5.

Likewise, the movement from K_1 to Q_1 in Figure 3.4 (due to the price increase in q) represents a movement along the compensated demand curve $D_H(U_1)$ from K_1 to Q_1 in Figure 3.5; the movement from Q_1 to K_0 represents the change in income or income effect. The equivalent variation of a price change is equal to area a in Figure 3.5, which is identical to $m_0 - m_2$ in Figure 3.4.

Finally, the change in consumer surplus due to the increase in the price of q is given by the appropriate area under the Marshallian or ordinary demand function, namely, area $(a + b)$ in Figure 3.5. Hence, we have the following relation between consumer surplus and the true measures of welfare change:

$$EV < CS < CV.$$

Suppose that, instead of increasing the price of q, the price of q falls from P_1 to P_0. Then, the compensating variation of the reduction in price is given by $m_2 - m_0$, while the equivalent variation is given by $m_1 - m_0$ (Figure 3.4), as we have already indicated. Since U_1 is now the original or starting level of utility, compensating variation is given by area a in Figure 3.5; the equivalent variation of the price reduction is then given by area $(a + b + c)$. Since consumer surplus remains unchanged and equal to area $(a + b)$, the relationship between it and the true measures of consumer welfare is now

$$CV < CS < EV.$$

Finally, we need to ask whether or not this distinction between EV, CV, and CS is worth all the fuss we have accorded it. For example, the reader may question why there are two *true* measures of consumer welfare, and yet they are not equal. The reason is that the two measures depend upon the assignment of property rights. Further, while consumer surplus is the only measure that can be estimated from actual data, it is not a theoretically valid measure of welfare. Nonetheless, CS is often very close to CV or EV. In practice, the difference between all three measures is very small. Further, for certain functional forms of the utility function, the three measures are identical.[2] Therefore, when it comes to market data, CS is, generally, a useful measure of consumer welfare, despite any theoretical problems that may exist with this measure.

Compensating and equivalent variation are important concepts, however, when it comes to measuring the value to consumers or consumer welfare of certain goods and services that are *not* traded in markets. In such instances, it is necessary to employ either the CV or EV concept if one is to obtain any measure of value whatsoever. This will become apparent in later chapters, which deal with the measurement of nonmarket values. These include values of recreational experiences, scenic amenities, preservation values (e.g., of old-growth timber and certain wildlife species), and so on.

Measures of Changes in the Welfare of Producers

A producer is willing to supply a commodity at the prices determined by the marginal cost of production – the marginal cost (MC) curve is the same as the producer's supply curve. Assume that, in Figure 3.6, the market equilibrium price for good q is P. Thus, the producer receives an amount OP for *each* unit that he or she sells. Suppose that the producer supplies an amount given by OQ'. He/she is willing to sell this amount for OP', which represents the marginal cost of the last unit produced. Since the producer actually receives a price of OP, the 'excess' or surplus that the producer receives for the marginal unit of output is approximated by $PQ' - P'Q'$. Actually, area $Pcda$ in Figure 3.6(a) represents the surplus on sales of OQ'; total revenue (PQ') minus total cost (the area under MC or area $OadQ'$). Given a market price of OP, the producer will supply OQ units of the good, thereby realizing a total surplus given by area abP – the shaded area. This surplus is referred to as *producer surplus*.

The producer surplus can also be identified in terms of the more familiar average variable cost (AVC) curve. Given that the price is OP in Figure 3.6(b), the return from producing OQ units is P times Q or the rectangle $OPxQ$. Now, the variable cost of producing OQ units of the output is given by the product of the average variable cost (OK) and output, that is, the rectangle $OKyQ$. The producer surplus or quasi-rent is simply the difference between these areas, namely, the shaded area $KPxy$. The shaded area in panel (b) of Figure 3.6 is identical to the shaded area in panel (a).

Producer surplus is, therefore, simply the difference between total revenue and total *variable* cost. (Notice that it is identical to quasi-rent as defined in Chapter 2.) This is not an ambiguous measure of welfare, and, hence, there is no counterpart to the CV and EV concepts of consumer welfare measurement.

Societal Welfare

The concepts of welfare defined in the previous sections are used to evaluate the economic efficacy of government programs and policies. By assuming that all individuals are to be treated equally, whether they are producers or consumers or whether they are rich or poor, it is possible to determine the gains and losses of various public decisions simply by summing all of the welfare measures. Gains and losses accruing at different points in time are weighted depending upon when they accrue. This is called discounting and is considered further in Chapter 5 under cost-benefit analysis. At this point, we assume that all the welfare gains and losses occur in the same time period.

Figure 3.6

Defining producer surplus

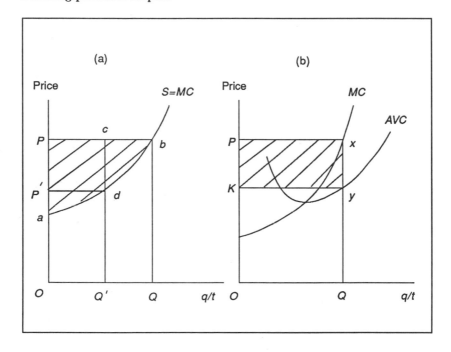

To illustrate the usefulness of the welfare measurement concept, consider the case where the government invests funds in research and development (R&D) aimed at improving milk yields either through new drugs (hormones) or more productive breeds of cows. The government wishes to know whether or not such research yields net benefits to society, that is, that benefits exceed the cost of the R&D activity. As a result of the R&D activity, the marginal cost of producing milk falls. This is represented by a rightward shift of the supply function in Figure 3.7 from S to S'. Ignoring problems associated with trade and market distortions, how do we measure the net benefits of the government decision?

Figure 3.7

Summing producer and consumer surpluses

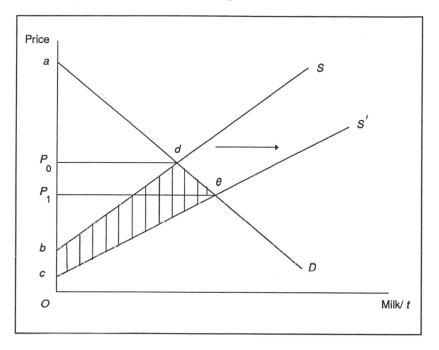

As a result of the supply shift, the price of milk falls from P_0 to P_1. The net gain to consumers is measured by the change in consumer surplus (CS). This is as follows:

$$\Delta\ CS = \text{area } (P_1ae) - \text{area } (P_0ad).$$

This is simply the new consumer surplus minus the original consumer surplus. Likewise, the change in producer surplus (PS) is given by

$$\Delta\ PS = \text{area } (P_1ec) - \text{area } (P_0db).$$

The net gain (or loss) to society is given by $\Delta CS + \Delta PS$ minus the cost of the R&D program. This is area *(cedb)* – the shaded area – minus the R&D cost.[3]

Of course, if it is not possible to estimate the supply and demand functions, then other procedures must be used to obtain the desired welfare measures. For example, the change in net revenues of milk producers provides an excellent alternative measure for producer surplus, as already noted. Thus, one would only need to estimate the demand function for milk as opposed to both demand and supply. (Estimation of supply and demand simultaneously is a difficult task due to identification problems. The same data are used to identify two functions.) In this example, it would be difficult to obtain measures of consumer welfare changes without actually estimating the demand function, although it is possible to avoid having to estimate supply. However, there are cases, particularly in land economics, in which other techniques are available for estimating consumer welfare changes. These techniques are related to the concepts of compensating and equivalent variation.

Public Goods and Welfare Change

Public goods such as clean air and water, or a scenic environment, are not traded in the marketplace.[4] However, government decisions or policies do affect the amounts of these goods and services that are provided. How do we measure welfare change when there is a change in the provision of a public good? What measures do we employ in these circumstances? Let us denote the public good by Q and all other goods by G. The indifference curves and budget line for this situation are indicated in Figure 3.8. Notice that the indifference curves have the usual shape, but the budget line is a horizontal line equal to some given level of income $m_0 = G_0$, since income is measured by G. There is no price for the public good, and this is the reason that the budget line does not have the familiar downward slope.

Assume that the initial level of the public good is given by Q_0, and that government policy causes the amount of the good to increase to Q_1. For example, suppose that, as a result of new automobile emission standards, the level of clean air increases (but the cost of automobiles does not). By increasing the availability of the public good, the individual is able to attain a higher level of utility (moving from level U_0 to U_1). The CV measure of welfare change asks what quantity of G must be taken away in order to return the individual to the original level of utility. The answer is that it is the amount given by distance AB in Figure 3.8.

One can also ask how much compensation the individual requires in order to relinquish the option of having the higher quantity of public goods. This is the EV measure of welfare change that is based upon the individual's right to the higher level of utility. The EV of the increase in quantity is given by the vertical distance CD in Figure 3.8.

Figure 3.8

CV and EV for a public good

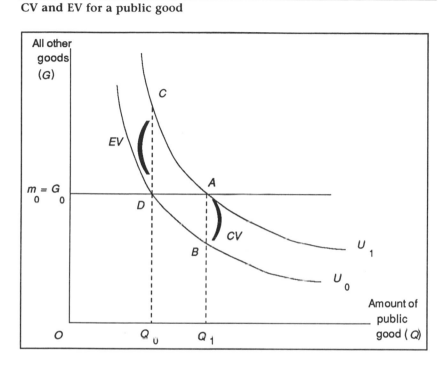

The appropriate measures of welfare change can also be found directly from the individual's marginal willingness-to-pay function for the public good. This function is derived as the *inverse* Hicksian (or inverse compensated) demand function. An inverse demand function gives own price as a function of own quantity rather than quantity as a function of price. Thus, we can write the inverse compensated demand function for the public good as

$$w = D_H^{-1}(Q; P_G, U),$$

where w is the marginal willingness to pay for changes in the quantity of the public good (Chapter 7). The benefit to the individual of an increase in the supply of Q is given by the area under the inverse compensated demand function, as indicated by the shaded area in Figure 3.9. This welfare measure is the compensating variation of the quantity change and, hence, is equal to the CV measure indicated in Figure 3.8 (i.e., vertical distance AB).

Figure 3.9

CV of change in provision of a public good

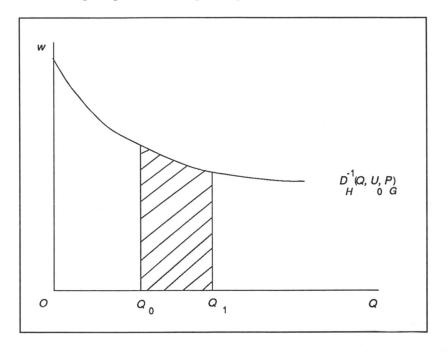

Now, if the level of the public good were to be reduced from Q_1 to Q_0, the opposite would be true. The *CV* measure now asks how much of good G would be required as compensation for the individual to put up with less of the public good (i.e., *CV = -EV*); the *CV* measure is now vertical distance *CD*. The *EV* measure indicates how much of good G would need to be taken away in order for the individual to be as well off with the original quantity of the public good as with the new (lesser) quantity. This is vertical distance *AB* and, thus, the *EV* in this case would equal the negative *CV* from moving in the opposite direction.

4
Property Rights, Market Failure, Externality, and Environmental Economics

Markets and Property Rights

Market economies function because individuals are, in general, motivated to maximize their income (profit) or welfare (utility). They willingly enter into market transactions because these are to their mutual benefit. Prices are the barometer of the values that individuals place on the goods and services that are traded. However, there are situations in which trades are not possible because *property rights* are not clearly specified. For example, a rational and well-informed individual would not be willing to purchase an automobile from another person without knowing whether or not that vehicle could be legally registered in the jurisdiction where it is purchased. Without a guarantee that this would indeed be possible, the current owner of the vehicle would have a difficult time selling the vehicle and would not consider that he or she had an exclusive right to it. What, then, is meant by the term property right?

A property right establishes legal ownership of a resource and specifies limitations on the way one can use resources. It exists only if the following conditions are met.

(1) Property rights must be *completely specified*. This implies that ownership is clearly delineated, and that restrictions upon the rights of ownership and penalties for violation of those rights are specified. Restrictions upon ownership must accompany property rights in order to avoid the confusion that would result if everyone used the things that they own in any way that they pleased.

(2) A property right implies *exclusive ownership*. This is the right to determine who, if anyone, may use the property and under what conditions. But all rewards and penalties in the exercise of the right accrue to the owner.

(3) Property owners have the right to *transfer* their property. In the example above, transfer was impeded by the vehicle registration process. Restrictions on the transfer of property lead to inefficiency – to market breakdown. It is important to recognize that *rights* are transferred as opposed to just material property. When buying land, one purchases the right to use that land, but the land is not physically moved. The same is true when you purchase an item at the store; even though the item is removed, it is the right to use the item that is purchased. Removal can be accomplished by shoplifting, but this does not constitute a transfer of the ownership rights; rather, ownership rights are violated.

(4) Property rights must be effectively *enforced*. Without enforcement, a system of property rights cannot be considered useful. If enforcement is imperfect, as it always will be in the real world, then the expected value of penalties must exceed any possible gains a violator can hope to make.

Finally, market transactions involve costs – information, contracting, and policing costs. Transactions costs are the costs expended in transferring property. (Avoiding transactions costs is one reason that firms will integrate into forward or backward markets. Theory suggests that an internal organization will supersede a market if the market transaction costs are greater than the costs of making the same transactions within a single organization.) It is important to recognize the existence of market transaction costs because we sometimes mistake the need for public intervention with high transaction costs. In this case, public intervention could be costlier than the benefit gained by correcting some perceived misallocation.

Externality: The Rationale for Public Intervention

Externality takes three different forms. Each type of externality constitutes an example of a market imperfection, of market failure. Externality is also considered to be at the 'heart and guts' of resource economics and a major reason for public intervention in private markets. However, it should be made clear from the outset that the existence of market failure, in and of itself, is not sufficient justification for government intervention. In addition, it needs to be demonstrated that government intervention enhances the welfare of society. There are four kinds of externality but only three of these have implications for welfare measurement, as is indicated in the following discussion.

Technical Externality

Technical externality results whenever the long-run average cost (LAC) curve falls over the relevant range of output – to the point where all demand is satisfied. A falling long-run average cost curve indicates that there are *economies of scale* in production. This is illustrated in Figure 4.1, where the demand function intersects the LAC curve before the LAC turns upward. In this case, as is shown in the diagram, the long-run marginal cost (LMC) function lies everywhere below LAC. Examples of industries or situations in which this phenomenon occurs are public utilities (telephone, water and sewage, cable TV, etc.) and bridges. Efficient allocation of resources occurs whenever marginal social valuation of a good or service is equal to the marginal social cost of providing that good or service. Marginal value is generally represented by the market price, except, for example, when there are subsidies. In the case of falling LAC, the situation where price is equal to marginal cost ($P = LMC$) results in losses, because the average cost of production lies above the average return or market price. Thus, firms will lose the shaded area in Figure 4.1 if they set price equal to marginal cost.

The situation depicted in Figure 4.1 will lead to a natural monopoly if the good or service is provided privately. Since a monopolist determines the quantity to sell by setting marginal cost equal to marginal revenue and then determining price from the demand curve, the market price will lie above marginal cost and inefficient allocation results. Since monopoly leads to inefficiency, and competition results in losses, public intervention is required. This intervention can take several forms.

The most common form of intervention is *government regulation*. Regulation of private or autonomous public utilities is a common method of preventing price from rising to the monopoly level. In this case, a divergence between price and marginal cost is tolerated, and regulation attempts to keep this difference at a level that enables firms to recover their fixed costs and earn a rate of return comparable to that available in other sectors of the economy – the *normal rate of return*.

The second approach is that of *public provision*. In this case, the good or service is provided by the government. It sets price equal to marginal cost and uses a lump sum tax to pay for the fixed costs of providing the good or service. For example, taxes are used to build bridges, and, once a bridge has been built, the marginal cost of getting a vehicle across the bridge is essentially zero (at least to the point of congestion). The appropriate charge to levy is zero. A toll may be employed, but once again the primary purpose of the toll is to recover the fixed cost: the toll is not meant to allocate the bridge's services most efficiently by setting price equal to marginal cost.

Figure 4.1

Technical externality

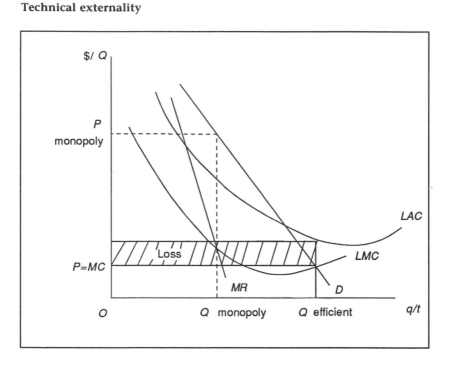

For services such as sewage treatment, residents may be charged a hook-up fee to connect them to the main sewer line; it is equal to the marginal cost of making the connection. A *system development charge* may be added to the hook-up fee. This charge is not meant to pay for the existing sewers and sewage treatment plant, because these have already been built. Rather, the day will come when hooking up another household or firm will result in the system's capacity being exceeded. Rather than letting this last household or firm incur the cost of replacing the treatment plant, the system development charge is levied so that all users contribute to the cost of replacing the plant.

Public Goods Externality
A second form of externality is the public good. A public good is one that, no matter how much one consumes of the good, there is still enough for everyone else. Everyone has access to the public good at the

same time so that *no one can be excluded from consumption once it is provided.* Examples of public goods are sunshine, clean air, national defence, and scenic amenities. There are few pure public goods because most have a private element to them. There are also many private goods, that are not purely private, as indicated by the discussion concerning property rights. Certain recreational activities have a high degree of publicness to them, while other goods have a very high degree of privateness. Further, not everything that is publicly provided is a public good. For example, the water fountain in a university building can be used by anyone, but my use precludes your using it at the same time. The same is true of water skiing on a reservoir: I am free to ski but may be prevented from doing so by other boats and skiers. These types of goods and services are referred to as *collective goods.*

Public goods are an important form of externality, because there is no incentive for individuals to provide them. The reason is obvious: once they are provided, no one can be excluded, so there is no way private individuals can sell such goods. There are no private property rights with respect to public goods. As a result, it falls upon the government to provide public goods. No private individual or firm would be willing to provide national defence services. Likewise, no private person would have an incentive to provide clean air or water. In many cases, there are also no incentives to change one's behaviour to prevent the befouling of air and water. In the absence of incentives, incurring costs to prevent pollution is the same as attempting to provide the public good (clean air) privately. As discussed below, this is one problem of environmental economics.

The public goods argument for government intervention also occurs in discussions concerning open spaces such as meadows and parks. Open space is a public good because others cannot be excluded from enjoying it. The public goods argument is also used by those contending that we need to ensure the long-term sustainability of agricultural production. But long-term sustainability of agricultural output is often invoked as an argument by those who are really interested in open space. This discussion is pursued further in Chapter 11, where provision of open space through zoning is considered.

Ownership or Technological Externality
The final type of externality is that which is usually meant when the term is discussed. A technological externality occurs whenever the actions of one economic agent are felt by a second (external) economic

agent, but this effect is not taken into account by the first agent in making his or her decisions. That is, the external agent incurs a cost, or receives a benefit, as a result of the actions of the first agent, but these effects are not taken into account by the first agent. Thus, while economic processes are *physically* linked, the economic effects are separated. For example, pollution by a factory affects the success rate of downstream fishers, but this is not taken into account by the factory when it makes decisions regarding output and, hence, the amount of effluent it releases into the river. It is clear that, in this and similar situations, the factory would take into account its actions upon the downstream fishery if it also owned the fishery. It is the separation of ownership that causes us to use the term *ownership externality* to characterize these cases.

While there are certain measures that can be taken to mitigate this type of externality, it is not possible to eliminate all technological externality. Rather, the objective is to find the optimal amount of externality to permit in order to ensure that the welfare of society is enhanced. In finding solutions, it will be shown that clear specification of property rights is particularly important.

Pecuniary Externality

Policy analysts and critics of land use and natural resource policy often confuse the pecuniary effects of externality with the real effects. Pecuniary effects concern income transfers and are not the same as the welfare measures identified in Chapter 3. Pecuniary externality results whenever the actions of one agent affect another agent through the market. For example, suppose that a laundromat has trouble hiring labour because a pulp mill has recently moved into town. The pulp mill offers higher wages, and employees at the laundromat will remain in their current employ only if their wages are increased. The laundromat must either pay the higher wages or go out of business. Unless higher prices can be charged for laundry services, the laundromat may experience a reduction in net earnings. However, this is not a real loss to society; it is an income transfer that favours labour. A real externality occurs if the pulp mill operation affects the production function of the laundromat, requiring it to employ more soap and/or labour to obtain the same output as previously or to purchase a dryer where laundry could earlier be hung out to dry.

Externality and Environmental Economics

In recent years, concern over the environment has become more pronounced, and economists have an important role to play when it comes to these concerns. The types of externality that are of concern when talking about environmental problems are technological externality and public goods externality. In this section, the focus is on the former.

External Economies and Diseconomies

What does economic efficiency mean in an environmental context? We tend to know more about the *costs* of environmental improvement than we do about the *benefits* of environmental improvement. For example, biochemical oxygen demand (BOD) is a measure of the harmfulness of wastes. It is a measure of the amount of oxygen required by the wastes and, thus, unavailable for supporting aquatic life. It is easy to reduce BOD by 85 per cent, but tertiary treatment to reduce it beyond 85 per cent is expensive. Thus, the marginal cost curve is rather flat and then takes a sharp upward turn, as is indicated in Figure 4.2.

Figure 4.2

Marginal benefits and costs of reducing pollution

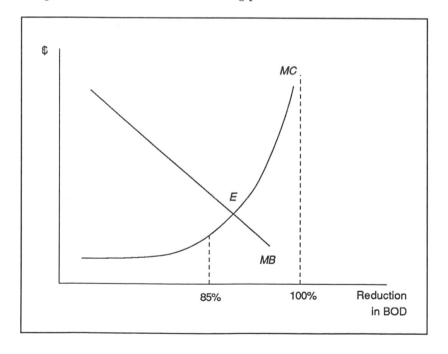

What, then, are the benefits of reducing BOD? There is little evidence regarding the marginal benefits of environmental improvement, although these benefits seem to be great when the environment is improved by a small amount. One role of the economist is to provide society with enough information concerning the marginal benefits (MB) and marginal costs (MC) to get us to some sort of equilibrium, such as E in Figure 4.2. In some sense the economist is a detective, seeking enough information to determine E, if not precisely, at least within some range of values. If we cannot attain E in this environmental market, then the market is economically inefficient. Economic efficiency is discussed later in this chapter.

When it comes to environmental goods, public action or intervention is often required. However, we must be able to justify public intervention as leading to greater economic efficiency. Further, environmental policy leads to a redistribution of income. Because of this, and as a result of the need to assign property rights, economic analysis often leads to value judgments.

Consider the following example of technological or ownership externality. The production function for the output of industry A is given by

$$A = f(X_1, X_2),$$

where X_1 and X_2 are inputs into production and f is the production function. The production function for industry B is

$$B = h(X_1).$$

The externality enters via the following relationship:

$$X_2 = g(B).$$

One consequence of producing B is the production of the externality X_2. This 'by-product' may be something 'good' or it may be environmentally 'bad.' Whatever the case, it is clear that B has an impact on the level of A's production via X_2. A has no control over the output of X_2. Hence, B is the acting party and A is the affected party.

Whether the production of X_2 is 'good' or 'bad' depends upon whether X_2 increases or decreases as B increases and whether an increase in X_2 results in a decrease or increase in the output of A. In mathematical language, it depends upon the signs of the derivatives of the foregoing functions. Four cases can be distinguished.

(1) $dX_2/dB > 0$ and $\partial A/\partial X_2 > 0$. This says that an increase in output B

will increase the amount of X_2 available for use in the production of A. An increase in X_2 will, in turn, cause an increase in the output of A. Since increases in B's output are beneficial to A, this is termed an *external economy*. (Of course, we can replace the word 'increase' with 'decrease,' but the idea remains the same: the fact that B produces is beneficial to A.) The product X_2 is something considered to be 'good.' An example of external economy occurs where B is a honey producer and A an apple producer. An increase in honey production requires more bees that, in turn, will pollinate more of the apple blossoms, thereby increasing the yield of apples.

(2) $dX_2/dB < 0$ and $\partial A/\partial X_2 < 0$. In this case, the second term indicates that X_2 is harmful to the production of A; that is, the more X_2 that enters into the production of A, the less A is produced. However, as a result of B's output, the availability of X_2 is actually reduced, as is indicated by the first term. The product or input X_2 adversely affects A, but B's output reduces it. Hence, we have an external economy once again.

(3) $dX_2/dB < 0$ and $\partial A/\partial X_2 > 0$. Again, the availability of X_2 is reduced by an increase in output B, as is indicated by the sign on the first term. However, unlike the previous case, a decrease in X_2 will cause a decline in the output of A. (The denominator in the second expression is negative, as is the numerator, thereby making the term positive.) Since the presence of output B is harmful to A, we refer to this as an *external diseconomy*.

(4) $dX_2/dB > 0$ and $\partial A/\partial X_2 < 0$. The first expression indicates that availability of X_2 rises with increases in B; the second expression indicates that more X_2 results in a reduction in A. Thus, production by B is harmful to A, and we have an external diseconomy. An example is the case of a pulp mill polluting a river, thereby decreasing the number of fish caught by downstream fishers.

If either $dX_2/dB = 0$ or $\partial A/\partial X_2 = 0$, or both, there is no externality.

Now let us introduce some economic magnitudes into the foregoing analysis. This is done by introducing prices P_A, P_B, r_1, and r_2 for outputs A and B and inputs X_1 and X_2, respectively. It is well known that economic agents make decisions at the margin. Firms will employ an input (e.g., labour) as long as the marginal benefit of the hired input exceeds its marginal cost, with optimal employment occurring where the marginal benefit is exactly equal to marginal cost. In competitive markets, the marginal cost of an input is simply its price (viz., wage rate). The marginal benefit is less straightforward but is also rather easy to find.

It is equal to the additional product attributable to the employment of an extra unit of the input *multiplied* by the price of the product. Hence,

$$P\ MP = r,$$

where *P* is output price, *MP* is the marginal physical product attributable to the input and *r* is the price of input. The left-hand side of the foregoing relationship is also known as the value of the marginal product of the input.

Returning to our externality problem, private evaluation of the amount of inputs to hire (amounts of output to produce) are given by the following relations for industries *A* and *B*, respectively:

$$P_A \cdot MP_{X_1 \text{ in } A} = r_1 \tag{4.1}$$

and

$$P_B \cdot MP_{X_1 \text{ in } B} = r_1. \tag{4.2}$$

Now, *A* does not have any direct control over the amount of X_2 it uses; availability of X_2 is determined by *B*. In this sense, the technology can be considered *asymmetric*.

Society as a whole is concerned about efficiency in both industries. Thus, society would like industry *B* to take into account the effect production of *B* has on *A*'s output. Social valuation of the amounts of input X_1 to be hired by *A* and *B*, respectively, would be as follows:

$$P_A \cdot MP_{X_1 \text{ in } A} = r_1, \tag{4.3}$$

$$P_B \cdot MP_{X_1 \text{ in } B} + (dX_2/dB)(\partial A/\partial X_2)P_A = r_1,$$

or

$$P_B \cdot MP_{X_1 \text{ in } B} + (dX_2/dB)(P_A \cdot MP_{X_2 \text{ in } A}) = r_1. \tag{4.4}$$

Whereas each producer could solve his/her own equilibrium condition to find out how much X_1 they should hire in the case of private evaluation, conditions (4.3) and (4.4) must be solved simultaneously when the externality is taken into account. The signs on the terms dX_2/dB and $MP_{X_2 \text{ in } A}$ (or $\partial A/\partial X_2$) will determine whether we have an external economy or diseconomy.

The second term on the left-hand side of (4.4) is not taken into account by *B* in making private production decisions. In order to arrive at optimal resource use from society's perspective, it is necessary to get

B to consider this term in his/her decision calculus. A number of alternative methods have been suggested.

(1) If we have an external diseconomy, then we must tax individual *B* to get him or her to make decisions that are closer to the social optimum. If, on the other hand, we have an external economy, then we need to subsidize firm *B* in order to get the firm to make decisions that are optimal. This solution to the externality problem is referred to as the *Pigou tax or subsidy solution.*

(2) The *Coase property rights solution* requires that property rights be correctly specified. Property rights could be specified so that *A* bribes *B* to take into account the damages (or benefits) accruing to *A*, or they could be arranged so that *B* would be required to pay compensation for damages inflicted upon *A*. Specifying property rights involves legal wrangling and other transaction costs.

(3) Another solution is *merger.* Take, for example, the case of pulp mill pollution that damages a downstream fishery. If the company that owns the pulp mill were also to own the fishery, then, in making its decisions, it would take into account the impact of the pollution generated by the pulp mill upon the landings of fish.

(4) The final option is for the government to *nationalize* both industries *A* and *B*. In this case, the effect that firm *B* has on output *A* would be taken into account by the public manager. However, this may be the least desirable of all solutions, as is indicated by the environmental degradation that has taken place in the centrally planned economies of Eastern Europe.

Whatever policy is pursued, it is necessary to recognize that, if firm *B* does not take into account its impact upon the output of *A*, inefficiency exists in the economy; society's overall welfare is lower than it could be. Only when a proper social evaluation occurs – when *B* takes into account its actions upon *A* – will an efficient resolution to the externality problem result.

Are Externalities Relevant?

Consider two individuals, Mr. Smith and Mr. Jones, who share a common property line along their backyards. Through his family room, Mr. Jones has an unimpeded view of the mountains beyond the front of Mr. Smith's house. Currently, there is no fence separating the two properties. However, Mr. Smith wishes to install a swimming pool, and, in order to prevent Mr. Jones viewing him while he is swimming in the nude, he wishes to build a fence. As Mr. Jones has a dog that has recently

Figure 4.3

Example of ownership externality

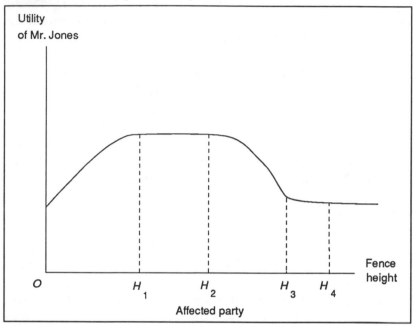

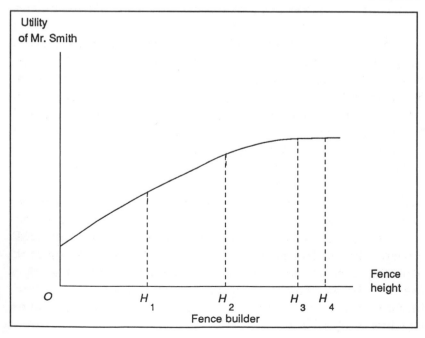

managed to get into trouble with Mr. Smith, the former is more than willing to have a fence between the two properties. However, the fence height that is required by Mr. Smith to prevent Mr. Jones from viewing him while he is swimming is higher than that required to prevent the dog from getting into Mr. Smith's garden. The situation is illustrated with the aid of Figure 4.3.

Mr. Smith is the fence builder. His utility increases with fence height until the height of the fence is at H_4. Beyond H_4, Jones is unable to view Smith while he is swimming, and there is no added utility to Smith from building a higher fence. However, the utility function has curvature to it, because, as the fence height approaches H_4, Mr. Jones finds it more difficult to be able to peer into Mr. Smith's yard; therefore, a fence height somewhat lower than H_4 would prevent most of Mr. Jones's viewing.

Mr. Jones, on the other hand, gets utility from increased fence height over height zero and up to a fence height of H_1. This height of fence is sufficient to contain his dog. Between fence heights of H_1 and H_2, Mr. Jones is indifferent as to what height of fence is built, because his view is unaffected. Beyond a fence height of H_2, Mr. Jones loses utility, because his view of the mountains is increasingly impeded as the fence increases in height. Beyond fence height H_3, however, Jones becomes indifferent regarding further increases in fence height, because his view is entirely impeded by the fence.

Since Smith is the fence builder, he can be considered the acting party, while Jones is the affected party. A *relevant externality* exists whenever the affected party has a desire to induce the acting party to modify his/her behaviour with respect to the activity, in this case, fence building. An externality is relevant whenever the affected party is not indifferent to the activity. Thus, in terms of Figure 4.3, a relevant externality exists between zero fence height and a fence height of H_1. This is because the utility of Mr. Jones is affected by (in this case, benefits from) the fence building activity of Mr. Smith.

An *inframarginal externality* exists over the range H_1 to H_2, because Mr. Jones is indifferent to any fence height between H_1 and H_2. He receives no increase or decrease in utility as fence height increases in that range. However, the very fact that fence height increases hastens the time that his utility does get affected, namely, after a fence height of H_2 is reached. Likewise, an inframarginal externality exists beyond fence height H_3, because a reduction in fence height will affect actions, as we now indicate.

A *Pareto relevant externality* exists when it is possible to modify the activity of fence building in such a way as to make the affected party, Mr. Jones, better off, without making the acting party, Mr. Smith, worse off. (A *Pareto improvement* is defined as any action or policy that increases the welfare of one person (output of one commodity) without, at the same time, decreasing the welfare of any other person (output of any other good).) If Mr. Jones values his loss in utility to a greater extent than Mr. Smith values his increase in utility as fence height increases, then it is possible for Mr. Jones to compensate Mr. Smith for building a fence that is smaller in height in such a way that Mr. Jones is better off. This possibility exists only in the range of fence height H_2 to H_3. It is in this range that a Pareto relevant externality exists.

It is only when a Pareto relevant externality exists that one party will approach the other party to cause a change in behaviour; in that case, there is a possibility to improve society's welfare. In the cases of relevant externality and inframarginal externality, there may be no need to modify the behaviour of any of the economic agents, because there will be no improvement in welfare. Existence of externality is not sufficient justification for government action. Nor, as this case illustrates, need government intervention be optimal. Under existing laws, the individuals should be able to resolve this problem.

Environmental Pollution and Solution Alternatives

It is possible to demonstrate a number of economic concepts concerning environmental pollution using the example of a pulp mill and a downstream fishery. The pulp mill pollutes a river, thereby affecting the catch of the fishers. We have a two-actor world, namely, fishers who want clean water that translates into more fish and an industrialist who dumps pollutants into the water, thereby killing the fish. For convenience, we assume linear cost and benefit functions. The benefits are those resulting from cleaner water, while the costs are those of cleaning up the water. How the socially optimal solution is obtained is not our primary concern; that is, we ignore the fact that the costs are the industrialist's problem and that the benefits accrue only to the fishers.

In Figure 4.4, waste withholding is plotted along the abscissa, while dollars is plotted along the ordinate. The marginal benefit (MB) curve represents the marginal benefits to the fishers as wastes are withheld. The marginal cost (MC) curve represents the marginal costs to the industrialist of withholding wastes. The problem is an asymmetric one, since only the pulp mill can prevent or clean up the pollution. An economically efficient solution or Pareto optimal[1] occurs at point C, where the costs to the industrialist are given by area $OACX$, and the costs to the fishers in terms of lost fish revenues are given by XCD.

Figure 4.4

Waste withholding and the social optimum

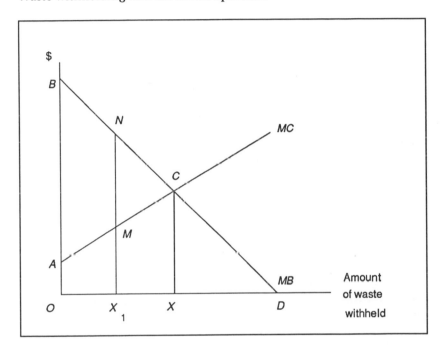

Consider waste withholding of some amount less than X, say X_1. In this case, the costs to the industrialist are given by area $OAMX_1$, while the foregone benefits to the fishers are given by area X_1ND. The sum of areas $OAMX_1$ plus X_1ND exceeds that of areas $OACX$ plus XCD. The amount by which the social costs of waste withholding to level X_1 exceed those of waste withholding to level X are given by area NCM.

The problem that remains is: how does a society arrive at equilibrium point C, the Pareto efficient solution? A number of cases can be considered and these depend upon who has the property rights, the fishers or the industrialist.

Coase Solution

Consider the case where the fishers have the property right. If there is no waste withholding, then the pulp mill will have to compensate the fishers an amount equal to area *OBD*, that is, the entire area under the marginal benefit curve. Given that the amount the industrialist must pay the fishers is initially much larger than the costs of withholding wastes, as given by the marginal cost curve, the industrialist will withhold waste until equilibrium point *C* is reached. There the marginal cost of withholding waste is equal to the marginal payments that the industrialist would have to make to the fishers.

Now reverse the property rights so that they reside with the pulp mill rather than with the fishers. In this case, the fishers will pay a 'bribe' (make a side payment) to the pulp mill that exceeds the costs that the pulp mill incurs in withholding wastes. Once again, movement is towards the equilibrium point *C* which is Pareto efficient.

Regardless of which actor has the property rights, in this world where there are no transaction costs, the area *ABC* in Figure 4.4 is a surplus that can be earned by reducing the amount of waste emitted into the system (i.e., withholding an amount *OX* of wastes). The two parties will negotiate to determine how much of the surplus each gains, with the result depending on the respective bargaining abilities and, likely, on the assignment of the property rights (the one with the property rights would appear to have a decided advantage).

There are a number of factors that prevent actors from negotiating to achieve a Pareto optimal solution in the face of externality.

(1) Property rights may not be clearly defined. For example, who owns the rights to the river or, for that matter, who owns the rights to a lake, ocean, or the air? Who has the incentive to modify his/her behaviour?

(2) Negotiation between the parties often leads to litigation, and court procedures are both costly and time consuming.

(3) The benefits of environmental improvement generally tend to be widely dispersed, and those who benefit from environmental improvement are generally unable to get together to discuss strategy, size of required bribes, and so on.

(4) Problems in technical information gathering often exist. Irreversibilities may be present. Many effects are nonmarket in nature and, therefore, extremely difficult to measure. As mentioned, many effects are widely dispersed, and more than one geographic and/or political unit is affected.

(5) Finally, pollutants have threshold levels. The effects of pollution are often negligible over some range, but they become critical beyond

a certain level. For example, an area may be able to handle five industrialists polluting the atmosphere, but pollution levels may become unbearable once a sixth industrialist enters and the threshold is passed. Who is to blame and who is to pay? Is it just the sixth or all of them?

Pigou Solution

Now consider the case of state involvement or the so-called Pigou solution. In this case, state intervention is assumed to be necessary to get society to the Pareto optimal point. Again, we must consider who has the property rights. First, let us take the case in which the fishers have the property rights. This situation can be illustrated using Figure 4.5, which is similar to Figure 4.4. Now the state would tax the industrialist according to the marginal benefit curve of the fishers. In effect, this causes the marginal benefit curve to become a marginal benefit of tax avoidance curve (MB_{TA}). Without a side bargain, the marginal benefit of tax avoidance will lead the industrialist to the socially efficient amount of waste withholding represented by the intersection of MB_{TA} and MC or amount OX.

Now, if it is still possible for the industrialist and the fishers to somehow get together, then the fishers may be able to bribe the industrialist to increase waste withholding beyond OX. That is, there may still be room for Coase-type side payments; indeed, the government intervention has created a surplus area for the two parties to negotiate over, although it is not surplus to society as a whole.

We can represent this situation in Figure 4.5 by adding to the marginal benefit of tax avoidance curve the original marginal benefit curve. This is represented by the curve labelled $MB_{TA} + MB$. By moving from OX to OX^N, the benefits to the fishers plus industrialist consist of the area under the $MB_{TA} + MB$ curve, namely, area $C + D + E$, which consists of the benefits of tax avoidance (area E) plus the benefits to the fishers (area $C + D$ = area E). The costs of this move to the two parties is $D + E$ (although the cost is incurred by the industrialist). The area C is a surplus over which the two actors will bargain, although it is not a surplus from the point of view of the rest of society. Thus, if side payments are possible in addition to the tax, it is likely that the two parties will agree upon waste withholding of OX^N. State intervention moves the economy to X, but bargaining will move the resulting equilibrium to X^N, which is not socially optimal, since society is worse off, by the shaded area D.

Figure 4.5

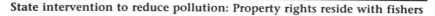

State intervention to reduce pollution: Property rights reside with fishers

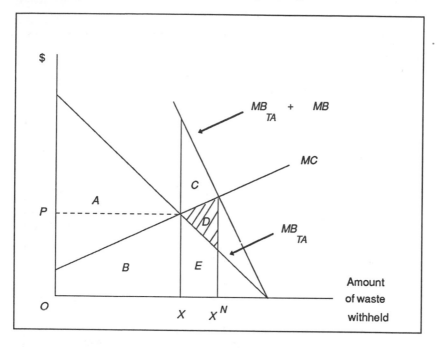

Rather than taxing the pulp mill according to the marginal benefit function of the fishers, the government could simply impose a charge of *OP* per unit of waste discharged. The industrialist will equate his/her marginal cost of withholding waste with the marginal benefit (= *OP*) of doing so. The optimal solution is again *OX* amount of waste withholding. Of course, the government will likely need to vary the charge in a trial-and-error fashion to find the optimal solution, but that would create uncertainty.

Now suppose that the property right resides with the pulp mill. In this case, the state would subsidize the industrialist an amount *ab* in Figure 4.6 (= *OP* in Figure 4.5), thereby making *MC'* the effective marginal cost curve facing the industrialist. In and of itself, the subsidy will create an incentive for the industrialist to withhold an amount of waste equal to *OX*. Additionally, if it is possible for the parties to come to some sort of agreement, they will move to *OX^N* amount of waste withholding. In moving from *OX* to *OX^N*, the industrialist incurs an actual cost equal to area *T* (although the cost to society is area *R* + *S* + *T*), fishers gain area *S* + *T*, and the parties bargain over area *S*. However, taxpayers are

worse off by area $R + S$, and the social loss is area R, which corresponds
to the shaded area in the previous figure (Figure 4.5).

Figure 4.6

**State intervention to reduce pollution: Property rights reside
with industrialist**

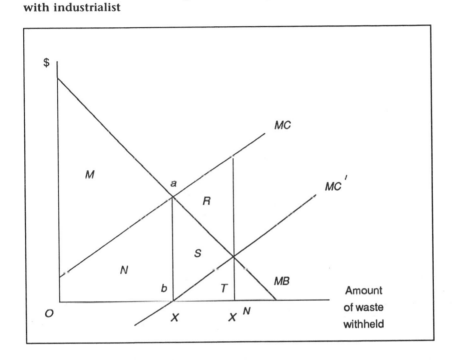

Merger
A third solution to the externality problem is to merge the activities of
making pulp and catching fish. While this is of course unrealistic, it
would get the pulp mill to take into account its effect on the downstream fishery. A merged firm would immediately recognize that the
number of fish being caught is reduced as a result of pulp production.
In making decisions regarding the pulp mill division of the merged firm,
the impact upon fish catch would be taken into account.

Discussion
The foregoing example of externality, with the pulp mill affecting the
profits of the fishery, illustrates a number of important points. First,
there still remain external effects, even at an economically efficient
equilibrium. Second, the fact that externalities exist does not necessarily

mean that we are not at a Pareto optimal. Existence of externalities is a necessary but not sufficient condition for government intervention. State intervention can only be justified if there is no possibility of Coasian side payments *and* if the costs of intervention (administration, policing, etc.) are less than the benefits (e.g., as given by area *ABC* in Figure 4.4). State intervention is circumvented if a Coase solution is still possible, despite an active role by government. Thus, if a Coase solution is at all possible, it would be a mistake for the government to intervene. In fact, the shaded area in Figure 4.5 (or area *R* in Figure 4.6) needs to be added to the administrative, monitoring, and policing costs of government intervention to determine the true cost of public action. Third, putting a correct tax on the industrialist does not necessarily get us to an economically efficient equilibrium. The best solution from society's point of view can be circumvented if it is still possible for the two parties to bargain.

Finally, it is important to note that the Coase solution discussed above is not a correct interpretation of what Ronald Coase himself said. That is, the foregoing discussion assumes that, for economic efficiency, it does not matter to whom the property rights are given, although it may matter from a political and egalitarian point of view. However, Coase provides no such argument. Indeed, he indicates that the assignment of property rights does matter, with one assignment leading to a different result than another. The proper assignment of property rights, according to Coase, is the one that leads to the least (most) overall costs (benefits) to society. This is discussed later in this chapter.

Consumers, Producers, and Externality

The pulp mill/fishers example is one of *producer/producer* externality. This case illustrates the effect of one firm's output decisions on the production function of another. There are also *consumer/consumer* and *producer/consumer* types of externalities.

An example of a consumer/consumer externality is that of smoking. Scientific evidence indicates that smoking is a definite cause of lung cancer, that smoking is linked to cancer of internal organs and to heart disease, and that smoking is harmful to non-smokers. In one province of Canada (Saskatchewan) during the 1980s, the provincial government collected approximately $17 million per year from cigarette taxes but spent $21 million per year on lung cancer alone. Given the fact that smoking is linked to other types of cancer and heart disease, and is harmful to non-smokers, it is obvious that the smoker does not pay a fair share of the costs of medical expenses. These costs are borne by non-smokers, and this is both inefficient and unfair. The solution is to tax cigarettes so that smokers bear the true costs of smoking, and this policy has been actively pursued by governments in recent years.

Smokers also endanger the health of non-smokers. Currently, non-smokers must bribe smokers not to smoke. By changing the law so that smoking is prohibited in a public place, and assuming this is somehow enforceable, property rights are effectively changed. Enforcement could take place by way of litigation, for example. The smoking example can be illustrated in diagrammatic fashion in Figure 4.7. The amount smoked by any individual smoker is plotted along the horizontal axis. The marginal benefit curve measures the benefits that the smoker derives from smoking. The curve labelled $MC_{private}$ is the private marginal cost of smoking. It is the cost that the smoker pays; it includes the price of cigarettes, the costs of more frequent cleaning of draperies, the costs of painting more often, and so on. The curve labelled MC_{social} is the marginal cost to society of that person smoking. It includes both the private cost of smoking and the cost to non-smokers. Thus, there is a divergence between the private and social costs of smoking. The smoker will smoke an amount given by Q_P, whereas society would prefer that the smoker smoke amount Q_s. Notice that, in order to attain a social optimum or economically (Pareto) efficient point, it is not necessary that the amount individuals smoke be reduced to zero. Yet, the intention of government appears to be to eliminate all smoking; this is an inefficient solution, unless the intersection of MB and MC_{social} occurs at a non-positive value for the amount smoked.

An example of a producer/consumer externality is coal unloading in a port city. The coal unloading activity results in the dirtying of laundry hung out to dry, the more frequent washing of windows, and so on for residents near the facility. The coal company could add to its costs payments to residents in order to put up with the coal unloading facility, or the residents could pay the coal company to choose an alternative site. Who pays depends upon the assignment of the property rights. The only problem is that the transaction costs of bringing residents together could outweigh the benefits, and a change in property rights could reduce these transaction costs. The diagram employed for the smoking example, Figure 4.7, could apply in this case as well. Rather than labelling the horizontal axis as the amount smoked, we simply re-label it as the amount of coal unloaded. Once again, there is a divergence between private and social costs, with the social costs being higher than the private costs. By getting the coal company to take into account the costs it imposes upon nearby residents, less coal will be unloaded at the facility.

Figure 4.7

Smoking: An example of consumer/consumer externality

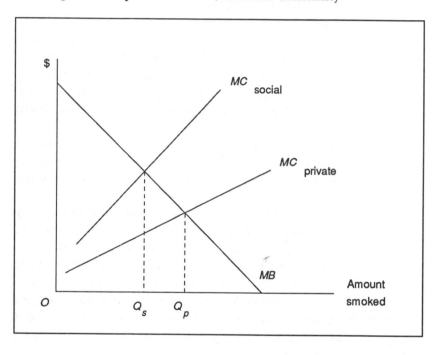

The example of the coal unloading facility also illustrates the concept of *threshold*. The increased cost or reduction in the amount of coal unloaded may be such that the owner of the coal unloading facility would prefer to shut the facility down and move it to another place.

Standards, Charges, and Other Institutional Alternatives

The problem of environmental pollution is characterized by many polluters and even more sufferers from pollution. Thus, the transaction costs of arriving at a Coase-type solution are enormous and generally prevent that type of solution. In order to achieve an economically efficient solution, it is necessary for public intervention. Government action is usually a set of institutions that provides incentives of one form or another to reduce pollution. One might ask what characteristics such institutions should have. A number are considered.

(1) Institutions must somehow reflect the external costs and benefits of the activity. For example, a surface mining reclamation board should not consist only of coal mining people. It should represent all individuals involved or affected by the decisions that are made.

(2) The institutions should be able to influence behaviour by either providing incentives or through direct control or regulation.

(3) Government institutions should be set up in ways that enable society to take advantage of economies of size. For example, waste disposal is characterized by economies of scale in the treatment of multiple types of wastes. Various waste materials can better be treated together than separately, and institutions should be developed that enable one to exploit opportunities to reduce treatment costs.

(4) Institutions must be constructed to take into account extra market or nonmarket benefits such as those arising from recreation, scenic amenities, and so forth. Measurement of nonmarket benefits is the subject of Chapter 7.

(5) Institutions must be concerned with a physically and economically relevant geographic area. A good example is the Rhine River in Europe. Germany wants a clean Rhine in Germany, but it does not care if the Rhine running through Holland is polluted. The same is true of the Colorado River, which crosses into Mexico as a stream of salt water. An institution developed to reduce pollution in these two rivers must have *effective* representation from Holland and Mexico, respectively, and not just from Germany and the United States.

(6) Institutions should be capable of adapting to changes in technology. Unfortunately, institutions generally have no mechanism for changing things once they are in place. The cost and benefit curves tend not to stay constant through time. Given that there are changes occurring over time, it is necessary that institutions be able to adapt to such changes.

(7) Finally, institutions must operate by a set of rules that are considered to be fair by a majority of people. Otherwise, they will fail, because they are not politically feasible.

Methods of arriving at a Pareto efficient solution have already been considered. These methods can be viewed as instruments and three of them will now be discussed in greater detail as well as compared from an efficiency standpoint.

Regulation or Standards

A standard requires that every firm limit its effluent or discharge to some prescribed level. There are two basic types of standards. An effluent standard focuses on the quality and content of the effluent that is dumped into the atmosphere or into a river. It is also possible to prescribe conditions for the receiving medium. By this we mean that air cannot contain more than some prescribed per cent of sulphur, or that water cannot contain more than some per cent of a particular type of pollutant. For attaining an efficient solution (where marginal cost is equal to marginal benefit), regulation does not always work. It is a satisfying method that works best over a particular range of waste withholding. In Figure 4.8, the standard for waste withholding is set at *OW*. It is generally not possible to set the level of waste withholding at a point that will enable attainment of the Pareto efficient solution (point *E*) because of the onerous informational requirements. The loss to society due to an inability to achieve *E* is given by area *MNE*. Even if the standard were set to attain *E*, standards are a once-and-for-all instrument and difficult to change. If the marginal cost and marginal benefit curves change, then point *E* may change. This requires that the standard be flexible.

Standards tend to be uniform across a country, province, or state. This is inefficient, because what applies in one region may not apply in another. For example, a car pollution standard applicable in Los Angeles or Vancouver may be too stringent for cities located in Saskatchewan or North Dakota. In these low-population areas, the standard is set beyond *E* in Figure 4.8. Thus, buyers in cities located in low-population centres will pay too much for automobiles. Similarly, a standard achievable in the lower level of a river basin may be below that already existing in upstream regions. There is no incentive, then, to get upstream users to reduce their pollution. Finally, regulation provides no revenues for the monitoring and enforcement of standards.

Payments

Government payments can be made to firms in order to get them to reduce their pollution. Such subsidies should reflect the social benefits of pollution control. There are a number of problems with payments, however. First of all, they are expensive, since there is no source of revenue. Further, government institutions may be open to extortion. A firm may pretend to start producing some output, declaring an intention to pollute the river. It is then paid not to produce. Finally, pay-

Figure 4.8

Achieving environmental objectives with a standard

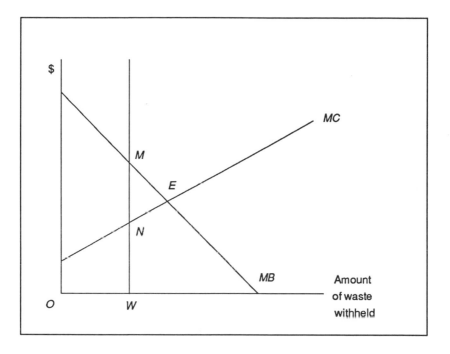

ments do not appeal to people's sense of equity and, as a result, may not be politically feasible.

These objections to payments do not seem to apply to agriculture, where producers are often paid hefty subsidies in order to prevent soil erosion. As an example, consider the $57 million outlay by the govern- ments of Saskatchewan and Canada, in 1989, to reduce soil erosion. As indicated in chapters 10 and 12, such expenditures may be wasteful; yet, agricultural producers have been able to convince governments of their need for subsidies in order to reduce the adverse environmental impacts of agronomic practices.

Charges
Charges are generally preferred by economists for a number of reasons. These are: (1) Charges can be less demanding in terms of informational requirements if the charge is varied by trial and error until the desired, but not necessarily optimal, level of waste withholding occurs. Yet, by levying an appropriate charge, the outcome will be the same as it is in

the payment system. (2) A system of charges generates revenue for the government. (3) Charges appeal to people's sense of equity. (4) Finally, charges are efficient from an economic standpoint.

Suppose that two firms, *A* and *B*, are polluting a river. Each firm has a different marginal cost curve for waste withholding as indicated by MC_A and MC_B. Now assume that society wishes to have waste withheld to some point *E*, as is indicated on the horizontal axis in Figure 4.9.

Figure 4.9

Charges to reduce pollution: Comparison with a standard

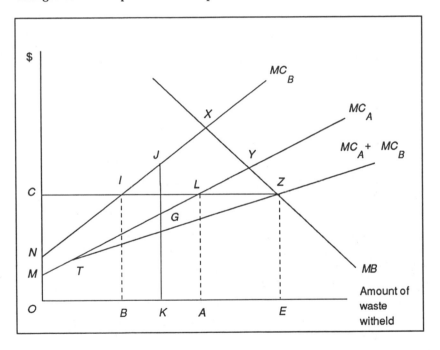

If an equitable standard is used to achieve waste withholding of amount *OE* (by trial and error), then each firm would withhold *OK* amount of waste, such that two times *OK* is equal to *OE*. The cost of waste withholding to society is given by the area *ONJK* + *OMGK*. If, instead of a standard, a charge of amount *OC* were used, firm *A* would withhold *OA* amount of waste and firm *B* would withhold amount *OB*. Notice that *OA* + *OB* = *OE*. The cost to society of waste withholding in this case would be area *ONIB* + *OMLA*. This area would equal *OMTZE*, that is, the area under the sum of marginal costs curve (MC_A + MC_B). This cost is less than the total cost that would be incurred under regulation. The less efficient waste withholder (firm *B*) would withhold less waste than would the more efficient firm *A*. Therefore, charges are preferred. Further, they provide incentives to change products, processes, and so on, as marginal costs change over time. Because firms are always trying to avoid being charged, they tend to respond quickly to technological change.

It should be noted that the preceding analysis holds when the marginal cost and benefit curves are linear. If this is not the case, then the result of charges being preferred to regulation *may* no longer be true. Perhaps this explains why some countries employ pollution regulation, while, elsewhere in their economy, they advocate the use of markets.

Discussion

The Greater Vancouver Regional District (GVRD) is a political jurisdiction that is responsible for planning and coordinating land use in the Vancouver region of British Columbia. To improve air quality in the region, the GVRD uses a combination of regulations (e.g., automobile emission standards and testing) and incentives. A draft GVRD air quality management bylaw recommends the use of permit fees for any firm or industry that discharges more than 100 kg (kilograms) of carbon monoxide per day or more than 5 kg per day of air contaminants such as nitrogen oxides, sulphur oxides, particulates, and volatile organic compounds. The taxes would be levied at the source, so that gasoline service stations would, for example, be required to pay for emission permits. The size of the emission fees that have been recommended are as follows: $1 per tonne for carbon monoxide, $34 per tonne for sulphur oxides, $50 per tonne for nitrogen oxides, $50 per tonne for volatile organic compounds, and $84 per tonne for particulates. It is unclear how these values were arrived at, but, if emissions are to be at an efficient level, the GVRD would want to balance the benefits of emissions reductions or damages caused against the costs of reducing emissions at the margin.

There are problems related to regulation of emissions and taxes that have not been considered in this chapter. However, in Chapter 9, we return to this issue in the context of global warming. There, the question relates to the design of appropriate policies for reducing emissions of carbon dioxide and other greenhouse gases on a global scale. Further, regulations and taxes are compared under conditions of uncertainty, transferable emission permits are examined as a policy instrument, and the problem of tax revenues are discussed. Before doing so, however, we need to reconsider policy designed to bring social and private costs into line.

Divergence of Social and Private Costs: A Reconsideration

One of the two essays for which Ronald Coase was awarded the 1991 Nobel Prize in economics was the paper 'The Problem of Social Cost' (1960). However, for the following four reasons, he is generally opposed to the 'solutions' to externality described above: (1) the policy prescriptions are based on comparisons between a state of laissez faire and an ideal world, (2) they do not take into account effects in other areas of the economy, (3) they fail to recognize that current legislation and common law already provide the needed correctives, and (4) they do not consider the possibility that corrective action may result in higher rather than lower social costs. We have tried to demonstrate the latter point, albeit in the restrictive framework of the ideal world.

Using actual court cases, Coase demonstrates that existing legislation and common law already resolve many externalities. Individuals do not have the right to unlimited use of their property. Further, efforts to correct for perceived divergences between social and private costs are going to cost more than they return in benefits. A tax solution cannot be imposed without, at the same time, determining what is to be done with tax revenues. Using pollution taxes to compensate those harmed by pollution (according to the damage suffered) is not the same as simply turning those revenues into the general tax account. The solutions in these cases are not the same, and the actual costs and benefits to society also differ. (This is discussed further in Chapter 9, with regard to carbon taxes.) Further, taxes will distort the optimal equilibrium. For example, a tax on automobile emissions in a region may induce in-migration and a higher population compared to the situation where there is no tax. Which of these results is preferred?

Finally, Coase argues that the correct course of action is to start the analysis 'with a situation approximating that which actually exists, to examine the effects of a proposed policy change and to attempt to decide whether the new situation would be, in total, better or worse than the original one' (Coase 1960). That is, the value of the total production of goods and services (widely defined to include nonmarket commodities) with the corrective policy in place must be compared with that in the absence of such a policy. It is Coase's contention that many tax and subsidy schemes would not lead to an increase in society's overall welfare. That is because existing institutions, along with market forces, already lead to an optimal allocation of society's resources.

Part Two:
Project Evaluation and Economic Development

Introduction to Part Two

In this section, we focus upon issues related to project evaluation and regional economic development. Throughout, there will be substantial emphasis on water resources because project evaluation developed in response to development of these resources and because they are important for economic development, particularly in arid countries. The western half of the North American continent, for example, is characterized by uneven distribution of water resources, low precipitation, and water shortages. The major water use in this region is for agriculture, with irrigation characterizing agricultural production in most western U.S. states and the Canadian prairie provinces of Alberta and Saskatchewan. As a result of uneven distribution of water, there are also grand schemes to divert water from one river basin to another, with some of these having been implemented and others, more grandiose, on the drawing boards (Pearse, Bertrand, and MacLaren 1985). The latter are, primarily, schemes designed to divert water from northern regions in Canada to the southwestern U.S. states. Investments in major diversions are unlikely in the foreseeable future because they are simply too costly. However, investments in smaller projects, that are large in and of themselves, continue to be made. It was as a direct result of exploitation of water resources in North America that tools for evaluating public investments in resource development projects and for analyzing regional development were devised.

The purpose of this section is to address methodological issues related to the historic development of water resources, namely, the economics of public investments in natural resource development. In Chapter 5, project evaluation methodology is introduced; the main tool used to evaluate such investments is social cost-benefit analysis. Although the discussion is focused primarily on water resources, the methodology discussed is applicable to any public investment – to any investment where the perspective is that of maximizing social welfare. Examples from areas other than water resource development are also provided.

A second tool used in the evaluation of resource development projects is input-output analysis, and that is the topic of Chapter 6. Input-output analysis is used in the evaluation of water resource developments because it provides a means of determining regional impacts – the effect on economic activity. Input-output analysis addresses the problem of regional development; it provides information on the changes in business activity, government revenue, gross regional product, employment, and so on. While it is useful when examining income transfers, the input-output methodology does not provide measures of welfare change or of the net benefits to society of resource development projects. However, the impacts measured by input-output models have, in many evaluations, been erroneously added to cost-benefit results in order to provide justification for the development of certain water-related projects (as well as others). These issues are discussed further in Chapter 5, and, to a greater extent, in Chapter 6.

Finally, obtaining measures to be used in cost-benefit analysis is difficult because, while the values of some goods and services can be determined directly from market transactions, others are not traded in the marketplace. These *nonmarket* values include such things as recreational facilities, scenic amenities, and the preservation of wilderness, and they must somehow be determined before it is possible to compare the values of a pristine river valley with the values provided by a reservoir created by a dam. The latter values include electricity, increased crop production from irrigation, and so on, but the former include scenic amenities, biodiversity, and so on. How does one determine whether timber production, for example, is more valuable than wildlife grazing when there is no apparent yardstick by which to measure the values of these activities or uses of land? This is the topic of Chapter 7. In particular, we wish to determine the recreational value of land and the value of wildlife (in terms of their being hunted and viewed). The theory and issues of valuation are considered in Chapter 7. The discussion is necessarily cursory due to the extent of available techniques and research.

Chapters 5, 6, and 7 are somewhat lengthy because they deal with theory, technical detail, and policy concerns. Nonetheless, many topics in these chapters are either omitted or only briefly touched upon, and the reader is directed towards the vast literature in the area, some of which is cited at the end of the book for applicable chapters. It is hoped that the reader will at least get a flavour of the methodologies and the issues.

5
Social Cost-Benefit Analysis: Evaluation of Resource Development Projects

Since planners and decisionmakers are frequently required to choose between two or more alternative programs or policies, project evaluation plays a key role in private and public investment planning. Social cost-benefit analysis, or simply benefit-cost (B-C) analysis, provides a logical and clearly defined basis for evaluating projects. However, unless the practitioner is fully cognizant of the methodology and underlying theoretical foundation of B-C analysis, there may be confusion about what needs to be measured and how; for example, one may have trouble distinguishing between the economic *benefits* of a project and the economic *impacts* of a project. The former refers to a welfare measure, while the latter is a measure of economic activity, but that has no meaning for welfare as defined in the previous chapters.

In this chapter, we describe the methodology of B-C analysis and consider its role in water project evaluation; the methodology pertains to the *social* valuation of all land and resource projects. The reason we focus on water projects has to do with a result of the history of B-C analysis. The methods and issues discussed in this and the following two chapters will, it is hoped, clarify problems that might be encountered in the analysis of certain projects.

Policy Evaluation and the Role of Government
Government intervention in the economy through direct investment appears to be taken for granted. In economics literature, however, the only accepted reason for government intervention in the economy, either via regulation or public expenditure on the provision of goods and services, is the existence of externality (Chapter 4).

Water resource development projects are characterized by elements of both public goods externality and technical externality. That is, for resource development projects, the socially desirable level of the goods or services will not be provided without government intervention. Although there are benefits, such as navigation, flood control, and water supply, the major benefits of water resource projects are often electrical power generation, water for irrigation, and water for recreation. Electric power generation and irrigation projects have elements of *technical externality*, since they require enormous investments, and their benefits are frequently disbursed to a large number of individuals. Hence, they may not be provided privately, or, if they are, the amount provided is less than that desired (from a social point of view). Provision of recreation, on the other hand, is a proper function of government because of its *public good* characteristics; in particular, it is unlikely to be provided privately, since benefits frequently accrue to those who do not bear the direct costs of provision. Finally, public investment in water projects may serve as a catalyst for economic development. For these reasons, a strong case can be made for public investment in the development of water resources.

Although public investment in the economy is justified in many situations, this does not imply that the government should pursue all investments that might be deemed worthwhile, however the term 'worthwhile' is defined. Indeed, the government's ability to pursue certain investments is limited by the availability of funds. Therefore, given the limited amount of public funds, some method of determining which investments are worth pursuing and which are not must be agreed upon – and the mechanism for doing this is known as *project evaluation*. Unfortunately, there is quite a bit of confusion regarding what is meant by project evaluation, and it would appear that B-C analysis is often considered to be its equivalent. This is misleading, as B-C analysis is a more restrictive concept than is project evaluation.

Project evaluation is a term used to describe any consistent set of criteria that can be used to judge whether or not potential public investment projects are likely to achieve stated policy objectives. Examples of such objectives are to increase regional employment, to diversify the economy of a particular region, to increase the number of individuals living in a certain strategic location (e.g., the far North), to attain the largest net social economic benefit for the public expenditure, and so on. Only the restricted objective of economic or allocative efficiency – to achieve the greatest net *economic* benefit for society – is addressed by

B-C analysis. Other objectives cannot properly be considered in the B-C framework, as these are generally considered to be income transfers (viz., pecuniary externality) in applied welfare economics.

Whenever project evaluation is undertaken, it is important for the practitioner to recognize, and to clearly identify, the viewpoint that is represented. If the economic efficiency objective is adopted, then B-C analysis is the appropriate tool to employ. If a broader social policy point of view is taken, tools such as social impact assessment analysis and regional economic development analysis using input-output (I-O) models may be more appropriate. Evaluation from a social policy point of view may be important in the context of political acceptability and political feasibility. B-C analysis has been criticized because it is a tool to rank projects in terms of economic efficiency only, while the objective of most public programs is not simply, or even principally, economic efficiency. Some suggest that B-C analysis may be largely irrelevant or relevant to only a small part of the problem of evaluating public projects and programs. Many political scientists have also criticized B-C analysis on the grounds that it already embodies a political philosophy that may not coincide with that embraced by those who make decisions.

Nonetheless, B-C calculations are important, not only because they are one of the criteria used to evaluate projects, but because they provide data concerning the costs of pursuing objectives other than allocative efficiency. B-C analysis enables one to determine trade-offs among objectives.

There are two important points that should be made. First, economists trained in welfare economics frequently refuse to consider alternatives to economic efficiency as having any validity in policy analysis, since these approaches have to do with social and political matters that are beyond the scope of economic science. In fact, some economists stress that B-C analysis cannot embrace the wider considerations with which the political system must deal, but whether these criticisms relate to the economist's inability to quantify certain items is not clear. Yet, there is nothing wrong with a practice of quantifying the quantifiables and leaving the qualitative factors (sometimes referred to as 'intangibles') as additional considerations. This argument leads to the concept of *multiple accounts*, which is discussed in the next section. Second, and related to this, it is not possible to mix measurement tools, since this results in confusion about, and misrepresentation of, the project analysis. Thus, for example, it is not possible to construct a B-C ratio by including the regional development impacts resulting from the implementation of a water resource project as secondary benefits. A portion of such impacts may, however, constitute benefits from the project under special circumstances. This point is elaborated on in Chapter 6.

Brief History of B-C Analysis

As the government's role in the economy expanded, it was necessary for decisionmakers to develop guidelines to determine whether or not public funds spent on various government activities were achieving their aims. One guideline developed by U.S. legislators, in the Flood Control Act of 1936, required that the benefits of water development projects, 'to whomsoever they may accrue,' should exceed all the social costs related to the development of the projects. This requirement was subsequently expanded upon in the economics literature, culminating in what is now known as cost-benefit analysis.

As a result of the 1936 Flood Control Act, an Inter-Agency River Basin Committee, with representatives from the Department of Agriculture, the Army Corps of Engineers, the Bureau of Reclamation and the Federal Power Commission, was set up to develop procedures for testing whether or not benefits exceeded costs, as is required by the act. The Sub-Committee on Costs and Budgets published criteria for the appraisal of water resource projects in the so-called 'Green Book' of 1950. A revised edition of the 'Green Book' was published by the U.S. Inter-Agency Committee on Water Resources in 1958. In the same year, Robert McKean and Otto Eckstein each published procedures for evaluating the economic efficiency of projects. Since then, Ezra Mishan (1971), Arnold Harberger (1972), the Treasury Board Secretariat of Canada (1977), Peter Sassone and William Schaffer (1978), and many others have outlined procedures for conducting B-C analyses.[1]

In 1961, the U.S. secretaries of the Interior, Agriculture, Army, and Health, Education, and Welfare were requested to review evaluation standards for water and related land resources development projects. Their recommendation (1962) was that development, environmental preservation, and individuals' well-being should be considered equal objectives. The suggested approach was to formulate plans on the basis of economic benefits and costs but to be constrained by environmental considerations. The result was that preservation and well-being were not given equal status with development or economic efficiency. Subsequently, further effort was expended on the development of guidelines for conducting project evaluation.

The methodology for performing project evaluations, particularly social cost-benefit analyses, began to take concrete form with the U.S. Water Resources Council's 'Principles and Standards' (P&S) for water project evaluation, which appeared in the *U.S. Federal Register* in 1973 and 1979. In 1973, the Water Resources Council (WRC) identified the following four objectives for project evaluation.

(1) All the benefits and costs of a project had to be considered in the evaluation, regardless of who bore the costs and who received the benefits. This is the objective of national economic development.

(2) Impacts on the environment had to be calculated and included in the cost-benefit analysis. This implied that nonmarket benefits of recreation, environmental degradation, and so on had to be taken into account.

(3) The regional benefits of resource development projects were to be included explicitly in the analysis, making it possible to justify a project on the basis of its regional development benefits.

(4) Finally, the impact of a project on social well-being had to be taken into account. For example, the analyst or planner was to take into account the impact of the project on the poor (e.g., on blacks or on those with lower incomes). This objective, then, required explicit consideration of social issues in evaluating resource development projects.

The 1973 P&S for evaluating projects focused only on the first objective. The 1979 P&S attempted to extend the evaluation methodology to the second objective. It is clear that, for water projects, the measured benefits from recreation were to be included, while, for environmental programs, the benefits of improving air and water quality were also to be determined. (Methods of estimating nonmarket benefits are discussed in Chapter 7.) Unlike 1973, however, the 1979 P&S provided for an evaluation manual. The last two objectives were not addressed in the 1979 P&S, perhaps because the WRC did not feel that these could be adequately handled within the P&S framework then proposed.

In 1982, the 1979 P&S were repealed, only to be reincarnated in a somewhat downgraded form the following year. Given the requirements of various pieces of legislation relating to water (and other) resource developments, a method for including items 2, 3, and 4 in the evaluation process had to be found. Such a method was developed in the 1983 'Principles and Guidelines' (P&G); by recognizing non-commensurability among the various objectives, which was not explicitly done in the earlier P&S, the WRC adopted a *multiple accounts* approach to project evaluation. The 1983 P&G are currently in use.

The four accounts that are now identified in the P&G are similar to the four categories indicated above. The difference between the approaches is the recognition that the various accounts deal with different issues and are not commensurable. Thus, the 1983 P&G include a description of methods for displaying the different accounts. The four accounts can be summarized as follows: (1) national economic development (NED) account, (2) environmental quality (EQ) account, (3) regional economic development (RED) account, and (4) other social effects (OSE) account. B-C analysis is used only to evaluate those items that can be measured in dollar terms, namely, those found in the NED account and quantifiable components of the EQ and RED accounts. Methods for quantifying some of these components are discussed in Chapter 7. The items that cannot be monetized are to be presented in each of the EQ, RED, and OSE accounts and are briefly described in the following paragraphs.

The main tool used to analyze the RED account has, historically, been input-output analysis. This is the topic of Chapter 6. As discussed in that chapter, the main fallacy that has been committed in the past (and continues to be committed by many involved in project evaluation) is to include values obtained from input-output analysis in the cost-benefit values. The RED account recognizes that these items are not directly comparable – that benefits to a region may be costs to the nation as a whole, indicating that the RED account focuses upon income transfers. By separating the NED and RED accounts (and the other accounts as well), the incompatibility between economic efficiency and income distribution or equity is explicitly recognized.

According to the P&G, environmental items that are to be displayed in the EQ account are ecological, cultural, and aesthetic attributes. Ecological attributes include functional aspects of the environment (e.g., assimilative capacity, erosion, nutrient cycling, succession) as well as structural aspects such as plant and animal species, chemical and physical properties of air, water, and soil (e.g., pH of rainfall), and so on. Cultural attributes provide evidence of past and present habitation that can help in understanding and propagating human life. Aesthetic attributes include sights, scents, sounds, tastes, and impressions of the environment. It is clear that these attributes would be difficult to measure in monetary terms, although they can be measured in other ways. These include both quantity indicators that employ numeric and non-numeric scales and quality indicators such as 'good' and 'bad.' It is obvious, however, that the EQ attributes need to be presented in a clear and concise fashion if they are to be of use in the decision-making framework.

Several principles govern the planning process with respect to the environmental quality account. Both an interdisciplinary approach and public involvement are required in the planning process, although the means for involving the public is left at the discretion of the planning agency. The EQ account is designed to assist agencies in meeting the requirements of the U.S. National Environmental Policy Act (NEPA) of 1969 and the NEPA guidelines established by the U.S. Council on Environmental Quality. As such, the procedures established by the WRC are meant to facilitate water resources planning in order to satisfy the aforementioned requirements as well as environmental requirements under the Endangered Species Act (1973), the National Historic Preservation Act (1966), the Fish and Wildlife Coordination Act (1972), the Coastal Zone Management Act (1972), and their subsequent amendments. Finally, as discussed below with respect to costs and benefits (NED account), the EQ attributes need to be displayed in a way that highlights the comparison between the 'with project' and 'without project' scenarios.

The OSE account includes any items that are not included in the other three accounts but are important for planning. While the U.S. WRC's P&G provides no procedures for evaluating other social effects, it does indicate that such effects include 'urban and community impacts; life, health, and safety factors; displacement; long-term productivity; and energy requirements and energy conservation' (U.S. Water Resources Council 1983:12). They also include effects on income distribution, employment, population distribution, fiscal effects on state and local governments, quality of community life, and so on. While some of these effects can be measured in monetary terms and, thus, are included in the NED account, others need to be displayed using guidelines similar to those of the EQ account. It appears that public agencies have substantial freedom within the planning process to include whatever items they wish in the OSE account and to determine how they are to be displayed.

Since the publication of the 1979 P&S, the basic techniques of evaluation have been extended to the appraisal of all U.S. government projects and programs, particularly environmental regulatory programs. In Canada, guidelines for project appraisal were established in 1977 by the Federal Treasury Board Secretariat, but these are vague and, in most instances, not very useful to the practitioner. One reason for this may be that they appeared before the 1979 P&S were released in the U.S.;

alternatively, it is likely that the political system in Canada, which relies on income transfers via specified projects from the central government to the provinces, mitigates the development and use of strict evaluation criteria. Project evaluation guidelines have also been developed by most provinces, but many of these are internal documents and are not available to the general practitioner.

A review of project evaluation studies in Canada and the United States by the author indicates that B-C methodology is not strictly adhered to, despite the lip service paid to this technique. For example, there is no evidence that the U.S. Bureau of Reclamation used B-C guidelines in determining whether or not to construct many of the dams that were placed on rivers in the western U.S. during the 1940s, 1950s, and 1960s. Perhaps this is because social B-C methodology was in its infancy, but it could also be the result of political factors or project evaluation criteria other than social B-C analysis. Particularly in Canada, applications of B-C analyses are difficult to find in a published format, since much project evaluation is carried out internally by government or by consultants, with the evaluation usually considered confidential. The U.S. has increasingly required federal agencies to conduct evaluations according to strict guidelines, and the U.S. Office of Management and Budget has greater resources to monitor public spending and compliance with legislation than does the Auditor General of Canada. In large part, this is due to the fact that there is no separation of the executive and legislative powers in Canada (with the accompanying system of checks and balances), and that there is greater devolution of power to provinces than there is to states.

Mechanics of Benefit-Cost Analysis

In the remainder of this chapter, we focus on social B-C analysis as a tool for evaluating projects.[2] One could address such things as the utilitarian philosophy underlying B-C analysis, the assumption that either the Kaldor-Hicks or Scitovsky compensation test holds, the requirement that projects to be evaluated are not so large that they distort prices throughout the economy, and so on. However, while these are important and should be familiar to the analyst, it is beyond the scope of this text to consider them. We only provide a discussion of the methodology of B-C analysis and some examples of its use.

There are several important assumptions that should be pointed out even to the novice.

(1) Only marginal changes in the economy are to be evaluated. That is, the impact of projects to be evaluated is small compared to national output.

(2) There are no significant distortions in other markets. Those that exist must be taken into account either by using shadow prices or by measuring indirect net benefits or costs in other markets.

(3) The status quo or some other distribution of income is taken as given. Usually B-C analysis is based on the assumption that the existing distribution of income is the preferred distribution.

(4) The tastes, income, and wealth of the current generation are also representative of the desire and ability to pay of future generations. (Intergenerational equity is considered further in Chapter 17.)

(5) All individuals are treated equally, so that a marginal dollar accruing to a rich person is valued the same as is a dollar going to a poor person.

(6) Either uncertainty is absent or the public's attitude towards risk can be represented by changes in the discount rate.

It is clear that these assumptions impose limits on the interpretation of the results of project evaluation using B-C analysis. However, if these presuppositions are recognized, B-C analysis becomes a useful tool for analyzing public policies.

Economic efficiency is simply defined. First, it is necessary to calculate the present value of all the social costs (PVC) of a proposed project as

$$PVC = C_0 + \frac{C_1}{(1+r)} + \frac{C_2}{(1+r)^2} + \dots + \frac{C_T}{(1+r)^T}$$

$$= \sum_{t=0}^{T} \frac{C_t}{(1+r)^t},$$

where C_t refers to *all* of the project-related costs incurred by society in year t, the life of the project is T years, and r is the rate of discount. The costs are those that are encountered in every year; these are costs over and above those that would be encountered in the absence of the project. The *with-without* principle of B-C analysis is important, since it illustrates the economic concept of opportunity cost. The term C_0 is sometimes referred to as the capital or construction cost.

Likewise, it is necessary to calculate the present value of all the social benefits of the project (*PVB*) as

$$PVB = B_0 + \frac{B_1}{(1+r)} + \frac{B_2}{(1+r)^2} + \dots + \frac{B_T}{(1+r)^T}$$

$$= \sum_{t=0}^{T} \frac{B_t}{(1+r)^t} ,$$

where B_t refers to *all* of the benefits that result from the project in year t, regardless of who in society receives them. Again, benefits are defined as the difference between benefits that accrue with the project as opposed to without it.

The discount rate reflects time preference, the fact that a dollar today is worth more than that same dollar one year from now. An important issue in B-C analysis concerns the appropriate discount rate to use and is discussed later in this chapter.

The next step in determining economic efficiency is to calculate the difference between *PVC* and *PVB*; the present value of net social benefits or simply net present value (*NPV*) is defined as

$$NPV = PVB - PVC.$$

If $NPV > 0$, then the project adds to the welfare of society and is deemed to be economically efficient. If $NPV < 0$, the present value of costs is greater than the present value of benefits and the project should not be pursued, because society will be a net loser. Such a project should only be undertaken if the attainment of some other objective, such as income redistribution, warrants the overall loss to society.

The formula for making B-C calculations is straightforward. Problems occur in the choice of discount rate and in measuring the actual costs and benefits. In particular, there is controversy about what is to be included in the measurements. The concept of economic surplus (discussed in Chapter 3) is important in this regard.

For a given project, one could identify three types of benefits or costs: (1) benefits and costs for which market prices exist and for which these prices correctly reflect social values; (2) benefits and costs for which market prices exist, but these prices do not reflect social values (e.g., labour input that would otherwise be unemployed); and (3) benefits and costs for which no market prices exist because the commodities (e.g., recreation, water quality, historic sites) are not generally traded in the marketplace. The first two types of benefits and costs are most easily included in a B-C analysis, while the last category of benefits (or costs) is frequently presented as additional considerations, because these values are difficult to obtain.

What constitutes a benefit (or a cost) is very much conditioned by the accounting stance of the decisionmaker. A private versus a public or social B-C analysis can be differentiated partly on the basis of the accounting stance.

All projects with a positive NPV should, in principle, be undertaken because they add to the welfare of society, but budget constraints prevent this from happening. Therefore, a project with a positive NPV may not proceed because an alternative project has a higher NPV. When there are a large number of projects and programs available to decisionmakers, with a limited budget, it is necessary to rank projects. This is done by comparing the social benefits on a per $1 basis of social costs; a B-C ratio can be constructed for this purpose, namely,

$$B/C = \frac{PVB}{PVC}.$$

As long as $B/C > 1.0$, the project is worth undertaking since, for every $1 society spends, it gains more than $1. While all projects yielding a B-C ratio greater than 1.0 should be developed, if there are a number of different projects competing for limited funds, the B-C ratios can be used to rank the projects. Projects are then chosen from the highest to the lowest B/C, until either all of the available funds are expended or there are no more projects with a $B/C > 1.0$.

What is confusing is that other B-C ratios may be constructed to examine particular aspects of a project. It may be useful to determine the benefits accruing to each $1 spent by the government. In this case, one subtracts from benefits the private costs and divides the result by public costs only; that is,

$$B/C = \frac{PVB - PVC_{private}}{PVC_{public}},$$

where PVB is defined as previously, $PVC_{private}$ and PVC_{public} refer to the present values of private and public costs, respectively. Thus, a distinction is made between costs incurred by the private sector and those incurred by the government.

If it is necessary to distinguish between capital costs and the costs associated with the operation, maintenance, and routine replacement (OM&R) of a facility, the B-C ratio might be written as

$$B/C = \frac{PVB - PVC_{OM\&R}}{C_0},$$

where $PVC_{OM\&R}$ is the present value of the OM&R costs, and C_0 represents the capital or construction costs of the project. (If construction of the facility requires a period in excess of one year, then C_0 can be thought of as the present value of capital costs.)

Finally, one might wish to determine the impact of each $1 of project costs only. The present value of associated costs (AC) is then subtracted from social benefits and divided by project costs. An example of associated costs are the increased on-farm costs that result when a water resources project is built for irrigation purposes. Then the B-C ratio can be written as

$$B/C = \frac{PVB - AC}{PVC_{project}}.$$

This concept of the benefit-cost ratio can also be interpreted as the 'direct costs' B-C ratio.

None of these representations of the B-C ratio should replace NPV and the social B-C ratio; they can be presented as additional considerations. Attempts to do otherwise will be construed as evidence that the project is not economically efficient from society's point of view.

It is not important in determining a project's economic efficiency whether the project is funded locally or by taxpayers outside the project region. However, in the latter case there will be additional benefits that need to be evaluated but only if the outside funds are tied to that particular project and would not be available under any other circumstances. Even in this situation, however, the benefits are difficult to measure, constitute a transfer from individuals outside the region, and may not even accrue to current residents in the region. Therefore, they are correctly ignored by applied welfare economists.

However, the one thing that should not be ignored in the evaluation of public projects is government inefficiency. Not only can the marginal excess burden of tax collection be onerous, but the costs of making funds available for projects often add further costs that are overlooked in determining the actual costs of a public project. These costs are also neglected in determining an appropriate discount rate, as is discussed later in this chapter.

B-C Analysis: Choosing a Dam Size for Flood Control

Suppose that a low-lying agricultural area is prone to periodic flooding, with the extent of damage dependent on the severity of the floods. Based on historical records and current yields and prices for commodities grown in the region, it is possible to construct a discrete probability distribution for damage (Table 5.1). Assuming that there is no change expected in the hydrological cycle, and ignoring possible future price and yield changes, it is possible to recommend various investment projects (dams) to reduce the losses due to flooding. The dam sizes vary from a weir, to prevent minor flooding, to a full-scale earthen dam that eliminates the possibility of flooding altogether (at least as experienced in the historical record). The investment alternatives correspond to the 'cases' indicated in Table 5.1 – that is, seven dam sizes from small to large will prevent flooding, as is indicated by the cases in Table 5.1.

Table 5.1. **Hypothetical probability distribution for flood damage**

Case	Cost of flooding ($)	Probability (%)	Cumulative probability (%)
1	10,000	8	8
2	20,000	12	20
3	30,000	30	50
4	40,000	26	76
5	50,000	12	88
6	75,000	8	96
7	100,000	4	100

To keep the analysis simple, we assume that, whatever dam is built, its life is infinite, and that there are no OM&R costs. Under these assumptions, there is only a capital cost; the present values of benefits are determined by finding the annual benefit and simply dividing the result by the discount rate.[3] The annual benefit is an *expected* value determined by multiplying the loss times the probability of occurrence. Any dam size greater than the smallest will not only prevent flood damage of the amount related to that 'case' but will also prevent lesser amounts of flood damage. The PVCs, PVBs, NPVs, and B-C ratios for a discount rate of 10 per cent are provided in Table 5.2. As an example of how to calculate the present value of benefits, consider case 3. The annual benefit is $12,200 (= 0.08 x $10,000 + 0.12 x $20,000 + 0.30 x $30,000); then PVB = $122,000 (= $12,200/0.10).

While any of dam sizes 3, 4, 5, or 6 yields a positive NPV, the optimal size dam to build is the one that yields the greatest NPV and the highest B/C. This is dam size 4. It is important to notice that preventing all possibility of flooding is an option that is not economic and, indeed, yields substantial losses to society. For dam size 7, the investment yields a return of 77.2 cents for every dollar that is invested, or a loss of 22.8 cents for every dollar of construction costs! Thus, it is economic to suffer the more devastating floods that are likely to occur 4 years out of 100; it does not pay to spend money to prevent them.

Table 5.2. **Crude cost-benefit analysis of alternative flood control investment projects**

Alter-native	Capital cost (PVC) ($'000s)	Present value of benefits (PVB) ($'000s)	Net present value (NPV) ($'000s)	Benefit-cost ratio (B/C)
1	15	8	-7	0.533
2	40	32	-8	0.800
3	100	122	22	1.220
4	150	226	76	1.507
5	250	286	36	1.144
6	340	346	6	1.018
7	500	386	-114	0.772

While the foregoing analysis gave the correct answer (choose dam 4), there is something amiss. Suppose that alternative 4 was not available. In deciding between 3 and 5, the B-C ratio indicates that alternative 3 should be chosen, while the NPV criterion requires one to choose 5. (The same contradiction occurs if one is required to choose between alternatives 1 and 2.) The problem is that none of the investment opportunities in Table 5.2 uses the same investment funds. In the choice between alternatives 3 and 5, alternative 3 costs $100,000 while 5 costs $250,000. What happens to the $150,000 difference between these investments? It is assumed that this money can be invested in its best alternative at a rate of return of 10 per cent. Therefore, the correct approach to valuing the various alternatives presented in the previous two tables is to assume that $500,000 is available to be invested. Thus, alternative 3 consists of an investment of $100,000 in flood control and a $400,000 investment at a 10 per cent rate of return; alternative 5 consists of $250,000 invested in flood control and a similar amount invested at 10 per cent. Likewise for the other alternatives. Making this adjustment gives the result in Table 5.3. Alternative 4 remains the preferred choice, but there are no contradictions between the NPV and B/C criteria. Notice also that incorrect application of the B-C methodology can lead to mistaken impressions concerning the profitability of investment projects.

Table 5.3. **Cost-benefit analysis of alternative flood control investment projects: Equal capital investment amount**

Alternative	Cost of dam ($'000s)	Capital cost (PVC) ($'000s)	Present value of benefits (PVB) ($'000s)	Net present value (NPV) ($'000s)	Benefit-cost ratio (B/C)
1	15	500	493	-7	0.986
2	40	500	492	-8	0.984
3	100	500	522	22	1.044
4	150	500	576	76	1.152
5	250	500	536	36	1.072
6	340	500	506	6	1.012
7	500	500	386	-114	0.772

B-C Analysis of Optimal Fertilizer Applications

Agricultural scientists have investigated banding of phosphate fertilizer versus broadcasting. As illustrated in Figure 5.1, banding places a concentrated amount of fertilizer with or near the seed, whereas broadcast applications make fertilizer available over a large area, namely, the entire field. Banding is successful because fertilizer is concentrated near the growing plant roots, but, as a consequence, the roots do not explore much of the soil volume (less than 3 per cent). This is not the case with broadcast applications, although it does not provide the initial impetus to growth that occurs with banding. Further, since fertilizer (especially phosphorous) tends to be immobile, the plant does not benefit as much as it could with broadcast applications, but there is residual fertilizer left for following years. Large one-time broadcast applications of fertilizer are important, because they supply nutrients for future crops under zero or minimum tillage systems. Soil scientists are interested in knowing whether or not, for a particular region, it is better to use a one-time broadcast application of fertilizer or annual banding in such tillage systems. (In practice, a combination of broadcast and seed-placed applications of fertilizers is often recommended.) This can be done using cost-benefit analysis.

Figure 5.1

Methods of fertilizer placement

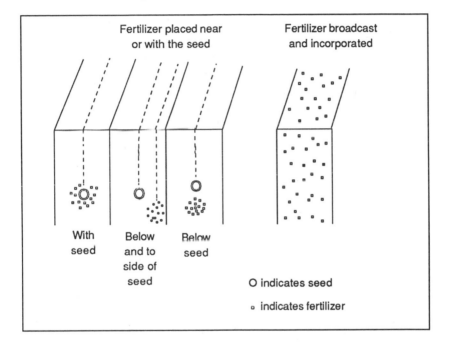

In one study, soil scientists at the University of Saskatchewan used field trial data and simulated fertilizer costs, grain prices, and discount rates to determine what would be the optimal fertilizer strategy for grain producers to adopt. The data are based on a five-year study. The net present values of returns for the single broadcast fertilizer application (Equation 5.1) and consecutive banded fertilizer placements (Equation 5.2) were calculated as follows:

$$NPV_{\text{broadcast}} = \sum_{t=0}^{4} (P \; \Delta y_t)(\frac{1}{1+r})^t - FC \qquad (5.1)$$

$$NPV_{\text{banding}} = \sum_{t=0}^{4} (P \; \Delta y_t - FC_t)(\frac{1}{1+r})^t \qquad (5.2)$$

where   P   = price of grain ($/kg),
      t = time (year),
      Δy_t = yield increase over control (kg/ha),
      r = discount rate, and
      FC = fertilizer cost ($/kg) + application cost ($/ha).

Notice that, since the change in yield is defined with respect to the control study (conventional recommendations of fertilizer applications), the *with-without* principle of benefit-cost analysis is employed.

The research study found that, for central Saskatchewan, one-time broadcast applications of large amounts of fertilizer (more than 80 kg/ha) yielded NPVs that exceeded equivalent applications of seed-placed (banded) fertilizers. The difference in NPVs varied from $23/ha to $70/ha, depending upon assumptions regarding prices and interest rates. However, the study neglected certain aspects of social cost-benefit analysis. In particular, externality effects of large fertilizer applications (pollution of groundwater), and input and output price subsidies were excluded from the analysis.

B-C Analysis: Ozone Damage and Opportunity Cost

Damage to crops in the Fraser River Valley of British Columbia occurs as a result of ozone (O_3) concentrations that exceed certain critical levels at various times during the growing season. Ozone is the result, primarily, of automobile emissions and is found to diminish very little in concentration with distance, even 100 km from the pollution source. The crops that are most sensitive to damage in the Fraser Valley are green beans, while potatoes and forages are not affected very much by ozone pollution. The most common method of measuring damage is to multiply the reduction in crop yields by the output price. However, this is not correct and could lead to overestimates of actual ozone damage. The following discussion illustrates some of the pitfalls that need to be avoided.

Agricultural production is often subsidized by government, although the actual degree of subsidy depends upon the particular crop. Some crops receive no direct subsidy while others are highly subsidized, with the farmer receiving as much as double the market price. Market price may be what the commodity trades for locally, in which case the government effectively subsidizes consumers, or it may be the world price (adjusted for transportation costs). The correct price for valuing crop damage is the market or world price – the price for which consumers could obtain the commodity if there were no restrictions (e.g., import quotas or tariffs) on their purchases.

Further, the government frequently subsidizes purchases of inputs by farmers. This is done either through the tax system or through actual subsidy payments to agricultural producers or input suppliers (Chapter 12). If ozone damage occurs, the inputs, and *the change in input use*, need to be valued at their opportunity cost, not the price that the farmer pays. In this case, the original net revenue received by the farmer needs to be reduced, and the damage from ozone pollution is less than otherwise indicated.

Finally, the concept of opportunity cost requires that adjustment be made for alternative land use. Suppose that land in the Fraser Valley can be used to grow either beans or potatoes. The annual net revenue from beans is $600/ha, but it is only $550/ha if potatoes are grown. As a result of ozone damage, assume that net revenue from beans declines to $450/ha. If one continues to grow beans, then one would say that the cost of ozone pollution is $150/ha per year. However, suppose that, for the same ozone concentrations, the net revenue from potatoes falls to only $500/ha, because they are less sensitive to ozone. If this is the case, then the real damage from ozone pollution is not $150/ha, but, rather, $100/ha, because farmers can grow potatoes instead of beans when they know that ozone damage is likely to occur.

Further Issues in Benefit-Cost Analysis
In this section, we consider some additional aspects of B-C analysis, although in a somewhat cursory fashion. It is recommended that the reader wishing to obtain more information about the intricacies of B-C analysis consult the references listed at the end of the chapter. The topic of nonmarket benefits is left to Chapter 7.

Internal Rate of Return Criterion
The internal rate of return (IRR) criterion is an alternative to NPV and B/C in selecting the most efficient projects. It is not widely used by natural resource economists, although it is used in private industry. In principle, IRR yields the same ranking of projects as does NPV and B/C. (As noted above, if care is not taken in specifying reinvestment alternatives, NPV and B/C can lead to contradictory selection.) The IRR is found by setting NPV equal to zero and solving for the discount rate or IRR:

$$0 = B_0 - C_0 + \frac{B_1 - C_1}{1 + IRR} + \frac{B_2 - C_2}{(1 + IRR)^2} + \dots + \frac{B_T - C_T}{(1 + IRR)^T} \, ,$$

where T is the length of the time horizon. To find IRR requires solving a higher-order function and, although simple to accomplish numerically on a computer, this is the main reason for the unpopularity of the IRR criterion. The basis for project selection is to compare the internal rate of return with an appropriate discount rate; if IRR is greater than the selected discount rate, the project is desirable. This criterion can then be used to rank projects.

Rate of Discount

Since $1 accruing today is worth more to an individual than that same dollar received at some future date (say one year from now), it is necessary to discount future benefits and costs. The calculation of NPV and the B-C ratio is sensitive to the rate of discount (interest rate) that is employed in the B-C analysis. What, then, is the appropriate rate of discount to use in weighting future costs and benefits?

Consider, first, whether a nominal or real rate of discount is to be employed. While a nominal rate might be used in cases in which one wishes to examine cash flows, it is generally not appropriate to use a nominal rate of discount because it requires that inflation be taken into account. This requires that the rate of inflation be predicted over the project's time horizon, and that might be 100 years. Since it is not possible to predict inflation, the appropriate discount rate to employ is one that abstracts from inflation, namely, a *real* rate of discount.

A low discount rate favours capital intensive projects, whose returns accrue further in the future; a high rate favours projects with high returns in the nearer term and/or returns that are less capital intensive (costs spread more evenly over the time horizon). An example of the former is the construction of a hospital, while an example of the latter is the seeding of forest clearcuts to domestic forages. A high rate of discount also discourages conservation of natural resources. Some types of investments are not undertaken privately because they do not yield returns until much farther in the future, but public investment displaces what some consider to be more worthwhile or profitable private investments. To express this disparity of views, four discount rates have been proposed.

(1) *Rate of Return on Private Investments.* Since the rate of return on private investments (in the range 15-25 per cent) represents the return

that one could potentially obtain on dollars invested by the public, this is also the appropriate rate to use in discounting future costs and benefits of public investments. The problem is that this rate is very high and, thereby, works against investments that have a high initial outlay, such as schools, roads, and hospitals. In addition, people indicate that they are willing to invest in government securities (e.g., T-bills, savings bonds) that yield returns well below the private rate of interest. Finally, not all of the funds available to government constitute a displacement of potential private investments (see 3 below).

(2) *Rate of Return on Long-term Government Bonds.* This tends to be a very low rate of interest (approximately 3-5 per cent in real terms) and favours public investments in projects that have high initial costs, with benefits accruing much farther in the future; this is sometimes referred to as a *front-loaded* project. The problem with this rate of discount is that lenders do not consider the riskiness of the individual projects that the government undertakes, because they know the government will not default on its obligations. Hence, this rate is likely inappropriate.

(3) *Opportunity Cost of Capital.* Money that is used by the government for investment purposes does not constitute a displacement of private investment opportunities alone. Governments obtain revenues from both taxes and borrowing. In order to determine the opportunity cost of public funds, it is necessary to find out from where the marginal dollars were diverted. The opportunity cost of capital is a weighted average of the alternative rates of return. Suppose that a public investment project costs $100. Assume that this money is raised through taxes – $40 from taxes on private firms and $60 from taxes on individuals. Suppose further that the rate of return in the private sector is 20 per cent, but that individuals are found to invest money in deposits that yield 10 per cent. (We abstract from risk in this example.) Then the opportunity cost of capital is 14 per cent (= 0.40 x 20% + 0.60 x 10%). The main difficulty in deriving the opportunity cost rate is that it is not easy to determine where the *marginal* tax dollars originate. Further, not all government revenues come from taxes; the government borrows funds (same problem as in 2) and earns money through charges, tariffs on imported goods, and so on.

(4) *Social Rate of Time Preference.* The social rate of time preference is an arbitrarily chosen low discount rate that reflects a social viewpoint in favour of capital intensive projects – projects that are weighted towards future generations (e.g., preservation of species, construction of schools and hospitals, and nature preserves.) Arguments in favour of

this approach are as follows. First, observed discount rates are high because individuals always face the threat of death, but this is not true for society as a whole. Second, society has an obligation to future generations; this is a paternalistic argument. However, since future generations have always been materially better off than preceding generations, some argue that the use of an arbitrarily low rate results in income transfers from poor to rich. Third, the marketplace does not reflect individual preferences, since, collectively, we are in favour of a particular action (e.g., some speed limit) but, individually, we act contrarily. Finally, there is the public goods argument that a low discount rate (perhaps even 0 per cent) is required to provide for things that would never be provided privately.

Given the pros and cons of each of the rates discussed above, there appears to be no consensus on the discount rate to use in selecting public investment projects. Some have argued that the rate should be adjusted, depending upon who the benefactors and beneficiaries are, (presumably) to favour the poor, to take into account differences in time horizons among projects if an arbitrary cut-off is chosen (a lower rate for projects with longer time horizons), and to take into account differences in riskiness of projects (for riskier projects use a higher discount rate). The discount rate has also been adjusted to take into account issues such as soil erosion. Perhaps a sensible approach to follow is to conduct *sensitivity analysis* – calculate the NPV and B/C for all alternative projects under consideration using a range of discount rates[4] – and judge whether or not there needs to be concern about the value of the discount rate employed. In the final analysis, the decision to select or reject a project is political and is based on evaluation guidelines that include B-C analysis as one of a number of criteria (viz., multiple accounts).

Efficiency versus Income Distribution

Income distribution constitutes an objective other than economic efficiency, and it traditionally refers to the distribution of water resource development projects among regions – regional income distribution. Thus, it is appropriately included in the RED account if a multiple accounts approach is adopted. However, income distribution might also refer to distribution among income categories (viz., rich versus poor) and, thus, would be included in the OSE account.

During the 1970s and 1980s, considerable debate concerning the methodology for including distributional considerations in B-C analysis took place. Two aspects of this debate are considered, namely, (1) the use of distributional weights in the evaluation of projects and (2) the issue of whether secondary effects (as measured by value-added) are an appropriate measure of benefits and should, therefore, be included as a measure of regional benefits.

(1) *Employing Distributional Weights in B-C Analysis.* The literature pertaining to the integration of income equality and economic efficiency in project evaluation is substantial. In this literature, distributional weights are employed to weight benefits and/or costs depending upon the particular region, income class, or group that benefits or bears the cost. The theoretical derivation of these weights is known to economists, but actually determining the income distributional weights is not a trivial task. To obtain knowledge about the weights amounts to discovering society's trade-off between economic efficiency and income distribution. This task is identical to discovering society's welfare function, which is impossible, as the economist Kenneth Arrow demonstrated in 1951 in a theorem known as the 'Impossibility Theorem.' Thus, most economists do not consider it proper to include income distributional considerations within the B-C framework.

The problem is that any weighting of benefits and costs introduces value judgments that cannot be handled within the B-C environment. As it is, the concept of economic efficiency is normative, albeit acceptable to society. The introduction of value judgments via a weighting of beneficiaries and benefactors results in a departure from acceptable and known evaluation practices, thereby making B-C analysis less impartial. The use of weights is an attempt to hide what really should be made explicit via the political process. That is, any departure from economic efficiency should be justified on grounds other than economic development, particularly since these might include a desire to distribute income in favour of one's constituents, whether these are rich or poor.

(2) *The Role of Indirect or Secondary Effects.* With regard to the secondary or regional 'benefits' of water resource projects, where such benefits were a topic of debate, issues concerning income distribution become involved. As early as 1955, Ciriacy-Wantrup concluded that secondary or indirect effects of resource development should not be included in project evaluation, although such effects are certainly relevant to repayment – that is, such effects have distributional consequences.

More recent research is emphatically critical of studies that include indirect effects as a measure of benefits. While the current method for identifying and measuring indirect effects, namely, via I-O models, may be appropriate, these effects are not to be confused with benefits.

Indeed, using regional 'benefits' generated from I-O models in the B-C analysis is wrong because the technique requires the mixing of different methodologies – B-C analysis is a normative model, the foundations of which lie in welfare economics, while input-output analysis is unrelated to welfare economics. The relationship between B-C analysis and input-output analysis is discussed further in Chapter 6.

6

Input-Output Models for Regional and Community Development

The purpose of inter-industry or input-output (I-O) models is to show the income or output relationships that exist between the sectors or industries within a province, region, or country and external 'trade' links with other economies. These models are useful as policy tools in analyzing, for example, the effect of decisions regarding land-use planning that would affect industry output or input patterns. In this chapter, a basically non-mathematical description of I-O analysis is presented; the necessary mathematics are contained in the appendix to this chapter.

I-O models are particularly useful to government agencies concerned with regional or community development. While I-O analysis is used to determine the economic impacts on a particular region or community of the development of new exports, it can also be used to evaluate the income redistributional effects of some government policies that affect industry structure and/or output. An understanding of the often cited 'multiplier effect' associated with governmental or industrial programs is also provided in this chapter.

Methodology of the Square Input-Output Model
An input-output model is simply a method of double-entry bookkeeping that permits the tracing of commodity values as they move through a given economy, so that inferences can be made concerning the economic interdependence of the various activities within the economy. (The relationships are really built up from production functions, as is discussed in Figure 6.1 below.) A brief exposition of the workings of a square I-O model follows.

An I-O or transactions table for a hypothetical region is illustrated in Table 6.1. All business activity has been aggregated into sectors A through E, where each sector (industry) corresponds to a collection of firms producing similar products and using approximately the same inputs. Although only five business sectors are included in the hypothetical example, actual I-O tables may be disaggregated to a much greater degree. While a high degree of disaggregation is useful for descriptive purposes, data limitations, costs, and the very structure of the economy determine the number of sectors delineated. As a result, actual I-O models that exist for various countries, provinces, or regions are not directly comparable.

The first five rows and first five columns of Table 6.1 constitute the 'processing sector.' Production activities (sales) are found on the left side of the table; sectoral purchases of goods and services are read across the top of the table. In order to determine how much firms in sector C sold to firms in sector E, for example, we first find sector C on the left side of the table. Reading across row 3 (for sector C), we find, from column 5, that firms in sector C sold $47 million worth of goods and services to firms in sector E.

How much did firms in sector C buy from firms in sector E? Now we locate sector C across the top of the table. Reading down column 3 we find that firms in sector C bought $29 million worth of goods and services from sector E firms. Intrasectoral sales and purchases are located on the diagonal. Hence, firms in sector D sold $9 million worth of goods and services to other firms in the same sector.

The remaining sectors on the left side of the table, sectors 6 through 9, are called the payments or primary inputs sectors. These sectors receive payments from the sectors listed at the top of the table. Hence, firms in sector C purchase $194 million of labour from households, paid for in the form of wages and salaries, dividends, interest, and so on. (Sector C is located at the top of the table; reading down column 3, sector C payments to households, for example, are found in row 6.) These firms also purchase $40 million from governments (taxes, licences, etc.), $337 million outside the region, and claimed $16 million for depreciation of capital goods and reduction of inventories of raw materials and final goods. Excluding imports, payments to households and governments constitute *value added*.

Columns 6 through 9 across the top of the table constitute the final demand sector. The final demand sectors purchase goods and services produced by the sectors located on the left side of Table 6.1. Thus, sector A sold $12 million worth of goods and services to households, $12 million to governments, and $110 million to areas outside the economy. An additional $75 million was spent on investment – fixed capital formation and increases in inventory. These values are found by reading

Table 6.1. **Transactions table for a hypothetical regional economy ($ mil.)**

		PURCHASING ACTIVITIES								
		Processing sector					Final demand sector			
Outputs	(1)	(2)	(3)	(4)	(5)	(6)	(7)	(8)	(9)	(10)
	A	B	C	D	E	House- holds	Gov't	Export	Invest. & in- vent. change	Total output
Inputs										
PRODUCING ACTIVITIES										
Processing Sector										
(1) Sector A	72	3	0	8	7	12	12	110	75	299
(2) Sector B	36	63	13	0	0	50	7	248	130	547
(3) Sector C	56	30	82	51	47	235	24	96	111	732
(4) Sector D	2	25	21	9	6	188	13	99	27	390
(5) Sector E	21	7	29	21	35	438	26	49	36	662
Payments Sector										
(6) Households	57	155	194	126	105	7	315	217	32	1208
(7) Government	13	94	40	21	26	186	21	0	0	401
(8) Imports	30	127	337	141	423	92	151	0	119	1420
(9) Depreciation and negative inventory change	12	43	16	13	13	0	1	0	0	98
(10) Total inputs	299	547	732	390	662	1208	570	819	530	5757

across row 1, with investment expenditure by a firm treated as a purchase from itself.

Transactions between the payments sector and the final demand sector may also occur. Thus, households paid $186 million to governments as taxes (row 7, column 6), and governments paid $315 million to households as wages, salaries, and transfer payments such as those used for welfare programs (row 6, column 7). Households bought $92 million outside the hypothetical economy and intergovernment transfers amounted to $21 million. Households purchased $7 million worth of goods and services (e.g., as hired domestic labour) from other households (column 6, row 6).

The I-O table is essentially a system of double entry accounts, because what firms purchase must equal what they sell. Therefore, total output must equal total input for the processing sector and the totals for columns 1 through 5 must be identical to the corresponding row totals. The same is not true for sectors 6 through 9. However, for the region as a whole, total inputs must equal total outputs. These are the checks imposed by double-entry bookkeeping.

Technical Coefficients Table

A table of technical or trade coefficients can be constructed from the transactions in Table 6.1. Such a table is useful because it gives a good picture of the interdependence of the industrial and commercial sectors of the regional economy. The technical coefficients tell us how much input is required from the various producing sectors to produce one dollar's worth of output in a given industry (sector). A Leontief production function is assumed because the technical coefficients are fixed. The difference between a Leontief production function and the continuous production function of neoclassical economic theory is illustrated in Figure 6.1.

National I-O models are constructed by using secondary data obtained from the technical production relationship and the national accounts. Regional I-O models can either be constructed directly from the national model (i.e., using the technical coefficients in the national model) with adjustments or from primary data obtained via survey methods (survey-based regional I-O table). In the latter case, the coefficients are appropriately called trade coefficients. The terms input-output coefficient and (direct) input coefficient are also used. One major difference between national and regional models is the size of exports and imports relative to the rest of the economy.

Table 6.2 is derived directly from Table 6.1 by dividing each dollar

Figure 6.1

Comparison of isoquants for fixed-coefficients or Leontief and neoclassical production functions

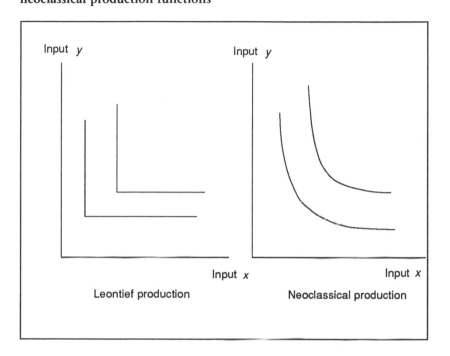

entry in a particular industry's column by the total value of output produced by that industry (i.e., the row or column total for that industry). Therefore, for each industry the column of technical coefficients represents the proportion of the total cost of production attributable to the inputs purchased from the various industries in the economy. Since the final demand sector does not produce any output, the calculations are carried out only for columns 1 through 5, that is, for the processing sector only. For example, 5½ cents of sector C's output are purchased by B firms for every $1 produced by sector B. This is obtained by dividing the entry in row 3, column 2, of Table 6.1 by the total for row 2, that is, 30/547 = 0.055. The result is a 5 x 5 matrix, frequently called the direct input coefficient matrix and denoted by A.

The household row coefficients for each sector are located at the bottom of Table 6.2 and are calculated by dividing the household values in Table 6.1 by the appropriate column or row total for the sector in question. Hence, the contribution by households (labour) to $1 of sector B's output is $0.283 (155/547). The use of these household coefficients in calculating various multipliers will be described later. Some analysts include all primary inputs to construct the trade or technical coefficients table; in this case, there will be additional types of multipliers (as noted below).

Table 6.2. Hypothetical technical coefficients

Selling sectors	Purchasing sectors				
	A	B	C	D	E
(1) Sector A	0.241	0.006	0.000	0.021	0.011
(2) Sector B	0.120	0.115	0.018	0.000	0.000
(3) Sector C	0.187	0.055	0.112	0.131	0.071
(4) Sector D	0.010	0.046	0.029	0.023	0.009
(5) Sector E	0.070	0.013	0.040	0.054	0.053
Households	0.191	0.283	0.265	0.323	0.159

Direct and Indirect Coefficients Table

Whenever a particular sector expands (contracts) its output, that sector will buy more (less) inputs from the producing sectors in the economy. The increase (decrease) in the output of these suppliers will affect their own input purchases. They will, in turn, purchase more (less) from their respective suppliers. This process repeats itself through as many rounds as are necessary to achieve a new equilibrium. The results of these inter-actions are found in the table of *direct and indirect coefficients* (Table 6.3) for our hypothetical regional economy. The table of direct and indirect coefficients shows the direct (immediate) impacts of a change in output plus the additional indirect effects. Because the direct and indirect input requirements for a $1 expansion of final demand for each processing industry are indicated in Table 6.3, the coefficients in this table will be larger than those in Table 6.2 (which shows direct effects only). A math-ematical derivation of Table 6.3 is presented in the appendix to this chapter.

For a $1 change in the final demand for the output of a sector listed across the top of Table 6.3, the sectors listed along the side will have their output changed by the value of the coefficient. For example, a $1 change in the demand for the output of sector A will cause an 18.5 cent change in sector B, a 30.4 cent change in sector C, and so on. The sum of each column shows the total change in business output for a $1 change in the output of the respective sector. This sum is often referred to as the *output multiplier*. For sector A in our hypothetical economy, the value of the output multiplier is 1.958. This particular form of the output multiplier is known as a Type I output multiplier because the household sector is considered exogenous. A Type II output multiplier is estimated when households are considered to be endogenous to the model.

There is also the option of endogenizing the government sector in addition to the household sector. In this case, one can develop Type III multipliers in a fashion similar to that discussed for Type II multipliers.

Table 6.3. **Direct and indirect coefficients for a hypothetical economy (household sector exogenous)**

Selling sectors	Purchasing sectors				
	A	B	C	D	E
(1) Sector A	1.322	0.011	0.002	0.030	0.016
(2) Sector B	0.185	1.133	0.023	0.007	0.004
(3) Sector C	0.304	0.083	1.137	0.164	0.090
(4) Sector D	0.032	0.056	0.035	1.030	0.013
(5) Sector E	0.115	0.023	0.051	0.068	1.062
Type I output multiplier	1.958	1.306	1.248	1.299	1.185

Use of the Input-Output Tables

In order to illustrate the use of an I-O model, one can trace through the impacts of a change in the final demand for a particular sector's output in our hypothetical economy. Consider sector C. We can identify the intersector and intrasector sales of firms in sector C by reading across row 3 in Table 6.1. We can determine how much sector C firms purchased from each sector by reading down column 3.

Suppose that the final demand for sector C's products is increased by $1 million. This could come about by increased government purchases from firms in sector C, for example. By multiplying the increase in output by the trade coefficient for each cell in Table 6.2, we can determine by how much sector C firms increase purchases from the other sectors. Purchases from households by sector C firms would increase by $265,000 (= 0.265 x $1 million). But these are only the first-round effects. To determine the total increase in output generated in the regional economy due to a $1 million increase in the output of sector C, we must refer to Table 6.3. By multiplying the $1 million increase in output by the output multiplier for sector C (1.248), we would obtain an estimate of the total increase in output generated in the region of $1,248,000. The impact of changes in the level of final demand for other sector's outputs can be analyzed in a similar way.

Derivation of Income Multipliers

Although the output multiplier is often cited by persons analyzing the impacts of government or business policies, policymakers are frequently more interested in increases in household income than output when there is an increase in regional economic activity. The two basic methods for determining the household income multipliers are discussed below. The approach used will depend on the importance of the household sector in the local economy. Where the household sector is a major component of the economy, as it is in most rural economies, the second approach is of more interest.

Exogenous Household Sector

The direct and indirect income change that results from an increase in the final demand for any sector can be determined as follows. Suppose there is a $1 increase in final demand for sector D. Sector D firms will increase purchases from sector A by $0.030 (Table 6.3). The household coefficient for sector A is 0.191 (obtained from Table 6.2), and the resulting increase in household income is $0.006 (= 0.191 x 0.030). Tracing the $1 increase in final demand for sector D through each sector, and using the appropriate household coefficients, results in an increase in household income of $0.395. The direct and indirect income change coefficient applies to a single sector only but does not give the total change in household income; that is, the additional spending of other sectors is not accounted for. The Type I household income multiplier estimates the total change. It is obtained by dividing the direct and indirect income change for a sector by that sector's household coefficient (i.e., direct effects). The Type I household income multiplier for sector D is 1.22 (= 0.395 ÷ 0.323).

Endogenous Household Sector

In small regional economies, the household sector constitutes an important component of the economy in relation to total intraregional activity. In such cases, the household sector cannot be treated as exogenous but can be treated as endogenous. This implies that households are included in the processing sector. The weakness with this approach is that it assumes labour is the 'output' of household production and that consumption is the 'input,' which is clearly not the case; therefore, it likely overestimates the multiplier effects. The technical coefficients table now has six rows and columns, and is calculated in the same manner as it is when households are exogenous. The household row and household column totals in the transactions table are made to be equal in this case, which is not a requirement when households are treated as exogenous. The table of direct, indirect, and induced coefficients, when the household sector is endogenous, is shown in Table 6.4. Table 6.4 includes not only the direct and indirect effects but also the induced income effect from re-spending of income, because households are included as part of the processing sector. The increase in household consumption due to an increase in household income – the induced effect – is thereby taken into account.

The household row in Table 6.4 gives the direct, indirect, and induced income change associated with a \$1 increase in the output of the sector located at the top of the table. For example, a \$1 increase in sector D's final demand will, after a new equilibrium is attained, result in an increase in household income of \$0.508. This value is the single sector multiplier (for sector D).

Table 6.4. Direct, indirect, and induced coefficients for a hypothetical economy (household sector endogenous)

Selling sectors	Purchasing sectors					
	A	B	C	D	E	House-holds
(1) Sector A	1.335	0.022	0.012	0.042	0.022	0.031
(2) Sector B	0.215	1.159	0.047	0.036	0.018	0.071
(3) Sector C	0.457	0.218	1.258	0.310	0.165	0.369
(4) Sector D	0.126	0.139	0.109	1.119	0.058	0.225
(5) Sector E	0.333	0.216	0.223	0.275	1.167	0.525
(6) Households	0.533	0.472	0.422	0.508	0.259	1.288
Type II output multiplier	2.999	2.226	2.071	2.290	1.689	2.509

Once again, the single sector multiplier does not capture the increase in total household income. A \$1 increase in D's final demand will increase the demand for A's products. A will not only buy more from D but will also buy more from all the other sectors. The Type II household income multiplier attempts to capture these effects, as does the Type I multiplier in the case in which the household sector is treated as being exogenous. The Type II income multiplier is obtained by dividing the value across the bottom of row 6 of Table 6.4 by the corresponding household coefficient (that is, direct effects from Table 6.2). For sector D, the Type II income multiplier is 1.573 (= 0.508/0.323). A comparison of the Type I and Type II income multipliers is presented in Table 6.5.

The Type II output multiplier is obtained from the column sum of the coefficients in Table 6.4 and is given in the bottom row of Table 6.4. For the earlier example of a $0.5 million increase in the final demand in sector C, the Type II output multiplier gives an estimate for the increase in total business income generated in the region of $1,035,500 (= 2.071 x $0.5 million).

Table 6.5. **A comparison of Type I and Type II income multipliers**

	Activity (sector)				
	A	B	C	D	E
Household coefficient (direct income)	0.191	0.283	0.265	0.323	0.159
Household exogenous					
Direct and indirect income change	0.414	0.367	0.328	0.395	0.201
Type I multiplier	2.168	1.295	1.236	1.222	1.265
Household endogenous					
Direct, indirect, and induced income change	0.533	0.472	0.422	0.508	0.259
Type II multiplier	2.791	1.668	1.593	1.573	1.629

Note that the Type II multipliers (output and income) are larger than the Type I multipliers. This is due to the additional economic activity that is accounted for when the household sector is treated as endogenous. The Type III multipliers will be larger yet.

The Rectangular Input-Output System

In the I-O methodology of the previous section, it is assumed either that each industry produces only one commodity, or that the output of the various commodities produced by each sector can be combined into a single aggregate commodity that is unique to that particular industry. A rectangular I-O system improves upon these assumptions in that both inputs and outputs of the various sectors of an economy are classified by commodity type; thus, the number of commodities produced can be unequal to the number of processing sectors or industries. A mathematical treatment of rectangular I-O systems is presented in the appendix to this chapter.

A simplified example of a rectangular I-O transactions matrix is presented in Table 6.6. In this example, there are three processing sectors or industries (A, B, and C) producing five types of commodities (1-5). As in the square matrix, each element of this transactions matrix is in dollar terms. The first five columns indicate the industries producing the five commodities (the *make* or *output* matrix). In addition to the three regional industries, commodities one through five may be imported from outside the economy. Imports can originate either from outside the country or from other regions in the country; these imports are known as competitive imports.

Table 6.6. **Hypothetical rectangular input-output system (households exogenous)**

		Commodities					Industries			Final demands			Total
		1	2	3	4	5	A	B	C	P	G	X	
Commodities	1						3	3	1	3	1	7	18
	2						7	4	2	2		1	16
	3						2	2	1	5			10
	4						8	10	4	5	3		30
	5						3	3	1	2	3		12
Industries	A	15	7	4	1								27
	B		1	4	25								30
	C			2	3	11							16
Imports (non-competing)							1	1	1				3
Wages & salaries							3	3	2	9			17
Government								4	4				8
Imports (competing)		3	8		1	1							13
TOTAL		18	16	10	30	12	27	30	16	17	16	8	200

The elements in the bottom or *total* row for columns one through five represent the total regional supply of the commodities. For example, for commodity 2, there is a total supply of $16 of this commodity in the hypothetical economy. Of the total supply of this commodity, $7 is produced by industry A, $1 by industry B, and $8 is imported from outside the region (reading down the column).

A description of the source of the inputs used by the three regional industries (the *use* matrix) is provided in columns 6 through 8 (under industries A, B, and C). Inputs are composed of both locally produced and imported quantities of the five types of commodities produced in the region. The industries also utilize *noncompeting* imports, that is, imports of commodity types that are not produced in the region. As in the square I-0 system, the producing industries can also purchase inputs from the primary sector. In this example, the primary sector is represented by the household ('wages and salaries') and government sectors.

Columns under industries A, B, and C represent the total payments made by these industries for various factors of production. For example, industry A used $27 worth of inputs – $3 of commodity 1, $7 of commodity 2, and so on. In addition, $1 of noncompeting imports was used in the production of A's outputs, and $3 was paid to the primary sector. Note that, as in the square system, the value of inputs used in production equals the value of commodities produced as outputs. It is assumed that there are no profits in this hypothetical system.

The last three columns represent final demand. This final demand is similar to that described under the square I-O system. In the present example, the final demand is composed of personal expenditures (P), government expenditures on goods and services (G), and exports (X). In this example, households are treated as exogenous. The columns under industries A, B, and C, plus those of the final demand (although final demand could be excluded), for rows 1 through 6 constitute the *use* or *absorption* matrix.

Estimating the Technical Coefficients Matrix

Two basic assumptions should be recognized. The first assumption is that, if the output of a commodity is increased, all industries producing that commodity get a fixed share of the increased production. The second assumption is that, for each dollar of an industry's output, certain fixed amounts of commodity inputs are required. This is equivalent to the assumption that the inputs consumed by an industry occur in fixed proportions that do not vary with the level of industrial output (although one could adjust the technical coefficients).

These two assumptions allow for the interindustry and commodity transactions table (Table 6.6) to be used in the derivation of a technical coefficients matrix similar to Table 6.2. The only difference between the technical coefficients matrix in the rectangular and square I-O systems is that, in the rectangular system, instead of having selling sectors, the inputs to production are delineated by commodity type. Table 6.7 presents the technical coefficients matrix; these are also referred to as the production coefficients or use coefficients. The coefficients in this table represent the value of each commodity used as an input for each industry per dollar of industrial output. The individual coefficients are derived by dividing the value of each commodity input of an industry by the total value of the output of that industry.

Table 6.7. Technical coefficient matrix for the rectangular
input-output system

		Industry		
		A	B	C
Commodity	1	0.111	0.100	0.063
	2	0.259	0.133	0.125
	3	0.074	0.067	0.063
	4	0.296	0.333	0.250
	5	0.111	0.100	0.063
Imports (non-competing)		0.037	0.033	0.063

The level of inputs used by an industry is proportional to the output of the industry as a result of the second assumption. Because one delineates both industries and commodities in the rectangular system, there is a need to determine the contribution each industry makes to the overall production of a particular commodity in the economy. The first assumption with respect to proportionality of commodity output allows for such a delineation. The contribution of each industry to overall regional supply of a particular commodity is represented by a market shares matrix. The value of production of a particular commodity by an industry is divided by the total value of the regional supply of the commodity to determine the market share of that industry (Table 6.8). For example, using Table 6.6 we see that industry B produces $1 of commodity 2 that has a total supply of $16. This implies that industry B's market share of commodity 2 is 0.063. The market shares (make) coefficients do not sum to one for commodities 1 through 5, because there are competitive imports.

Table 6.8. Market shares matrix for the rectangular input-output system

		Commodity				
		1	2	3	4	5
Industry	A	0.833	0.438	0.400	0.033	-
	B	-	0.063	0.400	0.833	-
	C	-	-	0.200	0.100	0.917

Using information contained in the market shares and industry technical matrices, one can determine the impacts on all commodities and industries in the economy of a change in the final demand for a particular *commodity* or group of *commodities*. That is, unlike the square I-O system, final demand is expressed in terms of commodities *and* the output of the primary sector. Before such an analysis is possible, several problems must be addressed.

First, when secondary or published data are used in constructing the technical coefficients matrix, it is usual for the data to reflect total expenditures on commodities by each industry. There is, in general, no mention of the proportion of a particular commodity input purchased from *foreign* firms (e.g., competitive imports). One may know the total amount of competitive imports, but the level of commodity imports used as inputs by each industry are usually not specified. As noted in the square system, imports are considered exogenous to the I-O model and, as a result, should be netted out from the technical coefficients matrix.

The usual procedure is to compute *self-sufficiency* ratios for each commodity. These ratios represent the proportion of total supply of each commodity that is produced in the country or region of concern. The computation of these self-sufficiency ratios may not be easy, but, assuming such information is available, multiplying the purchases of each commodity by an industry by the commodity's self-sufficiency ratio results in a netting out of leakages due to competitive imports. This assumes that each industry imports the same proportion of a particular commodity input (except noncompetitive imports) as do other industries in the economy. The value of these competitive imports must then be aggregated with the noncompetitive commodity categories.

Second, the price of any product can be expressed either as that charged to the purchaser or that received by the producer. The important point is that anyone using a rectangular I-O system must make sure that the final demand and technical coefficients are conformable (e.g., using the same type of price). The usual procedure is to express final demand in terms of producer prices. This necessitates the conversion of the values of commodities purchased and produced to the value of the same commodities using producer prices.

The difference between the producer and purchaser prices is represented by commodity taxes and wholesale, retail, and transportation charges. These four categories of charges must be removed from purchaser prices and used as output for the appropriate commodities (e.g., retail margins, transportation, etc.). The usual procedures are to determine the proportion of purchaser prices that are producer prices and the various margins for each commodity. One then multiplies each commodity's distribution between these margins by the values in the technology matrix to net out the various margins and then allocates the charges to the appropriate commodity category.

Example of the Rectangular Input-Output System

Tables 6.7, 6.8, and 6.9 are used in working through a simple example of a rectangular I-O system to determine the impacts on the hypothetical economy of changes in the final demand for a *commodity* or group of *commodities*. In this example, assume that all prices are producer prices. This assumption eliminates problems associated with converting purchaser prices to producer prices.

There still exists the problem of determining the relative amounts of competing imports that must be netted out of the technical coefficients matrix. One can determine the proportion of a particular commodity that is a competing import from tables 6.6 and 6.7. For example, $3 of commodity 1 is imported, which represents 16.7 per cent of the total supply, implying that 83.3 per cent of commodity 1 is produced locally. Table 6.9 presents the self-sufficiency ratios for the five commodities produced in this region.

Table 6.9. Self-sufficiency ratios for commodities 1 to 5

Commodity	Self-sufficiency ratio
1	0.833
2	0.500
3	1.000
4	0.967
5	0.917

Leakages is a term applied to the dollars that leave an economy in return for imports. This is an appropriate term, because money will continue to circulate until it leaks from the system and does not return. Leakages must be subtracted from either the market share coefficients or the technical coefficients, thus transforming them into trade coefficients (Table 6.10). Theoretically, each element of the coefficients matrix (Table 6.7) could be adjusted for leakages with a unique leakage coefficient; in practice, the data requirements are too large. Instead, coefficients are usually developed for each commodity without regard to the sector purchasing it. The most common approach is to use the base year ratio of imports to total demand as an estimate of future leakages.

Using Table 6.9, Table 6.7 is modified to net out the effects of competitive imports. This is accomplished by multiplying each commodity row by the corresponding self-sufficiency ratio. The modified technical coefficients matrix is presented in Table 6.10. This implicitly assumes that each industry imports the same proportion of each commodity used as an input as do other industries in the economy. Likewise, the market shares matrix (Table 6.8) is adjusted by multiplying each commodity row by the corresponding self-sufficiency ratio.

Table 6.10. **Modified technical coefficients matrix accounting for competitive imports**

Commodity	Industry		
	A	B	C
1	0.093	0.083	0.052
2	0.130	0.067	0.063
3	0.074	0.067	0.063
4	0.286	0.322	0.242
5	0.102	0.092	0.057

Now assume that there is a \$1 increase in the final demand for commodity 3. What is the overall impact on the economy? According to the market share assumption, \$0.40 of final demand will be produced by industry A, \$0.40 by industry B, and \$0.20 by industry C. The first-round indirect impacts of the production of the three industries are in terms of the intermediate input demands, as is shown by the modified technical coefficients in Table 6.10. Each input coefficient of industry A is multiplied by \$0.40, industry B by \$0.40, and industry C by \$0.20. The results are found in Table 6.11.

Given these first-round impacts, the total production of each commodity requires additional indirect production by industries A, B, and C that, in turn, require more commodity inputs. The impacts of this first round of effects on industrial output are found by multiplying the adjusted market shares (adjusted Table 6.8) by the corresponding row total in Table 6.11; the results are presented in Table 6.12.

Table 6.11. **First-round (direct) impacts of a \$1 change in final demand for commodity 3**[*]

Commodity	Industry			
	A	B	C	Total
1	0.037	0.033	0.010	0.081
2	0.052	0.027	0.013	0.091
3	0.030	0.027	0.013	0.069
4	0.115	0.129	0.048	0.292
5	0.041	0.037	0.011	0.089

[*]This excludes the \$1 change in final demand for commodity 3.

Table 6.12. Changes in industrial output resulting from first-round changes in commodity demands

Industry	Commodity					
	1	2	3	4	5	Total
A	0.056	0.020	0.028	0.009	0	0.113
B	0	0.003	0.028	0.235	0	0.265
C	0	0	0.014	0.028	0.075	0.117

The first-round impacts result in industrial output increases of $0.113, $0.265, and $0.117 for industries A, B, and C, respectively. These increases in output require additional inputs, as given by Table 6.10. As in the square I-O system, the multiplier effects eventually die out. The total impact on the five commodities produced in this hypothetical economy of a $1 change in the final demand of commodity 3 are given in Table 6.13 (e.g., column 3). For commodity 3, a $1 increase in its final demand results in a $0.157 increase in commodity 1, a $0.168 increase in commodity 2, a $1.134 increase in commodity 3, and so on.

Table 6.13. Direct and indirect effects of a $1 change in the final demand of commodities 1 to 5 on commodity output

Commodity	Commodity				
	1	2	3	4	5
1	1.120	0.043	0.157	0.147	0.094
2	0.147	1.051	0.168	0.137	0.103
3	0.099	0.036	1.134	0.124	0.096
4	0.409	0.148	0.578	1.566	0.393
5	0.132	0.047	0.172	0.162	1.103

Besides changes in the final demand for a single commodity, there are likely to be changes in the final demand for all commodities. The direct and indirect effects of $1 changes in all of the commodities produced within the region are also presented in Table 6.13, with the calculations found in the appendix. The impacts of a given change in the final demand of a particular commodity can be determined by multiplying the change in the final demand for that commodity by the coefficients in the column corresponding to that commodity.

Besides measuring the impacts of a change in the final demand of a commodity in the level of this and other commodities produced in the economy, the impacts of such a change on particular industries or primary inputs can also be analyzed. This is a major difference between the rectangular and square I-O systems. The matrix of direct and indirect effects of $1 changes in the final demand of the five commodities on industries A, B, and C, and on imports, wages and salaries, and government payments, is presented in Table 6.14.

Table 6.14. **Direct and indirect effects of a $1 change in final demand of commodities 1 to 5 on industrial output and primary input usage**

Industry	1	2	3	4	5
A	0.937	0.305	0.708	0.311	0.194
B	0.436	0.189	1.004	1.388	0.408
C	0.203	0.073	0.469	0.350	1.010
Imports	0.754	0.240	0.506	0.127	0.141
Wages & salaries	0.174	0.094	0.674	1.053	0.304
Government payments	0.049	0.027	0.496	0.446	1.368

Multipliers in the Rectangular I-O Model

As in the square I-O model, various multipliers can be computed for the rectangular I-O system. The theoretical definitions of the various multipliers are the same under both systems, although the actual computations are dependent on the type of system being used. In addition, under the rectangular system, the various multiplier effects can correspond to changes in the output of the commodities produced in the region (or they can correspond to changes in sectoral outputs). Again, this is in contrast to the change in *industrial* output being represented in the square I-O system.

Type I multipliers are obtained by assuming households are exogenous; Type II income multipliers are obtained by assuming the household sector is endogenous. In the latter case, total gross output of the household *sector* is taken to be the direct plus indirect plus induced effects of the level of final demand for the various commodities. The direct effect on households of a change in final demand is assumed to be the level of final demand for the household *commodity*. The Type II income multiplier is then computed as the ratio of the direct, plus indirect, plus induced effects and the direct impacts on households of the given vector of final demand.

An income *pseudo-multiplier* measures the total change in household income per dollar of output delivered to final demand. This multiplier should be contrasted with the Type II income multiplier that represents the total change in household income per $ of *income* generated directly by final demand. That is, if the amount of labour income created directly by final demand can be estimated, the Type II income multiplier will enable one to estimate the total impacts on household income. Alternatively, the income pseudo-multiplier enables one to estimate total household income impacts when only the aggregate level of output of final demand is known.

Income is likely less a concern than are jobs, even though the two are related. Hence, it makes some sense to construct job multipliers in addition to income multipliers. Gross output requirements can be translated into employment, say person-years, per dollar of sectoral output. For the square matrix in section 6.1, let $J = [e_1 \dots e_5]$ be a 5 x 5 diagonal matrix of employment coefficients. Then $[J(I - A)^{-1}]Y$ is the vector of total employment in each sector associated with demand vector Y (appendix). It is also possible to construct occupation coefficients for each sector, so that the inputs of changes in demand on various occupations is taken into account.

Similar to the income multipliers, there are also value added and pseudo value-added multipliers. Value added is defined as payments to the primary inputs, which include labour, capital, and government. The value-added multiplier is defined as the total value added divided by the direct value added, resulting from a given level of final demand. Again, total value added is defined as above. Direct value added is the level of primary inputs used directly in the generation of final demand. The value-added multiplier enables one to estimate the total change in payments to primary inputs, if the direct payments to these primary inputs are known.

As in the case of the income multipliers, pseudo value-added multipliers can be estimated, assuming the structure of final demand does not change. The pseudo value-added multiplier allows one to estimate the total effect on payments to primary inputs, given the total value of final demand. It is calculated by dividing the total value added by the total value of the final demand that generates that value added.

The output multiplier generated within a rectangular I-O system is similar to the output multiplier generated in a square system. It defines the total change in output (net of household production) of a change in final demand. Again, it is computed as the total regional output (not including output of households) divided by the value of final demand or, in other words, the sum of output delivered to final demand (not including the households).

The rectangular input-output system has one major advantage over the square I-O system; namely, it overcomes the problem of allocating all outputs of any specific commodity to a particular industry, even though there may be a major producer of a commodity in another SIC (Standard Industrial Classification) category. Most I-O models used today have adopted the rectangular format.

Discussion

Many multipliers can be derived from an I-O model, but they must be used cautiously. Although it is possible to determine the final change in local output as a result of a private or government action, nothing is known about the time distribution of the change or how long it takes to achieve the new equilibrium. The analysis is essentially static. The final change in household income will also be quite different from that predicted by the model's multipliers. During the period required to achieve a new equilibrium, the structure of the economy will likely change.

The multipliers discussed in this chapter are the most frequently used, mainly because they are easy to obtain. But multipliers can be considered useful as indicators only. Not only is their construction rather ad hoc, but the value of various multipliers is sensitive to whether the household sector is chosen to be endogenous or exogenous. This decision depends on the degree of openness in the region; that is, on the extent to which the local economy depends on trade with other regions. The more open the economy or the more dependent the region is on trade, the more appropriate it is to make the household sector endogenous.

Because I-O models are static, economic judgment is required to analyze any deviation from the current situation. As an example, consider an agricultural processing sector that purchases half of its inputs locally and the other half from farmers in another region. This is reflected in the coefficients of the I-O model. Now suppose that the amount of agricultural output produced locally doubles. If this produce is all sold to the local processors, the existing I-O model is no longer strictly applicable. Unless purchases from farmers in the other region also double, the coefficients in the relevant tables should be changed. Only if the change is small will the current model remain appropriate.

Regional models may be constructed from the national I-O models by including those sectors that are not present in the regional economy in the trade sector. The coefficients between the remaining sectors are simply the technical coefficients between these sectors as found in the national model. This procedure may be unrealistic, since a regional sector may use different production relations than would a national sector. Survey-based I-O models can be used, but these are subject to sampling errors that can only be assumed to be small and insignificant. Alternatively, regional self-sufficiency data can be used to adjust the national coefficients.

One issue of concern in the construction of regional models relates to the treatment of existing residents versus immigrants. Immigrants from other regions or countries may bring different skills, education levels, or even cultural experiences than those possessed by current residents. One way of distinguishing between current and new residents in I-O models is to employ average consumption coefficients for the former and marginal consumption coefficients for the latter; newcomers exhibit different spending patterns than do longer-term residents, perhaps spending a larger proportion of their income on housing. Average coefficients can be obtained from the existing transactions or trade table, but marginal coefficients will need to be estimated using information from other sources.

Finally, I-O models can be constructed to take into account the impacts of economic activity on the environment. Environmental concerns can be addressed by adding columns and rows of coefficients that indicate, respectively, how much waste material the economic sectors release into the environment per dollar of output and how many natural resources are used up per dollar of production. Focusing on pollution only, it is possible to account for environmental pollution generation and abatement associated with interindustry activity. Let $v^* = vX$, where v^* is a vector of pollution levels and v is a matrix of direct pollution input coefficients. Matrix v could be derived from a matrix of specified pollution outputs. Then, $v^* = [v(I - A)^{-1}]Y$, where the term in square braces is the matrix of total impact coefficients – an element in this matrix is the total pollution impact generated per dollar of final demand presented to the economy. Note the similarity with jobs. The matrices J and v could represent any factors associated with interindustry activity that are assumed to vary linearly with output – employment, pollution generation, or energy consumption.

Role of Input-Output Models in B-C Analysis

Input-output analysis is able to identify the increase in value-added activity throughout the economy. However, changes in value added are a measure of changes in economic activity and are not a measure of benefit (or cost) in the welfare economics sense; they are merely the upper limit on the opportunity cost of the resources employed in the various activities that generate the value added. One possible approach to valuing the opportunity cost of a project is to compare the indirect effects of the alternative use of the funds, as generated by an appropriate I-O model, with those generated by spending the available funds on the resource development project under consideration. These might be thought of as project-specific opportunity costs and might be positive, zero, or negative. If some alternative project gives rise to secondary impacts greater than those generated by the project being evaluated, the inclusion as benefits of the initial project's indirect impacts minus the opportunity cost of the best alternative may lead to a reduction in the net benefits of the resource development project. This is contrary to the increase regional analysts often expect when they include the indirect effects of a project as a benefit. The economic efficiency of the resource development projects is overstated if these arguments are ignored; secondary or regional impacts can be used to generate higher B-C ratios, thereby justifying public investment, but the analysis is likely to be incorrect.

It has also been argued that, when resources are not fully employed, their shadow or true value is not given by the observed price (e.g., wage rate of the employed labour force). If there is persistent unemployment of resources, particularly labour, then the indirect benefits of a project should be included as a benefit to the project. But there are a number of arguments against this view:

(1) It needs to be determined if unemployment is indeed persistent, and, if it is, whether the cause is structural (e.g., a poorly trained labour force) or not.

(2) If unemployment is not structural, it is not clear that resource development projects are the best way of reducing unemployment. Macroeconomic policies may be more effective in reducing unemployment. Further, the time required between authorization and construction may mitigate against the use of resource development projects as a method for reducing unemployment.

(3) Finally, if the shadow price of labour is zero, then the opportunity cost of capital must also be higher than is evident from the observed rate of return to capital. The reason is that returns from capital must be diverted to support unemployed labour. Therefore, since the discount rate is determined by the opportunity cost of funds used in the project, the discount rate to be employed in the B-C analysis must be higher than calculated. The higher discount rate militates against water and other resource projects, and it offsets the sup-

posed benefits due to secondary or regional impacts.

If a public project is funded by an increase in local taxes, an interesting question that arises for B-C analysis is whether or not the same multiplier would be used to measure the contractionary impacts of those taxes as is used to measure the expansionary impacts of the project itself. Use of the same multiplier would result in offsetting impacts, although it is likely that the overall impact would be negative, since there are inevitable leakages – the amount of revenue required to fund the project will be greater than the project costs. The discussions in this chapter indicate that different taxes will have a different multiplier impact than will project outlays. The difference in these impacts might be considered a project benefit or cost.

The problem with economic evaluation of regional development projects is that methodological errors are committed in applying tools of analysis.

Many of the more serious misapplications of these tools [of cost-benefit and I-O analyses] are not in the mainstream professional literature but in the myriad of environmental impact statements, forest timber plans, community development analyses, and other applied impact studies. These studies often represent the attempts of regional planners, semiprofessional economists, or project promoters to apply tools and concepts learned or mislearned from professional economists. (Hamilton et al. 1991:335)

Further discussion of the problems of cost-benefit analysis is provided in Chapter 5.

Appendix: Mathematics of Input-Output Models
In this appendix many of the concepts regarding square and rectangular input-output models are illustrated in mathematical terms.

Square Input-Output Models

Let x_{ij} =   purchases of sector j from sector i
           =   sales of sector i to sector j.

The flow matrix is

$$x_{ij} = \begin{bmatrix} x_{11} & x_{12} & \cdots & x_{1n} \\ x_{21} & x_{22} & \cdots & x_{2n} \\ \cdot & \cdot & \cdots & \cdot \\ \cdot & \cdot & \cdots & \cdot \\ \cdot & \cdot & \cdots & \cdot \\ x_{n1} & x_{n2} & \cdots & x_{nn} \end{bmatrix}.$$

All the flows are in monetary terms and are evaluated at producer prices.

The total output of sector i, X_i, is defined as the sum of the elements in the ith row of x_{ij} plus the final demand for sector i, Y_i. Hence,

$$X_i = \sum_{j=1}^{n} X_{ij} + Y_i, \qquad (A.1)$$

where $Y = C + I + G + E$,
C = consumer spending,
I = net capital formation,
G = government expenditures, and
E = net exports.

Therefore, the vector of gross output is

$$X = \begin{bmatrix} X_1 \\ X_2 \\ \cdot \\ \cdot \\ \cdot \\ X_n \end{bmatrix},$$

and the vector of final demands is

$$Y = \begin{bmatrix} Y_1 \\ Y_2 \\ \cdot \\ \cdot \\ \cdot \\ Y_n \end{bmatrix}.$$

Technical (Trade) Coefficients Matrix and Leontief Inverse Matrix
Dividing each column entry of the flow matrix by the corresponding
gross output gives the matrix of technical (trade) coefficients,

$$A = \begin{bmatrix} a_{11} & a_{12} & \cdots & a_{1n} \\ a_{21} & a_{22} & \cdots & a_{2n} \\ \cdot & \cdot & \cdot & \cdot \\ \cdot & \cdot & \cdot & \cdot \\ \cdot & \cdot & \cdot & \cdot \\ a_{n1} & a_{n2} & \cdots & a_{nn} \end{bmatrix},$$

where $a_{ij} = x_{ij}/X_j$. Therefore, we can rewrite (A.1) as

$$X_i = \sum_{j=1}^{n} a_{ij} X_j + Y_i. \tag{A.2}$$

In matrix notation this becomes

$$X = A X + Y. \tag{A.3}$$

Solving for X gives

$$X = (I - A)^{-1} Y, \tag{A.4}$$

where I is the identity matrix. The matrix $(I - A)^{-1}$ is the matrix of direct
and indirect coefficients and is often referred to as the Leontief matrix.
For predicted levels of final demand (Y^*), equation (A.4), can be used
to project the levels of total output (X^*) as

$$X^* = (I - A)^{-1} Y^*. \tag{A.5}$$

Multipliers

Let

$$(I-A)^{-1} = B = \begin{bmatrix} b_{11} & b_{12} & \cdots & b_{1n} \\ b_{21} & b_{22} & \cdots & b_{2n} \\ \cdot & \cdot & \cdot & \cdot \\ \cdot & \cdot & \cdot & \cdot \\ \cdot & \cdot & \cdot & \cdot \\ b_{n1} & b_{n2} & \cdots & b_{nn} \end{bmatrix}.$$

If the household sector is exogenous, the output multiplier is found by summing down a column of $(I - A)^{-1}$; that is, the Type I output multiplier for sector r is

$$M_{out} = \sum_{i=1}^{n} b_{ir}. \tag{A.6}$$

Suppose that the household sector is exogenous. Let $H = (l_1 l_2 \ldots l_n)$ be a row vector of household coefficients determined by $l_j = h_j / X_j$, where h_j is the amount of labour services purchased by sector j. The Type I income multiplier for sector r is

$$M_{Ir} = \frac{\sum_{i=1}^{n} l_i b_{ir}}{l_r}. \tag{A.7}$$

Suppose that the household sector is chosen to be endogenous. If the last row in the Leontief inverse matrix is derived by including the household sector, then the Type II income multiplier for this sector, r, is defined as

$$M_{IIr} = \frac{l_{nr}}{l_r}. \tag{A.8}$$

The Type II output multiplier is defined as in (A.6), although there is an additional row and column in the Leontief inverse matrix when the household sector is endogenous.

Rectangular Input-Output Systems

The general accounting framework for the rectangular system is presented in Figure A.1. Compared with Table 6.6, in this figure competing imports (the next to last row in Table 6.6) are deducted from final demand rather than being considered as a positive supply of commodities. Consequently, the total for a commodity row and column represent the domestic production rather than the total supply of the commodity. Therefore, in the mathematical derivations, the competing import sector is first ignored. Then, the formulae are corrected to take into account the degree of self-sufficiency in the economy. It is the latter formulae that apply to the tables in the text, as is demonstrated in the discussion below.

The following notation is used in Table A.1:

NC = number of commodities,
NS = number of sectors or industries,
NF = number of final demand sectors, and
NR = number of primary inputs.

The matrices and their sizes are explained in the figure and the reader should compare this outline with Table 6.6 (which includes an extra row). The matrix V is often referred to as the *make* matrix, while U, or U and F (taken together), constitute the *use* or *absorption* matrix.

The rectangular I-O system is based on the assumption that the total value of commodity outputs must equal the value of commodities used by the local industries as inputs and the level of final demand. That is,

$$q = Bg + e, \qquad (A.9)$$

where B is an $NC \times NS$ matrix analogous to the technical coefficients matrix, and e is an $NC \times 1$ vector of final demands for each of the commodities (each element is the sum of the rows of F). Commodity output, in turn, is also related to industrial output by the market shares matrix

$$g = Dq, \qquad (A.10)$$

where D is an $NS \times NC$ matrix of market share coefficients.

Substituting (A.10) into (A.9) yields

$$q = BDq + e, \qquad (A.11)$$

Table A.1. General accounting framework for the rectangular input-output system

	Commodities 1...NC	Sector (industry) 1...NS	Final demand 1...NF	Total
Commodities 1 . . NC	xxxxxxxxxxxxxxx xxxxxxxxxxxxxxx xxxxxxxxxxxxxxx xxxxxxxxxxxxxxx xxxxxxxxxxxxxxx	U Intermediate demand	F Final demand	q Total commodity output
Sector or industry 1 . . NS	V Market share	xxxxxxxxxxxxxxx xxxxxxxxxxxxxxx xxxxxxxxxxxxxxx xxxxxxxxxxxxxxx xxxxxxxxxxxxxxx	xxxxxxxxxxxxxxxx xxxxxxxxxxxxxxxx xxxxxxxxxxxxxxxx xxxxxxxxxxxxxxxx xxxxxxxxxxxxxxxx	g Total sector output
Primary inputs 1 . . NR	xxxxxxxxxxxxxxx xxxxxxxxxxxxxxx xxxxxxxxxxxxxxx xxxxxxxxxxxxxxx xxxxxxxxxxxxxxx xxxxxxxxxxxxxxx	Y Primary inputs by sectors	YF Primary inputs by final demand agencies	P Value-added
Total	q' Total commodities input	g' Total sectors input	E Total final demand	

which implies that

$$q = (I - BD)^{-1} e. \tag{A.12}$$

Alternatively, substituting (A.9) into (A.10) and solving for g yields

$$g = (I - DB)^{-1} D e. \tag{A.13}$$

Given equations (A.12) and (A.13), two multiplier matrices can be identified. These are given by equations (A.14) and (A.15).

$$M_C = (I - BD)^{-1} \tag{A.14}$$

$$M_I = (I - DB)^{-1} D \tag{A.15}$$

M_C is an $NC \times NC$ matrix, representing the direct plus indirect effects on each commodity of a one dollar change in the level of final demand for each commodity. For example, element $M_C (2, 3)$ represents the direct and indirect effects on commodity 2 of a \$1 change in final demand for commodity 3. M_I represents the $NS \times NC$ matrix of the direct plus indirect effects on each industry of a \$1 change in the level of final demand for each commodity. Neither of these multiplier matrices takes into account competing imports, however.

When there are competing imports, the above multiplier matrices must be modified. Given that C represents an $NC \times 1$ vector of competing imports (next to last row in Table 6.6), the total supply of competing commodities in the region is

$$S = \text{domestic supply} + C,$$

where S is an $NC \times 1$ vector of the total supply of commodities (equal to q in Figure A.1).

Define the following diagonal matrix of coefficients, whose elements are the ratios of competing imports to total supply, S, for each commodity (i.e., the self-sufficiency ratios of Table 6.9):

$$\theta_{ij} \begin{cases} = 0 & \text{if } i \neq j \\ = C_i/S & \text{if } i = j \text{ and } C_i \neq 0 \\ = 1 & \text{if } i = j \text{ and } C_i = 0 \end{cases} \tag{A.16}$$
$$i,j = 1,\ldots,NC.$$

Then $D^* = D(I - \theta)$ is an $NS \times NC$ matrix of adjusted market shares (Table 6.8); D^* is calculated as the proportion of the total supply of each commodity. Also $B^* = (I - \theta)B$ is the modified technical coefficients (or trade coefficients) matrix (Table 6.10). This compares to the definition of D as the proportion of total domestic production of each commodity obtained from a particular industry. The sum of the coefficients for any commodity (column) in D^* need not be equal to 1.0, due to competing imports. This sum will represent the proportion of the total supply of a particular commodity that is obtained from domestic production.

Substituting these results in equations (A.12) and (A.13), respectively, gives

$$q^* = (I - B^*D^*)^{-1} e \qquad\qquad (A.17)$$

and

$$g^* = (I - D^*B^*)^{-1} D^* e, \qquad\qquad (A.18)$$

which implies

$$M_C^* = (I - B^*D^*)^{-1} \qquad\qquad (A.19)$$

and

$$M_I^* = (I - D^*B^*)^{-1} D^*. \qquad\qquad (A.20)$$

Equation (A.19) generates Table 6.13 in the text, while equation (A.20) generates the top half of Table 6.14. The bottom half of Table 6.14 is generated from $(I - T)^{-1} D^*$, where T is the technical coefficients matrix for primary inputs and is determined by dividing each element in Y by its respective column total.

Income Multipliers
In matrix notation, the Type II income multiplier is computed as

$$M_{II} = \frac{Y_H}{e_H}, \qquad\qquad (A.21)$$

where Y_H is the total output of the household sector and e_H is the final demand for the household sector's output. The income pseudo-multiplier is computed as

$$H_{II}* = \frac{Y_{H_i}}{e_i},$$

(A.22)

where e_i is the final demand for sector i's output.

7
Valuing Nonmarket Benefits

Inclusion of the costs and benefits of changes in the availability of commodities not normally traded in the marketplace, such as recreational services and clean water, is an important component of cost-benefit (B-C) analysis. It is also important in land-use planning, where multiple uses of land exist and trade-offs need to be made. Such trade-offs can only be properly evaluated if the value of land in each of its uses is considered, and that includes taking into account the values of goods and services not traded in the marketplace. Nonmarket values are explicitly recognized in B-C analysis and are to be included in the National Economic Development account, according to the U.S. Water Resource Council's (1983) 'Principles and Guidelines' for project evaluation. In this chapter, methods for estimating nonmarket costs and benefits are examined. The discussion is cursory due to the nature of the topic – there are many methods available and research in this area is prolific.

To assess the benefits of an improvement in water quality, for example, the values placed on the change in water quality by individuals is to be measured and summed over all individuals. This value can be approximated by consumer surplus when it is possible to estimate a Marshallian demand function for the good or service in question; but the correct measure is either the compensating or the equivalent variation of the change – the area under the income-compensated (Hicksian) demand function fixed on the initial or the final level of utility, respectively. An estimate of benefit can be found, therefore, by determining a demand function for the activity or by using a survey instrument to elicit either the compensating or equivalent variation.

It is possible to distinguish indirect and direct approaches to obtaining information about nonmarket goods and services as well as about public goods. The *expenditure function approach* relies upon a relationship between private goods (that are traded in the marketplace) and public goods in order to draw inferences about the demand for the public good. This approach is sometimes referred to as the *indirect approach*; it is indirect because information on goods and services traded in markets is used to value the nonmarket good or service under consideration. Other *choice-based models* employ related information about an activity in order to provide estimates about the value of the activity itself. Examples of this method include the *travel cost method* for valuing recreational sites and voter behaviour. In the United States, citizens frequently go to the polls to vote on government budgets that deal directly with expenditures on public goods. This information can be used to say something about the value of the public good in question. This approach is referred to as *voter referendum*.

The *direct approach* uses questionnaires or surveys to directly elicit an individual's *willingness-to-pay* (WTP) for more of a public good or his/her *willingness-to-accept* (WTA) compensation to have less of the public good (e.g., clean air). Therefore, it is also referred to as the *income compensation approach*. WTP is equivalent to compensating variation under certain circumstances, while WTA is often the same as equivalent variation (Chapter 3). Since this approach requires individuals to respond to hypothetical questions in a survey setting, it is also referred to as the *contingent valuation method* (CVM) if actual values are requested, or the *contingent behaviour method* if a behavioural response is desired. One variation is *conjoint analysis*, which simply requires that individuals choose between alternatives.

Although there is some overlap in classification of techniques, in this chapter, we examine these approaches to measuring the benefits of goods and services for which explicit markets do not exist – that is, nonmarket or extra-market benefits.

Expenditure Function Approach

There are two major ways to observe data about unpriced or nonmarket values – through physical linkages or through behavioural linkages. Estimates of the values of nonmarket commodities can be obtained by determining a physical relationship between the nonmarket commodity and something that can be measured in the marketplace. This is done via *damage functions*. A damage function provides physical information about how damage from, say, pollution is affected by emission levels, and it relates damages to monetary values. For example, damage functions for soil erosion for the Palouse region of eastern Washington and western Idaho (as well as for Saskatchewan) have been estimated. The physical component of the damage function provides information about the estimated yield loss when topsoil is removed. Then, using data on the amount of soil erosion caused by a certain agronomic practice and given crop prices, it is possible to estimate the cost of soil erosion from the estimated physical damage function. It is possible to assess the value of topsoil, a commodity not traded in the marketplace, using information about crop yields, costs of agronomic practices, and crop prices. (The economics of soil erosion are discussed in Chapter 10.)

Behavioural linkages, on the other hand, are traced through individual utility functions. These then appear in the marketplace as demands for market goods. By considering the effect upon the demands for related private goods, it may be possible to say something about the value of public goods.

Market Valuation of Public Goods via Physical Linkages

There are situations where the public good, Q, is a factor input in production. An example of this was illustrated in Chapter 5, where ozone damage to crops was considered. In that example, an estimate of the benefits of cleaner air is given by the loss in net returns from the farmland, basically the loss in value due to reduced crop yields. In the case where a public good is a factor input, the production function for output X can be written as

$$X = f(K, L, N, Q),$$

where K refers to inputs of capital, L is labour, N is land, and Q is the public good (perhaps clean air or water).

What effect will a change in Q have on the production of the good in question? This will depend, in part, on the effect that a change in Q has on the output price of X. Suppose that there are constant returns to scale, and that Q does not affect returns to scale. (Constant returns to scale implies a horizontal supply function.) Also assume for the moment that the changes in the output of X are sufficiently large to affect output price, that is, that the demand for X is downward sloping. An increase in the availability of Q only decreases the cost of producing every level of output by the same amount. A good example is that of irrigation; an increase in Q might represent a reduction in water salinity. Although the costs of producing crops are unaffected, yields will increase because water is less saline. The supply or marginal cost function is a horizontal line, as is shown in Figure 7.1. An increase in Q reduces marginal cost, causing a shift in supply from S to S'; all of the gain from the reduction in the price of X accrues to consumers in the form of consumer surplus (the shaded area in Figure 7.1). Thus, the demand for the market commodity X provides information about the benefit of an increase in the availability of Q.

Figure 7.1

Increase of public good with constant returns to scale production

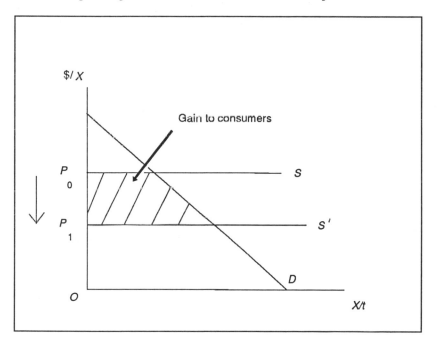

A second situation occurs when an increase in Q does *not* affect the price of the final output X. For example, a reduction in the salinity of irrigation water in a region is unlikely to have an impact on crop prices, since these are determined in a much larger market. Thus, the demand function for X is a horizontal line, as is shown in Figure 7.2. A reduction in the marginal costs of producing X (from MC to MC'), resulting from an increase in Q, will provide no benefits to consumers. All the benefits, indicated by the shaded area in Figure 7.2, accrue to producers or, rather, to the owners of the fixed factors of production. But how does one measure the shaded area?

Figure 7.2

Increase in public good with infinite elasticity of output demand

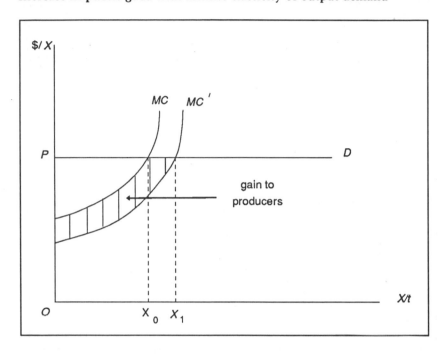

If producers are price takers in output markets, they are likely price takers in input markets as well; then the benefits of an increase in Q accrue to owners of the fixed factor – land. (The owner of the fixed factor is the residual income claimant, as is seen in Chapter 2.) The benefits of an increase in Q are simply equal to the change in profits or fixed factor income – the increase in rent. Since increases in rent are capitalized in land values, changes in the land values of those farmers now using less saline water constitute a good measure of these benefits. If the production unit is small relative to both input and output markets, then changes in land values are a good indicator of the change in producer benefits. Otherwise, farm budget studies are needed to reveal the required data.

Finally, consider the case in which an increase in the availability of Q significantly increases the availability of X (local fresh vegetables), thereby shifting supply from S to S' and causing the price of X to fall (in the local market). Then there is both a change in consumer surplus and producer surplus due to the change in Q (purer irrigation water).

Figure 7.3

Increase in public good with local supply and demand

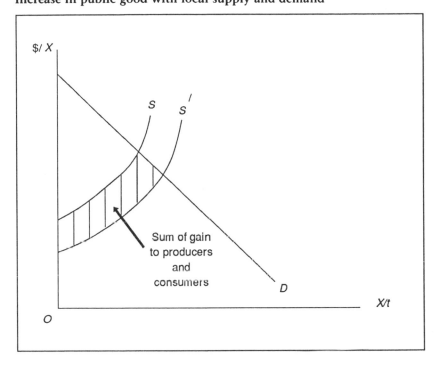

In Figure 7.3, the shaded area represents an estimate of the total benefits of increasing Q. How does one estimate this area in practice? To obtain an estimate of the change in consumer surplus, it is necessary to estimate the ordinary demand function and, under it, to calculate the appropriate area. The producer surplus is determined in the fashion discussed in the preceding paragraph. It is measured by the change in the net income of factor inputs.

If government agricultural policies support crop prices, then actual or market prices overstate social benefits. In this case, farm budget studies are required in order to determine the extent of producer benefits. Consumer benefits can be calculated in the same manner as above, but it will be necessary to include in the calculations the government support payments themselves as a cost to taxpayers. In all cases, it is worthwhile recalling the concept of *opportunity cost* and using it as a guide in calculating the benefits and costs of changes in the availability of a public good.

Market Valuation of Public Goods via Behavioural Linkages
Another example of the damage function approach occurs when individuals purchase in-house filtration systems in order to reduce their exposure to air pollution. Such expenditures provide a lower bound on estimates of the benefits of reducing air pollution. These expenditures are known as *defense expenditures*, referring to the fact that they are made to counteract or prevent the adverse effects of the externality. The degree to which such expenditures are truly representative of the benefits of reducing air pollution depends on the degree of substitutability between the privately purchased goods and the public good (clean air).

Behavioural linkages are more common than are physical linkages, but they require a behavioural response to changes in the nonmarket commodity, and this response must somehow be measured. If there is no response to marginal changes in water quality, for example, then it is not possible to determine its value, even if it has value on average. There are two methods for measuring value via behavioural linkages.

The first approach is to use information about market values, as is discussed below. The second approach is to obtain values for nonmarket commodities directly, using contingent valuation and behavioural methods. CVM and contingent behaviour are discussed later in this chapter.

Market valuation of public goods via behavioural linkages assumes that an individual's utility function includes the public good (Q) as the argument[1]

$$U = U(X_1, X_2, ..., X_n, Q),$$

where X_i ($i = 1, ..., n$) represents a good or service that is traded in the marketplace. The inverse Hicksian or compensated demand function can be found, as is indicated in Chapter 3, with the total benefit to an individual of an increase in the supply of the public good Q given by the appropriate area under the demand function (Figure 3.9). This benefit is either the compensating or equivalent variation of the change in the supply of the public good, depending on whether the person has the property right to the original or final level of the public good, respectively.

It should be obvious to the reader that the tasks we are engaged in amount to detective work – we are attempting to measure the value of a change in the availability of a public good that is not traded in the marketplace using market data for related or affected goods and services.

However, there are the inevitable problems associated with any investigation of this kind. The problems that are encountered in this particular piece of detective work concern the method by which the public good Q enters the utility function. Several cases are discussed.

Separability
A particular good is said to be separable within the utility function if changes in the availability of that good have no effect on the marginal rates of substitution among any of the other goods; changes in the availability of one good do not affect price ratios among any of the other goods. Nor do such changes affect the amounts of other goods and services that are purchased. This is important for the current discussion, because, if Q is separable within an individual's utility function, then the purchases of other goods are unaffected by changes in the availability of Q. Thus, while changes in the provision of the public good affect the level of utility, it is impossible to find a record of this impact in the marketplace, because goods and services traded in the market are unaffected by changes in Q.

Complementarity
Suppose that there is some degree of complementarity between the market commodity X_1 and the public good Q. For example, there is complementarity between water quality and fishing or between water quality and demand for water skiing. Then, if the demand for X_1 (water skiing) is zero, the marginal utility of Q (water quality) is zero (assuming that water skiing is the only private good or service that depends on water quality). An increase in the availability of the public good must cause an outward shift in the demand function of the complementary good X_1, so that the area above market price and between the new and old demand curves for X_1 serves as an estimate of the benefit of increasing Q. This benefit is indicated by the shaded area in Figure 7.4. Without some form of complementarity, there would be nothing to measure.

Substitutes
The case of substitutes has already been mentioned; in-house filtration systems are a substitute for clean air, albeit an imperfect one. Defence expenditures provide an estimate of the potential benefits of increases in the availability of cleaner air. However, for the case of air purifiers in one's home, it is obvious that, while averting behaviour is a substitute for Q in an individual's utility function, these expenditures are not a

Figure 7.4

Shift in demand of private good when level of public good changes

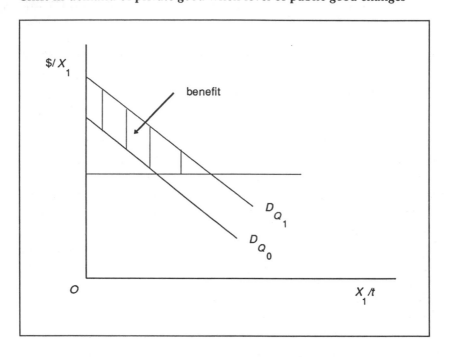

perfect substitute for Q. After all, what is preferred: a gas mask or clean air?

Property Values, Benefit Estimation, and Hedonic Pricing

A particular example of the approach to measuring nonmarket values via market transactions for other goods is provided from studies of property values. The notion that property values are related to environmental quality was discussed earlier in this chapter. Studies have found little evidence of a relation between agricultural land values and environmental pollution, primarily because, besides pollution, other factors (e.g., proximity to market) affect land rents. (Farms located near large cities are affected most by air pollution, but such farms also tend to be sufficiently close to the market that the mix of crops grown yields a higher net return than does land of identical quality farther from market but experiencing less pollution.) However, there does appear to be a significant relationship between air quality and the price of housing.

This relationship has been studied in order to determine the benefits of improving air quality in urban environments.

Hedonic pricing is one technique that can be used to measure the benefits of improving environmental quality; it measures changes in Q through impacts on property values. When Q is considered a parameter in individual utility functions, it is implicitly assumed that the amount of the public good available is the same for all individuals. However, individuals are often free to choose the level of Q that they want. This freedom to choose is exploited by the hedonic price technique.

The best example of individuals choosing the amount of public goods they want occurs with respect to the choices they make concerning house purchases. People choose to live in areas that have cleaner air or less crime, they choose to live near airports or along highways, and they choose to live on quiet or on busy streets. The choice is determined by the amount they are willing and able to pay for housing. Hedonic pricing exploits these choices by estimating implicit prices for house characteristics that differentiate closely related housing classes. In this way, it is possible to estimate demand curves for such characteristics (or public goods) as air quality and noise levels.

Hedonic pricing is a two-stage procedure. In the first stage, the price of a house is determined as a function of private housing characteristics (c_i) such as size of lot, number of rooms, age, number of bathrooms, and liveable floor space plus public good characteristics (Q_i) such as nearness to a fire station, crime rate, air quality, and noise levels. These public goods are somehow measurable; for example, air quality and the neighbourhood crime rate can be measured, as can distance to the nearest fire hall or fire hydrant. Thus, in the first stage, the following function is estimated statistically:

$$P_{house} = f(c_1, \ldots, c_n; Q_1, \ldots, Q_m),$$

where there are n private characteristics related to the house and property, and there are m public good characteristics that can be measured. The foregoing function is referred to as the *hedonic* or *implicit price function*.

The implicit price of a private characteristic of housing in the region of concern is found by partially differentiating the hedonic price function with respect to that characteristic. If c_1 is the number of rooms in a house, then

$$\frac{\partial P_{house}}{\partial c_1} = \text{implicit price of a room.}$$

This is the amount that an additional room will add to the value of a house. Likewise, it is possible to determine the marginal value of improved air quality or a reduction in crime rate. Let Q_1 be air quality. Then

$$\frac{\partial P_{house}}{\partial Q_1} = \frac{\partial f}{\partial Q_1} = g_1(c_1, \ldots, c_n; Q_1, \ldots, Q_m).$$

This is the expenditure on housing required to get a unit increase in clean air. Notice that $g_1(\cdot)$ is a function of Q_1, which is only possible if $f(\cdot)$ is not linear in Q_1. If $f(\cdot)$ is linear in Q_1, then the implicit price of an increase in air quality would be the same regardless of how good or bad the air quality is – the marginal value of air quality does not change according to the level of air quality. This is unrealistic, since the value of an additional unit of clean air (measured by a reduction in surface ozone or a reduction in particulate fallout) is certainly worth more when air quality is poor than when it is very good. It is only when $g_1(\cdot)$ is a function of Q_1 that it is possible to proceed to the second stage of the hedonic pricing technique.

Given implicit prices of air quality (observations of different prices for different houses), the second stage of the hedonic method requires that these prices be regressed on family income and Q_1 (air quality). The following function is then estimated:

$$\frac{\partial P_{house}}{\partial Q_1} = h(Q_1, \text{income, other relevant personal variables}).$$

This is the demand function for Q_1 (as illustrated in Figure 3.9), and the area under it is a measure of the benefit that results when a change in the provision of the public good (air quality) occurs due to some government policy.

From an empirical point of view, housing studies are plagued by simultaneity and identification problems. These do not occur with regard to the hedonic travel cost method discussed below.

Other Choice-based Methods

In this section, the earliest method for estimating nonmarket values is examined, namely, the travel cost method. This method was used to value recreational demand, and variants of it are still employed in this task. In addition, the hedonic method as applied to recreation demand is also briefly discussed.

The Travel Cost Method and Recreational Demand

The earliest problem of evaluation of nonmarket benefits came about shortly after the Second World War. The U.S. National Parks Service wished to obtain more money from Congress, but, in order to justify the additional funds, the service was required to demonstrate that the social benefits of the additional funds exceeded the social costs (i.e., that the funds generated a return to tax dollars). An economist with the National Parks Service, A.E. Demaray, contacted a number of prominent economists to find out how one might go about valuing the services provided by national parks. He received three types of responses:

(1) The problem defies quantification which, of course, was not true.
(2) The value of the parks is what the parks do for the economy of nearby towns. Using this reasoning, the economies of Jasper and Banff townsites in the Canadian Rockies provide an indication of the value of the respective national parks by those names. This is wrong for reasons similar to those considered in the discussion about the use of input-output models for evaluating economic benefits (Chapter 6).
(3) A letter from Harold Hotelling suggested that a Von Thünen model could be used to find the value of the recreational services provided by parks. One of the distinguishing features between visitors to parks is the distance that they travel (and hence the travel costs they incur) to get to the park or recreational site. This information could be exploited by assuming that travel costs and entrance costs are treated alike.

Demaray did not understand what Hotelling meant and, upon examining (1) and (2), decided that nothing could be done. Ten years later, Marion Clawson, a former director of the U.S. Bureau of Land Management, independently formulated the travel cost method for evaluating recreational resources along lines similar to those suggested by Hotelling.

How does the approach work in principle? Consider the following example. Suppose one wished to value a park located at a particular site. One would approach the individuals using the park and ask them, among other things, where they came from. In this example, the park's users are divided into three zones according to distance travelled and comparable travel costs. The travel costs from each zone, the annual number of visitors, and the total population in each zone are determined in Table 7.1. The cost of travel from a zone is easy to determine – it is a function of distance and cost per unit distance travelled – and could include costs associated with travelling time.

Table 7.1. **Travel zones, travel costs, and visitors to hypothetical park**

(1) Zone	(2) Travel cost/visit	(3) Number of visitors	(4) Population	(5) Visits/1,000 population
1	$1	1,800	3,000	600
2	$2	2,400	6,000	400
3	$3	2,000	10,000	200

A 'demand' relationship is established by plotting column (2) in Table 7.1 against column (5), as is shown in Figure 7.5, but this is not a true demand function. How do we derive the demand curve for the park? Assume an admission charge that is considered to be identical to travel costs by the users. If the entry fee is $1, then people from zone 1 will

Figure 7.5

Visitor relationship for hypothetical park

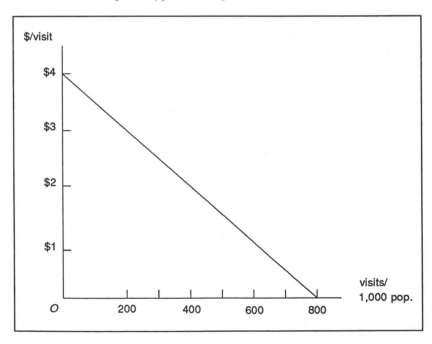

incur costs of $2 rather than $1. From Figure 7.5, we find that only 400 individuals per 1,000 population will visit the park if they incur travel plus entry costs of $2. Hence, only 1,200 individuals from zone 1 will visit the park if there is an admission charge of $1. The results for all zones and admission charges are provided in Table 7.2. Plotting the entry charge against the totals provided in the last row of Table 7.2 gives the demand relation for the hypothetical park, as is drawn in Figure 7.6. In the absence of an entry fee, the total area under this demand curve constitutes the benefit to that particular recreational site.

Figure 7.6

Demand for hypothetical park

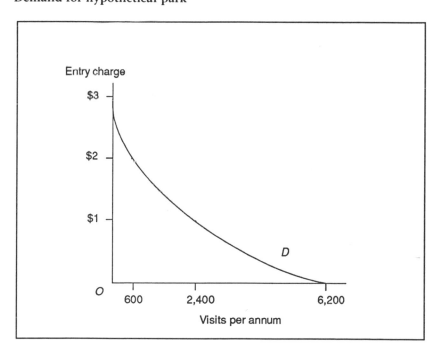

Table 7.2. **Impact of an entry charge on visitors to hypothetical park**

Zone	Entrance charge			
	$0	$1	$2	$3
1	1,800	1,200	600	0
2	2,400	1,200	0	0
3	2,000	0	0	0
Total	6,200	2,400	600	0

The criticism of the travel cost method as presented above is that the demand curve that is derived is not a true demand function after all; it is simply a statistical demand relationship and cannot be used to make welfare judgements. The reason is that it is not based on a well-developed and meaningful theory of consumer demand – utility maximization. Such a theory is illustrated with the aid of Figure 7.7.

Figure 7.7

Constructing a theoretical recreation demand model

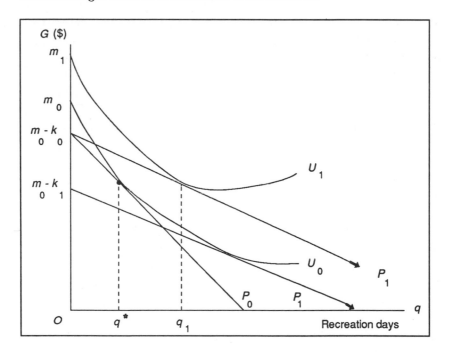

Assume that there is a single recreational site and that consumers have the option of staying home or travelling to the site and recreating. All other goods and services (G) are plotted on the vertical axis and the number of days spent recreating at the site (q) is plotted on the horizontal axis. Since recreation is not a *necessity* in the sense that individuals can live without it, the indifference curves do not intersect the horizontal axis; however, they do intersect the vertical axis, since some amount of one's budget must be spent on 'all-goods-other-than-recreation' in order to survive.

Now assume that the individual starts with some amount of income given by m_0 (and equal to an equivalent amount of G if the price of G is 1.0). Further, suppose that the cost of getting to the site (the travel cost) is K_0, and the entry fee or price of q is initially P_0. If recreation is to take place, the budget line begins at the point labelled $m_0 - K_0$, because this is the amount of budget available for recreating at the site once one takes into account the cost of getting to the site. Given that the indifference curve through m_0 (namely, U_0) is tangential to the budget line with slope determined by P_0, the person is indifferent between staying home and going to the site and recreating for q^* days. If the entrance fee to the park were greater than P_0, then the person would stop visiting the site altogether. That is, for prices less than P_0 the individual will participate in recreation but not for prices above this critical value. Thus, q^*, K_0, and P_0 are critical values for the given budget, travel cost, and entry fee – the individual will either recreate for q^* or more days or will not recreate at all.

Now, if the entry price were reduced to P_1 ($< P_0$), the individual would take q_1 days of recreation at the site, enabling him or her to get on an indifference curve (U_1) that is higher than that going through m_0. The equivalent amount of income to this level of indifference is given by m_1.

Finally, the travel cost itself influences decisions. At a price of P_0, an increase in the travel cost to K_1 will prevent the person from recreating. If the entry fee were subsequently reduced to P_1, then the individual can still attain U_0, but he or she remains indifferent to staying home or recreating.

It is clear that the graphical analysis in Figure 7.7 can be used to derive a demand curve in a fashion similar to that used to derive the Marshallian demand curve in Chapter 3. However, in this case, not only does income shift the demand function – so does travel cost. The point is that the approach discussed with reference to Figure 7.7 can be used to formulate a demand function that can be empirically estimated: demand is a function of entrance fees, consumer income, travel cost, and the prices of complements and substitutes. In principle, data can be collected on each of these variables. Furthermore, welfare estimates that are subsequently derived make sense from a theoretical standpoint.

The basic travel cost methodology has, subsequently, been modified in a number of directions. Issues regarding site quality, visits to multiple sites, congestion, and the opportunity cost of a recreationist's time, particularly travelling time, have been incorporated into the models. But the basic idea underlying the methodology is that described above.

Site Attributes and the Hedonic Travel Cost Technique

The hedonic pricing method can also be applied to recreation demand estimation, but the problems involved are complex. Simply, total household expenditures on recreation at a particular site take on the role of property value in the hedonic or implicit price function. Expenditures by a large number of households recreating at more than one site are regressed on a variety of private and public characteristics of the various recreational sites. Again, by partially differentiating the hedonic price function with respect to any of the public attributes, an implicit price for that attribute is obtained. In the second stage, the implicit prices are regressed on household characteristics, particularly income, and the amount of the attribute available, howsoever measured. The resulting equation is the demand function for the attribute. The area under the demand function can then be used to obtain benefit measures for changes in the amounts of the public good. In practice, it is not easy to implement hedonic pricing.

The hedonic travel cost method seeks to identify the demand function for the flow of amenities associated with the physical attributes of recreational sites and, thereby, the benefits of changes in site attributes. In this respect, it is similar to the hedonic price method described in conjunction with the value of housing. However, the hedonic travel cost method is more closely aligned with the travel cost approach described above. Indeed, it is possible to derive the benefits of a change in attributes using the travel cost approach, but this requires that one estimate the demand for a site before and after the change in attributes occurs. This is illustrated in Figure 7.8.

In Figure 7.8, the curves labelled $V(P;z)$ represent the demand for recreation visits as a function of travel costs P, where P includes travel cost, time and entry fees, and site attributes z (the demand shifter). In the diagram, attributes shift the demand function; thus, the demand for visits when site attributes are z_2 lies outside the demand when attributes are z_1, and likewise for z_3. Suppose there are two sites that the recreationist might wish to visit. Site 1 has a travel cost of P_1, while site 2 has a travel cost of P_2. The demand functions for the two sites differ according to the level of physical attributes available at each site; suppose the demand functions are $V(P;z_1)$ and $V(P;z_2)$ at sites 1 and 2, respectively. Then the net benefits of recreating at site 1 are given by area ABP_1, while the net benefits of choosing site 2 are given by area XYP_2. If site 1 is chosen over site 2, then area ABP_1 must be greater than area XYP_2.

Figure 7.8

Valuing recreational site attributes

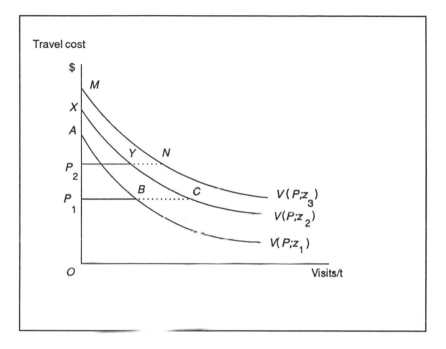

Now suppose that the attributes at site 1 change so that the demand curve associated with site 1 is no longer $V(P;z_1)$ but $V(P;z_2)$, which is identical to that for site 2. Since site 1 was chosen previously, it will be chosen again. The net benefit of the improvement in attributes at site 1 is given by area $(XCP_1 - ABP_1)$ = area $AXCB$. If, on the other hand, attributes at site 2 were to change from z_2 to z_3, so that the new demand function is $V(P;z_3)$, then the benefit of such a change will depend upon whether or not the recreationist shifts away from site 1. If site 1 continues to be the preferred site, the benefits of the improvements at site 2 are essentially zero. If site 2 is now chosen over site 1, then the measure of benefits is given by area MNP_2 minus area ABP_1.

While the travel cost method is based on a marginal utility condition describing the choice of the number of visits to a site, the hedonic travel cost technique is based on a marginal utility condition describing the choice of site quality and, implicitly, the actual site itself. The travel cost method requires observations on a wide range of recreationists, who have come various travel distances in order to be able to identify the demand curve for trips. With regard to the demand for attributes, the travel cost method works best if site choice remains fixed as the visit level changes.

The hedonic travel cost procedure works best when the visit level remains fixed as the site choice changes. The hedonic method seeks to measure the demand for site characteristics or attributes directly. It requires only that the sample of users be spread around at various sites within a recreational area (e.g., national park or forest area) so that they face various costs of using a particular site. These costs vary due not only to travel distances but also due to the physical attributes of the sites. In this way, a demand function for site attributes can be identified.

While the theoretical model upon which the travel cost method is based does not really permit visits to more than one site, it can easily be modified in practice to allow for the use of several sites. The same is not true of the hedonic price approach. It requires that individuals select only one site out of the ones that are available.

The foregoing approaches require that the researcher interview individuals in order to obtain the needed information for implementing the model. This may be a drawback because interviews are expensive; while that may prevent policymakers from getting information on nonmarket values, it is sometimes possible to obtain, simultaneously, the information required for implementing more than one of the approaches discussed in this chapter. The problems encountered when conducting surveys are discussed in greater detail in the next section.

The Direct Approach

The contingent valuation method explicitly elicits information concerning the minimum level of compensation required by an individual to forgo receiving a particular level of a public good or the maximum amount the individual would be willing to pay to obtain the nonmarket good or service. Contingent valuation has become prominent in recent years, because the U.S. Department of the Interior has approved its use in regulations implementing the Comprehensive Environmental Response, Compensation, and Liability Act of 1980. The contingent behaviour method simply asks individuals to respond to questions concerning their behaviour. Unlike CVM, therefore, the contingent behaviour approach requires additional detective work in order to assign value to the public good.

Income Compensation or Contingent Valuation Methods

Contingent valuation is a method of directly eliciting an individual's compensating or equivalent variation for a change in the availability of a public good. As a result, this approach is often referred to as the direct approach in contrast to the indirect approach of determining the value of nonmarket commodities from information about market transactions for other, related goods and services.

> Contingent valuation devices involve asking individuals, in survey or experimental settings, to reveal their personal valuations of increments (or decrements) in unpriced goods by using contingent markets. These markets define the good or amenity of interest, the status quo level of provision and the offered increment or decrement therein, the institutional structure under which the good is to be provided, the method of payment, and (implicitly or explicitly) the decision rule which determines whether to implement the offered program. Contingent markets are highly structured to confront respondents with a well-defined situation and to elicit a circumstantial choice upon the occurrence of the posited situation. Contingent markets elicit contingent choices. (Cummings et al. 1986:3)

The individual values obtained from the survey are then summed to obtain a value for the unpriced or nonmarket commodity. These values are either the CV or EV of the hypothetical change (Chapter 3). The contingent valuation method has been criticized because it requires an individual to respond to hypothetical situations. As a result, various types of bias may occur, and these biases can only be removed through proper design of the contingent device and proper training of those who are responsible for gathering the required data.

Contingent valuation surveys fill a need, because they enable economists to measure things that cannot be measured in any other way. These are commodities and services that do not leave a footprint in the marketplace, either because they are separable from privately traded goods and services in individuals' utility functions or because they are separable in the production function. Surveys enable one to get at the correct theoretical measure in a direct fashion.

A major weakness of an economist's training concerns primary data gathering. For one thing, poor survey design and execution affect the response rate. A good contingent valuation survey (1) communicates the attributes to be valued, (2) communicates the terms of the bargain (see below), and (3) is consistent with economic theory (Chapter 3). If the mechanism for obtaining responses is not consistent with economic theory, then it is not clear what the resulting responses mean. Some problems with CVM are as follows.

(1) The survey approach places individuals in hypothetical situations with which they may be unfamiliar. They are unable to respond in a meaningful manner to the questions that are subsequently posed about these situations. To prevent this, the interviewer can use explanation, pictures, or other props to clearly identify the hypothetical situation to which the respondent is required to respond.

(2) The relationship between the respondent and the interviewer may influence the values provided; the problem is that the observer is in the picture, influencing outcomes. Questions pertaining to willingness-to-pay (WTP) to have access to a resource or to have more of some public good and questions pertaining to the willingness-to-accept (WTA) compensation for being denied access or having less of the public good are subjective, and the respondent often provides answers that he or she thinks the interviewer wants to hear. Thus, the respondent is not a *neutral* participant. This problem is likely the easiest to overcome through the proper training of interviewers.

(3) The respondent is not neutral to the hypothetical situations that are laid out. He or she may either *bias* the results up or down, depending upon whether he/she thinks that the responses will prevent others from accessing a recreational site by making it either too expensive or less attractive. Responses may also be given in such a way that the value of the contingency is overstated, because the respondent knows that he or she will not bear the cost of providing the public good; or the respondent may purposely understate his or her WTP in order to escape charges. This form of bias can be prevented by the inclusion of a realistic payment device, whereby the respondent recognizes that he or she will, indeed, be required to pay for the proposed change.

(4) *Starting point bias* is a problem in some instances. This refers to the value that is, initially, suggested by the researcher to the respondent. If the value is lower than that which the respondent had in mind, the respondent may revise values downward; likewise, they may be revised upward. This problem can be prevented by determining realistic starting point values from pre-tests of the survey

instrument or by using open questions (i.e., not suggesting starting values).

There are several approaches to asking valuation questions. The first is simply to let the respondent provide the values and not suggest values to him or her (e.g., sealed bid). It is also possible to ask a single question regarding whether the individual will accept a certain value or not. For example, the respondent simply answers 'yes' or 'no' to: If you were to be charged an additional five dollars to use this park once more trees are planted, would you pay it? Another approach is to ask individuals to choose between two values (dichotomous choice). Finally, since none of these approaches permits the researcher to hone in on an individual's minimum WTA compensation in order to forgo consuming more of the public good (or equivalent variation), or maximum WTP for more of the public good (or compensating variation), a *bidding procedure* can be employed. The interviewer suggests a particular value and then increments this value up or down (depending upon the respondent's answer) until the actual WTP or WTA compensation is found for the contingency in question.

Different types of surveys are also available to researchers.

(1) Mail surveys cost about $10-15 per case if they are appropriately done. However, such surveys encounter problems associated with sample selectivity that might be corrected to some extent by using econometric tools for testing and correcting for sample selectivity bias. Other problems occur because 20-25 per cent of those in the 21-25 age category cannot read beyond a grade 8 level, and overall illiteracy rates are high. This is one factor that accounts for low response rates. Further, it is difficult to get accurate lists of names for survey purposes, and one does not have control over the survey itself (although some follow-up could be used to offset this).

(2) Telephone surveys cost about $30-40 per case. Although the interviewer can respond to questions regarding clarification, interviewer bias does enter in. One problem concerns choice of respondent: rather than choosing the person who answers the phone, the interviewer can ask for the person in the household who is, say, over age eighteen, and whose birthday is next up. Call-back based on a household listing obtained at first contact is the most expensive method. Another problem is that of information overload. Questions must be kept simple so that individuals can easily keep track of items over the telephone. Finally, the preponderance of

telemarketing has, to some extent, 'poisoned the well' for telephone surveys.

(3) In-person surveys are the most expensive ($250-300/case), but they have the highest response and 'success' rate. The major problem with this method is bias that arises due to personal contact.

It is important to pre-test any contingent valuation survey, sometimes requiring forty or fifty versions. Using focus groups in one's pre-test helps the researcher to understand how and what people are valuing. Further, samples should be split so that the dimension of a particular item in the questionnaire can be asked in different ways. It is then possible to test whether or not the phrasing of the question affects the answer or value provided.

The purpose of contingent valuation surveys is to get individuals to reveal values that correspond to the actual values that people put on commodities in real markets. Doing so is referred to as validity. If respondents do not answer honestly or meaningfully, validity is threatened. There are three kinds of validity tests.

(1) *Content* validity focuses on the wording of questions in the actual survey. Questions need to clearly identify and focus on the items to be valued and the 'terms of the bargain.' The latter refers to the mechanisms regarding how actual payment occurs, to whom the payment is made (from whom funds are received), in what form monies are paid or received, and how any funds raised are to be used in implementing the contingency.

(2) *Construct* validity results when a survey's questions are consistent with economic theory; the responses can be related to meaningful theoretical concepts. One measure of validity in these cases is to compare values from the contingent valuation survey with values obtained from market methods such as hedonic pricing. For example, hedonic methods, using house prices, must give higher values for clean air than for contingent values; otherwise, people would move to homes that are located in areas that have less air pollution.

(3) Finally, *criterion* validity relies upon comparisons with laboratory experiments. For example, one might wish to compare hypothetical responses to WTP and WTA compensation for hunting permits with those obtained from a simulated market for permits. Some comparisons of simulated market values and contingent values are provided in Table 7.3.

There are problems with contingent valuation surveys that are often

Table 7.3. Contingent values and simulated market values

		Dollar values	
Commodity	Valuation method	Contin- gent	Simulated market
For compensation demanded			
Goose permits	Dichotomous choice	$101	$63
Deer permits	Sealed-bid auction	833	1,184
Deer permits	Dichotomous choice	420	153
For willingness to pay			
Goose permits	Dichotomous choice	21	--
Deer permits	Sealed-bid auction	32	24
	Sealed-bid auction and bidding	43	19
Deer permits	Dichotomous choice	35	31

Source: Bishop and Heberlein (1990:97-8)

overlooked by economists, although psychologists have focused attention on them. Psychologists argue that CVM should not only be consistent with economic theory but, perhaps more importantly, should be consistent with psychological measures of value. They criticize contingent valuation methods on the basis of possibilities for individuals to distinguish among items to be valued. Four possibilities occur: (1) preferences exist and are stable, well-defined, and easily measured; (2) preferences exist and are stable but are not easily measured, because some of the resulting measures are biased; (3) preferences exist and are stable, but all measurements are biased; and (4) preferences may not exist in many situations, or, if they do exist, they are not stable or well formed. The main criticism is that the CVM creates preferences and bias because context or familiarity does matter.

It is possible to rank or value items with which one is familiar, but this ability declines as the degree of familiarity falls. For example, consider the following items listed from highest to lowest degree of familiarity (familiarity declines as one goes from category 1 to 7): (1) groceries, (2) appliances, (3) automobiles, (4) homes, (5) recreational activities, (6) air and water quality, and (7) nature (environment and species preservation). Valuing changes in the hypothetical availability of commodities in each of these categories becomes increasingly difficult as one moves from categories 1 through 7. It is likely impossible to place dollar values on hypothetical changes in the availability of commodities in categories

6 and 7. This problem is discussed further, with respect to preservation values.

Contingent valuation responses vary according to whether questions have to do with a return to the status quo or whether one is responding to questions concerning attainment of a higher level of quality (preservation, etc.) than previously. A major problem in this context concerns *preference reversals*. Consider the example in which you are faced with two gambles, as follows:

Gamble A: 0.9 chance to win $6
Gamble B: 0.2 chance to win $30.

What is the maximum price that you would pay for each of these gambles? Choose the one that you wish to play.

In experimental settings, psychologists found that Gamble B tends to elicit a higher price, because its expected return is higher ($6 versus $5.40). Most people choose to play gamble A over B, with 40-50 per cent assigning a higher value to B but still choosing to play A. This is an example of a reversal. Similar tests, involving things such as an upgrade to a television or computer versus an upgrade in the environment, yielded similar results.

Another problem with the contingent valuation approach is that researchers have found a wide divergence between compensating and equivalent variation or between WTP and WTA compensation. This divergence is greater than that predicted by theoretical considerations and has been attributed, by some, to psychological attachment to a particular property right.

What is Being Purchased? Preservation Values and Moral Satisfaction

An important use of contingent valuation surveys is to determine preservation values for such things as old-growth forests, particular wildlife species, wild rivers, and scenic amenities. Preservation value includes *option value*, *existence value*, and *bequest value*. Option value is the amount of money that an individual who anticipates visiting an old-growth forest, for example, would pay to guarantee future access to that forest, even though he or she is uncertain as to whether or not they will ever make such a visit. Existence value is the amount a person is willing to pay for the knowledge that a natural environment, such as a forest, is preserved in a particular state (viz., old-growth). Bequest value is defined as the willingness to pay for the satisfaction derived from endowing future generations with a natural environment.

Preservation values can be substantial. For example, researchers found that a reduction in water quality in the South Platte River basin of Colorado due to increased mining activity resulted in a welfare loss of $61 million per year to residents in Colorado. Preservation benefits for wildlife were estimated by Canadian economists to be in the neighbourhood of $68 million per year for Alberta residents. This evidence suggests that ignoring preservation values in the management of natural resources could lead to substantial misallocation of these resources; in particular, it results in improper use of public lands.

However, recent research on endowment effects and on purchase of moral satisfaction raises serious questions about the values individuals place on nonuse consumption. One problem concerns the 'embedding' of values within a questionnaire. Thus, an individual may respond that he or she is willing-to-pay $25 per year towards preserving grizzly bear when asked only about this particular species. Summing over individuals leads to a large value for grizzly bear. If the same individual were asked about his/her willingness to pay to preserve all wildlife species, the answer may also be $25/year. Out of that amount, the person may only be willing to pay $15/year towards the preservation of big game species; out of the $15, the individual may only be willing to contribute $5/year to preserving grizzly bear. The conclusion is that individuals state that they are willing to pay some amount towards preservation of species in general or preservation of a particular species, but what they really wish to purchase is the moral satisfaction of having made their contribution towards saving the environment, helping defeat cancer or heart disease, and so on.

If it is moral satisfaction that individuals are actually purchasing, and not the contingent commodity, this raises questions about the validity of contingent valuation surveys. If the criticism is correct, the WTP or WTA compensation values that are solicited via questionnaires have no meaning and cannot be used in cost-benefit analysis. Currently, economists are divided into two camps on this issue, and research into resolving this debate is ongoing.

The Contingent Behaviour Method and Conjoint Analysis
Unlike CVM, the contingent behaviour method does not require survey respondents to value hypothetical situations, but are simply asked to make choices between situations. For example, an individual will be

asked to choose between alternative recreational sites or activities. Conjoint analysis can then be used to infer the importance of the attributes that characterize each alternative within one's preference function. Conjoint measurement is a marketing technique that uses revealed choice among goods with different characteristics (as in hedonic pricing) with a survey that asks people to choose among or rank hypothetical alternatives in order to impute the values of the characteristics. Its main advantage is that direct monetization of benefits is not required; thus, trade-offs can be derived without using market information. Other advantages and disadvantages are similar to those of using any survey technique and relying on hypothetical choices. Attribute valuation is important because of its use in prediction. With conjoint analysis, one attempts to estimate individual utility functions and to use these to predict individual choices with respect to, for example, the development of new recreational opportunities.

Where individuals are simply asked whether or not they would take part in a particular hypothetical activity, regression techniques can be used to infer something about the ranking and value attached to various activities. However, these methods of valuation are fairly recent, and more research is required if these techniques are to be used to value public goods in the future.

Discussion

Given that procedures for obtaining estimates of nonmarket values (mainly via surveys) can be expensive, and that they are not without controversy, is there a practical, less expensive approach that can be followed? In many settings, the cost of maintaining land in its natural state is small, and B-C analysis can aid in identifying this cost. At the individual project level, rather than trying to estimate the benefits of allocating resources in ways that explicitly account for nonuse values, it may be better simply to determine those costs and benefits of alternative policies for which market values do exist. (Perhaps sensitivity analysis can be used to determine the range of positive net benefits.) Then one can determine whether or not the opportunity cost of deciding against projects that favour extra-market values is worth it. For example, one study shows that logging of the Stein River Valley – a pristine wilderness area in western Canada – results in a loss of $7.7 million to society, even when recreational and existence values are ignored. The logging companies are willing to log the Stein only because tax write-offs make it profitable to do so. There are other projects involving resource use that yield negative or negligible net benefits to society, even when the opportunity costs associated with nonmarket values are ignored. Therefore, estimation of nonmarket values (particularly preservation or existence values) is often not required in order to determine whether or not resources should be allocated in ways that favour nonuse consumption of resources; in many cases, a proper social cost-benefit analysis, using available market data, will suffice for making decisions.

But, in other situations, preservation values may be important. For example, since pristine forestlands in northern Canada are among the largest in the world, preservation demand may be an important consideration with respect to decisions regarding future development. Research is required in order to determine the economic value of the global weather regulator and water storage functions of boreal (and other) forests. Here, there is an opportunity to develop theoretical and empirical methods that will enable countries such as Canada to better manage their vast forest regions for multiple use. To the extent that nonuse (preservation) values accrue to foreigners, it may be necessary to focus on mechanisms that might be used to get foreigners to bear some of the costs of preserving both northern and tropical forestlands. One such mechanism is a globally tradeable CO_2 emission permit – an idea discussed further in Chapter 9.

Part Three:
Land Use and Sustainable Development

Introduction to Part Three

After their initial recovery following the Second World War, the developed economies of the Western world entered into a phase of sustained growth. Near the end of that phase, towards the end of the 1960s, the environmental movement gained strength as the public became increasingly concerned about the direction that economic growth was taking. Not only was there concern about rapidly depleting nonrenewable resources, particularly oil, but also about water and air pollution, the externality effects of agricultural chemicals that accompanied the Green Revolution, nuclear war, and the apparent inability of the African nations to feed themselves. These fears were largely pushed aside or forgotten in the early 1970s, with the success of the OPEC cartel in increasing oil prices fourfold and the *commodity crisis* that accompanied it. The recession that followed focused attention on jobs and inflation, not the environment.

In the early 1980s, the environment once again became the centre of attention. This time the focus was less on the diminishing supply of nonrenewable resources, since conservation, newly discovered sources of oil, and alternative fuels mitigated these problems to some extent. Rather, the focus was on acid rain – caused by emissions of sulphur dioxide from automobiles and industrial plants (e.g., coal-fired generators), depletion of ozone in the upper atmosphere, soil degradation, climate warming, the disposal of hazardous wastes and domestic garbage, and the extinction of wildlife species through the destruction of their habitat. All these concerns fall under the rubric of *sustainable development*.

Sustainable development is a concept that became popular with the publication of *Our Common Future* (1987), the title of the report of the World Commission on Environment and Development (WCED), headed by Gro H. Brundtland, then prime minister of Norway. Sustainable development is defined in the report as 'development that meets the needs of the present without compromising the ability of future generations to meet their own needs' (p. 43). This definition is not particularly enlightening, and *Our Common Future* never really resolves the issue of biological versus economic sustainability. However, it does depart from 'doomsday' or Malthusian thinking that characterized the Club of Rome's Project on the Predicament of Mankind (Meadows et al. 1972); *Our Common Future* is rather more optimistic and also appears to be willing to exchange irreversible loss of some ecological resources for economic growth. Unfortunately, this does not appear to be the direction taken by later writers on sustainable development.

It should be noted that the ideas espoused in *Our Common Future*, and similar and follow-up reports, are really nothing new. Similar treatments of the ecological problem, for that is what it is, are found in, for example, E.F. Schumacher's *Small is Beautiful* (1973). Many seem to think that sustainable development is a new approach to thinking about environmental and ecological problems, but, in the discussion that follows, we show that economists have long thought about these concepts. The one thing that all the rhetoric surrounding *Our Common Future* has done is to draw attention to the problem of ecology and the idea that this is a global problem. Solutions to the global problem will be difficult, if not impossible, to achieve. The main reason has to do with the unwillingness of individuals and countries to give up a particular standard of living in order to transfer income to those in other countries. Likewise, countries are unwilling to give up security in order to combat the problems of the environment.

In this section, we begin, in Chapter 8, with a discussion of what sustainable development means and with an examination of theoretical issues; these include the economic ideas of conservation, a safe minimum standard, and preservation (but from a different point of view than that presented in previous chapters). Given the importance that scientists attach to ecosystems, in Chapter 9, we consider the atmosphere as a particular global ecosystem. It is demonstrated that the economic models of externality developed in Chapter 4 can be insightfully used to study climate change. Effects of climate change on land use are examined from a Canadian point of view.

An important issue associated with sustainable development and land use concerns soil erosion. Is soil erosion a problem? Does neglect of the soil result in large losses to farmers? Why do Canadian reports of the on-farm costs of soil erosion exceed those of the on-farm costs in the United States? What about the off-farm or external costs of soil erosion? In Chapter 10, the economics of soil erosion or soil conservation are examined, and the confusion about the on-farm versus off-farm costs of soil erosion is clarified. Methods of measuring on-farm costs and yield-soil depth relationships are considered. The yield-soil depth relationship is really another form of a crop production function. Since such functions are affected by technological change, the influence of technology on policy concerning soil erosion is also examined.

8

Conservation, Sustainable Development, and Preservation

In this chapter, the relationship between the now-popular term *sustainable development* and concepts that have appeared in the natural resource economics literature since at least the mid-1950s is illustrated. The prospects of future resource scarcity are also examined, because scarcity is a notion that is tied to the concept of sustainable development. We begin by examining the concept of sustainable development. What exactly does it mean? Also considered are the notions of *conservation* and a *safe minimum standard* of conservation, and how these relate to sustainable development. Finally, the concept of *coevolutionary development* is examined; it extends the biological notion of coevolution to include human institutions. Future resource scarcity and land preservation are also discussed. In all cases, we are concerned with how these definitions relate to that of sustainable development and what role economics has to play in these areas.

What is Sustainable Development?

To what extent is sustainable development a new concept for economists? The concept of sustainable development is found in the definition of economic conservation and in the notion of a safe minimum standard of conservation. More recently, the idea of coevolutionary development has been proposed as a way of integrating human beings and nature from an economics point of view. In this section, each of these concepts is defined.

Sustainable Development I

While there is consensus that sustainable development concerns intergenerational transfer of natural resources, if not wealth, there are differing views about what sustainable development really means. There are now more than sixty definitions of sustainable development. The definition provided by the Brundtland Commission in *Our Common Future* is not very helpful: 'development that meets the needs of the present without compromising the ability of future generations to meet their own needs' (1987:43). This definition of sustainable development is probably more ambiguous than is the concept of stewardship, which, for a resource such as land, implies that it be used in such a way that long-term productivity is not diminished.

It is possible to classify definitions of sustainable development according to whether one subscribes to the constrained economic growth or to the maintenance-of-the-resource point of view. Economists are familiar with the former, whereas the second is characterized, at its extreme, by groups that advocate absolutely no interference in the environment. The idea of maximizing economic growth subject to environmental constraints is a position often attributed solely to neoclassical economists. Its detractors argue that such a view condones the kind of growth that resulted in environmental deprecation to begin with. But the idea of growth is not unique to neoclassical economics, as institutional economists have also argued that there are no limits to growth outside of human innovation.

The following definition of sustainable agriculture appears to be a useful starting point with respect to how one might define 'sustainable development':

> [Sustainable] agriculture is a systems approach to farming that seeks to develop a multiyear practice that takes advantage of whatever is produced or can be produced on the farm, including naturally occurring beneficial biological interactions, to ensure soil fertility and to keep losses from pests, weeds, and animal diseases within acceptable levels. The aims are adequate productivity and profitability, conservation of resources, protection of the environment, and assured food safety. (Hileman 1990:27)

A number of different terms are used interchangeably to describe sustainable agriculture – alternative, low-input, organic, ecological, regenerative, and so on. Sustainable agriculture is not simply a return to the past (as some view it), although some of the practices of the past may be resurrected. Agronomic practices that contribute to sustainable agriculture differ from conventional methods in that they do not use high inputs of chemicals and machinery, and they do not focus on a small number of similar crops (monoculture). The above definition of sustainable agriculture is also sufficiently general to encompass conservation of wildlife.

While the foregoing definition is somewhat clearer than others, there remains an inherent contradiction in the term 'sustainable development.' Can development really be sustainable, or does growth preclude sustainability or maintenance of the resource base? What is required for development to be sustainable? These issues are not really addressed by proponents of sustainable development. Fortunately, the economics literature sheds some light on the issue.

Conservation

Economists have attempted to interpret the term conservation. One approach defines conservation as a redistribution of use rates into the future. Depletion is then a redistribution of use rates towards the present. This definition of conservation, which is attributed to S.V. Ciriacy-Wantrup (who is considered to be the father of resource conservation), requires that there be some benchmark distribution of use rates for a resource. Consider a hypothetical coal mine. There are four planning periods, as is indicated in Table 8.1, and four alternative plans for removing coal. The first alternative is the benchmark, perhaps the current rate of extraction. Relative to the benchmark rates of extraction, the second alternative is resource-conserving, since it redistributes use rates into the future – more of the resource is available in the future. The third alternative is resource-depleting, as use rates are redistributed towards the present – less coal is available in the future. The third alternative has greater current consumption than does either the benchmark alternative or the second alternative.

A problem arises in attempting to categorize plan 4. It is not clear whether plan 4 can be considered conserving or depleting, since the net change in use rates is zero and there is no clear indication that all changes are either into the future or towards the present. Whenever there are a large number of pluses and minuses in the row that indicates how the plan's use rates have changed from those of the benchmark plan, it is necessary to employ a weighting scheme. The weighting scheme should account for the need to discount the future. Thus, weights should increase as the distance from the present time period increases. If the weighted change in use rates is positive, then there is resource conservation; if it is negative, depletion of the resource occurs.

Consider a system of weights similar to discount rates. Assume the

Table 8.1. **Extraction or use rate for a coal mine**

	Planning period			
	1	2	3	4
Alternative plan	(tonnes/year)			
#1 (benchmark)	4	3	3	2
#2 (conservation)	3	3	3	3
Change in use rate	-1	0	0	+1
#3 (depletion)	5	4	2	1
Change in use rate	+1	+1	-1	-1
#4 (unclear)	5	1	3	3
Change in use rate	+1	-2	0	+1

weights begin with 1.0 and increase by 10 per cent for each period. Then, the weighted change in use rates for alternative 4 is given by

$$+1 + (1.1)(-2) + (1.1)^2(0) + (1.1)^3(+1) = 0.131.$$

In this case, alternative 4 is resource-conserving. However, this conclusion depends, crucially, upon the weights that are chosen. Some would argue that stewardship requires that resource availability in the future be weighted exactly the same as that in the present. In that case, the weighted change in the use rates for alternative 4 is simply given by the sum of the changes, and this must always equal zero. Of course, this criterion is not very helpful. But it is unlikely that people will ever agree upon an appropriate weighting scheme. The point is that conservation is a relative concept, and one cannot judge whether something is conserving or depleting without reference to some benchmark.

The foregoing definition of conservation (depletion) concerns the degree of conservation and its measurement. Another definition that relates more directly to that of sustainable development has been provided by Anthony Scott:

Conservation is a public policy which seeks to increase the potential future rates of use of one or more natural resources above what they would be in the absence of such policy, by current investment of the social income. The word investment ... covers not only such policies as investing the social income in restoration, education, and research, but also policies of reservation and hoarding of stocks. (1973:30)

Scott's definition is based on six conditions, including that, as a practical point, focus should generally be on a single resource within a defined geographical region, and that conservation should be measured in physical as opposed to monetary units (as does Ciriacy-Wantrup). Further, Scott's definition is confined not to natural resources alone, recognizing the necessity of trade-offs between investments in natural capital (e.g., preservation of ecosystems) and investments in human-made capital and knowledge. It also recognizes that conservation is a political, as well as a biophysical and economic, concept. This definition of conservation appears to be synonymous with sustainable development. It is clear, therefore, that economists have been thinking about sustainable development long before it became popular.

In Table 8.1, the resource is to be completely exhausted at the end of the planning horizon. Does this fact of exhaustion violate the concept of sustainable development? It may well be that the activity of exhausting a nonrenewable resource does violate the concept of sustainable development, but only if the ability of future generations to meet their needs is compromised. Are such needs compromised? What are the needs of future generations? Can technological advance be counted upon to satisfy those needs even though less conventional resources are available? Can the experience of past advances in technology be used to justify exploitation of resources and the environment? There is an additional concept, also attributable to Ciriacy-Wantrup, that is important to consider, namely, the notion of a *safe minimum standard* of conservation. Perhaps it, or the concept of *coevolutionary development*, can shed additional light on sustainable development. These concepts are considered next, but they also relate to an additional notion, namely, that of *quasi-option* value, which is discussed later in this chapter.

The Safe Minimum Standard of Conservation
Ciriacy-Wantrup first used the term 'safe minimum standard of conservation' and urged its adoption to allow for uncertainty in resource development and to increase 'flexibility in the continuing development of society' (1968:253). The safe minimum standard of conservation expands upon the *minimax* principle of game theory, as is illustrated in Table 8.2. Two states of nature or outcomes, denoted by 1 and 2, are possible, but their occurrence is uncertain. Society has two strategies for coping with uncertainty: extinction (E) occurs, for example, when the resource is exploited, while the strategy SMS (safe minimum standard) leaves the resource in its current state. The decision is determined in this

'game' by choosing the strategy that minimizes the maximum possible loss, that is, choosing E if $x > y$ and choosing SMS if $x < y$, with equality of x and y indicating indifference.

Table 8.2. Matrix of losses

Strategies	States		Maximum losses[*]
	1	2	
E	0	y	y
SMS	x	$x - y$	x

[*]assumes $x, y > 0$

There are problems with the game-theory approach: (1) it is conservative, with the SMS chosen if its costs (x) are only slightly less than the losses (y) to society under the worst conceivable future outcome; (2) payoffs (and costs) are assumed to be known with certainty, while the distribution of income is ignored – it does not matter who gains or loses; (3) it is static, because the probabilities of each state of nature are unknown and have no effect upon the decision to be taken – there is no learning effect as time passes; and (4) more importantly, it fails to recognize that a decision not to develop a resource (e.g., construct a dam that floods a valley, harvest old-growth timber) constitutes a deferral – development can still take place in a future period.

The safe minimum standard of conservation modifies the minimax principle. The modified decision rule is: adopt the SMS unless the social costs of doing so are unacceptably large. It is clear that this rule places the development of natural resources beyond routine trade-offs, although the safe minimum standard of conservation does not permit deferral or nondevelopment at a cost that is intolerably high. Failure to recognize that there are intolerably high costs to not developing a resource in some cases inevitably leads to dangerous conflicts within society (e.g., between loggers and environmentalists). Decisions regarding what level of costs is considered 'intolerably high' and what trade-offs are acceptable are political.

The purpose of cost-benefit analysis is to determine the costs and benefits of alternative strategies for the resource, whether deferral, preservation, or development. While cost-benefit analysis can appropriately identify the efficiency consequences (and the gainers and losers), its recommendations need to be constrained by the safe minimum standard of conservation. When it comes to decisions concerning resource development and preservation, cost-benefit analysis constrained by the safe minimum standard of conservation is certainly a tool of analysis warranting serious consideration in policy debates.

Coevolutionary Development

Coevolutionary development is a concept that is derived from the biological notion of coevolution. Coevolution refers to evolution based on reciprocal responses of two or more closely interacting species; it refers to the interaction of two or more plant and/or animal species over time. Impacts or changes in one species have an effect on other species that, in turn, impact on the former. Coevolutionary development extends the notion of coevolution among plant and animal species to include social as well as ecological systems. That is, coevolutionary development integrates the cultural or social realm, and all its human-made institutions, with the biological sphere. The concept is illustrated in Figure 8.1. Humankind's activities impact upon nature, which, in turn, has a feedback effect upon humans through the institutions that are created and the activities that can possibly take place. However, the feedback effects continue in what becomes an infinite loop between the cultural and natural realms.

The idea of coevolutionary development originates with a concept of time that is alien to 'mechanical philosophy' or Newtonian models. In classical models, time is not really present, since all processes, even dynamic ones, are reversible and, thus, static. In thermodynamics, time is continually running down, since entropy – the amount of energy unavailable for work – increases over time. Nonetheless, time is still parametric, since the system's location depends upon the starting point, and it is possible to select alternative starting points. In this sense, time is still reversible. A contradiction to thermodynamic time occurs with the concept of evolution, which states that there is greater, not less, order as time advances. For human beings, time is extremely important and it is irreversible.

It is irreversibility that is important in environmental systems. As Richard Norgaard explains:

> The basic assumptions of the neoclassical model [of economics] do not fit the natural world. The model assumes that resources are divisible and can be owned. It acknowledges neither relationships between resources in their natural environments nor environmental systems overall. It assumes that both the economic and environmental system can operate along a continuum of equilibrium positions and move freely back and

forth between these positions. Markets fail to allocate environmental services efficiently because environmental systems are not divisible, because environmental systems almost never reach equilibrium positions, and because changes are frequently irreversible. (1985:382-3)

Figure 8.1

Coevolutionary development or ecological economics

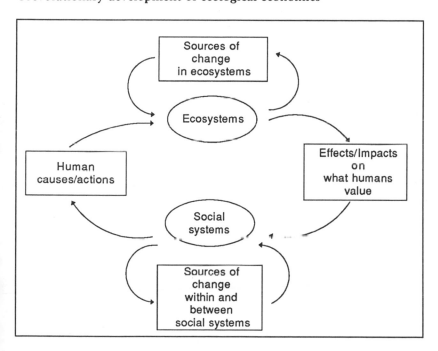

The solutions to the kinds of environmental problems that we examined in Chapter 4, especially the Pigou tax/subsidy solution, presume a mechanistic, equilibrating world. But irreversibilities and disequilibria are facts of life in ecological systems.

When it comes to environmental pollution, multiple pollutants prevent equilibrium from occurring. For example, methyl compounds and mercaptans are fairly safe by themselves and are individually benign. However, they combine to form methylmercaptans, which are deadly, even at low concentrations, and are malign. In the example of the pulp mill and the fishers (Chapter 4), the waste from the mill likely causes irreversible changes in the river's ecosystem. Further, it is unlikely that these are the only agents affected by the activity of polluting a river; for example, recreationists and municipal water users will be affected. The model presented in Chapter 4 assumes an equilibrium can be found within some optimal institutional framework based on a realignment or proper specification of the property rights. But reality is much more complicated.

Coevolutionary development takes a view that is more encompassing (holistic?) than that of mainstream or neoclassical economics. Consider agricultural activities in which humans impact upon the ecosystem in order to satisfy their needs, intervening in nutrient cycles and disturbing the equilibrating mechanisms present in the natural system. Coevolutionary development occurs faster, or is perhaps only possible, if the cultural or human system compensates for these losses in the natural system. This response is in the form of fertilizers, pesticides, crop rotations, legumes, and so on, that, in turn, result in further response (perhaps in the form of surprise) from the ecosystem that requires further compensation from, or adjustment within, the institutions that humans use to organize their life.

This interaction between the systems of nature and those of human beings – the feedback mechanisms between the two – leads to a number of questions. What form and nature will the adjustments take? Is the development 'sustainable'? Are the cultural and physical responses mutually destructive? An attempt to answer these questions is provided by briefly considering Amazonia. This example provides a notion of the complex interactions that occur in the real world – interactions that make it difficult to implement policy.

By the early 1990s, events in the Amazonian region of Brazil had become a focal point of criticism for the world's environmentalists. The Brazilian government had provided public infrastructures, such as towns, schools, public buildings, and roads, as well as incentives to cattle ranchers in order to develop the region into one capable of producing large numbers of cattle for export. (Brazil needed exports in order to pay back international loans that, in an effort by banks to circulate petro dollars, were made without due regard to project risks.) This resulted in the rapid denuding of the tropical forests, with a consequent loss of unknown numbers of wildlife species and added atmospheric carbon dioxide (a cause of global warming) due to burning of the forest. As early as 1981, Norgaard argued that the agricultural development being promoted in Amazonia results in interactions between the cultural system and the ecosystem that are mutually destructive. Swiddon or 'slash and burn' agriculture is preferred, as it is sustainable in a coevolutionary sense. However, swiddon agriculture cannot support the same size population as other, more exploitive, forms of agriculture, at least in the short term. If the region is to support a larger population, new institutions need to evolve – institutions that are more efficient in their use of natural resources per unit of economic activity.

Examples such as these do not occur only in low-income countries. In later chapters, we will consider sustainability and land use in western Canada's grain belt. In this region, government subsidies to agriculture have encouraged agricultural development that is not sustainable in the coevolutionary sense. Further, despite increasing farm size and a declining rural population, governments continue to provide incentives that create public infrastructure in declining rural communities and promote intensive agricultural production where other land uses (e.g., for cattle or wildlife) are more appropriate. The investments that result are inefficient from a societal point of view and are harmful to the region's ecosystems.

Coevolutionary development is now immersed in a new discipline called *ecological economics*. While ecological economics is in the process of carving out a niche for itself in science, it is not clear that it differs from environmental and resource economics in any substantive way. Therefore, it is not clear that, outside of the notion that greater care must be accorded to the interaction between nature and culture, the concept of coevolutionary development can be thought of as a foundation for deciding upon sustainable development.

Sustainable Development II
Sustainable development appears to include ideas that economists have been considering for quite some time – conservation, the safe minimum standard of conservation, coevolutionary development, and so on – but the concept remains ambiguous. Coal, petroleum, natural gas, and minerals are examples of resources that are, by their nature, subject to exhaustion. If consumption continues at current rates, there will come a point in time when these resources are no longer available, although technical advances may delay that time somewhat. Obviously, from the definitions of conservation and depletion, sustainable development cannot imply that nonrenewable resources are prevented from being depleted or even kept at the current or some other level. It will be necessary to replace the flow of services from these nonrenewable resources with services obtained from renewable resources. At the same time, it will be necessary to reduce the amount of services provided by

natural resources and the environment per unit of standard of living. This implies greater reliance on human capital or knowledge and additions to the stock of human-made capital. Human-made capital is important, even though it is resource-using, because it can substitute, to some extent, for natural capital; human-made capital can reduce society's reliance on natural resources by increasing the usefulness of each unit of service provided by the nonrenewable and renewable resource stocks. For example, greater fuel efficiency in the transportation sector is already available, but old capital stocks in this sector still need replacing.

The degree of substitutability between natural capital (whether renewable or nonrenewable) and human capital is limited, although knowledge is useful for helping to increase the elasticity of substitution. As resources become scarce, their relative prices will rise, which leads to conservation and substitution towards alternative resources and technologies. The change in prices will have this impact even if a shrinking resource base causes future generations to have lower incomes because their resource endowment is smaller. Thus, rising relative prices will result in a substitution away from those resources that are becoming scarce. Some might argue that this is unlikely, given the extent to which the resource base is currently being damaged. However, evidence indicates that this is exactly what has happened in the past and what continues to occur today. For example, the technology to produce electric automobiles that are capable of travelling distances of 150-300 km on a single charge is already available. What is preventing the adoption of such technology is the relatively low price of gasoline.

In the case of nonrenewable resources, it is possible for an economic system to sustain economic growth (i.e., sustainability with respect to aggregate output growth) but, at the same time, to consume the resource (as in Table 8.1). Initially, it appears impossible for the system to be sustainable with respect to growth and nonsustainable with respect to a nonrenewable resource if we maintain the assumption that the nonrenewable resource is a necessary factor of production. However, as discussed above, there may be sufficient substitutability between reproducible capital and the nonrenewable resource so that economic growth can be sustained while generating a continuous decline in the nonrenewable resource stock. From a policy perspective, the fact that aggregate output growth can be sustained, despite nonsustainability of the resource stock, hardly constitutes grounds for government intervention in order to halt the depletion of the resource stock. This is an example of how sustainability of aggregate output growth can lead to nonsustainability of a nonrenewable resource.

In addition, there often exists a sustainable backstop technology that is based on sustainable resource use (e.g., solar or wind power). A relatively plentiful nonsustainable resource (say, oil) may be used in the beginning of the growth process, but, as it becomes increasingly scarce and more expensive, the sustainable resource (say, solar power) is used as the substitute technology. In this case, the economic system itself supplies the incentives for the system to proceed from a nonsustainable to a sustainable system. Policy intervention is hard to justify in such a situation and may even lead the economy onto a nonsustainable path, when it was on a sustainable one to begin with.

One of the main obstacles to sustainable development is an unwillingness to adopt economic incentives that cause individuals to change their behaviour with regard to resource use. Too often we expect the government to solve problems that are outside its capacity to solve, except where its role is to set up appropriate market incentives. Unfortunately, the government fails to take appropriate measures, because the majority of individuals in society are against them, and groups conduct rent-seeking activities to avoid paying the cost of its responsibility for sustainable development. Too often the sustainable development process results in recommendations to make incremental changes to existing policies, along with suggestions to collect more information and to improve existing management of resources. Unfortunately, the recommendations cover familiar territory, where the thinking and positions of various interest groups are well staked out – there is often no real change in economic institutions and incentives that would truly lead to sustainable development.

What, then, might an appropriate approach to sustainable development look like? There are several rules of thumb that might help to achieve sustainable development.

(1) For a given technology, the rates at which renewable resources are to be used must always be less than the available flows; as technology advances, rates of use could increase. Further, renewable resources must not be driven to extinction – a safe minimum standard of conservation for renewable natural resources must prevail. This rule does not permit society to rely upon possible future technological advances to overcome problems created today. However, it does not require, for example, that every animal or plant species be preserved from extinction, because not every species is essential

to human welfare, and loss of some species may enable humans to learn more about the benefits of those that remain. Further, the economic costs of preserving all species from extinction are large compared to the benefits. Similar arguments can be made for other renewable resources.

(2) Waste flows must be kept below the assimilative capacity of the environment.

(3) With regard to the stock of nonrenewable resources, these should not be allowed to be depleted or exhausted as long as the economic benefits of maintaining that stock at some (minimum or sustenance) level exceed the costs of so doing. Examples of this were provided in Chapter 2.

(4) Excessive government intervention in the economy causes development that is not sustainable. The reason is that large, bureaucratic governments are, themselves, wasteful of resources and are targets of rent seeking by political self-interests. By circumventing markets, governments misallocate resources and create an atmosphere that is not conducive to sustainable development. The role of government has been discussed in previous chapters: it is to set rules of law that encourage individuals and firms to make decisions that lead to sustainable development of the world economy and that treat all economic actors equally. It should encourage investment in human and human-made capital that reduces reliance on natural resources and the environment, while redistribution of income towards the poor must be conducted in a manner that is fair and that does not distort resource use.

Failure to implement these simple rules need not be catastrophic, but it could substantially lower current standards of living. Perhaps it is necessary to learn the lesson of the ancient Israelites. God had commanded them to leave the land fallow every seven years; nothing was to be done to the land during that year because the land needed to replenish itself. Old Testament prophets frequently accused Israel of failing to meet this requirement, of failing to practise stewardship. However, the Israelites neglected to comply with that simple command for a period of some 490 years. As a consequence, they were taken into captivity by the Babylonians for a period of seventy years, one year for each year that God's command had not been followed. Is there a Babylonian captivity on the horizon for this world?

Resource Scarcity?

About two hundred years ago, Robert Malthus argued that, since population growth was geometric while growth in food production was arithmetic, the world was doomed to a sustenance level of existence. Humankind would never be able to progress beyond a primitive state because resource scarcity (in this case food) would prevent it. Ever since, there have been Malthusians who have predicted a variety of catastrophic world events that follow from the biophysical limits to growth – the fact that we are consuming nonrenewable resources and, in some cases, driving renewable resources into an irreversible critical zone (e.g., loss of species, soil erosion, and desertification caused by cultivating marginal lands). In each case, the limits to growth have been circumvented through technological advances and other circumstances that were unforeseen at the time the predictions of scarcity were made.

Economists study resource scarcity by examining commodity prices. If the real (inflation-adjusted) prices of a resource increase, this is a sign of increasing scarcity; if real commodity prices fall, this is evidence that either the demand for the resource has fallen or that there is an abundant supply. Resource commodities are inputs into the production of final products. Thus, timber is an input into housing construction and paper production, while oil and natural gas are used for transportation and heating. The demand for a resource commodity falls whenever less of the resource is required to achieve the same or a greater level of final product than previously. More efficient means of harvesting timber and processing logs into lumber, and greater use of a tree's mass (i.e., less waste), increases the supply of wood products available from the same forestland. Planting faster-growing species also increases timber supply. New discoveries, secondary or enhanced recovery, more efficient ways of extracting oil from tar sands, and the ability to pump oil from deep-sea wells increase the supply of oil and gas. Fuel efficiency and alternative fuels (e.g., electricity, solar, and wind) have reduced the demand for oil and gas. As a result of such changes, the real prices of many nonrenewable resources have either remained stationary over time or have actually fallen. This provides evidence that there is no reason to expect an impending resource shortage.

It is interesting to note that, in 1891, the U.S. Geological Survey predicted that there was little or no chance of finding oil in Texas. In 1926, the U.S. Federal Oil Conservation Board predicted that the U.S. had only a seven-year supply of oil left, leading some to argue that the price of a gallon of gasoline would soon rise to $1. Similar predictions were made in 1939 and 1949, but none ever materialized. The so-called energy crisis of the 1970s occurred, primarily, because price controls on oil in the U.S. (implemented by the Nixon Administration) meant that there was no incentive to encourage conservation (reduce demand), exploration for new sources of oil (increase supply), or investment in alternatives to fossil fuels (reduce demand). The energy crisis abated rapidly once price controls began to come off in 1979. Deregulation of prices was complete in early 1981. As a result, energy consumption declined by 20 per cent during that year, and drilling activity increased by 50 per cent. The resulting fall in energy prices led to the eventual collapse of the OPEC oil cartel.

In Canada, the National Oil Policy of 1961 guaranteed western oil producers a market for oil by preventing consumers west of the Ottawa River Valley from purchasing oil from sources other than western Canada. This resulted in Ontario prices for western crude that were 25 to 35 cents per barrel higher than what they would otherwise have been. When world oil prices increased dramatically in 1973 as a result of OPEC, the federal government responded by freezing the price of all oil at $3.80/barrel. Taxes on exports and oil company profits were used to subsidize oil imports east of the Ottawa River Valley. Although the oil producing provinces (primarily Alberta) increased their royalty rates to capture a large portion of the resource rents, the low Ontario price and the export tax kept these rents well below their potential. In an attempt to offset the power of the western producing provinces and increase the available supply of oil, the federal government encouraged and subsidized exploration outside the producing provinces in northern and coastal areas.

Throughout Canada the low-price oil policy weakened concurrent policies to conserve energy, adopt energy efficient technologies and alternative fuels, and reduce polluting activities in general. Later, when domestic and world prices converged, these policies were, inadvertently, to give Canada's industry a competitive disadvantage relative to its trading partners, who had already adopted energy-saving technologies. Although the federal government was forced to back off its price freeze when Alberta decided to reduce oil production in 1980, the National Energy Program that was introduced in 1980 did not go the full step. It slowly increased domestic prices to the world level via phased-in price increases. The producing provinces and the primarily foreign oil companies continued to object to this policy, because the resource rents available to them remained lower than what they would have been under a free market. This redistribution of resource rents was objected to as a matter of discriminatingly unfair income redistribution, but it was the rent dissipation among Canadian consumers, in the form of lower than world prices, which likely led to inefficiency and resource misallocation.

In retrospect, it appears that attempts to control prices of resource commodities lead to their scarcity. An examination of oil, wood products, aluminum, copper, zinc, nickel, and other resource commodities indicates that, while consumption has increased, real prices have either remained relatively constant or even declined. This indicates that there has been both an increase in the availability of the resource in situ and greater efficiency in mining and production. One is forced to conclude that, with few exceptions, there does not appear to be an impending shortage of natural resources.

To reach the same conclusion about ecosystem resources that are not priced in the marketplace is not possible. However, what the foregoing discussion does indicate is that, by somehow pricing ecosystem services, the chances of maintaining these resources will be greatly enhanced.

Economics of Preservation: The Example of Biodiversity

Ecologists have identified a number of reasons for maintaining biological diversity or biodiversity. Each of these reasons (and others) have been the subject of study by economists.

(1) There is the possibility that unknown species contain genetic material that may someday be valued as a factor input into production, as a cure for disease, and so on. By not maintaining biodiversity (and allowing such species to go extinct), these economic benefits are lost forever.

(2) Some so-called 'minor' species serve as an ecological indicator, warning society of environmental changes that could be costly to correct, much like canaries warned miners of high levels of dangerous gases.

(3) The web of species is needed to generate soil, regulate fresh water supplies, dispose of wastes (*waste receptor* function), and maintain atmospheric quality.

(4) Finally, biodiversity is significant because it is important to avoid irreversibilities.

Biophysical scientists frequently fail to recognize the difference between commercial values and economic values. Jobs and regional development are often incorrectly identified as the economic benefits of resource development (as noted in Chapter 6), but these have nothing to do with economic efficiency or welfare. Commercial values refer to those goods and services that are traded in markets – that have commercial value. Economic values can be assigned to anything that has value to people, even if these are not traded in the marketplace. As long as individuals would be willing to pay some amount to have, keep, or avoid the 'thing' (even if payment does not actually occur), it has an economic value that contributes to the overall welfare of society.

There is a substantial economics literature pertaining to the preservation of endangered species, wildlands, and biodiversity (see References and Suggested Readings at the end of the book). Resource extraction is the main cause for development of wildlands and the destruction of habitat. In the Pacific Northwest, concern centres around endangered species (viz., Northern Spotted Owl) and the preservation of old-growth forests; in the tropics, deforestation is blamed for the destruction of ecological systems and the subsequent loss of unknown numbers of plant and animal species; in the Great Plains region of North America, conversion of wetlands to agriculture forever alters both the landscape and the ecology. Preservation in each of these examples, as well as in many others, is related to *uncertainty* and *irreversibility*.

Uncertainty is a problem because we do not know if the plant or animal species that became extinct contained information that may have enabled us to find an alternative source of liquid petroleum, a perennial variety of corn, or a cure for cancer. The benefits from any of these discoveries could be enormous. Consider, for example, the savings to society from the discovery of a perennial hybrid of corn. This would result in savings from not having to plough and seed the 28 million hectares that are currently planted to corn in the U.S. every year. It would also lead to a reduction in soil erosion, because annual ploughing is no longer required and perennials are better able to bind the soil during periods of rain and/or wind. Another example is a wheat-like salt grass discovered in the Colorado River delta. Through selective breeding, yields increased from several kilograms per acre to as much as a tonne per acre. The plants grow best when irrigated with full-strength sea water, making it valuable in arid and saline areas. Pharmaceutical values foregone by loss of biodiversity are considered by many to have immense, albeit unknown, value. By delaying the development of wildlands, it is quite possible that new information about the existence or value of a particular endangered species will become available.

Irreversibility has both a biophysical and economic dimension to it.

From a biophysical point of view, there are some environments that can never be restored to their original state once development has occurred. In some cases, reclamation procedures and time might restore an exploited ecosystem to some semblance of its former state, but the discriminating observer will be able to notice that the original state has not been attained in all of its diversity and beauty. Intra- and interspecies variety has value to individuals simply because they get pleasure from observing such variety. Along with these benefits of preservation, ecosystems such as wetlands provide basic biophysical services that contribute to the support of human life, and this certainly has value. Farming too close to wetland areas or draining them is an irreversible process that has consequences for the hydrological cycle and the ability of land to absorb harmful pollutants and take them out of the system, thereby increasing humans' exposure to these pollutants. Indicator species are valued as early warning 'devices' regarding changes in the ecology (e.g., the brown pelican, osprey, and bald eagle alerted us to the dangers of DDT). When such warnings occur, by acting immediately rather than later, a substantial sum can be saved ('an ounce of prevention is worth a pound of cure').

Economic irreversibility occurs when development has left an environment in a state that can be restored to the original only at a cost that exceeds that of preventing the degradation to begin with – this is the concept of *conservable flow* (Chapter 2.) Thus, if restoration to an original state is excessively costly, either in terms of the resources that must be allocated or the time required, economic irreversibility has occurred. However, in this case, the value of preserving the original state can be explicitly recognized. It is only when the consequences of a decision can be readily altered at negligible cost to society that a decision can be said to be reversible.

It is clear that there is some value to delaying development in the current period if more becomes known about future benefits and costs in the next period. That is, the expansion of choice by delaying development of wildlands and endangered species represents a welfare gain to society. The value of this welfare gain is known as *quasi-option value*. By the same token, a reduction in the options available to society represents a welfare loss. Quasi-option value is a slightly different concept than the option value defined in Chapter 7.

To expand on this idea, consider the following example. If the current and future returns from the decision to harvest an old-growth forest are uncertain, then, in general, it is not correct to replace the uncertain returns by their expected values in calculating the present value of the decision to preserve said old-growth forest. By waiting until the uncertainty is resolved, the actual value of the benefits of preserving the forest will be known, and this value will be different from the expected value. By using expected value in calculating the next period's benefit of preserving old-growth forest, the value of preservation is likely underestimated. The difference between the value obtained using expected values and the true value once the uncertainty is resolved – the shortfall – is quasi-option value. This is the loss of options that an irreversible decision entails. Thus, if there is any chance that some uncertainty is resolved by delaying development, the decision to develop or preserve favours the preservation decision. But this does not imply that preservation will always be the preferred strategy. The safe minimum standard approach implies a similar bias favouring preservation, but the costs of preservation cannot be onerous.

The economic consequences of irreversibility can be demonstrated using the simple model of Figure 8.2. Environmental amenities (E) are plotted on the abscissa, while produced goods (G) are plotted on the ordinate. In the first time period, the production possibility frontier is given by curve MK_1. A tangency between the social indifference map and the frontier occurs at point A. Societal preferences are assumed to remain constant from one period to the next, although, in practice, they are likely to shift in a way that favours environmental amenities. Such a shift would reinforce the results discussed here. Now, as a result of technical change, the economy's ability to produce more goods increases in the next period, but the amount of environmental amenities remains constant *as long as no development takes place*. This is illustrated by the production frontier MK_2. A new optimum occurs at B. At this point, the relative price or value of environmental amenities has increased, as is indicated by the increase in the (absolute) slope of the tangent line (slope = $-p_E/p_G$, where p refers to price).

If development occurs in the first period, it is no longer possible to obtain an amount M of the environmental amenity in the second period (e.g., driving a species to extinction is irreversible). Assuming technical change, the production frontier shifts to NK_2. This frontier lies entirely inside the frontier resulting from the 'no-development' scenario, indicating that society is less well off. Only if technical change is significantly enhanced by first-period development will society be better off in the second period by permitting development to reduce environmental options. This could result from knowledge about the existence of plant or animal species that comes about as a consequence of development. This is indicated in the figure by the dashed production possibility frontier.

Figure 8.2

Development versus preservation: Increasing value of environmental amenities

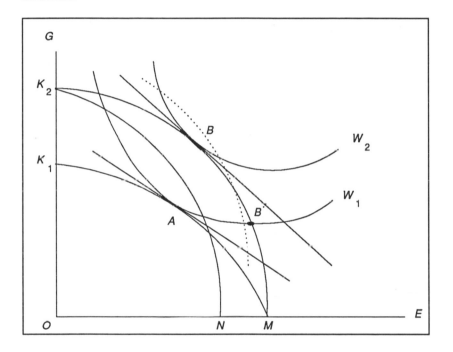

If preferences change over time to favour environmental amenities, then the results in Figure 8.2 will be even stronger. The reason is that a change in preferences will pivot the social indifference map in a way that causes the tangency point B to lie to the right and down the curve MK_2, say to B'. If irreversible development then occurs in the first period, technical change must be sufficient to shift the dashed line further to the right. However, if B' lies to the right of the dashed curve, then no amount of technical change can compensate for the lost environmental services.

To summarize, as time passes, the decisionmaker gets more and better information about the costs and benefits of maintaining land in its present, reversible state. Thus, if the decisionmaker has to choose between developing and not developing land (whether or not to harvest a stand of old-growth timber), he or she can obtain additional information about present and future returns of the options by delaying the decision. It is important to recognize that the problem's decision and information structure evolves through time.

The conclusion is that the discounted net benefits of development need to exceed the present value of the net benefits of preservation by a 'substantial' amount before development should proceed. The difficulty is measuring quasi-option value. Given that measurement is difficult or impossible, some small amount of development might proceed simply in order to obtain more information. For example, by cutting down some tropical trees, it may be possible to obtain information about the species and ecology of the region. Another possibility is simply to focus on the actual decision process; for example, it is possible to incorporate (Bayesian) uncertainty into the decision process by using stochastic dynamic programming or stochastic cost-benefit analysis.

Finally, what has been said about preservation of endangered species and wilderness applies equally to the residential development of agricultural land. This is an irreversible process. It is clear, however, that one should not look only at the current agricultural value of land in making the decision to convert it to residential development. Quasi-option value must be taken into account here as well.

Discussion

What contribution does economics have to make when it comes to *sustainable development*? From the discussion in this chapter, it is clear that economics is important in two ways. First, because economists have long ago addressed issues related to sustainable development (e.g., open access, conservation, safe minimum standard, etc.), they have a comparative advantage in giving meaning to the concept – something that is currently lacking. Second, implementing sustainable development will require developing policies (economic institutions and instruments) to bring about sustainable development. The economist has a comparative advantage in measuring costs and benefits of proposed policies and in examining alternative institutions and market incentives for attaining sustainable development. An illustration of how economic thinking can bring perspective to policy issues is provided through a consideration of the effect of trade.

Globalization of world trade has been blamed for tropical deforestation, destruction of wildlife habitat, and poverty in low-income countries. The argument is that global trade encourages less-developed countries to employ more land in the production of tradeables; these are not the products that *should* be produced. Forest products sold in international markets result in faster rates of deforestation, while agricultural land is diverted from production of commodities that provide food for indigenous peoples to production of commodities that have value to those with high incomes. It is implicitly, and erroneously, assumed that production of indigenous foods is somehow environmentally better than using the land to produce exportables. This is, of course, an empirical question.

One consequence of such thinking is that some European countries have banned imports of tropical hardwoods, because their harvest is considered unsustainable. Where it is not possible to distinguish between hardwoods from different countries, however, such a ban simply increases transportation costs, as goods are shipped in a non-optimal fashion in order to get around the ban. Alternatively, where the ban is effective, it leads to a reduction in the value of land used for timber production. This causes forestland to be converted to other uses more rapidly than was previously the case, as pressure for agriculture becomes greater due to the value of agricultural land having increased relative to its value in timber production. Hence, the ban results in a faster, not a slower, rate of conversion of the land from tropical forest to agriculture.

World trade also encourages developed countries to move environmentally unsound production processes to low-income countries, which must cope with their environmental costs. The chief economist of the World Bank has argued that it makes economic sense to locate 'dirty' industries in Third World countries. Such industries impose lower costs upon residents in those countries than in developed countries, mainly because the environment is valued less highly and contributes to economic growth. The World Bank should, therefore, encourage migration of dirty industries in that direction. While the idea that life in poor countries is worth less than it is in rich countries is morally detestable, the proposal has merit. The reason is that such a policy will enable individuals in poor countries to raise their standards of living (incomes) and life expectancy (e.g., avoid starvation) so that they *do* become concerned about environmental issues and *do* have the opportunity to worry about getting cancer at some future time. In terms of Maslow's hierarchy of wants, food, shelter, and clothing are currently of much greater concern to many in low-income countries than is the environment. Increasing incomes of individuals in those countries will do more than well-intentioned policies by developing governments to bring about sustainable development.

In the meantime, are low-income countries doomed to become a dumping ground for the rich world's hazardous wastes and 'dirty' production processes unless governments intervene? Not at all. Many companies have decided to turn their backs on the cost advantages of locating 'dirty' production processes in low-income countries as a result of the Bophal disaster. In that case, a chemical leak at a subsidiary of Union Carbide in Bophal, India, in the mid-1980s caused a large number of deaths and landed the company in protracted litigation. Indeed, there are an increasing number of examples of companies going out of their way to pursue higher standards than are actually required in poor countries. One reason is related to the issue of liability, but the other has to do with marketing. Companies that are considered environmentally friendly have an advantage in the marketplace.

While the General Agreement on Trade and Tariffs (GATT) permits countries to apply the same environmental regulations on imports as on domestic products, it does not permit countries to discriminate according to means of production. Exceptions under Article XX of the GATT are meant (1) to protect human, animal and plant life, and health (Article XX(b)) or (2) to conserve a country's exhaustible resources (Article XX(g)). Arbitrary discrimination or disguised trade restrictions are not permitted. Thus, for example, GATT would not permit the U.S. to discriminate against tuna caught by countries that exceeded U.S. regulations concerning the average number of dolphins killed by tuna boats. The grounds for rejecting U.S. discrimination were both technical and that the U.S. attempted to discriminate on the basis of production processes; the latter was not permitted because dolphins in the eastern Pacific were beyond American reach. However, as in similar situations, the GATT regulations can be circumvented by the eco-labelling of products. This is allowed because eco-labelling treats foreign and domestic producers equally and does not discriminate on the basis of production processes. No countries have challenged such labelling at the GATT.

The GATT is not concerned about harmonizing environmental standards, as is the European Community, for example. The GATT is concerned with liberalizing trade, although it has recently been considering the role of environment in trade. By liberalizing trade, however, the GATT is contributing to sustainable development and better land use. By making hardwood trees, exotic species, and other 'environmental' commodities more valuable, countries are provided with economic incentives to manage and conserve these resources. Neither the GATT nor the globalization of the world economy can be blamed for global or local environmental problems; indeed, freer trade promotes sustainable development, and barriers to trade are a hinderance to the attainment of a sound global environment.

9
Economics of Global Climatic Change

Global warming is the result of human or anthropogenic activities that have increased carbon dioxide (CO_2) and trace gases in the atmosphere (methane, chlorofluorocarbons, ozone in the troposphere, and nitrogen oxides), thereby intensifying the greenhouse effect. The sun's rays pass through the so-called greenhouse gases, but the gases prevent dissipative heat from escaping. While global warming is discussed in terms of CO_2, trace gases make a significant contribution to the greenhouse effect. A double-CO_2 atmosphere is expected between 2050 and 2100, depending upon one's assumptions. Trace gases hasten global warming, while the thermal inertia of oceans slows it.

Economists have been involved in the climatic change debate since the early 1980s. Recently, the focus of economists has shifted to estimating the costs and income distributional consequences of both 'business-as-usual' warming and the various policies which are meant to avert it. The focus of this chapter is on two important issues related to climatic change: (1) How is climatic change likely to impact on land use, and (2) what does economics have to say about climatic change and policies related to it? In this chapter, the economic side of the climatic change debate is presented. However, the chapter begins by describing the technical aspects of global warming. Later, the economics of climatic change are discussed and there is a review of land-use impacts from business-as-usual emissions of CO_2 and other greenhouse gases. The focus is upon the primary or resource sectors. Finally, policies recommended by economists for averting or abating global warming are considered.

Technical Aspects of Global Warming
The main greenhouse gases (GHGs) are CO_2, methane, nitrous oxides,

and chlorofluorocarbons (CFCs). Table 9.1 provides information regarding anthropogenic contributions to these greenhouse gases. Not all GHGs have the same radiative impact (power to warm the earth) or atmospheric life. As a result, it is important to express the effect of each of these GHGs in CO_2-equivalent units, which requires discounting for atmospheric life and taking into account emissions and atmospheric concentrations. The length of time each gas remains in the atmosphere and the relative instantaneous and total contributions of each of the gases are provided in Table 9.2. It is clear that CO_2 is the most important GHG, and that efforts to control warming will, for the most part, need to focus upon controlling CO_2 emissions. Given this focus on carbon dioxide, it also helps to know about the carbon content of various fuels, since these are used for comparison in determining where and how best to reduce CO_2 emissions. This information is provided in Table 9.3. It appears, from these tables, that the CO_2 problem is, primarily, a coal problem.

Table 9.1. Summary of key greenhouse gases affected by human activities

Atmospheric concentration	Carbon dioxide ppmv[a]	Methane ppmv[a]	CFC-11 pptv[b]	CFC-12 pptv[b]	Nitrous oxide ppbv[c]
Pre-industrial (1750-1800)	280	0.8	0	0	288
Present day (1990)	353	1.72	280	484	310
Current annual rate of change	1.8	0.015	9.5	17	0.8
- % rate of change	0.5	0.9	4	4	0.25
Atmospheric lifetime (years)	50-200[d]	10	65	130	150
Global warming potential[e]	1	21	4,500	7,100	290
Emission reductions to stabilize concentrations at current levels	>60%	15-20%	70-75%	75-85%	70-80%

[a]ppmv: parts per million by volume
[b]pptv: parts per trillion by volume
[c]ppbv: parts per billion by volume
[d]Absorption of CO_2 by oceans and biosphere is not known, so a range of values is provided.
[e]Based on release of 1 kg of gas in 1990 and 100-year horizon
Source: Grubb (1990:14-17)

Climate scenarios are generally described in terms of (double) CO_2-equivalent atmospheric concentrations, implying GHG concentrations equivalent to a double-CO_2 atmosphere. Some have argued that atmospheric concentrations of GHGs could result in even greater warming, but such arguments fail to recognize (1) that there are limits to the availability of fossil fuels, and (2) that there are ongoing efforts to reduce CFCs and other pollutants that contribute to the greenhouse effect because of their (non-warming) externality effects (e.g., California has introduced a timetable for implementing conversion to zero emission vehicles).

Table 9.2. **Contribution of GHGs to global warming**

Greenhouse gas	Atmospheric lifetime (years)[a]	Relative instantaneous contribution to warming[b]	Relative total contribution to warming[b]
CO_2	50-200[c]	53.2%	80.3%
Methane	10	17.3%	2.2%
CFCs	65, 130[c]	21.4%	8.8%
Nitrous oxides	150	8.1%	8.7%

[a]Grubb (1990:14-17)
[b]Nordhaus (1991:39)
[c]Absorption of CO_2 by oceans and biosphere is not known so a single value cannot be given. The atmospheric lifetime for CFC-11 is 65 years; for CFC-12 it is 130 years.

Climate scenarios are simulated using climate models, of which there are four types. The simplest are *integral-parameter or zero-dimensional*; these model mean temperatures on earth by equating the mean daily uptake of solar radiation by the earth's surface to the outgoing radiative heat flux. *One-dimensional* models add a second dimension of detail in terms of variations in a climate variable but only one dimension in terms of latitude, longitude, or vertical directions. The most common of these models permits variation in temperature by height above the earth's surface, but with reference to a particular surface location on earth (a particular latitude and longitude). *Two-dimensional* climate models are constructed using any two possible directions and, thereby, allow more detail on climate variables. These models are used for a variety of theoretical investigations.

Finally, the sophisticated *three-dimensional* global climate models are

Table 9.3. Carbon content of different fossil fuels

	Tonnes of carbon per million tonnes oil equivalent	Tonnes of carbon per 10^{12} joules
Natural gas	0.61	13.8
Crude oil	0.84	19.0
Bituminous coals	1.09	24.5
Anthracites	1.14	15.5
Oil products		
Gasoline	0.80	18.0
Kerosene	0.82	18.5
Diesel/gas oil	0.84	19.0
Fuel oils	0.88	10.0

Note:
1 barrel of oil = 0.136 tonnes
1 calorie = 4.2 joules (J)
1 British thermal unit (Btu) = 1.05 kJ (kilojoules)
1 kilowatt-hour (kwh) = 3.6 J
Source: Grubb (1990:26)

general circulation models (GCMs) that numerically simulate the day-to-day evolution of the large-scale weather system, including some form of representation of the interaction between the atmosphere and the ocean. There are now 14 GCMs that are used for analyzing climatic change. The best-known were developed by the Goddard Institute for Space Studies (GISS), Oregon State University (OSU), the Geophysical Fluid Dynamics Laboratory (GFDL), the United Kingdom Meteorological Office (UKMO), the National Centre for Atmospheric Research (NCAR), and the Canadian Climate Centre (CCC). The problem with such models is that they use coarse grids of 500 km by 500 km and, consequently, can not be used to model regional variations in climate. The models are extremely expensive to run and require the use of supercomputers. While water vapour is the most important GHG, it is often treated exogenously in GCMs, and clouds, the role of oceans, and precipitation changes (and, hence, expected soil moisture) are poorly modelled. While GCMs predict an increase in average global temperatures of 1.5-4.5°C under a double-CO_2 atmosphere, the timing of this increase is uncertain, average estimates have declined over the past several years, and northern latitudes are expected to experience the greatest temperature increases.

Measurement of current CO_2 emissions is also a problem because there is inadequate knowledge and/or uncertainty about sources of emissions, different GHGs, the role of human activities such as deforestation and wood burning, and the character of feedbacks that reduce atmospheric CO_2 (e.g., absorption by oceans and forests). Further, there is the problem of linking emissions to atmospheric concentrations of the GHGs and their ultimate contribution to warming (as discussed above). Globally, it is generally acknowledged that anthropogenic emissions of CO_2 amount to 4.8-5.9 billion tonnes of carbon (C) equivalent per annum. A recent estimate puts annual global emissions at 5.650 billion tonnes (Mt).

Canadian estimates of CO_2 emissions provide some indication of the problems that are likely to be encountered. Environment Canada provides an estimated total Canadian emissions of 128.435 million tonnes (Mt) of C in 1987 (Table 9.4), although a U.S. estimate places them at 111 Mt per year. If Canadian emissions are to be compared to the global figure cited above, it is necessary to make several adjustments to the Canadian total, including removal of CO_2 emissions from pulp and paper production, combustion of fuel wood, slash burning, and solid waste incineration. Then, Canadian emissions amount to 114.45 Mt of C annually. In any case, Canadian emissions are about 2 per cent of global emissions.

Table 9.4 provides several different estimates of Canadian emissions as well as projections for the year 2005. The provincial estimates by the Federal-Provincial-Territorial Task Force on Energy and the Environment were developed to determine Canada's ability to comply with a 20 per cent reduction in CO_2 emissions by the year 2005, as was called for by the 1988 Toronto conference on 'The Changing Atmosphere.' The task force 'concluded that achievement of a 20 per cent reduction in CO_2 emissions by 2005 from 1988 levels would cause significant economic dislocation and would require significant changes in lifestyle' (p. 17). It did not recommend action to bring about this reduction.

When it comes to reducing greenhouse gas emissions, the problem facing the Canadian economy can be illustrated by considering Quebec. Between 1973 and 1988, CO_2 emissions declined by 24 per cent and, in 1988, Quebec had the lowest rate of CO_2 emissions per capita (9.8 tonnes of carbon). However, these reductions were primarily obtained by replacing oil with natural gas and greatly increasing reliance on hydro electricity. Natural gas became available as a result of extending the trans-Canada gas pipeline in order to bring western gas to the province, while electricity became available as a consequence of the large James Bay Hydro Project. The latter project had questionable negative environmental impacts. Despite including the increase in hydro generating capacity from the Great Whale River Project (currently delayed due to environmental pressure on New York City, which was to buy the electricity), Quebec's emissions of CO_2 are forecast to rise by 16 per cent between 1988 and 2005 (Table 9.4).

Table 9.4. **Estimated and projected Canadian carbon dioxide emissions by province, 1987, 1988, and 2005**

Province	CO_2 emissions		
	Estimated 1987[a]	Estimated 1988[b]	Projected 2005[b]
	Millions of tonnes C equivalent		
Nfld.	2.3	2.0	3.3
PEI	0.4	0.4	0.5
NS	4.7	4.8	7.2
NB	3.9	5.3	8.2
Que.	17.4	18.2	20.9
Ont.	42.0	44.9	54.2
Man.	3.4	3.4	4.0
Sask.	8.4	8.7	10.2
Alta.	28.7	33.9	48.3
BC	16.7	23.1	28.1
Territories (incl. Yukon)	0.5	0.5	0.5
TOTAL CANADA[c]	128.4	145.2	185.4

[a]Jaques (1990)
[b]Federal-Provincial-Territorial Task Force (1990)
[c]Column total may not equal sum of items due to rounding.

The Greenhouse Effect and Economic Efficiency

A concept that is frequently overlooked or ignored in the climate debate is that of *opportunity cost*. The correct approach to determining the feasibility of any policy or action with respect to addressing global climatic change is to calculate what the state of the world would be with business-as-usual warming versus what it would with some policy in place. The term 'state of the world' refers to the total value of global output of goods and services, and this includes those goods and services, such as environmental amenities (values derived from clean air, watershed protection, scenic vistas, biodiversity, recreation, etc.) that are not traded in markets. A policy could consist of adaptation to global warming or a strategy to avoid warming. The difference in the value of global 'production' of goods and services is the benefit (or cost, if negative) of the action that is undertaken. If the discounted benefits from action exceed the discounted costs, then the action is worth undertaking. The approach that yields the greatest net benefits is the appropriate one to pursue. If the costs of a wrong decision are large, low-income countries, in particular, may be harmed, because they can least afford to lower their rates of economic growth.

Property rights to the atmosphere currently do not exist, and, thus, the atmosphere can be considered an *open-access resource*. While the cumulative effect of CO_2 and other GHG emissions may be negative, no one person or country has the incentive to reduce emissions, because the benefits of so doing are shared by others – the costs to others of one person's emissions are not taken into account by that person. Until the nations decide that the atmosphere is to be collectively owned and then determine an effective means for managing it, the atmosphere cannot be considered a *global commons*, because this term refers to global owner-ship and management for mutual welfare.

In making decisions, economic agents will emit greenhouse gases into the atmosphere as long as the private marginal benefits ($MB_{private}$) of doing so exceed the private marginal costs ($MC_{private}$). Since private marginal costs are less than social marginal costs (MC_{social}), there is a divergence between the socially and privately optimal levels of emissions (Figure 9.1). (Social costs subsume private costs and, in Figure 9.1, it is assumed that MB_{social} is equivalent to $MB_{private}$.) This divergence of social and private marginal costs results in excessive emissions from a global standpoint.

The important thing to notice from Figure 9.1 is that the globally optimal level of GHG emissions is not zero. (It may also be true that the optimal rate of global temperature increase is not zero.) From an eco-nomic standpoint, the least-cost solution to global climatic change is one that permits some level of emissions. Any level of emissions other than *OE* is inefficient: a reduction in emissions lessens benefits more than it diminishes costs, while an increase in emissions escalates benefits less than it raises costs. Consider the emissions level *OX* that corre-sponds to business-as-usual emissions. The social benefits of reducing emissions from *OX* to *OE* are given by area *C + D + F*, while the social costs are given by area *D + F*; the net gain is given by area *C*. That is, the net social benefits (costs) of emissions reduction are given by the area between the $MB_{private}$ and MC_{social} curves, as long as the former lies below (above) the latter. The policy objective is to provide incentives such that emissions are reduced from *OX* to *OE*.

Figure 9.1

Determining optimal GHG emissions

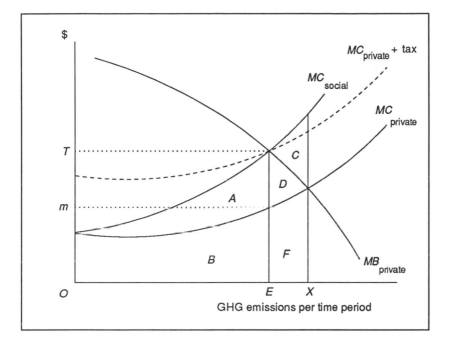

It should be noted that *OE* will change with changes in any of the MB$_{private}$ and MC$_{social}$ functions. Adoption of fuel-efficient technologies will shift marginal cost down and to the right, ceteris paribus, thereby increasing *OE*. Likewise, as society places greater value on an atmosphere with lower concentrations of GHGs, the marginal cost of emissions increases and *OE* will be reduced. This suggests that the instruments identified below will need to be flexible over time, adjusting to changes in the optimal level of emissions (assuming this level can be identified).

Figure 9.1 is drawn in terms of the marginal costs and benefits of activities that result in GHG emissions, with the divergence between MC$_{social}$ and MC$_{private}$ representing the costs to the atmosphere. In Figure 9.2, abatement and damages are treated directly. The horizontal axis measures GHG emissions as a proportion of the uncontrolled level of emissions. The uncontrolled level of emissions is determined from private decisions so that at *Y* in Figure 9.2 the laissez-faire abatement cost is zero. Economic theory indicates that the marginal cost of abatement function (MCA) must be concave; it rises on either side of *Y*. Abatement costs rise as one moves to the right or left, because costs are incurred when GHG emissions are increased or diminished. If it were possible to attain a lower level of emissions at less cost, society would take advantage of this possibility and move towards the origin. The marginal damage function (MD) represents the change in damages (caused by global temperature rise) from each unit change in GHG emissions. Damages can be avoided by reducing GHG emissions. Point E denotes an optimal level of emissions compared to the current level, because any emissions level below or above E leaves society worse off; that is, either costs exceed benefits (damage reduction) or damage is greater than the cost of reducing emissions.

Figure 9.2

Marginal damages and abatement costs from greenhouse warming

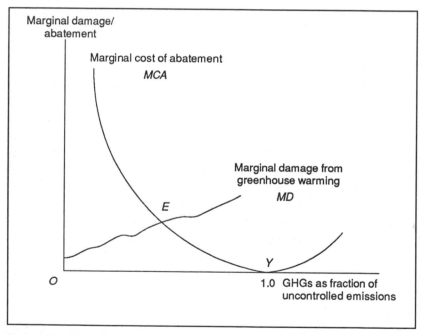

Source: Nordhaus (1991)

As one moves from point Y (the uncontrolled level) towards E, the marginal cost of abatement is, initially, quite flat, indicating that emissions can be reduced at relatively low cost over some range, but then marginal costs rise more steeply. Estimates of the functions in Figures 9.1 and 9.2 are based on measures of costs and benefits at one point in time. The purpose of these estimates is to find an optimal emissions level and, thereby, the appropriate level of taxes or quotas on emissions. More complicated models exist for determining the appropriate levels of taxes and quotas over time, but the underlying idea is not much different from that presented above.

Research has focused, primarily, on the marginal costs of abatement, using either an end-use approach (e.g., production of fuel-efficient automobiles, replacing incandescent with fluorescent light bulbs) or one that seeks to equate the supply and demand of energy in the global economy; these are referred to as the bottom-up and top-down approaches, respectively. Less research has focused on the marginal damages of climatic change. This explains why the MCA function in Figure 9.2 is rather smooth, while the MD function is drawn as a 'wavy' line (because it is just not well known).

Before one can advocate policy regarding reductions in GHG emissions, it is necessary to determine the benefits of such an action. Simply arguing that action is warranted because global climatic change is inevitable is unsatisfactory. It is necessary to demonstrate that: (1) global welfare (the value of output plus that of unpriced amenities) under an aggravated greenhouse effect is less than what it would be in the absence of warming; (2) the net value of this output exceeds the costs of averting anthropogenic warming (with the dollar values presented in present or terminal value terms, implying that discounting occurs); (3) the net benefits of averting anthropogenic warming are greater than the net benefits of adapting to the projected warmer climate; and, finally, (4) costs and benefits are determined at the margin, because reliance on average costs and benefits results in misallocation of resources. The latter point is demonstrated with the aid of Figure 9.1. The total private benefits at OX (given by the area under $MB_{private}$) might exceed the total marginal social costs (given by the area under MC_{social}). Then the average private benefit exceeds the average social cost, leading to the incorrect conclusion that OX is preferred to OE.

Some economists have attempted to summarize all known information about the marginal cost functions for reducing atmospheric GHGs. The focus has been on tree planting, reducing CFC use, and reducing CO_2 emissions. This information constitutes the marginal cost of abatement (MCA in Figure 9.2). Very little is known about the marginal benefits (i.e., marginal damage function) of slowing or averting anthropogenic global warming. Hence, constant levels of marginal damages are frequently assumed. Targeted levels of emissions reduction occur where the marginal cost of reduction of all GHGs intersects the marginal damages. One estimate indicates that reductions in GHG emissions of about 17 and 45 per cent are required for medium and high levels of damages, respectively.

These and other methods for determining the optimal levels of emissions reductions provide some gross estimates of value of carbon reductions. These indicate that 1 ton of carbon is valued at between $0.57 and $106.70 in terms of the global commons. In order to achieve reductions in GHG emissions, the cost will be in excess of $200 billion per year, or between 1 and 3 per cent of world output. It will be higher if inefficient policies are undertaken or if implementation occurs too rapidly.

Intervention to avert global warming is not costless; any money spent to reduce GHG emissions has an opportunity cost, namely, reduced investment in R&D, capital, debt reduction, and consumption. These costs are not inconsequential and could prove harmful to some economies. Aid from developed to low-income countries could alleviate some of the burden encountered by some countries, but income redistribution on a large scale creates additional problems for both the donor and recipient countries. Donors will attempt to minimize the amount transferred (e.g., by reducing other forms of aid), while, in recipient countries, this could lead to increased economic inefficiency and dependence.

Global Warming and Land Use

The sectors of the global economy that will be most affected by the greenhouse effect are agriculture, forestry, and coastline resources, although other natural resources (e.g., continental wetlands) and health and leisure will also be affected. In developed countries such as the U.S. and western Europe, agriculture and forestry account for about 3 per cent of the gross national product (GNP), although they account for a much higher proportion in developing countries. Data about the costs of business-as-usual warming are available only for the developed countries.

Agriculture

Studies of the welfare effects of climatic change on U.S. agriculture are sensitive to the GCM that is used. Researchers have found that, for the climate predicted by the GISS GCM, an annual gain of approximately $10 billion accrues to the U.S. agricultural sector; however, for the GFDL GCM climate, a loss of the same magnitude results. In both cases, a CO_2-fertilization effect was assumed; this effect is thought to increase crop yields by some 33 per cent. The U.S. results are not surprising, given that, for the central interior of North America, GFDL shows July soil moisture to be lower than normal, while GISS indicates that it will be higher. The total annualized loss could be as high as $36 billion, but only if there is no CO_2-fertilization effect. Naturally, the distribution of gains and losses varies from one region to another.

Researchers have also examined the adaptability of grain farmers in southern Minnesota to gradual global warming, using dynamic (transient) climate, crop, and economic relationships to reflect gradual adaptation to climatic change. It is misleading to simply compare cropping strategies under no warming with those under a double-CO_2 atmosphere, if one is interested in investigating adaptation. The research indicates that, in agriculture, adaptation is likely to be an important means of avoiding the adverse consequences of global warming. The main method of adaptation is for farmers to vary their crop mix among corn, soybeans, and sorghum and to choose from early, mid- or late-maturing cultivars. Despite the fact that no allowance was made for other crops, technical advance (e.g., new crop varieties), or, more importantly, a CO_2-fertilization effect, the research concludes that grain farmers can adapt to a changing climate – a climate which would be warmer and either wetter or drier. Indeed, adaptation is preferred to preventing warming.

At one workshop (the 'Coolfont Workshop'), national crop yields in the U.S. were projected to rise by about 15 per cent, while yields in the USSR would increase by about 40 per cent. The latter increase is greater than the former, because warming in northern latitudes is predicted to be greater; this is also the reason Canada's agricultural sector is likely to benefit from global warming. Similar increases in crop yields of between 15 and 40 per cent were projected for Australia, China, Brazil, and Europe as well as increased productivity in most fisheries as a result of coastal ocean up-welling. These results are dependent on the GCM used and, often, the stance of the researchers.

Global warming is expected to have a greater impact on northern latitudes and, thus, Canada should warm to a greater extent than the continental U.S. Economic studies of climatic change impacts on agriculture in Canada have focused primarily on the Prairies. Various GCMs gave mixed results concerning whether conditions will become more or less favourable to prairie agriculture. In all cases, the length of the growing season increases, usually by two weeks or more, but in some cases moisture deficits also increase and crop yields decrease. However, with the longer growing season, new cropping options become available to prairie producers (e.g., sweet corn, soybeans, sorghum), increasing crop diversity and reducing risk due to cropping decisions (but *not* risk from weather variability). However, the studies assumed no CO_2-fertilization effect. In some regions (such as southern Alberta), results show moisture to be insufficient to support these new crops, and that consequently, irrigation may be required.

In addition to changes in crop yields, changes in cropping area can be expected. Global warming could result in substantial increases in arable acreage, particularly in northern Alberta and BC, where adequate soils are available. This is illustrated by comparing Canada's ecoclimatic provinces under current atmospheric concentrations of CO_2 (Figure 9.3a) and under double CO_2 (Figure 9.3b). The grassland ecoclimatic region increases from 49.9 million hectares to 199.1 million hectares if transitional grasslands are included – almost a fourfold increase. The grasslands ecoclimatic province increases from 5 to 12 per cent of Canada's total land area, while transitional grasslands increase from 0 to 8 per cent. The entire increase in the former is located in the western provinces, while some of the latter is found in northwestern Ontario (Figure 9.3b).

The length of growing season, changes in precipitation, crop response, and potential for increasing arable area are all uncertain and depend on original assumptions concerning climatic change (i.e., GCM results) and the accuracy of crop simulation models. The result is mixed conclusions regarding the status of prairie agriculture under climatic change. However, models that account for the farm sector's ability to adjust to the changing conditions generally conclude that the Canadian Prairies will benefit from climatic change.

As a result of yield increases (caused by factors other than CO_2 fertilization), substitution of higher-valued crops, and seeding of 1.3 million additional hectares of arable land in the north, Canadian researchers estimate that climate-induced output expansion in Manitoba could result in a $1.5 billion increase in agricultural exports from that province alone, or a 190 per cent increase over current conditions. Even for scenarios with major crop yield losses, revenue increases could be achieved simply through the substitution of old with new crop varieties. Even in a worst-case scenario, net revenues declined by only 3 per cent, due to the ability to substitute crops with improved yields for crops with reduced yields, although this flexibility varied by region within the province. Results for Alberta and Saskatchewan show similar crop substi-

Figure 9.3

Ecoclimatic provinces of Canada: (a) 1990 or current; (b) 2050 or 2 x CO_2 scenario

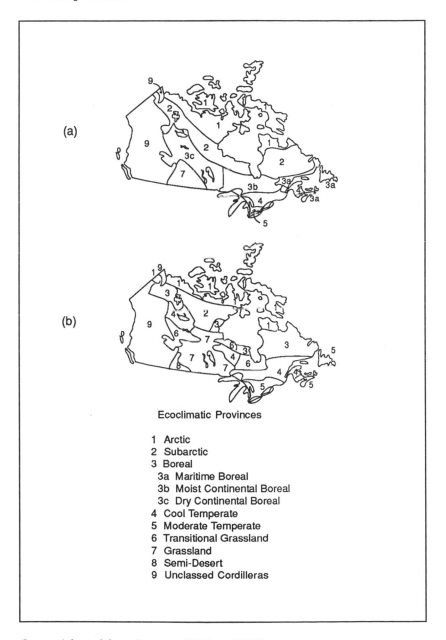

Ecoclimatic Provinces

1 Arctic
2 Subarctic
3 Boreal
  3a Maritime Boreal
  3b Moist Continental Boreal
  3c Dry Continental Boreal
4 Cool Temperate
5 Moderate Temperate
6 Transitional Grassland
7 Grassland
8 Semi-Desert
9 Unclassed Cordilleras

Source: Adapted from Rizzo and Wiken (1992)

tutions but slightly less potential for the introduction of new crops.

It is apparent that restructuring of western Canada's agricultural economy (as well as that in other regions of the globe) will be required over the next fifty to sixty years in order to adjust to climate warming. In some regions, agricultural expansion will be possible, while either retrenchment or greater reliance on irrigation will be required in other regions.

The conclusion is that there is a great deal of uncertainty concerning the measurement of agriculture's economic gains and losses due to climatic change. It is not clear that global warming will have only adverse economic consequences for agriculture. As a result of a CO_2-fertilization effect, agriculture in most countries will likely benefit from the greenhouse effect. Although adjustments will be required, possibly with interbasin water transfers and increased use of irrigation in some regions, the time frame is sufficiently long to permit the economic planning of agricultural outputs. Past experience and empirical findings indicate that agriculture can respond quickly to changes in either the physical or policy environment. However, it is likely that government agricultural policies, such as freight rates, grain subsidies, input rebates, and so on, will have a larger impact on the agricultural economy than will global warming, and that current interventionist policies could actually harm the long-term resilience of the agricultural sector.

Forestry

One unknown in the climatic change debate is the role of forests. In particular, it is not clear to what extent deforestation contributes to an increase in atmospheric CO_2. There are suggestions that deforestation adds some 1-2 billion metric tons of carbon to the atmosphere each year. Thus, policies to slow rates of deforestation or to increase the amount of growing vegetation worldwide might be considered.

The vegetative cover of the globe is a primary net CO_2 sink, with northern or boreal forests accounting for approximately one-quarter of this amount (Table 9.5). However, boreal forests account for only slightly more than one-tenth of the carbon that is sequestered annually by global forests. Temperate forests constitute about 60 per cent of the area of boreal forests, but account for only about one-half the carbon in vegetation, although they account for nearly the same net annual productivity in terms of carbon sequestration. In terms of importance, only the tropical wet and moist forest contains more carbon in situ and an annual absorption of carbon that is greater than the boreal forest (Table

9.5). However, boreal forests store significantly more carbon in their soils and associated peatlands than do tropical forests. This makes the boreal ecosystem much more important as a global carbon sink.

Studies of the impacts of global warming on forestry have focused primarily on location of forests, species adaptation, and pests and disease. As a result of global warming and a CO_2 'fertilization effect,' total forest biomass increases of 10 and 20 per cent have been projected for the U.S. and Russia, respectively. The southern boundary of the boreal forest zone is projected to shift northward by 250-900 km, while the northern limit could move some 100-700 km. The southern boundary is delimited by 1,300 growing degree days (number of days temperature is above 5°C, with each day multiplied by the number of degrees above 5°C), while the northern boundary is delimited by 600 growing degree days. Parts of the current boreal vegetation zone are projected to become aspen parkland and/or boreal temperate; even parts of the subarctic might become aspen parkland. Thus, in some areas, boreal species will come into competition with southern deciduous species, while grazing and farming may replace current forest activities in other regions.

Table 9.5. **Areas of major vegetation types, carbon in vegetation and soils, and net primary productivity of terrestrial ecosystems**

Region (description)	Area (10^8 ha)	Carbon in vegetation (10^{15} g)	Net primary productivity (10^{15} g C/yr)	Carbon in soil (10^{15} g)
(1) Tropical wet & moist forest	10.4	156.0	8.3	138.7
(2) Tropical dry forest	7.7	49.7	4.8	45.8
(3) Temperate forest	9.2	73.3	6.0	104.3
(4) Boreal forest	15.0	143.0	6.4	181.9
(5) Tropical woodland & savannah	24.6	48.8	11.1	129.6
(6) Temperate steppe	15.1	43.8	4.9	149.3
(7) Desert	18.2	5.9	1.4	84.0
(8) Tundra	11.0	9.0	1.4	191.8
(9) Wetland	2.9	7.8	3.8	202.4
(10) Cultivated land	15.9	21.5	12.1	167.5
(11) Rock and ice	15.2	0	0	0
GLOBAL TOTAL	145.2	558.8	60.2	1,395.3

Source: Jackson (1990:39)

In general, the economics of global climatic change on forestry have not been concerned with welfare gains, income redistribution, or adaptation. True, some researchers have estimated a small positive benefit to the forest products sector from global warming, while others have pointed out that international trade in forest products will play a crucial role in determining whether or not a country will gain or lose when its forest resources are affected by global warming. However, the main focus of economic research has been on the role played by deforestation in contributing to enhanced CO_2 concentrations in the atmosphere and the role of forestation policies in mitigating climatic change through carbon sequestration.

The main idea behind carbon sequestration is to develop plantation forests with faster growing trees than those that currently exist. These forests will sequester carbon from the atmosphere so that an increase in forest biomass will reduce the build-up of atmospheric CO_2. Once plantation forests reach harvestable age, prices of timber products will be driven down to unacceptable levels. One proposal is to use the wood as a biomass fuel, replacing fossil fuels. Other suggestions are to 'pickle' wood in structures by providing incentives for house construction, for example, or simply to bury the wood. Much of the timber that is harvested ends up in structures or landfills, where it releases its store of carbon only very slowly. In that case, carbon is not released to the atmosphere (as with burning), while the new plantations sequester additional carbon. Large subsidies will be required to implement any of these schemes, although firms or individuals could be required to purchase emission permits from those engaged in tree planting. The research indicates that carbon sequestration can be an economically feasible means of reducing the concentration of CO_2 in the atmosphere but only when compared to some other alternatives that have been considered. It may not be economically feasible based on damages avoided by abating climatic change.

Carbon budgets for the Canadian forest sector indicate that forests might be net absorbers of CO_2, and that the amount absorbed is of the same order of magnitude as is the case for total Canadian emissions. There remains controversy regarding estimates, because the role of organic matter in soils, either in storing or releasing carbon, is not well known. Estimates by the current author indicate that Canada's forests sequester about 157.1 Mt of carbon per annum. This figure is likely to remain relatively constant over the next few decades, because the forest area is not likely to change much. In 1987, the forest sector contributed about 17.7 Mt of carbon to the atmosphere through pulp and paper production, slash burning, and combustion of wood fuel, or about 13.8

per cent of total Canadian emissions (Table 9.4). Estimates of the role of the forestry sector for the years indicated in Table 9.4 are provided in Table 9.6. The net contribution of the forestry sector to removal of atmospheric CO_2 is about the same as that contributed by the rest of the Canadian economy. There is also evidence to indicate that Canada might actually be a net carbon sink, but, if it is, this is unlikely to continue in the future.

Table 9.6. **Global warming and Canada's forestry sector (mil. tonnes of carbon)**

Item/Year	1987	1988	2005
Atmospheric CO_2 added by forestry sector	17.7	20.0	25.5
Net CO_2 absorbed by forestry sector	139.4	137.1	131.5
Net CO_2 contributed by rest of Canada	110.7	125.2	159.9

Source: van Kooten, Thompson, and Vertinsky (1993)

Reforestation of denuded forestlands in temperate latitudes is, in some cases, not worthwhile, because the costs of site preparation and planting trees exceed the discounted benefits of future timber harvest, and because many sites would generate a stand of trees at some future date without human intervention. However, if the benefits of carbon sequestration are included, then sites that are not worth replanting from a private perspective may well be worth replanting from a social perspective.

Economic research on climatic change as it relates to forestry needs to focus on issues beyond the role of carbon sequestration, despite the importance of such research. Restructuring of the world forest economy is already underway, and climatic change will have an impact on this. One requirement will be to assess the changes that are likely to occur. Since agriculture and forestry are competing land uses in many regions, it is clear that changes in agricultural practices will affect forestry.

Large changes in temperature (increases of 4°C or more) and precipitation can cause vegetation zones to migrate by 400 to 600 km. Depending upon the sensitivity of individual species to such changes, it is possible that trees planted today are not suited to the climate and environment that will exist in the region in fifty to sixty years. This is a concern not only for silviculturalists but also for economists, because the income distributional impacts of planting 'wrong' species may have a large impact on the future of the forest industry in a region and, hence, on community viability. This is a problem that has not been adequately addressed in the literature, mainly due to a lack of appropriate economic models for dealing with this aspect of climatic change. There has been very little economic research into adaptation of the forestry sector to climatic change. Most has focused on biophysical aspects of climatic change, while economics has largely been ignored.

Coastal and Other Resources

Sea level is forecast to rise between 30 and 150 cm as a result of global warming, although some have argued that warming will actually lower sea levels. (The most likely scenario is a 33 cm rise between 1990 and 2050.) The countries most likely to be affected by sea level rise are the U.S., the Netherlands, the Maldives and other island countries, and Bangladesh. Little information is available about the costs that increases in sea level will impose; these costs include the loss of land, recreational opportunities, wildlife amenities (viz., coastal wetlands), and so on. One study suggests that costs of protecting coastal structures is small. For example, a sea level rise of 50 cm is thought to increase the costs of protective coastal structures over half a century by $25 billion for the U.S., $1 billion for the ex-Soviet Union, $25 billion for Europe, and small amounts for other countries. These costs need to be compared with costs of abating warming (see above). As with other natural disasters (storms, earthquakes, etc.), wealthier nations are better able to cope with a rise in sea level by building dykes and other protective structures than are poor countries; therefore, increasing the welfare or output of poor nations should be a top priority in debates about climatic change.

Wildlife habitats are also expected to be impacted by climate warming, but its precise effect on habitats and their location is not clear. Some coastal wetlands will be inundated, but new ones will be formed. Loss of waterfowl habitat in southeastern Saskatchewan, for example, has been attributed partly to the drought of the late 1980s, but it is not clear that this drought is the result of global warming. However, government programs have also been blamed for destruction of wetlands and other wildlife habitat (Chapter 13). Little or no information concerning the costs and benefits of the loss of habitat is available, although economists are examining this issue in contexts other than that of climatic change. Without this information, it will be difficult to determine what will be the exact benefits and costs of business-as-usual warming or policies to slow it, respectively – that is, whether prevention or adaptation is the preferred strategy.

Some economists correctly point out that there may also be a loss in ecological amenities as a result of global warming. An example of these is waterfowl habitat loss. There may also be losses in (unknown) species that may have contributed to the eventual cure of an existing or future disease as well as the potential loss of ecological diversity. These losses can be valued, although it is extremely difficult to do so.

Policies for Reducing Global CO_2 Emissions

In this section, economic policy instruments for reducing global emissions of CO_2 and other greenhouse gases are examined.

Command and Control Regulation

Command and control imposes restrictions upon individual economic agents, groups of agents (e.g., a sector of the economy), or a country. The authority might specify the actual level of emissions permitted at a particular source, require that certain standards be met for a sector (e.g., an automotive emissions standard), prohibit activities such as deforestation, or specify that certain equipment be installed at emission sources.

The problems with this approach are threefold. First, there are no incentives to do better than is required by the standard. This is important in the long term, particularly if overall emissions rise. Second, there are few incentives to achieve the standards at the lowest cost to the economy as a whole. Although each agent or sector achieves their emissions standard at lowest cost, opportunities to reduce economy-wide costs are foregone, because some sectors are not encouraged to reduce emissions further, while others reduce them beyond what is efficient (so that costs are higher than they should be). Thus, the marginal cost of further reductions is higher in one sector than in another, while efficiency considerations require that they be equal across sectors and across firms within a sector. Related to this is the difficulty of determining an economically efficient standard for an entire industry. Finally, the costs of monitoring and policing such a system may be expensive and, in some countries, not even feasible.

Economic Incentives

Economic incentives, on the other hand, harness the power of markets in order to achieve emission reductions at the least cost to society, both in the short run and the long run, by providing incentives for innovation. Economic incentives include subsidies and taxes (or charges). They can also be employed in conjunction with quantity restrictions on the level of emissions, as in the case of tradeable emission permits.

Subsidies

It is possible to achieve the desired level of emissions reduction in an economically efficient manner by for example,providing firms with subsidies per unit reduction of carbon emissions. In contrast to taxes, subsidies are often politically more acceptable. A subsidy of amount mT (Figure 9.1) has the effect of shifting the $MB_{private}$ inward by that amount, since continued emissions result in foregone subsidy. The new, private marginal benefit function intersects private marginal cost at emissions level OE rather than OX. While this results in the desired level of emissions in the short run, there is a problem in the long run, because the authority does not know the actual marginal benefit and cost functions. Subsidies are calculated on the basis of some benchmark level of emissions. Individual economic agents are encouraged to raise this benchmark by investing more than they otherwise would in those sectors that receive subsidies. This could be particularly troublesome where subsidies are provided to low-income countries. Even contemplation of subsidies could encourage some countries not to implement currently feasible GHG reductions, while implementation of subsidies will stimulate investment in those sectors receiving them. Finally, a practical difficulty with subsidies is that they are often tied to a specific, proven technology, which could reduce efficiency and flexibility.

Taxes

A tax on CO_2 emissions (carbon tax) of mT (Figure 9.1) would cause individual agents to equate the marginal benefit of their CO_2 emissions with their marginal private cost plus the amount of the tax. That is, the $MC_{private}$ will shift up in parallel fashion by amount mT (to the dashed curve $MC_{private}$ + Tax in Figure 9.1), intersecting $MB_{private}$ at the socially desired level of emissions, OE. In effect, firms (countries) avoid the tax by reducing emissions to the point where the marginal net benefit (marginal benefit minus marginal cost) to the firm (country) of further emissions reduction is equal to the tax. This is further illustrated with the aid of Figure 9.4.

In Figure 9.4, NMB denotes private net marginal benefits ($NMB = MB_{private} - MC_{private}$), the tax is OP ($= mT$ in Figure 9.1), and distances OE and OX are the same as in Figure 9.1. (The subsidy of mT ($= OP$) can also be examined via Figure 9.4. Now $NMB' = MB_{private} - MC_{private} - OP$, where the last term constitutes a foregone benefit whenever carbon is emitted. This marginal net benefit function intersects the horizontal axis at OE. Any reduction in $MC_{private}$ or increase in $MB_{private}$ increases emissions beyond *OE*. With no tax, production results in emissions of *OX*, where *NMB* = 0. With the tax, the private net marginal benefit function shifts to *NMB'* and emissions fall to *OE* (where *NMB'* = 0).

Figure 9.4

Net marginal benefits and costs: Taxes and quantity quotas

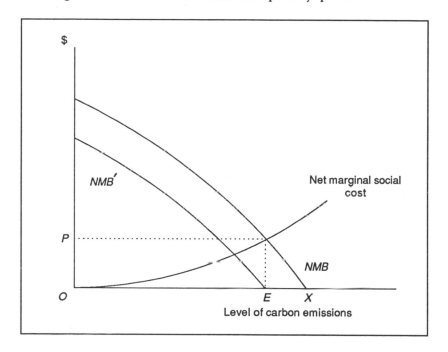

The main advantage of a tax scheme is that firms with lower abatement costs will reduce carbon emissions to a larger extent than will firms with high abatement costs, and all economic agents have an incentive to reduce the costs of their emissions in the long run. Another benefit of a carbon tax is that it generates revenue for the government, which could be used for policing, tax collection, and monitoring. If the authority looks to maximize revenue from the tax scheme, it may not wish to increase taxes to the required level, and, in particular, it may not want to increase the size of the tax over time. The reason is that higher tax rates might result in lower revenues.

Emission Permits
Finally, transferable emission permits may be used in conjunction with quantity restrictions to achieve the desired level of carbon emissions,

OE. Experience in the U.S. indicates that tradeable emission permits are more politically acceptable when permits are issued free to existing polluters on the basis of their current emission levels. Existing markets for emission permits (e.g., sulphur dioxide emissions from thermal power plants) have functioned less than perfectly, because they have been thin (few transactions) and/or dominated by single buyers or sellers. But this is unlikely to be a problem with respect to GHG emissions, because markets would not be confined to a single, small region – climate warming is a global problem. However, there is the question of whether it is ethical to provide 'legal rights' (permits) to harm the atmosphere.

Offsets and Private Markets
Under a system of tradeable emission permits, a new emission source should have the option of either purchasing emission permits or buying carbon offsets. The new source can purchase carbon sequestration services as opposed to emission permits. The benefit of such a system is that, even if a country decides to restrict emissions unilaterally (no international greenhouse protocol), it could permit emitters to purchase *new* carbon sequestration services worldwide. Likewise, private individuals or groups may wish to avert global warming by purchasing new forest reserves or plantations. This approach has been used successfully by various agencies (e.g., Ducks Unlimited to preserve wetlands, the Nature Conservancy to purchase threatened ecosystems, and World Vision to aid development), but the magnitude of the greenhouse problem limits the long-term success of this approach.

Uncertainty
Uncertainty is unavoidable when it comes to economic policies and the atmosphere. Not only are the marginal costs and benefits of GHG abatement (or the functions in Figures 9.1 and 9.4) unknown, but estimation of the impacts of global warming are uncertain. This uncertainty has policy implications. Setting a quantitative emissions target (say, at *OE*) and issuing permits to attain that target results in the same potential savings as does a system of carbon taxes (set at $OP = mT$). However, with uncertainty regarding greenhouse damages and with marginal costs that rise rapidly as emissions are reduced, the regulated target could result in much higher (perhaps unacceptable) costs than those originally envisioned. Thus, taxes may be preferred.

On the other hand, if the effects of anthropogenic warming are *not* known with certainty *and* there is concern about critical levels of atmospheric GHGs, then direct control via an emissions target may be the preferred instrument for dealing with this problem. Taxes may be set too low, and, therefore, emissions would be too high to avoid a critical zone for atmospheric concentrations of greenhouse gases. A quantitative target may, therefore, provide the authority with greater control.

Policy Choice in a Global Commons
The economic policy issue is further complicated when one considers that the greenhouse problem is global and requires cooperation among all nations. It would not be effective for a single country or subset of countries (e.g., OECD members) to pursue emission reductions in isolation. While solitary pursuit of reduced GHG emissions would establish a moral example, the climate warming problem is beyond the scope of a single country or group of countries to resolve, regardless of their economic might. In this section, the predicament of global policy is considered.

International Agreement
The first obstacle to overcome is that of achieving an international agreement on emissions reduction. In all probability, it will be much more difficult to achieve an agreement on CO_2 than it was to achieve an agreement on CFCs. One might consider four positions that nations have adopted concerning CO_2 emissions.
(1) The *cautious* countries (principally the U.S.) argue that there is not enough information available about global warming to warrant undertaking costly policies in order to avert it. Only 'no-regrets' strategies that produce benefits in addition to those of mitigating global warming (e.g., reducing harmful automobile emissions) should be pursued.
(2) A number of countries, primarily in western Europe, have adopted an *activist position*. These countries support the view that temperatures are rising and feel that the benefits of averting global warming outweigh the costs. Many of the countries in this group are unlikely to meet their stated targets, with their positions having been adopted in preparation for the anticipated negotiation of an international accord.
(3) Some countries are currently *unable to act*, because their economies

are not capable of bearing the burden of complying with any international agreement (e.g., countries of the old Soviet empire and those in eastern Europe).

(4) Finally, there are the low-income nations that are both *unable and unwilling to act* on an agreement regarding GHG emissions. These countries argue that the developed countries are responsible for global warming, and that they should be the ones to do something about it.

A global agreement to reduce GHG emissions is unlikely to be successful at preventing an aggravated greenhouse effect from occurring, because it will take quite some time to reach an agreement and then to actually curtail emissions. Delay in reaching an agreement will result because it will be difficult to convince those in categories (3) and (4) to commit to an agreement. Then it will be necessary to put in place the required institutions, technology, and so on that will cause GHG emissions to start to decline. These processes will take time and probably mean that global warming will be unavoidable. Therefore, adaptation may become a necessity. Efforts will likely be required to increase the resilience of many economies, particularly those of low-income countries.

World Carbon Taxes

If only the countries in categories (1) and (2) above were to impose taxes, the demand for fossil fuels in those countries would fall. This would increase the supply of fossil fuels to non-participating countries, effectively reducing prices in those countries. This would encourage greater emissions by consumers, who would tend to use more polluting (i.e., older) technology and increase investment in sectors that emit more CO_2. The net result might be very little change in global emissions.

There are two additional considerations pertaining to a carbon tax, even if some form of international agreement is possible. First, is the tax to be levied at the producer or consumer level? It is unlikely that countries will agree to producer taxes that will substantially increase the revenue of the OPEC nations (who collect the tax), particularly after the problems caused previously by a flood of petro dollars and the political instability of the Middle East. Yet, levying taxes on consumers could force countries in the Middle East to increase oil production in order to maintain their revenues. This would cause oil prices to fall, partly offsetting the effect of the carbon taxes in reducing CO_2 emissions.

Second, there remains the other problem of tax revenues. Countries may become more concerned about revenue maximization than about reducing carbon emissions. Suppose countries can avoid 'revenue temptation.' The developed countries who will collect the largest proportion of world revenues must be careful what they do with this windfall. Redistribution of the tax revenue to low-income countries is usually preferred, but transfers to low-income countries are often subject to political riders by the 'donor' countries, as now happens with foreign aid. Further, observers argue that income transfers need to target offending sectors in the low-income countries, but this counters the tax and might inadvertently lead to increased investment in those sectors, thereby offsetting gains in emissions reductions. It is unlikely that a redistribution of tax revenue of this magnitude would be acceptable to citizens of developed countries.

Carbon taxes can be used to offset other sources of government revenue, mainly revenue from income taxes. By so doing, economic growth might even be enhanced as distortions caused by income taxes are reduced. At the same time, there is an incentive for the economy to reduce reliance on fossil fuels that result in pollution.

Quantity Restrictions and Emission Permits
An international agreement on GHG emissions will likely employ country emission targets or direct control with emission permits. Countries with insufficient emission permits could purchase rights to emit GHGs from those with surplus rights, paying an annual rental fee to those countries. But several problems remain. First, effective use of a system of permits requires a certain level of expertise and administrative capability that is not found in many countries. Second, on a global scale, no institution exists for ensuring compliance – there is no global policeman. Third, there remains the problem of how to allocate permits. Some have suggested that these be distributed according to the size of the adult population, and that they be vested in governments and not private individuals. This creates three problems: (1) developed countries are unlikely to pay the enormous rents that would be required; (2) there is the possibility that recipient governments might use monies in ways that lead to greater emissions of GHGs (e.g., purchase warplanes); and (3) governments lack the information about emissions which is needed in order to exploit the gains of trade made available from permit trading.

Discussion

Although there appears to be a general consensus that anthropogenic emissions of greenhouse gases will bring about an aggravated greenhouse effect, the empirical evidence for this is weak. Indeed, conclusions regarding this process are based primarily on a belief that global warming will come about (a belief reinforced by the climate models) and a genuine concern that the atmosphere could enter into a critical zone. However, there are a number of prominent scientists who do not subscribe to the theory that global warming will come about. Clearly, policy decisions must be made in an uncertain environment.

The current generation passes wealth to future generations in the form of human capital (knowledge), human-made or physical capital (e.g., energy-efficient power plants), and natural resources (pristine wilderness, an atmosphere with low concentrations of GHGs, etc.). When society makes investment decisions, it is inconsistent to use a low discount rate when deciding to invest in projects that reduce GHG emissions, but to use a high rate when deciding on capital investments; this leads to economic inefficiency. Faced with the choice between investments in climate and capital investments, the efficient policy is to invest heavily in the high-return options and use the proceeds to slow climatic change in the future. That is, investments in human and physical capital that result in a greater ability, on the part of an economy, to cope with the adverse impacts of climate warming may make more sense than do uncertain and low-return investments with respect to averting climatic change.

This introduces two additional concerns. Given that climatic change cannot be avoided entirely, should avoidance strategies (e.g., taxes or emission permits) take precedence over policies that provide greater scope for adaptation in the future? The economist answers that one should allocate investment funds between avoidance and adaptation strategies until the marginal benefit from allocating another dollar on avoidance is equal to that from spending another dollar on adaptation. This requires the use of equivalent discount rates in evaluating choices.

The focus of the discussion in this chapter has been on government intervention. However, experience indicates that it would be a grave error to place the task of maintaining or enhancing the welfare of future generations in the hands of the state. One characteristic that appears to be common to all countries is that they have mortgaged the future in order to pay for present consumption. If the Canadian experience is any indication, governments have been more than willing to jeopardize the welfare of future generations in order to enhance their own chances of staying in power.

In conclusion, what is to be done about the greenhouse effect? Based on available cost and benefit data, and because of the uncertainties of global warming, a reasonable response is to pursue the following three measures: (1) expand knowledge through continued research and development; (2) seek to reduce externalities, such as air pollution from automobiles, because these are worthwhile pursuing despite their benefits in abating the greenhouse effect; (3) phase out the most powerful CFCs for a similar reason; and (4) plant trees. But it is important to consider the following advice offered by William Nordhaus:

> Those who paint a bleak picture of desert Earth devoid of fruitful economic activity may be exaggerating the injuries and neglecting the benefits of climatic change ... The threat of climate change is uncertain. It may be large, and might conceivably be devastating. But we face many threats. And don't forget that humans have the capacity to do great harm through ill-designed schemes, as the communist experiment clearly shows. Gather information, move cautiously, and fashion policies efficiently and flexibly so that you can respond quickly as new information becomes available on the gravity of greenhouse warming. (1990:196, 211).

10
Economics of Soil Conservation

Land degradation is a worldwide problem; it refers to soil erosion, loss of organic matter content and natural fertility, plus the destruction of the soil's structure due to, for example, compaction caused by heavy equipment. Unless economic analysis is correctly applied to the study of soil degradation, it will be difficult to determine appropriate and efficient policy responses. Economic research focuses on human as opposed to only non-human factors that cause degradation of agricultural lands; it centres on farming practices and on economic institutions and the signals (e.g., incentives) that farmers receive, all of which affect soil degradation. Soil erosion is the most readily identifiable form of land degradation, and for that reason it is the focus of this chapter.

Despite the fact that the problem of soil erosion has been well documented worldwide, farmers in some regions have been slow to change their agronomic behaviour in order to slow erosion. There are a number of reasons why this has been the case.

(1) Increased yields due to technical change have offset or masked reductions in yield resulting from soil erosion.

(2) Soils in the Great Plains region of North America are not susceptible to the rapid degradation that occurs in the shallower soils of the tropical rain forests. While one might expect farmers in North America to be less sensitive to land degradation than those in tropical regions, ceteris paribus, producers in the tropics may face institutional constraints and incentives that cause them to deplete the soil faster.

(3) As we argue in Chapter 12, government agricultural programs often have the unwanted effect of encouraging farmers to cultivate marginal lands – lands that might be most susceptible to wind and water erosion.

(4) Finally, degradation of soils results in two types of costs – on-farm costs and external or off-farm costs. The former cost is measured in terms of the forgone future productivity due to erosion today, and is borne by the farmer. Economic research indicates that these on-farm costs are often incorrectly measured and may be small. The second cost is the external or off-site costs of erosion that are difficult to quantify, although they may be large. The external costs are large, because, when soil erodes into water systems or the air, society bears the costs associated not only with soil particles but also with the chemicals that are attached to the soil. Together, the private or on-farm costs plus off-farm costs constitute the social costs of soil erosion. However, because external costs are not borne by the farmer, farmers lack an incentive to change their behaviour.

There are four basic concepts that must be kept in mind when assessing the damage due to soil erosion.

(1) The concept of opportunity cost requires that crop yields be compared using the principle of 'with versus without' conservation.

(2) Yield penalties that result from using conservation practices should not be confused with the assessment of erosion damage. If this is ignored, the cost estimates have little economic meaning.

(3) It is necessary to distinguish between *reparable* and *residual* yield damages. Reparable yield damage refers to fertility lost due to mining of the soil that can be restored by an increase in fertilizer and other inputs (*revolving fund*). Residual yield refers to erosion that affects the *conservable flow*. Residual yield damage results in reduced moisture infiltration, diminished rooting zone, and weakened soil structure.

(4) Finally, an economic assessment of soil erosion must separate the impacts of erosion from those of technology.

In this chapter, we expand upon these concepts. The discussion relies on both the definitions of rent developed in Chapter 2 and those of conservation and depletion found in Chapter 8. In addition, concepts from chapters 4 (externality) and 7 (nonmarket measurement) will prove useful. One objective will be to introduce readers to the concept of *user cost* and to demonstrate more clearly what is meant by *opportunity cost*. The objective is to provide a clearer perspective on economic issues related to soil erosion.

Soil Conservation and Depletion

Much of the controversy in soil conservation research is due to the various definitions of conservation advocated by opposing groups. Some argue that conservation is wise use of the soil resource, while others argue that conservation is the maintenance of the resource for future generations. Both of these views on conservation are based on value judgements regarding the meaning of the words *wise* and *maintenance*. Furthermore, neither definition provides a clear method by which to quantify conservation: How does one measure 'wise use of soil'? A more concrete and rigorous definition of conservation is required.

One definition of conservation was provided in Chapter 8. Another is provided by Arthur Bunce, who states that 'conservation of agricultural land appears to mean the maintenance of the fund of resources and the present level of productivity of the soil, assuming a given state of the arts' (1942:7). Buncian conservation implies the absolute maintenance of the soil in the state in which it was received. This view is akin to that of stewardship, but it is likely inconsistent with neoclassical economics, because it does not allow for trade-offs (e.g., between soil loss and long-run profitability). This view of conservation appears to imply nonuse, but, more correctly, it requires restrictions on use, much like the safe minimum standard of conservation restricts use in certain circumstances. Therefore, soil in excess of some minimum amount required to maintain productivity can be depleted, and it may be optimal to do so.

Contrary to Bunce's definition, Ciriacy-Wantrup's definition of conservation (Chapter 8) does not mean nonuse, but, rather, the *redistribution* of use rates in the direction of the future. This definition of conservation indicates a need to compare two or more time distributions of use, where one use is employed as a benchmark. For agriculture, it requires a comparison of alternative cropping strategies in order to determine both their effects on soil erosion and on farm profitability (or viability). The economist recognizes that it is technologically difficult, and seldom economical, to keep soils as productive as they were during the first few years after breaking the virgin sod. Thus, the cost of soil degradation is to be determined by comparing the offending cropping practices with the best soil-conserving alternative. This is the opportunity cost concept.

It is often assumed that soil erosion of any kind cannot be maintained indefinitely. However, soil does regenerate to some extent, and soil erosion can take place as long as it remains below the rate of natural regeneration or soil formation. To determine a 'tolerable' level of soil loss (equal to the rate of natural regeneration and known as the *T factor*), the Soil Conservation Service of the U.S. Department of Agriculture has calculated the rate at which the subsoil in a soil profile becomes topsoil. For most deep soils this occurs at the rate of one-thirtieth of an inch (0.85 mm) or five tons per acre (11.2 tonnes/ha) per year. Soils that are shallow to bedrock or groundwater, or that have some other obstruction to the rooting zone, can tolerate lower levels of soil loss – as low as one ton per acre (2.25 tonnes/ha) per year (six-thousandths of an inch or 0.17 mm per year). In tropical areas, soil forms at lower rates of about 0.01 to 0.50 mm per year. (This is why northern soils sequester more carbon, as is indicated in Table 9.5 of Chapter 9.) Exceeding the tolerable soil-loss rate threatens the productivity and fertility of the soil, in some cases this jeopardizes its ability to support vegetative cover. While U.S. lands have been classified according to T rates, the same is not true of Canadian agricultural lands.

Rates of soil loss also vary. Soils covered with natural vegetation lose less than 0.01 mm of topsoil per year in the Canadian Prairies, but they lose 0.02 to 1.00 mm of topsoil annually in the tropics. Converting grasslands to row crops increases erosion by a factor of 20 to 100 in the tropics and by as much as 300 times on the Prairies, while tillage summerfallow increases erosion by an additional factor of 5 to 6 over row crops (on the Prairies). Conversion of forests to row crops increases erosion by a factor of 20 to 1,000 times, with the higher rates occurring in the tropics. The problem with converting forests to crops is that the rate of soil formation is also reduced.

Opportunity Cost and the User Cost of Soil Erosion

What is meant by the *user cost of soil erosion*? The user cost of any natural resource is simply *the present value of future sacrifices implied by current resource use*. Therefore, the user cost of soil erosion is the impact of lost soil on future profits via the level of stock; that is, it is the present value of future revenues that are lost if we use a unit of soil today. How, then, does user cost relate to the *opportunity cost of soil erosion*? This can be illustrated using Figure 10.1.

Many researchers who have provided estimates of the on-farm (or private) costs of soil erosion have actually assessed the user cost of soil erosion. This is done by assuming that production can occur without any erosion taking place. Suppose that $R0$ in Figure 10.1 represents the discounted value of the path of net returns from growing a crop on a field where topsoil depth is somehow maintained at its existing level, which is probably unrealistic. Assume that $R1$ represents the discounted returns of an alternative cropping strategy, say, continuous row cropping or employing a two-year, wheat-fallow rotation to reduce risk, as occurs in some arid cropping regions. (Further returns end at the dashed vertical line, indicating that identical planning horizons are used.) The on-farm cost of the cropping system represented by $R1$ is then given as $R0$ - $R1$, but this is *not* the on-farm cost of soil erosion: it is the user cost of soil erosion. Farmers do not, however, make decisions based on total user cost. Since producers are able to switch from more erosive to less erosive cropping systems at any point in their planning horizon, they consider the *marginal user cost*, a concept discussed in conjunction with Figure 10.2 below.

Figure 10.1

User and opportunity costs of soil erosion

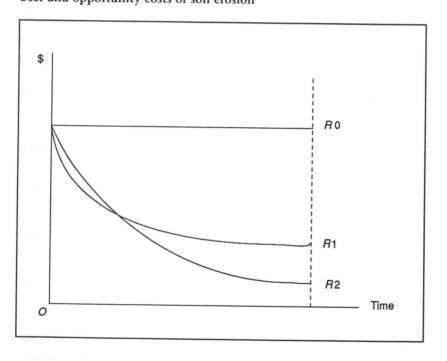

Estimates of total user costs ($R0$ - $R1$) have ranged between $468 million per year for the Canadian Prairies to $1 billion per year for Saskatchewan alone. Similar estimates for the United States are quite a bit lower, ranging from three-hundredths of one per cent to one-tenth of one per cent of total crop revenue per year. While it is not always clear as to how researchers obtain these estimates, they are estimates of user costs, and such estimates are sensitive to assumptions regarding rates of soil erosion, starting topsoil depths, the rate of discount and grain prices. For Saskatchewan, for example, empirical evidence suggests that total user costs range between $0.87/ha and $168.83/ha per year. That is, almost any 'cost' figure can be used, but such costs are not the opportunity or on-farm costs of soil erosion.

The correct measure of the on-farm or opportunity cost of soil erosion is determined by comparing the 'offensive' crop practice $R1$ with the best available, soil-conserving practice, say $R2$, where $R1$ and $R2$ refer to the respective discounted values of the paths of net returns for the two agronomic practices. Then the difference $R1 - R2$ constitutes the on-farm or opportunity cost of soil erosion. If $R1 - R2 < 0$, then there is an on-farm cost from using the erosive crop practice; if, on the other hand, $R1 - R2 > 0$, then the recommended, soil conserving practice ($R2$) is worse than the 'offensive' agronomic strategy ($R1$), and farmers who choose to employ the erosive techniques are behaving rationally. An example of this is provided in the next several paragraphs.

It is not always an easy task to identify an appropriate soil-conserving cropping strategy. In dryland cropping regions, a two-year, wheat-fallow rotation might be used as a means of conserving moisture (two years of moisture are used to grow one crop) and reducing risk. As the annual moisture deficit is reduced, so is the frequency of summerfallow (e.g., summerfallow may be practised once every three or four years rather than every second year). The alternative to these fixed rotations, which is used to calculate the aforementioned on-farm costs of soil erosion, is that of native pasture. To employ this alternative as a basis for measurement is unrealistic, because land is already under cultivation, and an agricultural economy, with a concomitant public and private infrastructure, is already in place.[1] But the recommended alternatives to the fixed rotations are to (1) continuous crop, (2) replace tillage fallow with chemical fallow, and/or (3) use reduced- or zero-tillage systems. The latter is, primarily, recommended in areas that receive adequate moisture, while the former two practices have been recommended in drier areas, such as southwestern Saskatchewan and southern Alberta, although it is not clear which is the better of the two alternatives for conserving soil. As noted, the true on-farm or opportunity costs of soil erosion are obtained by comparing returns under the cropping practice of interest with the best alternative (soil-conserving) practice.

Unless economic factors are properly considered, evidence often gives the impression that there are substantial benefits to be derived from conservation practices. Consider, for example, the results for Saskatchewan provided in Table 10.1. Simply looking at total yields over a 26-year period seems to suggest that continuous cropping is preferred to a fixed, wheat-tillage fallow rotation; continuous cropping also reduces soil erosion. However, if costs of planting and added moisture and fertilization benefits of tillage fallow are taken into account, the case for continuous cropping disappears. Economic calculations indicate that farmers would annually sacrifice between $32.84/ha ($13.30/ac) and $47.59/ha ($19.27/ac) by following the agronomic practice of continuous cropping that has been recommended for the purposes of soil conservation. Variability in annual returns is ignored in Table 10.1, and variability is much higher under continuous cropping, thereby making this recommended soil conserving practice a risky venture.

Table 10.1. **Total yields over 26 years and discounted annual net returns per hectare, Saskatchewan, for various soil types: W-F rotation vs. continuous cropping (price = $4/bu, discount rate = 5%)**

	Topographic soil class[a]					
	High		*Moderate*		*Low*	
	Yield[b]	Expected annual net return	Yield[b]	Expected annual net return	Yield[b]	Expected annual net return
W-F	43.7t	$117.45	42.2t	$112.74	34.1t	$87.29
Continuous	76.8t	69.86	76.7t	69.76	62.3t	54.45

[a] High, moderate, and low are Topo classes 2, 3, and 4, respectively.
[b] Total expected yield over 26 years in tonnes (t).
Source: Rennie and de Jong (1989)

Studies also show that chemical fallow and reduced and zero tillage are costly because chemicals are expensive. With only a few exceptions, these alternatives are not profitable compared to existing, more erosive practices, even over the long term. This is also true for rotations with chemical fallow as opposed to tillage fallow. Strip cropping, shelter belts, and so on are discussed by some observers, but these are not widely used in many areas; subsidies are often required to get farmers to adopt these conservation practices, but they have been abandoned as soon as there is an upward surge in crop prices. If no other feasible conservation practices are forthcoming, as appears to be the case for much of western Canada's grain belt, then the opportunity or on-farm costs of soil erosion are quite low. Why this should be the case can be seen with the aid of Figure 10.2.

A biological relationship between yield and topsoil depth is illustrated

Figure 10.2

Yield-topsoil depth relation

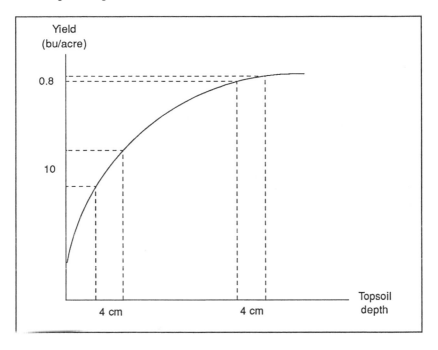

in Figure 10.2. The positive intercept on the yield axis indicates that it may be possible to achieve some crop growth even if topsoil depth is zero, because some plants are able to grow in subsoil, albeit not very well. This is an empirical issue, and the arguments presented here do not change if the yield-soil depth function passes through the origin. The degree of growth, if any, differs among soil types, location, and the type of plant. More important, as topsoil depth increases, the increase in yield from additional topsoil declines – the 'law of diminishing returns.' The reason is that, once the depth of topsoil exceeds the rooting zone, additional topsoil is not required for crop growth. The yield-topsoil depth relation drawn in Figure 10.2 also indicates that there is a limit to the amount of yield that can be attained, and the functional form demonstrates this by the fact that yield reaches an asymptote.

At higher levels of topsoil depth, the curve is flat, indicating that a rather substantial decrease in topsoil (say 4 cm) will not have a large impact on yields (a 0.8 bu/ac reduction) – the marginal product of topsoil depth is very small. When topsoil is relatively abundant, as it is on much *non-marginal* land, the value of the marginal product of soil is practically zero. At lower levels of topsoil depth, the yield-depth relationship is steep. In this case, a 4 cm reduction in available soil depth will result in a substantial yield loss (a 10 bu/ac reduction); the marginal product of soil depth is high.

Figure 10.2 can also be used to clarify what is meant by the marginal user cost of soil erosion (see appendix to this chapter). As a field is cultivated, the farmer notices that production slides down the yield-topsoil depth curve. Additional losses of soil entail greater yield losses – the marginal user cost of soil erosion rises. As production slides further down the curve to the left, and marginal user cost increases, the farmer's incentive to practise conservation on that field rises. The losses become sufficiently large to warrant expenditures in order to prevent them. As long as farmers are in the flat portion of the yield-topsoil depth function, they have little incentive to incur expenditures in order to prevent soil loss; but, when production occurs in the lower ranges of the relationship, the benefits of soil conservation increase. This explains why economists, for example, have found that farmers are unwilling to employ chemical fallow when topsoil depths are adequate, but that they would adopt this soil conserving method when topsoil depths decline to a much lower level. It appears that farmers do behave rationally; the evidence indicates that, for many prairie farmers, topsoil depths are currently at a level at which the marginal user costs of soil erosion are insufficient to warrant adoption of soil conservation practices.

Soil Erosion, Depletion of Soil Nutrients, and Technical Change
Some argue that the cost of soil erosion can be measured by the increased cost of fertilizer required to replace lost soil fertility, but this may be incorrect from an economic theory standpoint. The problem is complex. In order to discuss this, it is important to distinguish two factors related to soil: (1) the depth of soil needed to accommodate the roots of plants, and (2) the quality of soil, which refers to its natural fertility (in situ nitrogen and other nutrients) and its tilth (e.g., organic matter content). Depletion of replaceable soil nutrients concerns loss of organic matter and natural soil fertility, while soil erosion concerns soil depth. It is possible to destroy soil quality while maintaining adequate topsoil depth, but it would likely be difficult to maintain soil quality while losing soil. These concepts were discussed in Chapter 2, and one must not confuse them.

We observe that farmers tend to use more fertilizer on fields that have greater rooting zone capability (depth). That is, agricultural producers will expend more inputs and effort (time) on 'better' quality fields. Economic theory suggests that, as the marginal product of topsoil depth rises due to a loss of soil, the amount of fertilizer (and other inputs) used by a rational agricultural producer also declines, ceteris paribus. Assume that all factor prices (r_i, where subscript i denotes the type of input) and output price (P) remain constant, and that marginal product falls as input use increases. Consider the following well-known equilibrium condition:

$$\frac{P \, MP_{\text{soil depth}}}{r_{\text{soil depth}}} = \frac{P \, MP_{\text{fertilizer}}}{r_{\text{fertilizer}}}, \tag{10.1}$$

where MP_i refers to the marginal physical product of input i. A loss of soil depth implies an increase in its marginal physical product. Then, assuming that the marginal product of fertilizer is unaffected by the amount of soil depth available,[2] only a reduction in fertilizer use will increase its marginal product and, thereby, maintain equality in (10.1).

The situation is somewhat different if we consider soil quality, as represented by the amount of fertilizer available in the soil. In that case, the shadow price of soil fertility is given by $P \, MP_{\text{fertilizer}}$ – the value of the marginal product (VMP) of fertilizer. In the framework of (10.1), as natural soil fertility is depleted, the marginal product of fertilizer increases (because marginal product falls as input use rises). It is then necessary to increase the amount of applied fertilizer in order to get its marginal physical productivity back down and restore equilibrium in (10.1) (i.e., get back on the expansion path).

Only if the marginal product of fertilizer is affected by changes in topsoil depth can changes in fertilizer applications be used to provide information about the costs of soil erosion. However, in this situation, measurement is complex, and it is certainly not true that all of the increase in fertilizer costs can be attributed solely to the reduction in topsoil depth. Furthermore, if topsoil depth falls, thereby increasing the marginal productivity of soil, result (10.1) suggests that, rather than fertilizer applications increasing, they should be reduced. This makes sense, since farmers are more likely to apply greater amounts of fertilizer on more productive (deeper) soils. Once again, the effects of changes in the availability of one input on the marginal product of another complicates this conclusion. These notions are expanded upon in the following discussion.

Residual versus Reparable Yield Damage and Welfare Effects

In the previous section, it was assumed that the marginal physical product of fertilizer was unaffected by topsoil depth – that fertilizer and soil depth are independent. In such a case, farmers would not respond to changes in topsoil depth, except to reduce fertilizer use, as is indicated above. However, for other aspects of the soil, farmers might well respond to reductions in soil quality by increasing their expenditures on inputs. This is illustrated in Figure 10.3, where soil quality rather than topsoil depth is represented on the abscissa. Y_0 represents the yield

Figure 10.3

Residual and reparable soil damage

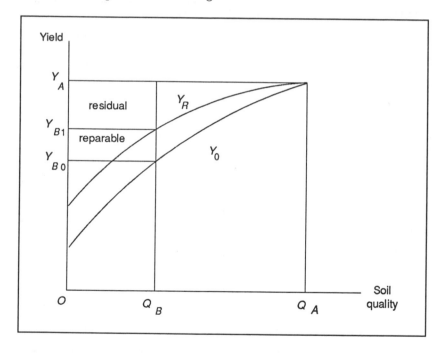

function, given constant input use (input use is unaffected by soil quality), and Y_R represents the restored yield curve (inputs from off-site replace in situ resources). Suppose that soil quality declines from Q_A to Q_B as a result of agronomic practices that degrade the soil, whether such practices are avoidable or not. Yields will decline from Y_A to Y_{B0}, which represents the total yield damage due to soil degradation, given that farm practices and/or input use do not change in response to the decline in soil quality. An amount $Y_{B1} - Y_{B0}$ of the lost yield can be recovered by changing farming practices and/or input use. This is the *reparable* yield damage and is equivalent to the revolving fund component of the soil (Chapter 2). (For example, as long as there is adequate topsoil, even losses in organic matter can be overcome by one or two years of 'green manure' – growing a crop that is then ploughed under.) This leaves the amount $Y_A - Y_{B1}$ that represents the *residual* yield damage. The residual yield damage is equivalent to either the conservable flow component of the soil (if it is worthwhile preventing soil degradation) or the expendable surplus component (if it is not worthwhile to prevent degradation).

Figure 10.4

Welfare effects of reduced soil quality on fertilizer use

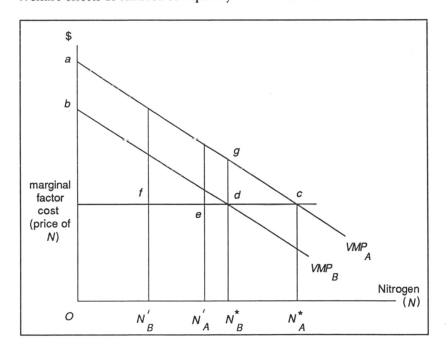

With regard to the welfare effects, these can be seen with the aid of Figure 10.4. Suppose that the component of soil quality of interest is nitrogen (N). Let VMP_A and VMP_B represent the values of the marginal products of N at soil qualities Q_A and Q_B, respectively. Let N_i^* and N_i' represent, respectively, the optimal amount of nitrogen required in production and the amount of nitrogen available in the soil prior to seeding for soil qualities $i (= A$ or $B)$. The difference between the optimal and available amounts of N can be made up by using artificial or inorganic fertilizers.

The net welfare effects of lost production due to a decline in soil quality from Q_A to Q_B can be found by determining welfare at Q_A and subtracting that at Q_B:

Welfare at Q_A: $W_A = \text{area}(OacN_A{}^* - N_A'yecN_A{}^*)$,

welfare at Q_B: $W_B = \text{area}(ObdN_B{}^* - N_B'fdN_B{}^*)$,

and $W_A - W_B = \text{area}(acdb + N_B'feN_A' - N_B{}^*dcN_A{}^*)$.

This is the net residual yield damage caused by a decline in soil productivity and is also equal to $P(Y_A - Y_{B0}) = VMP_A - VMP_{B0}$ (from Figure 10.3), where P is the value or price of output. It is difficult to show the welfare effect associated with the reparable damage via Figure 10.4, because this assumes that inorganic fertilizer use remains at $(N_A{}^* - N_A')$, not that the optimal amount of fertilizer use is $N_A{}^*$. However, the marginal welfare cost is given by $P(Y_{B1} - Y_{B0}) = VMP_{B1} - VMP_{B0}$.

The change in welfare between the two situations depends upon how much nitrogen is in situ in the soil under Q_A versus Q_B. Further, whether or not input use of inorganic fertilizer will rise or fall depends on the size of $(N_A{}^* - N_A')$ relative to $(N_B{}^* - N_B')$. If $(N_A{}^* - N_A') = (N_B{}^* - N_B')$ or $(N_A{}^* - N_B{}^*) = (N_A' - N_B')$, then the welfare loss is given by area $(acdb)$.

Economic Assessment of Erosion Damage with Technological Advance

Agricultural yields have increased in spite of soil erosion, and this persuades some farmers that erosion damage is insignificant and that there is little need to adopt soil conserving agronomic practices. Technology has boosted absolute crop yields in spite of declines in topsoil depth. However, the yield loss due to soil erosion – the loss farmers should be using in their conservation decisions – is the difference between the potential yields they could have if they had used conservation techniques and actual yields. This argument is illustrated in Figure 10.5.

In the figure, farmers are, initially, assumed to be on production function Y_0, producing at A. The function Y_1 represents the production function at some time in the future. Technical change enables the farmer to produce more wheat, say, for every level of topsoil depth. The way in which the two functions are drawn indicates that technical change provides a greater yield benefit on fields with more topsoil. As a result of soil erosion, from topsoil depth SD_0 to SD_1, the farmer finds that yields have declined from 58 bu/ac (point A) to 53 bu/ac (point B'), or by 5 bu/ac. The conclusion that one draws is that erosion damage has been partly offset by technical change. However, this conclusion is wrong *unless all technical change is induced by concern over erosion* – that is, that technical change is endogenous. However, if this is not the case, if technical change is exogenous, the correct comparison is between points A' (70 bu/ac) and B' (53 bu/ac), or 17 bu/ac. This is the correct measure of the erosion yield damage. With exogenous technical change, it is inappropriate to conclude that technical progress partly offsets erosion damage.

Figure 10.5

Erosion assessment damage with technical change

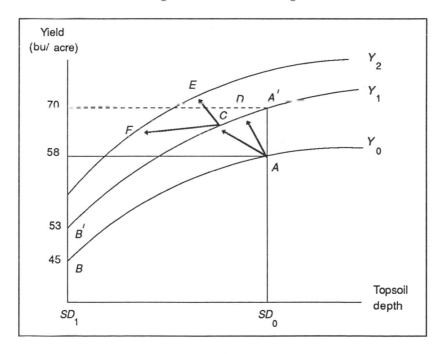

Farmers and policymakers can be lulled into a false belief that technical progress will continue to offset erosion damage. In the early years, agricultural producers will move along path A to C (Figure 10.5) by continuing to use erosive agronomic methods. With conservation practices, they would move along path A to D instead. Technical progress will continue, shifting the production function to Y_2, but continued use of erosive practices at point C will cause a movement along path C to F. In this case, yields decline in spite of technological improvements. Conservation could, however, provide a yield increase, as is indicated by the movement along path C to E.

Technical change that relates to soil erosion can be divided into two categories. (1) Technical change can be exogenous to erosion; in other words, enhancements in production take place independent of soil erosion. (2) On the other hand, induced technical change can take place in order to remedy soil erosion. Exogenous technical change can be divided into (a) land neutral, (b) land complementary, and (c) land substituting technical change.

Let the crop production function be

$$Y = f(SD), \tag{10.2}$$

where Y is crop yield and SD is topsoil depth. Then land neutral or additive technical change results in the production function (10.2) shifting up by the same constant amount for all soil depths, so that it can now be represented by

$$Y = f(SD) + A(t), \tag{10.3}$$

where $A(t)$ represents technical change as a function of time. With land neutral technical change, the true economic damage from soil erosion is no different than it would be if no technical change had occurred at all, but it is still possible for farmers to experience increased yields even though erosion has occurred. An example of land neutral technical change is provided by the introduction of large farm equipment, which allowed producers to farm a larger area.

Land complementary or multiplicative technical change is mathematically illustrated by modifying (10.2) as follows:

$$Y_t = B(t) f(SD), \tag{10.4}$$

where $B(t) > 1.0$ is the technical change factor. An example of land complementary technical change is provided by improvements in crop cultivars. This type of technical progress tends to increase yields for greater topsoil depths. It can be argued that land complementary technical change results in potential costs of erosion that are greater than would have been the case if the technical change had not taken place.

Land-substituting technical change means that there are greater increases in yields at shallower soil depths. An example of this type of technical advance is provided by tillage improvements that conserve soil moisture. It can be argued that land-substituting technical change actually decreases the potential costs of soil erosion.

The economic assessment of erosion damage, given the presence of erosion-induced technical change, is quite different from that encountered in any of the other categories. In this case, damage assessment should be based on yield with conservation and unchanged technology versus yield with erosion and induced technology. Therefore, the induced technology actually offsets some of the costs of soil erosion.

With this overview of technical change and its impacts upon the economic assessment of erosion, it is necessary to consider the following questions: What type of technical change has been most prevalent in agriculture? Is technical change different in its impact on crop yields and erosion damages in different regions of the world? The vast majority of technical change in North America, and likely elsewhere in the world, has been exogenous with respect to topsoil depth, since breeding to prevent lodging, improvements in inorganic fertilizers, and research into new cultivars have not been a reaction to eroding soils. Furthermore, it appears that the vast majority of the research in North America has been land complementary or multiplicative, which is not inconsistent with fundamental agronomic principles. Plant breeding research, among other objectives, strives to develop cultivars with greater genetic potential for converting available plant nutrients and moisture to harvestable grain. This, in itself, is not proof that technical change has been multiplicative, but empirical evidence does support this conclusion. A survey of 272 farmers in the Palouse region of southeastern Washington and northwestern Idaho indicated that they expected future yield increases on deeper soils to be three times those expected on shallower topsoils.

The previous discussion certainly indicates that the economic assessment of erosion damage is complex. Failure to heed the impact of technical change, confusion regarding the production function from which the yield costs are measured, and/or failure to take into proper account opportunity cost will undoubtedly lead to inaccurate estimates of the true costs of soil erosion.

Soil Conservation: Economic Research

Soil research can be divided into four categories: (1) short-run farm budget simulation, (2) analyses of farm business characteristics and farmer conservation decisions, (3) analyses of tenure characteristics, and (4) intertemporal modelling. The short-run farm budget simulation technique usually employs linear programming or farm management models that typically simulate various management strategies in order to determine the costs and benefits of soil conserving systems. These models are limited in that they compare cropping strategies that are fixed over time. In such models, cropping decisions are not responsive to changes in the biophysical state of the system. In these models, determining an optimal cropping strategy in order to balance concerns about profitability, risk, and soil conservation requires an exhaustive search of all possible cropping regimes.

The second category of research is useful because it sheds light on key variables that affect farmers' conservation decisions. This research is characterized by statistical analyses that prove or disprove various hypotheses. In fact, if done at specific time intervals in a farmer's planning horizon, these analyses could show how a farmer's attitude towards soil conservation changes over time.

Analysis of land tenure characteristics is interesting because it shows the contrast between the individual who owns his or her land and the individual who rents it. From a theoretical standpoint, one would expect the owner to exhibit better stewardship than would the land renter, because the owner may benefit from conserving soil through increased land values when he or she sells the land at some future date. However, these effects can be mitigated against if efficient tenure contracts are written.

Finally, intertemporal modelling of soil conservation decisions over time can be accomplished in two ways. (1) An intertemporal model may be just an extension of a short-run, farm budget simulator that is linked to run for successive years; or (2) optimal control methods can be used in order to determine the privately optimal path of soil depletion or optimal cropping strategy to employ in each period of time as a function of prices and the biophysical conditions of the agronomic system. Optimal control methods have the advantage that they are forward-looking; such techniques take into account the effect of current decisions upon the future state of the agronomic system. For example, a dynamic programming approach can be used to determine optimal cropping strategies when farmers are faced with uncertainty about the future state of the system and the effect that current agronomic decisions have upon it and upon net returns. The state of the system is described by such things as topsoil depth, soil moisture, weed infestation, and disease (e.g., crown rot).

The major problem with many dynamic optimizing models of soil erosion is that they assume that agricultural producers are able to directly control the amount of erosion on their fields. Of course, this is not the case, as soil erosion is a natural and uncertain phenomenon. What farmers can control are agronomic practices – the crops they grow, the types of tillage practices used (conventional, minimum, or zero tillage), contouring ploughing, construction of shelterbelts, and so on. Farm management models are now available that permit the economist to study the effects of cropping practices over time and to choose those practices leading to minimum rates of soil erosion, while, at the same time, permitting farmers to earn a livelihood. Complicated models in this genre can be constructed using advanced mathematical programming packages such as GAMS (General Algebraic Modeling System), which was developed by the World Bank for such purposes. The complexity of the models depends upon the number of states used to describe the system, the number of decisions, whether or not there is uncertainty and whether or not producer risk is then taken into account, whether the objective function and/or the constraints are linear or non-linear, whether or not more than one objective is to be optimized, and so on. The intertemporal approach has many advantages over the other approaches, since the impacts of soil erosion on productivity accumulate over time, and, therefore, current decisions affect decisions in later years. Intertemporal models are realistic because farmers make investment decisions with a definite planning horizon in mind; in addition, intertemporal models are used to relate information about farm tenure and land characteristics.

An examination of soil erosion time paths using field-level data for a sample of farmers in Saskatchewan indicated that a wheat-tillage fallow rotation would completely erode about 40 cm of topsoil in 93-190 years, depending on whether a high or low rate of erosion is assumed. The length of time required to erode the soil is substantially reduced if, rather than the erosive two-year, wheat-fallow rotation, cropping decisions are based on a flexcrop strategy derived from a dynamic optimizing model (plant wheat, if available spring soil moisture is above some critical level, otherwise plant fallow). The results for various prices, discount rates, and rates of soil erosion are provided in Table 10.2. They indicate that the application of a simple, advanced management technique can substantially improve the sustainability of soils.

Table 10.2. Erosion under flexcrop strategies in southern Saskatchewan

Item	Scenario							
Price ($/bu)	2.50	2.50	2.50	2.50	4.50	4.50	4.50	4.50
Discount rate (%)	0	5.0	0	5.0	0	5.0	0	5.0
Erosion rate	low	low	high	high	low	low	high	high
Years required to erode 36 cm of topsoil	285	269	157	135	373	362	195	185

Source: Weisensel (1988)

Advanced management techniques, such as those underlying flexcropping, can also be used to encourage cropping practices that are environmentally sound. This occurs where other crops or cropping practices and other agricultural activities, such as livestock production, are included in the array of possible decisions. It can be demonstrated that conservation benefits can be achieved while maintaining economic viability.

Construction of optimal and dynamic farm management models requires data that are generally not collected by scientists. It is clear that research is required both in terms of data gathering and demonstrating the usefulness of this approach to policymakers and agricultural extension agents. However, research indicates that the use of advanced farm management techniques offers an alternative approach to preventing soil degradation and moves in the right direction, namely, towards a sustainable agriculture.

Is Land Degradation a Problem?
Now consider the question: Is agricultural land degradation a problem sufficient enough to demand government intervention? To answer this question, we consider the on-farm and off-farm costs of soil degradation.

On-Site Costs
From an economic perspective, the on-farm costs of soil erosion in Canada (the main form of soil degradation) have been blown out of proportion, perhaps even to the point where policymakers are considering action that can only be considered detrimental to the farm community. Other forms of soil degradation, such as loss of organic matter and salinity, are related to soil erosion, because the factors that contribute to the latter (viz., monoculture and tillage summerfallow) also contribute to other forms of degradation. To some extent, each of these forms of degradation is reversible, with the degree of reversibility

decreasing from organic matter to salinity to soil erosion. Loss of natural soil fertility is also related to organic matter, salinity, and soil erosion, but artificial fertilizers can be brought from off-site in order to alleviate this problem and green manure can be used to restore lost organic matter.

The economics of soil degradation have been characterized by inadequate empirical evidence and/or improper economic reasoning. As already noted, one study of on-farm costs of soil erosion on the Canadian Prairies suggests that these are approximately $468 million per year, while another indicates that the costs to farmers of soil degradation in Saskatchewan alone are even higher – about $1 billion annually. The latter figure constitutes an incredible 30 per cent of average total cash receipts from crop production in that province and exceeds average net farm income for that period by 17 per cent! Other estimates are also unbelievably large. The reason has to do with poor economic analysis, namely, failing to focus on the true economic or opportunity costs of soil erosion.

In the September 1989 issue of *Scientific American*, Pierre Crosson and Nathan Rosenberg write:

> The U.S. is the only country in the world that has *reasonably* accurate and comprehensive estimates of soil erosion and its effect on productivity. Those estimates suggest that if current rates of cropland erosion prevail *for 100 years*, crop yields will be from 3 to 10 percent lower than they would be otherwise. Yield increases (resulting from technology) that are modest by historical standards would much more than compensate for such a loss ... Estimates of erosion have been made for other parts of the world ... [but] these evaluations have little scientific merit ... Apocalyptic scenarios ought to be evaluated sceptically. (p. 128)

The point is: While soil degradation may very well be a serious environmental and economic problem, the severity of the problem cannot be justified on the basis of supposedly large on-farm costs. A correct valuation of on-site costs indicates that they are small and are taken into account by farmers in making production decisions.

Off-Site Costs

Soil erosion from exposed land and dried lake beds, and run-off from forest and agricultural land is a non-point source of pollution. Its costs are not adequately taken into account by farmers in making agronomic decisions, and, therefore, inefficiency in resource use results. While government intervention is often advocated when there is an externality (e.g., subsidies or penalties), such intervention could lead to greater inefficiency unless the benefits of the action are known. However, measurement of the external costs or damages of water and wind erosion, and, thus, the benefits of policies to prevent it, is a difficult task. Research on off-farm costs gives some indication of their magnitude.

In general, two approaches have been used. The *hedonic pricing approach* relies upon differences in property values to determine the costs imposed by soil erosion. The *cognitive survey technique* uses questionnaires to elicit the monetary values that individuals place on the damages that they perceive. Money is used as a measure of welfare gains and losses. The impacts of the externality are measured so that the benefits of averting damage can also be measured. One technique for quantifying the benefits is the willingness-to-pay measure (WTP), while another is the willingness-to-accept (WTA) compensation (Chapter 7).

The total annual cost of *wind erosion* to residents of New Mexico was estimated to be $U.S. 465.82 million in 1984. Of this total, 98.2 per cent was incurred by households, 1.6 per cent was assigned to businesses, and the remainder was ascribed to the government sector. Damages per resident are slightly less than $U.S. one dollar per day. A Canadian study estimated the damages to society of wind-borne dust from the exposed lakebed caused by lowering the Upper Arrow Lake Reservoir in the interior of BC by more than 80 feet to be no more than $2 million per year. On a per resident basis, the damages may be as large as $200 per year; this estimate is less than that for New Mexico, because there are differences in severity of dust storms. The damages estimated in the BC study could not justify the capital construction required to prevent them.

Now consider *water erosion* from agricultural lands. One estimate indicates that the overall annual off-site costs of water erosion to the U.S. are $U.S. 6.1 billion, or about $U.S. 245 per resident. Another study examined the costs of water erosion as they pertain to treatment of surface water only. An increase in costs from sedimentation was found to average about $U.S. 3.83 per person per year. The study also found that a 25 per cent decline in upstream soil erosion would reduce annual treatment costs in Ohio by $U.S. 2.7 million annually. Thus, these communities should be willing to pay $U.S. 2.7 million per year to avoid excess sedimentation in their surface water.

Estimates of the off-site costs of soil erosion under conventional and conservation tillage practices in southern Ontario have also been made. Conservation tillage techniques were found to reduce soil erosion and, therefore, to raise sport fish stocks and lower the cost of water treatment and water conveyance. The total annual benefits resulting from the elimination of excess sedimentation from lakes and streams in southern Ontario for various fish species was $35 million. Conservative tillage practices also reduced surface water treatment costs by $10.2 million per year. In addition, the removal cost of sediment from municipal drains and provincial roads in Ontario was determined to cost taxpayers about $15.2 million annually. Thus, the annual damages from water erosion of soil in southern Ontario amount to about $7.50 per resident. The difference between the large U.S. estimates and the small estimates for Ontario arises because the Ontario study considered only the benefits (damages avoided) from using conservation tillage, while the U.S. study focused on total externality costs.

Estimates of the external costs of soil erosion in other parts of Canada have not been made. An estimate of the off-farm or external costs of soil erosion on the Prairies can be found as follows. Based on the foregoing discussion, external costs of soil erosion of $200 per person per year are likely an upper estimate of such values. Assuming 4.5 million residents, an upper estimate of the total annual external costs of soil erosion on the Prairies is $9 million per annum. Even if the actual total is one-quarter of this amount, the damages are large, indicating that the off-site or social costs of soil degradation are important – not the on-farm damages.

Other sources of land degradation have already been alluded to. Soil salinity is often included in estimates of soil degradation, as is loss of organic matter and natural or in situ fertility. While these are important, they are not likely to result in large economic losses (as was noted earlier). A more significant source of degradation occurs as the result of land conversion, either from an unimproved to an improved state or from cropland to urban use. The focus here is on the former. Loss of wetlands and associated uplands, native range, tree cover, and so on has an impact on ecosystems that is valued for its ability to assimilate farm pollution, provide scenic amenities, produce wildlife, and so on. These values are often external to the farm enterprise and constitute a real cost to society. Except for attempts to value ducks and other species that are hunted, no attempt has been made to measure these losses.

In a public policy document on soil erosion, the Canadian Agricultural Economics and Farm Management Society indicated that the on-farm costs of soil erosion are probably not a threat compared to the off-site costs, and it argued for greater focus on, and measurement of, the external costs of soil erosion. The position paper did not stress the losses mentioned in the previous paragraph, although it did indicate an awareness of these lost amenity values. When one compares Canadian and U.S. agricultural policy, it is clear that American programs are concerned about the external or environmental costs of farming activities, not the on-farm costs. Canadian programs, on the other hand, are focused on the on-farm costs because scientists have argued that these costs are enormous. This subtle difference in focus carries with it an important policy implication. As will be seen in Chapter 12, Canadian policy is driven by a desire to appeal to farmers, while U.S. policy is focused on taxpayers. Unless the underlying focus of Canadian agricultural policy with respect to the environment changes, soil degradation is likely to continue unabated.

Discussion

While soils in temperate climates are highly buffered and not in imminent danger of being depleted, there is physical and economic evidence to suggest that current rates of soil erosion are greater than are socially desirable. If farmers experience economic losses due to on-farm damages resulting from soil erosion, there is little justification for public intervention in order to prevent such losses. However, if there is a concomitant desire by society to protect the productive potential of the land for future generations, it could be argued that agricultural land is a public good, in which case government intervention to prevent erosion on private lands may be justifiable. But the idea of land as a public good is questionable, and, even if land can be considered a public good, government intervention may not be justified, because, in the past, such intervention has worsened rather than alleviated soil degradation.

It appears that off-site as opposed to on-site damages constitute the more significant problem. Public intervention in order to prevent soil erosion, via direct subsidies, regulation, or other means, is best justified on the basis of its externality effects – the costs imposed on the nonagricultural sectors of the economy. It is probably true that off-site damages are correlated with on-site damages, so that reducing erosion on the most erosive lands will also yield on-farm benefits in the form of increased future production capability, although this need not be the case. The point is that government farm policies to ameliorate the adverse environmental consequences of agricultural activities can best be justified on the basis of a reduction in the externality costs or off-site damages caused by soil erosion.

To argue that government intervention is required in order to prevent farmers from injuring themselves is insufficient justification for such intervention. Political acceptability of this argument will be difficult to obtain, and programs that are designed on the basis of this presupposition will probably not achieve the desired results (in terms of reducing erosion and protecting the environment). On the other hand, if a public role is justified on the basis of the external costs of agricultural land degradation, political acceptability by the nonagricultural sector will be easier to achieve. Only then might it be possible to commit the funds and effort (in terms of institutions and personnel) to achieve environmental objectives. This issue will be discussed further in Chapter 12 in conjunction with public control over private land-use decisions in agriculture.

The remaining problem is that of determining what policies are appropriate for reducing soil erosion. Given that society does not want to penalize farmers and prefers to subsidize production for reasons that have little to do with economic efficiency and everything to do with income redistribution, the only politically feasible courses of action are to redefine present government programs or to design new programs around reward systems. New programs would include, for example, compensating farmers for employing conservation practices (viz., conservation easements and leases) or taking land out of production and putting it into some type of conservation reserve. Politically feasible programs would be voluntary and, to reduce program costs, farmers would be required to bid on options in order to participate. The other approach to reducing land degradation is to tie subsidies to certain conservation practices; farmers are required to comply with certain regulations in order to remain eligible for farm program payments. Conservation or cross compliance takes the form of sodbuster and swampbuster provisions and registered farm conservation management plans, as will be seen in Chapter 12. Evidence from the U.S. suggests that conservation compliance is acceptable to both taxpayers and farmers alike. This evidence also indicates that greater efforts in farm management and extension will be required in order to implement conservation plans.

Finally, experience in other countries indicates that simply spending monies on preventing soil erosion is not, in itself, sufficient to ameliorate the problem. It is necessary to identify and target those lands that are not only the most erosive but are also those that will provide the greatest reduction in damages (as opposed to lost soil) per dollar of expenditure. This requires a much greater interdisciplinary research effort than has been the case in Canada in the past.

Perhaps the most sensible approach to the problem of land degradation is one that is based on the experience of agricultural producers. Sharon Butala, who lives in the southern Canadian grain belt (where early explorers had recommended against crop production) offers the following solution to land degradation in that region.

> Surely it would make more sense, in view of all the problems involved in farming the dryland prairie, to invest that annual billion dollars or more [in government subsidies] in turning ... farms back into the grassland from which they came – not every farm in the Prairie provinces, by any means, but many if not most in the Palliser Triangle and elsewhere in the Prairies where farming has always been marginal. Instead of fighting a losing battle for markets, instead of risking topsoil and environment ... it might be better to move out the farmers and close off these areas of marginal land ... to farming entirely. Perhaps it is finally time to admit that ... the settling of farmers on the dry, southern plains was an experiment that failed. Much of that land, in a slow and gradual process, might be turned into a national park ... Where soil and weather conditions make it feasible – parts of central Alberta, Saskatchewan, and southern Manitoba – sustainable agriculture geared to producing six million tonnes of wheat could be encouraged ... The vast expanses of regenerated prairie grassland, with rejuvenated wildlife stocks, could be successfully marketed internationally as a last-of-its-kind tourist attraction. (1990:38-9)

The issues discussed here are explored further in chapters 12 and 13.

Appendix: A Mathematical Model of Soil Erosion

Assume a farmer maximizes his/her net discounted revenues over time, cognizant of the fact that current soil erosion will reduce future yields. The dynamic optimization problem is written as

$$\underset{\{u_t\}}{Max} \ \sum_{t=0}^{T-1} \beta^t \left[p \cdot f(D_t, u_t) - c(u_t)\right] + \beta^T V(D_T),$$

subject to

$$D_{t+1} = D_t + M - g(D_t, u_t)$$

$$D_t, M \geq 0 \qquad 0 \leq u_t \leq 1$$

where: D_t is topsoil depth at time t;

u_t is the cropping intensity, with $u = 0$ indicating tillage fallow and $u = 1$ being the most intense, least erosive cropping practice;

p is output (crop) price;

$f(\cdot)$ is the crop production function or yield;

$c(\cdot)$ is the production cost function;

$V(D_T)$ is the value of land at the end of the planning horizon as a function of topsoil remaining at time T;

M is naturally occurring additions to topsoil (or tolerable loss);

$g(\cdot)$ is the rate of soil loss as a function of cropping intensity; and

$\beta = \dfrac{1}{1+r}$, where r is the discount rate.

The discrete time, current value Hamiltonian is (see Conrad and Clark 1987:33):

$$H(D_t, u_t, \lambda_{t+1}) = pf(D_t, u_t) - c(u_t) + \beta \lambda_{t+1}[M - g(D_t, u_t)].$$

Necessary requirements for a maximum are:

$$\frac{\partial H}{\partial u_t} = 0, \quad \beta \lambda_{t+1} - \lambda_t = -\frac{\partial H}{\partial D_t}, \quad D_{t+1} + D_t = \frac{\partial H}{\partial (\beta \lambda_{t+1})}, \quad \lambda_T = \frac{dV}{dD_T}, \quad \text{and } D_0 = \bar{D},$$

where $\bar{D}$ is topsoil depth at the beginning of the time horizon. Thus, the first-order conditions are:

$$p\frac{\partial f}{\partial u_t} - \frac{dc}{du_t} = \beta \lambda_{t+1} \frac{\partial g}{\partial u_t}, \tag{A.1}$$

$$\beta \lambda_{t+1} - \lambda_t = \beta \lambda_{t+1} \frac{\partial g}{\partial D_t} - p\frac{\partial f}{\partial D_t}, \tag{A.2}$$

$$D_{t+1} - D_t = M - g(D_t, u_t), \tag{A.3}$$

$$\lambda_T = \frac{\partial V}{\partial D_T} \quad and \quad D_0 = \bar{D}. \qquad (A.4)$$

In condition (A.1), the left-hand side (LHS) term is the profit to be gained in this period from allowing soil to erode from employing cropping intensity u; this is the marginal benefit of soil erosion. The RHS is the marginal cost of soil erosion, which consists of the shadow price of soil in the next period discounted to the current period $(\beta\lambda_{t+1})$ multiplied by the amount of soil that is lost when cropping strategy u_t is employed. The value $\beta\lambda_{t+1}$ reflects the effect that an incremental loss in D_t will have over the remainder of the planning horizon $(t + 1, ..., T)$ and is referred to as user cost.

The LHS of (A.2) gives the current value of the change in the shadow value of soil (marginal user cost). As soil erodes, the marginal user cost falls, so that the LHS of (A.2) is always less than or equal to zero. The reason for this is that, as soil becomes more eroded, further erosion has a declining (negative) effect on the objective function. As soil depth gets lower, *rates* of soil loss increase (i.e., $\frac{\partial g}{\partial D_t} < 0$). The value of the marginal product of soil depth $(p\frac{\partial f}{\partial D_t})$ is always positive. Both sides of (A.2) are negative, as required.

Condition (A.3) provides the biophysical dynamics of the soil system as a function of human activity (cropping intensity), while (A.4) gives the transversality (starting and end-point) conditions. In particular, the farmer takes into account the potential sale value of the farm at the end of the planning horizon in making current decisions. Finally, it is clear from (A.3) that, in a steady state, the rate of soil loss should equal natural regeneration $(g(\cdot)=M)$.

Part Four:
Economics of Land-Use Planning and Control

Introduction to Part Four

Government intervention in private decisions regarding land use is accepted by most citizens. However, it is important to determine both why public intervention is required and why intervention may be desirable. Economics is interested in determining efficiency and equity aspects of public policy in land use and the efficacy of institutions that are developed to exercise society's control over land use. In this section, these issues are addressed by examining the regulation of urban land use (Chapter 11), social control over and preservation of rural land (Chapter 12), and the role of water in agriculture (Chapter 13). The latter belongs in a section on the economics of land-use planning, because, without government subsidies and other economic signals, land use would be quite different.

In Chapter 11, the focus is on methods for analyzing land use in urban areas; land-use planning and social control over private land-use decisions are discussed. The effect that zoning has on land use and, more importantly, on efficiency and equity are investigated from an economics perspective. Because of its income redistributional effects, zoning is not a panacea for land-use planning, and alternative approaches that incorporate zoning within them are available to planners. Finally, transportation and urban land use are examined in Chapter 11.

In Chapter 12, the economics of preservation and conservation of agricultural land is considered. Preservation of agricultural land is also a concern of sustainable development, as is discussed in Chapter 8. Here, the concern is with public policy to preserve land and the institutions that have evolved for preserving agricultural land; that is, Chapter 12 is concerned with public control over land-use decisions in agriculture. Further, government agricultural programs and their impact on land use are discussed. Such programs have encouraged farmers to cultivate lands that would serve as habitat for wildlife, that might otherwise have been left in native pasture, or that are particularly susceptible to degradation (e.g., soil erosion). In return for payouts from government agricultural programs, farmers should be required to comply with certain environmental standards. Cross compliance is required in the United States but not in Canada. In Chapter 12, the issue of conservation or environmental compliance is also examined.

In Chapter 13, we look at a particular resource, namely, water. While much has been written about the arid western United States and its need for water, our concern is with interbasin water transfers and the sale of water between nations (viz., large-scale water diversion). The main topics in this chapter relate to the irrigation and destruction of wetlands in western Canada. While the use of cost-benefit analysis in water resource development was considered in Chapter 5, here the focus is on the extent to which irrigation has expanded, despite the fact that its economic feasibility is questionable. Also included in Chapter 13 is an examination of wetlands preservation in the pothole region of the prairie grain belt. The problem with maintaining wetlands on private agricultural land relates to social control over private land use and the role of government agricultural programs in the destruction of waterfowl habitat.

11
Efficiency and Equity in Land-Use Planning

Land-use planning and control are increasingly employed by governments in order to direct land development in ways that are considered socially desirable. For example, a land control and development commission controls all decisions regarding land use in the state of Oregon. In British Columbia, land-use control is exercised through the Agricultural Land Reserve (ALR), which was established as an attempt to preserve agricultural lands by freezing development on lands in the reserve. Both these examples indicate how social control over private land use is expanding. The question that one has to address is: what enables the state to exercise control over land that is considered to be private property? That is, are property rights inviolable?

British common law has never given anyone exclusive right to acquire, use, and dispose of property. In feudal England, no person, except the king (and, later, the state), owned the absolute right to property. In biblical Israel, all land was held as a trust from God, and property could only be leased to others, returning to the original owners or stewards in the fiftieth year, the year of Jubilee. Further, in Israel, the poor had a right to some of the produce of the land; they had a right to 'glean' the fields behind the harvesters. Early American settlements followed this biblical tradition in their own land-use planning.

With the age of individualism, there arose the view that property rights were inviolable. Since the 1770s and up to the mid-1960s, the U.S. courts considered property rights to be absolute. Since the mid-1960s, however, this attitude has changed, primarily because it has come into conflict with human rights. Externality in the acquisition, use, and disposition of property are the major reasons for social control over the use of private property; the social costs and benefits of land use are not the same as are the private costs and benefits. *Eminent domain* or *takings* illustrates the social limitations upon the private rights of ownership: eminent domain permits the government to take private property for public use but only if just compensation is provided. Not only does eminent domain apply to land, it also applies to any takings from individuals (e.g., taxes to pay for public welfare programs). While there are many ingenious arguments for taking things from individuals, political philosophers question whether or not many government actions justified under the 'takings' clause in the U.S. Constitution are, indeed, constitutional. Nonetheless, today there are many public institutions that regulate and exercise control over the use of land. Control is exercised either by direct regulation or through an incentive structure, such as taxes and subsidies, or through some combination of these. Takings are considered further later in this chapter and in Chapter 17.

Zoning is the oldest and most easily recognized form of planning. It was used as a means of separating activities of adjacent but dissimilar firms and households that imposed externalities upon each other. In general, zoning and land-use planning have been separated in both legislation and administration, although this is unfortunate, since they are not separate functions. We will examine zoning as a method of land use control and planning later in this chapter.

Land markets have been profoundly influenced by the impacts of public programs and policies, not just policies related to land use itself. Since they have a historic root, they have created land-use patterns that may not be desirable by today's standards. For example, urban sprawl caused by government policies in North America that favoured low-priced energy, ownership of single detached homes, and the consumption of open space may no longer be desirable because of their impacts upon land use. Sometimes public land-use planning is required to counteract the effects of other public programs and policies and to rationalize land-use conflicts arising therefrom. However, *simply demonstrating inefficiency in land utilization resulting from reliance on a market mechanism is insufficient justification for planning – for government intervention*. Planning must also lead to efficient land use.

A major problem with land use planning is that there are always conflicts among various interest groups. These groups include: (1) developers, speculators, builders, and lenders, who wish to maintain their present control over land use; (2) the coalition of environmental groups; and (3) groups interested simply in preserving the size and/or quality of their neighbourhoods or towns. Given such diverse groups, the goals of land-use planning agencies tend to be rather vague. For example, one could find the following goal statements for many public agencies that exercise control over private land uses: (1) to manage and control urban growth and confine it to the most suitable lands; (2) to control population distribution; (3) to preserve open space and scenic landscapes; (4) to lower pollution levels; (5) to preserve agricultural land, especially prime agricultural land; (6) to protect critical natural areas such as wetlands; (7) to provide decent, safe housing at affordable prices; (8) to provide more rational transportation systems; and (9) to provide an adequate economic base and employment opportunities. Goal statements are purposely vague, and very few would be opposed to any of the aforementioned goals. Indeed, the goals are much like 'motherhood and apple pie.' They are purposely vague in order to minimize conflict and, thereby, gain acceptance with interest groups.

It is important to distinguish between a *goal* and an *objective*. Everyone will agree with the goal of lowering pollution levels; but when one considers the objective of reducing pollution levels by one half, there will definitely be disagreement. The same is true when one considers the goal of providing more rational transportation systems. To one group this might mean providing a new freeway through a certain area. To another group it means providing greater and easier access to public transportation facilities, including, perhaps, the construction of light rapid rail systems. Obviously, the goal itself creates no conflict; but once the goal is stated as an objective, conflicts will arise.

Cost-benefit analysis is the major tool used in evaluating water resource development projects (Chapter 5). In the future, cost-benefit analysis will, increasingly, be the main tool for evaluating land-use developments. One of the problems with B-C analysis is that of determining benefits. While the costs of land-use planning are generally easy to identify, the same is not true of the benefits. The costs of land-use planning are (1) the costs of organizing, implementing, and administering land-use controls and (2) the social costs associated with restricting land use. For example, if land is zoned open space, its value will go down. This loss in value is a measure of the opportunity cost of using land for, say, housing. However, there remains one problem with this second cost: Does the market price of land exceed its social value or not? Land prices are generally higher than is suggested by productivity in agriculture. Perhaps this is because land serves other social functions, for example, as a hedge against inflation, as collateral on loans, and/or as an outlet for speculation. In addition, particularly in agriculture, government subsidies, tax incentives, and so on frequently become capitalized in land values.

What, then, are some benefits of land-use planning?

(1) A number of goals of land-use planning are environmental in nature. There are many studies suggesting methods of measuring benefits of environmental improvement. Further, environmental impact coefficients have been added to input-output models to assess environmental impacts associated with various economic activities.

(2) Outdoor recreational benefits are also tied to land-use issues. These include such things as hunting, hiking, camping, and scenic amenities.

(3) Benefits are also associated with population distribution. Some studies have looked at economies of scale in the provision of public services, while others have examined preferences regarding optimal town size.

(4) Preserving agricultural land is a benefit of land-use control, but little work has been done with respect to measuring these kinds of benefits.

What criteria are to be used to evaluate alternative land-use controls? One can consider a set of criteria that includes the following: (1) effectiveness in achieving planned objectives, (2) the effects on the distribution of costs and benefits, (3) the organizational and administrative costs, (4) political and legal acceptability, (5) the effects on the provision of other public services (e.g., financing), and (6) whether the controls are direct or indirect. Information-gathering costs under indirect controls tend to be higher for individuals than is the case under direct controls. This will be examined in greater detail below. However, it is important to note that *safe minimum standards* are best achieved by direct controls such as zoning. Therefore, we examine zoning in greater detail.

Before turning to zoning, we consider how land-use planning proceeds. In this regard, it is useful to distinguish between an informational model of planning and a blueprint model. The differences between the two models are illustrated in Figure 11.1. The informational model relies on a cybernetic or feedback approach to planning. As a result of uncertainty, the incremental approach to planning (as illustrated by the informational model) would be most appropriate for development planning. The incremental approach is often associated with Charles

Lindblom's concept of *muddling through*. Zoning appears to be representative of the blueprint model as opposed to the informational model. However, whether or not land-use planning has achieved its objectives is still a matter of conjecture.

Figure 11.1

Land-use planning models

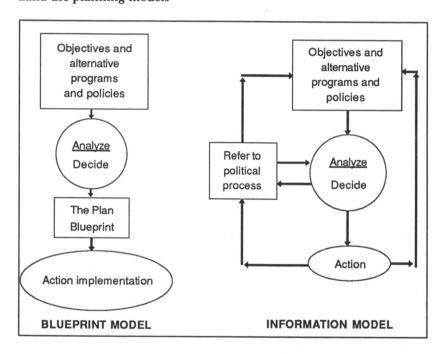

BLUEPRINT MODEL   **INFORMATION MODEL**

Direct Land-Use Control: Zoning

Land-use planning tends to rely on direct government controls, and zoning is the most common type of control available. A second type of direct control is the urban service boundary. The urban service boundary is designed to control urban sprawl, because the cost of providing public services, such as sewage, gas, electricity, and transportation escalates rapidly with urban sprawl. This method is designed to confine growth by increasing population density. The location of the urban service boundary can be modified through *appeals* and *variances* that tend to favour those who have better access to the political process. Finally, agricultural land reserves that are designed to preserve agricultural land are a form of direct control over land use.

Similar criticism arises with regard to zoning. First, zoning is considered to be ineffective. Critics tend to point to Houston as an unzoned city that developed land-use patterns that are no different from those found in zoned cities, particularly Dallas. (This is not a fair comparison, however, because Houston did employ other forms of direct land-use control). Second, the costs of zoning are borne by certain groups (e.g., the poor), while zoning is often aimed explicitly at protecting and promoting the value of private property – it has little to do with the social plan. Third, zoning is negative in that it only specifies what cannot be done. Finally, like the urban service boundary and agricultural land reserves, zoning is open to appeals and variances that favour larger and wealthier property owners.

When economists consider land-use planning and land-use issues, they look at three components. They consider (1) efficiency, which usually dominates their thinking, (2) equity, and (3) political acceptability. The latter is a very important but often neglected component, although each of these issues has an influence on land-use decisions. We will examine each in turn as it relates to zoning.

Efficiency

Efficiency is associated with externality, and, as was seen in Chapter 4, there are three types of externality that are of concern here: technological externality that is also Pareto relevant, public goods externality, and technical externality.

The objective of land-use planning is to eliminate or at least reduce Pareto-relevant externalities. The idea is to keep different land uses separate. Thus, some of the first zoning laws were passed in colonial Boston in order to keep polluting leather manufacturers out of residential areas. But, zoning is not an efficient way of eliminating this type of externality. Why? First of all, it is not always necessary that commercial enterprises be separated from residential zones. For example, a portrait painter may not create an externality. Further, land-use controls provide no incentive for reducing externality. Zoning does not, in and of itself, provide the needed incentives to eliminate or reduce noise, smoke, flashing signs, and so on. If the objective is to reduce traffic, zoning may be used to prevent commercial activities that are considered to result in increased traffic, but there is no incentive to get one's neighbour to reduce his or her driving.

In this regard, *performance standards* are a better alternative than is zoning. They are more flexible, provide an incentive to reduce the externality, and directly focus on the objectionable behaviour. For example, it may be desirable to zone an area in such a way that movement of heavy tr··cks is restricted to ten per day, say, or air or noise pollution is reduced to some maximum permissible level. Residential areas are no longer zoned according to criteria such as number of dwellings per lot but by the number of flashing signs, vehicle trips per day, and so on. Thus, a portrait painter may fit in, but a business requiring a large sign (whether it flashes or not) may be objectionable. There is no zoning according to heavy, light, and so on, but there are incentives to increase efficiency. The major problem with performance standards is that enforcement may be difficult, if not impossible.

Public Goods Externality: Preservation of Agricultural Land and Open Space

Two reasons are often cited for preventing the development of farm land. Each of these reasons has an element of public good to it. The first is the argument that prime agricultural land must be preserved for future food needs, while the second is open space. With regard to prime agricultural land, the idea that we should maintain an agricultural production potential has some properties of a public good. Sometimes, however, this argument is used by those who are really advocating more open space. Perhaps the prime agricultural land argument is not one of public good but, rather, one of option demand: society wants to keep land in agriculture so that its products will be available in the future, in the event that they are needed to feed future citizens. Should that be done? Private goods are certainly not valued by including their option demand as an additional consideration, outside their market price. Indeed, although individuals may be willing to pay some small amount to keep Cadillacs around just in case they may wish to purchase one in the future, this option is already built into the price of Cadillacs on the used-car market. Likewise, the future option on prime agricultural land may already be built into the price of land.

Empirical evidence suggests that the value of land as determined by its marginal productivity is often less than its current market value. People buy land, suffer low returns initially, but feel that returns will increase when agricultural output is worth more. Society is probably already exercising the option of preserving agricultural land; this is reflected in its high price compared to low productivity. Hence, it is questionable whether this is truly a public good argument. Preservation of agricultural land is discussed further in Chapter 12.

Open space is a public good because non-exclusion exists. One person's viewing does not exclude another person's viewing; one person's enjoyment does not exclude another person's enjoyment. However, it also has an element of a private good. Residents located around or near the green area have a more pronounced interest in the meadow, as is reflected in their property values, than do those travelling on the road through the meadow. The problem with public goods is that, if public goods are provided via zoning, the individuals who gain do not always bear the costs. The beneficiaries often overstate the value of such goods and often make no sacrifice, except through participation in the political process. Sometimes those who bear the cost and do not gain will fight back, but the tendency is otherwise. Zoning protects open spaces, but it is not clear that optimal levels of these goods are provided. The problem is that zoning does not get individuals to reveal their true willingness to pay or their true preference for open space.

As an example, suppose a hayfield can be turned into a shopping centre. What yardstick is required to measure one alternative, open space, against the other, the shopping centre? The alternatives available are: (1) we can let the government buy the hayfield and place an ad valorem tax on the property of nearby residences in order to get those who benefit the most to pay towards the purchase of the hayfield; or (2) perhaps nearby property-owners can be made to pay some of the cost, with the government paying the remainder, since some of the benefits accrue to others. By getting individuals to pay some of the costs, it is hoped that they will better evaluate the true worth of open spaces.

Regardless of whether preservation of prime agricultural land or simply need for open space is used as an argument, some form of public investment is necessary in order to have public goods of this nature provided. Land-use control is one method of providing such public goods.

Technical Externality or Public-Service Costs
It is expensive to provide people with police and fire protection, transportation services, sewer, water, electricity, and so on. A denser settlement pattern will economize on the costs of providing public services. The question is: What kind of economies of scale are present in the provision of public services? This question hinges on another question: What is the optimal size of a city? Studies indicate that optimal city size is somewhere between 50,000 and 150,000 residents, and this consti-

tutes an argument against aggregating smaller cities or entities into bigger ones.

The opposite could also occur. In one of Canada's less-densely populated provinces, Saskatchewan, each rural municipality has its own government. Since the population of many rural municipalities is very small, it would be better to aggregate their functions, thereby reducing the costs of many services. (Of course, not all of the costs are borne by the residents themselves, but certainly they constitute costs to the rest of society.) While rural municipalities have formed larger units in order to construct such things as recreational and medical facilities, considerable inefficiency remains in the way most services are provided, both because ad hoc committees are not as workable as single, all-encompassing entities and because the remaining functions are handled at the rural municipality level (e.g., clearing roads of snow in winter).

Zoning is a tool that can be used to get people to crowd together and, thus, to provide a denser population. Some people will, nonetheless, continue to want to live on acreages; but if we truly believe in consumer sovereignty, we should also make these people bear the full additional costs of providing public services such as school buses, fire protection, and construction and maintenance of roads. Marginal-cost pricing should apply to those who wish to live in the rural areas surrounding cities. They should be made to pay the added or marginal cost of providing the services they require. Even so, some of the fixed costs will inevitably be borne by society as a whole.

Equity

One problem with zoning is that it results in its own demise because it sets up incentives that lead to changes in the overall or ultimate plan. The reason is that zoning results in changes in the value of land. Consider Figure 11.2. Prior to zoning, all of the acres in the diagram are assumed to be valued at $2,000/ac. After the zoning ordinance has been passed, land values in the area zoned nondevelopmental are $500/ac, whereas those in the commercial zone are now $10,000/ac. Now suppose that commercial interests are having trouble finding appropriate land in the area zoned commercial. They purchase 100 ac of land in the area that is zoned nondevelopmental, as is indicated by the shaded area. The purchase cost for the 100 ac is $50,000. Now the developer has a vested interest in getting the zoning regulation or ordinance changed in his or her favour. The developer will be willing to pay some amount in what is termed *rent-seeking activity* in order to change the ordinance so as to permit commercial development on the 100 ac in question. If the zoning ordinance is changed, the land will be worth $1 million (100 ac x $10,000/ac). Given that the developer paid $50,000 for land, the difference of $950,000 is the amount that could be gained through the rent-seeking activity. The developer will gain, if it costs him/her some amount in lawyer's fees, bribes, and so on, less than $950,000 to change the law. It is obvious, therefore, that zoning provides incentives to change the zoning laws.

Figure 11.2

Impact of zoning on land values

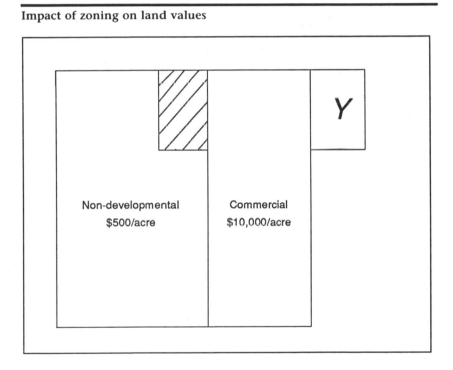

The second problem with zoning can also be illustrated here. In most cities, zoning jurisdiction comes from the municipal government. Zoning is circumvented simply by moving outside the zoned area or outside the urban service boundary, say to the area marked with *Y* in Figure 11.2. This, then, provides a major argument for land-use control at the provincial, state, or national level, depending on the size of the appropriate entity.

Figure 11.2 illustrates yet another problem with zoning, and this also has to do with equity. Zoning results in *windfalls* for some and *wipeouts* for others. Consider what happens to the land that is zoned in the foregoing example. Those in the commercially zoned area experience a windfall of $8,000/ac. They did nothing to earn this windfall – they were simply fortunate in terms of the location of their land. However, those in the other zone experience a wipeout of $1,500/ac. Obviously, issues of equity are involved. There have been two attempts to get around the problem of equity; namely, *zoning by eminent domain* (ZED) and *transferable development rights* (TDRs). We consider each of these in turn.

Zoning by Eminent Domain

The idea behind zoning by eminent domain is that windfalls should be taxed in such a way that wipeouts are covered. A capital gains tax attempts to do this by taxing gains and crediting losses. To some extent, taxing windfalls and compensating wipeouts lessens the incentives to change the ultimate plan. This can be seen with reference to our earlier example. If the zoning ordinance is changed, then a tax of $950,000 could be levied on the commercial developer who obtained the variance to the zoning ordinance described in Figure 11.2. This will reduce the developer's incentive to change the zoning ordinance; indeed, it reduces the incentive so that developers would base their appeals solely on site suitability. Although the idea of *windfall-for-wipeout compensation* is appealing, the chance that actual windfalls will balance wipeouts is remote.

Under zoning by eminent domain, the responsible authority designates different areas for residential, commercial, and industrial purposes. To guard against windfalls and, particularly, wipeouts, eminent domain procedures are employed. In essence, the zoning authority transfers the development rights from one set of landowners to another and enforces payment using procedures of eminent domain. The property that becomes more valuable as a result of the zoning ordinance is specifically assessed to recapture the incremental gain resulting from public action; those properties must pay for the associated development rights. The collection of windfalls is then used to compensate those experiencing wipeouts. ZED effectively entails public purchase and sale of development rights.

There are three problems associated with zoning by eminent domain. We consider each of these in turn.

(1) *Identification of windfalls and wipeouts*. Only those changes in land values resulting from zoning are to be treated. All other changes in value

due to individual or private market actions can be ignored. To separate the two types of changes is very difficult in practice.

A zoning ordinance produces both a direct effect and an indirect effect. A *direct effect* occurs when there are changes in use intensity on land that result in changes in the value of that land. An *indirect effect* takes place when the value of land is affected by changes in zoning regulations that apply to some other piece of land. For example, when preserving a farm as open space, it not only lowers the farmer's property values but increases the value of adjacent residential property. The direct effect is the actual lowering of the farmland value, while the indirect effect is the raising of adjacent residential property values. Direct effects are generally easier to identify than are indirect effects. Furthermore, losers will aid the authority in identifying their wipeouts, but gainers will not be as willing to assist in the identification of their windfalls.

(2) *Measurement of changes in the value of affected land.* The problem of measuring changes in the value of land affected by a zoning ordinance can be illustrated with the aid of Figure 11.3. Suppose that land is rezoned from use B to more restrictive use A. If the land value in use A at time $T_2 (= A_2)$ is compared with the land value in use B at time $T_1 (= B_1)$, then no compensation is indicated, which is obviously not true – our measure indicates that there is no loss of value in this case. Failure to account for the factors that cause the price of land to rise over time, such as the real rate of return on land in uses A and B as well as inflation, can cause problems. Now assume that the land is rezoned from use A to less restrictive use B. How does the time-lag in assessment affect the calculation of windfall recapture? Under full recapture, the owner would be assessed $B_2 - A_1$, when the true windfall is $B_1 - A_1$ at T_1 or $B_2 - A_2$ at T_2. In cases where land values are rising for both uses, the time-lag in assessment will understate wipeout compensation and overstate windfall recapture. As a result, both parties are unhappy.

What about assessing both parties at time T_2? Suppose the zoning change from B to A is significant in terms of its impact on future land values. Without rezoning, the time path of land values for B is given by the solid line; but with the zoning ordinance at T_1, it shifts to the dashed line. Then land assessments for use B rise to B_3 rather than to B_2. It is obvious that $B_3 - A_2$ may overstate the desired level of wipeout compensation for those zoned from use B to use A, since the correct compensation is $B_2 - A_2$ if measured at T_2.

(3) *Financial solvency.* It may well be that windfalls exceed wipeouts as a result of zoning; indeed, if zoning is to increase economic effi-

ciency, this should be the case. But measurement and transaction costs may prevent this. Hence, financial solvency of any windfall-for-wipeout plan may be in jeopardy, even if windfalls exceed wipeouts.

Figure 11.3

Measuring changes in land value due to zoning ordinance

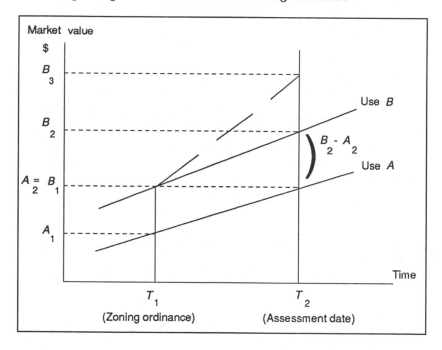

When to recapture windfalls is also related to financial solvency. Most ZED plans call for immediate recapture of windfalls and immediate compensation for wipeouts. However, owners of the land do not experience either until they sell their property. Setting up a tax and compensation scheme in such a way that the recapture or compensation occurs when the land is sold results in an incentive for the losers to sell their land as soon as possible and for the gainers to wait. This, then, places a financial burden on the system.

Transferable Development Rights

There are two basic property rights – the right to sell and the right to develop or improve a property. A system of transferable development rights attempts to separate the rights of development from the property right to sell. Unlike ZED, this separation does not subsequently vest the right to develop with the state; rather, it resides with private individuals. How can we take development rights away so as to ensure equity in zoning? How does a system of TDRs work?

Consider Figure 11.4. The previously unzoned area in the diagram has now been zoned into four areas. Those four zones are I - pure agriculture, II - single-family dwellings, III - multiple-family dwellings, and IV - commercial. Development increases from least developed to most developed in going from zone I to zone IV. Those in area IV experience windfalls, while those in area I experience wipeouts. Now assume that, initially, each piece of property has the same price and development potential. Each owner of land, regardless of what zone he or she falls in, is now assigned development rights based on the amount of land he/she owns. In order to develop a piece of property, an owner needs development rights. The TDR system is designed so that no one person in areas III and IV has enough development rights to develop their property to the limit permitted by the zoning regulation. A person in area IV may own 100 ac but only have enough rights to develop 35 ac. If the person's property is of value once it is developed, he or she will

Figure 11.4

Zoning of previously unzoned land: The case for TDRs

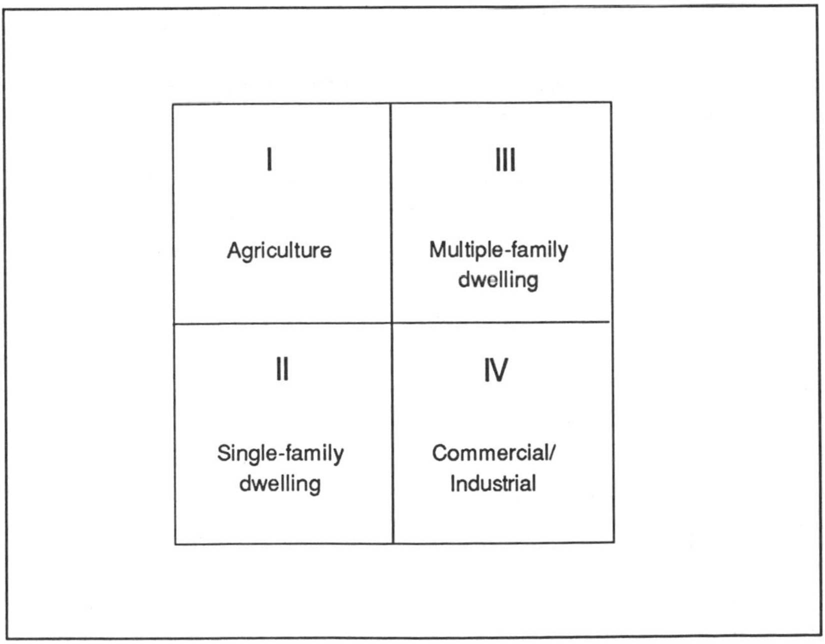

I	III
Agriculture	Multiple-family dwelling
II	IV
Single-family dwelling	Commercial/ Industrial

seek more development rights in order to allow him- or herself to develop that property. Where will those development rights come from? Those in area I will have development rights but will be unable to use them because their property is zoned to prevent development. Thus, individuals in area I are willing to sell their development rights to those in area IV, because the development rights are useless to them. It is in this way that a system of TDRs reduces windfalls and wipeouts that are associated with public policies regarding land use.

Consider Figure 11.5. In the region represented in the figure, land is either zoned for urban use (different types of urban land use are ignored) or as open space. The value of a unit of land in urban use is P_U (panel (b)), while land in open space is worth P_0 (panel (a)); obviously, $P_U > P_0$. Now the authority decides to re-zone some of the land designated urban use to open space. This is shown by a reduction in the supply of urban land from U_0 to U_1 in panel (b) and an equivalent increase in the supply of land for open space from L_0 to L_1. The price of urban land increases from P_U to P_U' because the demand for urban land is downward-sloping. For simplicity, it is assumed that the price of open space remains constant at P_0; this could be thought of as the agricultural value of the land. Landowners affected by the zoning ordinance – those whose land was zoned from urban use to open space – experience a reduction in the value of property (a wipeout). They will argue that the amount of the wipeout is equal to the difference between the current value of land and its value in open space (i.e., $P_U' - P_0$) or area $A + B$ in panel (a). However, the correct measure of the wipeout is given by area A only, or the difference between the pre-zoning ordinance value of urban land and its use in open space (P_U minus P_0).

The remaining owners of urban land are also affected by the zoning ordinance, albeit in an indirect fashion, because the value of their land has increased. They receive a windfall equal to area $P_U'abP_U$ in panel (b). If development rights are provided to those who are zoned open space, so that the remaining urban landowners cannot develop their land without the purchase of development rights, the windfall gain will be reduced or eliminated. If there exists a market for development rights (panel (c)), then developers of urban land will substitute structure for land. The demand for urban land is reduced, as is represented by the shift in demand from D_u to D_u'. As a result, the windfall area is reduced to the shaded area in panel (b). In fact, windfalls could be completely eliminated if the demand for urban land should shift far enough to the left. The final price of land will depend upon the density that is permitted and upon the number of structures allowed per unit of land. Indeed, we can even have wipeout for wipeout compensation if D_u shifts far enough down as a result of restrictive residential density limits. The compensation that is provided to those experiencing a wipeout is given by area E in panel (c).

Figure 11.5

Rezoning and use of TDRs

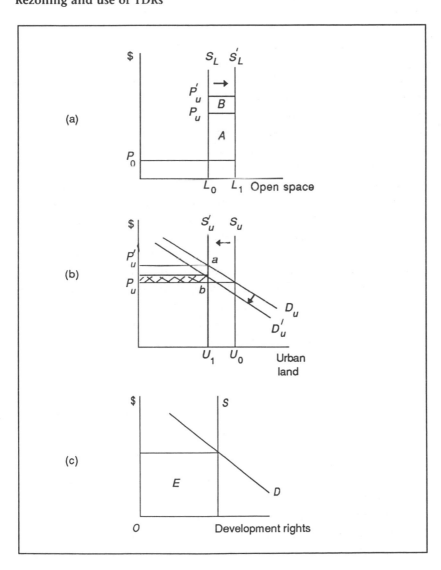

A system of transferable development rights is, of course, sensitive to the number of development rights that are issued. Issuing too many development rights negates their purpose. Perhaps it is a better strategy to issue too few development rights initially and, once the price reaches a particular level, to issue more in order to prevent the price from going higher. Problems associated with the issuance of development rights also have repercussions on the political acceptability of a TDR system.

Further, there is the issue of the conversion factor between TDRs and development. For example, one TDR might be worth X square feet of single-dwelling space, Y square feet of multiple-dwelling space and Z square feet of commercial space. The government can use the conversion factor to fine-tune the market; for example, the conversion factor can be reduced if there are too many development rights in the market. The problem is that changes in the conversion factor result in uncertainty, which, in turn, reduces political acceptability.

The final issue regarding transferable development rights concerns the basis for distributing them. We can examine this by considering the example in Table 11.1. There we have three one-acre plots of land, each with an agricultural value of $500. Their actual market or current values are assumed to be $600, $900, and $1,500, respectively. Assume that the authority issues thirty development rights, each valued at $50. Now we can consider four different mechanisms for distributing development rights to the owners.

(1) *Distribute development rights according to the number of acres that are owned.* The problem with this mechanism is that it does not reflect either the physical or the economic potential of the land. Thus, 100 acres of swamp would receive just as many development rights as would 100 acres of prime agricultural land located next to an already thriving commercial area, despite the fact that this land is now zoned open space. In terms of our example, each of the three owners would receive ten development rights. Thus, each is compensated to the tune of $500. As is indicated in row 4 of Table 11.1, the compensated value of land is $1,000. This consists of the $500 value in agricultural land plus $500 in development rights. Obviously, this system is unfair to the third owner, as he/she is only compensated $1,000, whereas the market value of that land prior to zoning was $1,500. Both owners 1 and 2 are overcompensated.

(2) *Development rights could be distributed according to the physical potential of the land.* Scientists can determine the development potential and

Table 11.1. Wipeout compensation under alternative mechanisms
for allocating TDRs

Item	Owner of 1-acre plot		
	1	2	3
(1) Current value ($/ac)	600	900	1,500
(2) Agricultural value ($/ac)	500	500	500
Compensation according to acres owned			
(3) Number of TDRs	10	10	10
(4) Compensation* ($)	1,000	1,000	1,000
Compensation according to land value			
(5) Number of TDRs	6	9	15
(6) Compensation* ($)	800	950	1,250
Compensation according to opportunity cost			
(7) Number of TDRs	2	8	20
(8) Compensation* ($)	600	900	1,500

*Each TDR is worth $50. Compensation is determined Row 2 plus the value of
the TDRs.

distribute development rights accordingly. The problem is that this
leaves out economic factors. Land suitable for development may be
uneconomic for any other activity. For example, steep hills may be
suitable for multiple-unit housing but certainly not for agriculture. Thus,
this criterion for distributing development rights simply misses the
mark.

(3) *Development rights could be allocated according to land value.* This case
is illustrated in rows 5 and 6 of Table 11.1. The distribution of development rights in this case is based on the current value of land. Owners
1, 2, and 3 would be given 6, 9, and 15 development rights, respectively.
The value of the development rights that the individuals are given is
determined by multiplying this number (row 5) by $50, the value of one
development right. When that value is added to the agricultural value
of the land ($500/ac, as is found in row 6), we notice that owners 1 and
2 are overcompensated, while owner 3 remains undercompensated by
$250. As with the first mechanism, this system is unfair to individual

3, while individuals 1 and 2 would support it. Again, distributing development rights according to land values misses the mark, because it is changes in land values in which we are interested.

(4) *Distributing development rights according to opportunity cost for loss of value.* This implies that development rights be distributed on the basis of the difference between current land (market) value and agricultural value. Owners 1, 2, and 3 would receive 2, 8, and 20 development rights, respectively. The value of those development rights is determined by multiplying the numbers in row 7 by $50. As can be seen from row 8, the owners are compensated in a way that is equitable, at least in terms of preserving the status quo distribution of income.

Now notice that, in the above example, if the price of development rights exceeded $50, everyone would be overcompensated, and eventual home buyers and those who lease or own commercial property would suffer. They might suffer even more if there were no system of TDRs to mitigate against the adverse distributive effects of zoning. If the price of development rights was less than $50, landowners would be undercompensated.

Let us return to this idea of windfall-for-wipeout compensation. The system of transferable development rights emphasizes the importance of windfall-for-wipeout compensation. However, this should, perhaps, be de-emphasized for the following reasons. First, it is difficult to establish what constitutes a windfall and what constitutes a wipeout – measurement is difficult. Second, in most cases windfalls do not equal wipeouts, although the converse is implied by the expression 'windfall-for-wipeout compensation.' Third, payments made for development rights are not a windfall recapture, as often seems to be implied.

To make these concepts somewhat clearer, consider two examples: (1) Mr. A buys a piece of land. A year later, a highway is built nearby and the value of the land doubles. Mr. B thinks that Mr. A has received a windfall, but A argues that this is not the case. He has researched the growth potential in the area and has spent some effort in recognizing that a highway was needed. It is clear that, in this case, trying to recover windfalls might be a misguided effort. (2) Mr. Jones owns land in a region zoned agriculture only. He feels that the zoning ordinance has wiped him out. Several farms in his area were sold to speculators at high prices in recent years, and his farm has been assessed higher than its agricultural value. However, no one has ever made Jones an offer, since his farm does not have a view. Has he really experienced a wipeout? How is it to be measured if he did, in fact, experience a loss?

Political Acceptability

Public intervention in the private use of land is justified when private land use imposes costs or confers benefits upon others. Such public intervention takes place through instruments such as zoning, regulation of permissable land uses, taxes, subsidies, and so on. The 'takings' clause in the U.S. Constitution requires that compensation be provided whenever the government uses its eminent domain power to restrict land use; Canada does not have a takings clause in its constitution, but provincial laws prevent governments from expropriating property rights without compensation. (Where private land-use activities impose real costs on others, common law provides that compensation be paid to those that are affected, as is discussed in Chapter 4.) If land-use control is accomplished by zoning, at least partial compensation for the loss of valuable property rights may be necessary in order to make land-use control politically acceptable and, indeed, legal.

Even if zoning is a politically acceptable means of exercising social control over land use, problems regarding the distribution of the costs and benefits of land-use control may limit the usefulness of such methods of social control. Part of the problem concerns appeals and variances and the perception, whether based in fact or not, that the system or plan can be tampered with if one is sufficiently rich or well connected. Tradeable development rights are one means of mitigating the adverse income distributional effects of zoning and of providing for some compensation. Unfortunately, development rights have never truly been implemented on a large scale, and eduction may be needed to make this mechanism more appealing. However, a system of tradeable development rights might well become politically attractive for dealing with a number of issues related to public control over land use. One such example, pertaining to public transportation, is discussed in the next section.

Transportation and Urban Land Use

Transportation is a major land use in urban areas; typically, cities in developed countries relinquish one-third or more of their land to motor vehicles for roads and parking lots. In the United States, about 0.6 ha (1.5 ac) of land per capita are paved; if China were to pave land at the same rate, about 64 million ha would be required, which is equivalent to more than 40 per cent of the country's cropland. While land use has been altered by the automobile, there are other costs associated with the private use of motor vehicles as well. Not only are automobiles responsible for much of the ozone and other pollution (including CO_2 emissions) in urban areas (Table 11.2), but the high rate of traffic injuries and fatalities imposes a large social cost on society; there are almost 50,000 fatalities per year in both the U.S. and Europe. Further, private automobiles are an inefficient means of moving people (Table 11.3).

Table 11.2. Pollution emitted from typical work commutes in the United States[a]

Mode	Hydrocarbons	Carbon monoxide	Nitrogen oxides
	(grams per 100 passenger-kilometres)		
Rapid rail	0.2	1	30
Light rail	0.2	2	43
Transit bus	12	189	95
Van pool	22	150	24
Car pool	43	311	43
Auto[b]	130	934	128

[a]based on national average vehicle occupancy rates
[b]based on one occupant per vehicle
Source: Lowe (1990:14)

Attempts to get individuals in North America to choose alternative modes of transportation have been largely unsuccessful. The reason is that the problem of private automobile use and the resulting congestion, traffic accidents, pollution, and adverse impacts on land use have never been seriously addressed. One reason is political: the political will to spend large sums of taxpayer money to construct rapid rail or light rail transit systems and to tax private automobile use in order to take into account its externality effects is lacking. In the past, governments appeared to favour freeway construction, but it is now recognized that this only encourages urban sprawl and, eventually, exacerbates the problems of traffic congestion, pollution, and lost hours due to commuting. As a result of conflict between vested interests (environmental groups, developers, and local residents) and inappropriate institutional structures for dealing with transportation problems (viz., a transportation board with no power over zoning), the political system in many urban areas is deadlocked – politicians are unwilling to make difficult decisions pertaining to transportation. Nothing gets done about resolving transportation issues, even though these affect the living environment of the entire region; urban areas continue to grow in an ad hoc fashion.

Table 11.3. **Number of persons per hour that one metre-width of land can carry, selected travel modes**

Mode	Operating speed* (kilometres per hour)	Persons* (per metre-width of land per hour)
Auto in mixed traffic	15-25	120-220
Auto on highway	60-70	750
Bicycle	10-14	1,500
Bus in mixed traffic	10-15	2,700
Pedestrian	4	3,600
Suburban railway	45	4,000
Bus in separate busway	35-45	5,200
Surface rapid rail	35	9,000

*ranges adjusted to account for vehicle occupancy and road speed conditions in developing countries
Source: Lowe (1989:22)

One of the challenges facing decisionmakers is that of encouraging individuals to adopt other forms of transportation, whether public transportation or alternatives such as bicycles. Evidence from European countries, such as the Netherlands, indicates that a 'carrot-and-stick' approach is needed. One cannot impose penalties on the private use of motor vehicles (e.g., gasoline taxes, high parking rates) without, at the same time, providing alternative modes of transportation that are competitive with private vehicles. In cities such as San Francisco and Vancouver, where house prices fall as one moves farther into the suburbs and commuting distances increase, the burden of penalties falls upon those in the relatively low-income categories, who cannot afford housing close to their jobs in the city. European experience indicates that, since time is a major factor in commuting and is highly valued, penalties must be very high indeed before a commuter chooses to take public transit that increases commuting time.[1] Therefore, it is necessary to employ the stick of high penalties with the carrot of a good public transportation system. In 1988, for example, the Dutch government announced a policy designed to reduce the number of automobiles from the current 5 million to just 3.5 million in 20 years, compared to the forecast number of 8 million. The policy will increase the costs of buying and operating an automobile by about 50 percent, but $5.7 billion per year will be spent on improving public transportation.

Similar comments can be made about the use of bicycles. In many low-income countries, where there is greater reliance on bicycles because motor vehicles are too expensive for many citizens, high rates of traffic fatalities are the result of collisions between bicycles and motor vehicles. Data from cities in developed countries indicate that, unless bicycles can be physically separated from motor vehicles, only a small proportion of daily vehicle trips will be made by this environmentally preferred mode of transport. For example, 50 per cent of daily passenger trips in the city of Groningen in the Netherlands are made by bicycles, compared to 20 per cent for Copenhagen, Denmark. The main reason has to do with the adoption of a pro-bicycle policy designed to separate bicycles from motor vehicular traffic in the former city.

The economic viability of public transportation systems and their being chosen by commuters depends upon a variety of factors that are related to land use. Urban densities and commuting choices are provided in Table 11.4. It is clear that the higher the urban density, the more likely that a commuter will choose public transport. However, public transport must also be available. On the other hand, it is unlikely that rapid rail transit will be a viable option in areas of low-density housing – urban sprawl. Then, in order to make transit viable in the long term, it is necessary to use zoning and other land-use incentives to increase the population density along rail transit corridors and to encourage a denser population that is more tightly bound to the urban centre. It is also necessary to change land-use regulations in order to permit development of office towers and other places of employment close to rapid transit stations. Thus, by exercising its control over land use, the authority can make public transportation more feasible than it currently appears.

Likewise, tools of land-use planning, particularly changes in zoning regulations, can be used to compensate those who may be adversely impacted by the development of transportation corridors in their backyard. Residential areas close to, and impacted by, the rapid rail corridor could be re-zoned to a higher-valued use, thereby providing both compensation to current owners and opportunities to develop land along the corridor for commercial use (i.e., employment). Purchase of transit rights of way can be facilitated by appropriate land-use policies, for example, that enable the owner of the right of way to construct developments that might straddle the future rail line. Even where the owner is not a developer, the land would be more valuable and the owner could receive compensation in addition to that provided under eminent domain procedures.

Table 11.4. **Urban densities and commuting choices, selected cities, 1980**

City	Land-use intensity	Private car	Public transport	Walking and cycling
	(pop. + jobs/ha)	(per cent of workers using)		
Phoenix	13	93	3	3
Perth	15	84	12	4
Washington	21	81	14	5
Sydney	25	65	30	5
Toronto	59	63	31	6
Hamburg	66	44	41	15
Amsterdam	74	58	14	28
Stockholm	85	34	46	20
Munich	91	38	42	20
Vienna	111	40	45	15
Tokyo	171	16	59	25
Hong Kong	403	3	62	35

Source: Newman and Kenworthy (1989)

In the next two chapters, we examine public policies relating to rural land use, particularly to the conflict at the urban/rural fringe, and between agriculture and other rural uses of land. Conflicts on public forestlands are considered in Part Five.

12
Land Preservation and Conservation

Urban residents are becoming increasingly concerned about agricultural land use. In some cases, there is a concern about the loss of agricultural land, because loss of high quality land is perceived to reduce the future capability of the country or the region to feed itself. Preservation of agricultural land in the rural/urban fringe may simply be an argument to justify open space, as is seen by the willingness of some to permit development of golf courses on designated agricultural land. It is not clear that those who are opposed to such developments are opposed because they see golf courses as a loss of agricultural land or because they would like to see the land eventually used for wildlife habitat and not agriculture. (Golf courses are also opposed because they benefit the better-off in society.) The issue of preservation of agricultural land is discussed in greater detail in this chapter, because it deals with government planning of and control over rural land use along the urban fringe.

Urban taxpayers are also becoming increasingly concerned about agricultural practices that degrade the environment. Included in these concerns are soil erosion and loss of wildlife habitat. Soil degradation (i.e., concern over future agricultural potential) was discussed in Chapter 10, while loss of wildlife habitat is considered in Chapter 13. Given the size of agricultural subsidies, taxpayers in the U.S. demand that farmers comply with certain environmental standards in return for government agricultural subsidies. In Canada, specific subsidies to prevent land degradation are pursued. Other policies to prevent land degradation are also under consideration or are actively pursued. In any case, governments are attempting to control the private use of land.

The chapter begins with an examination of agricultural land classification and the urbanization of agricultural land in Canada. Preservation of rural land and economic issues related to land preservation are then discussed. As an example of the effect that government agricultural programs have on land use, we look at Canadian programs in the grain growing region of western Canada, and, finally, we will address means for preserving and conserving agricultural lands, including cross compliance.

Agricultural Land Classification and Urbanization of Land

In this section, two issues related to land use are examined. The first pertains to the classification of land according to its capacity to produce agricultural outputs. This provides an indication of the availability or supply of cropland. Related to this is urban or suburban development of agricultural land. It is reasonable to assume that society would prefer to develop land of low rather than of high agricultural capability. The expansion of urban development onto agricultural land is the second topic to be considered.

The Canada Land Inventory

Rural land is classified according to its productive capability in agriculture, in forestry, and in other uses; land is classified according to its use, based on its physical rather than economic attributes. The Canada Land Inventory (CLI) is a computer-based information and mapping system that identifies, classifies, and records the *current* and *potential* uses of Canadian lands. The joint federal/provincial CLI program was initiated in 1961 under the guidance of the Agricultural Rehabilitation and Development Act. Canada's participation in the World Land Use Commission after the Second World War, along with growing regional economic disparity, poor land stewardship, and increasing land-use conflicts, motivated the creation of the Canada Land Inventory.

The CLI land capability classification and Britain's Land Use Capability Classification are based on the U.S. Department of Agriculture's (USDA) Soil Conservation Service land capability assessment, which incorporates slope angle, climate, flood and erosion risk, and soil properties. USDA used eight classes, each with subclass information. The latter contains 'capability unit' subdivisions to indicate the severity of the subclass limitation. The CLI classification has one less class but more subclasses and includes series for forestry, recreation, and wildlife (ungulates and waterfowl) in addition to agriculture. USDA did not use the method for forestry, recreation, and wildlife.

The potential land-use inventory incorporated in the CLI entails capability assessments for Canada's habitable areas. Classification series do not consider current use, other use capabilities, or *economic factors*. The respective assessments are represented in ratings ranging from class 1, the 'best' for the particular use, to class 7, or no capability for that use. Assessments are based on limiting factors at the particular land sites. For example, arable land is classified according to the soil's potential and limitations for sustained production of 'common' field crops, using mechanized production. Class 1 has no significant limitations for field crop production, classes 2 and 3 have some limitations, class 4 is marginal land, classes 5 and 6 lands are suitable only for pasture (with improvements to class 5 considered feasible), and class 7 has no agricultural capability. Each class, except class 1, has subclasses indicating limitations and their intensity. These include: adverse climate, poor soil structure or characteristics, erosion, low fertility, inadequate moisture, inundation by streams or lakes, salinity, stoniness, low soil depth, topography, cumulative minor adverse characteristics, and excessive water. Limitations are considered a barrier to improvement, at least without major investments in reclamation. Forestry assessments are based on the land's potential for producing indigenous tree species at full stocking under good management. CLI maps are available at the 1:50,000 scale and are stored on computer at the 1:250,000 scale as part of the Canada Land Data System.

The CLI classification system for *actual* land uses was undertaken in 1963 by the Geographical Branch of the Federal Department of Mines and Technical Surveys and was motivated by (and based on) the World Land Use Commission's World Land Use Survey, which was presented to the 1952 International Geographical Union Congress. This survey was, in turn, based on Britain's 1931 First Land Utilization Survey. The CLI uses ten broad land-use classes: urban; horticulture, poultry and fur operations; orchards and vineyards; cropland, improved pasture, and forage crops; rough grazing and rangeland; productive and unproductive woodland; swamp, marsh, or bog; land that will not support vegetation; and water. British Columbia's Agricultural Land Reserve (see below) designations are based on these classifications.

A distribution of agricultural land capabilities by province is provided in Table 12.1. Although the majority of class 1 or best agricultural land is found in Ontario, Saskatchewan has the largest share of good agricultural land (classes 1-3). A drawback of this land classification scheme is that both economic and climatic factors are ignored. The CLI is based on soils and does not adequately account for climate. Researchers have

Table 12.1. **Distribution of Canada's agricultural lands by CLI agricultural capability class and by province (hectares)***

Province	CLI Class		
	Best land Class 1	Good land Classes 1-3	Arable land Classes 1-5
Nfld.	0 (0)	1,851 (0.0)	109,981 (0.1)
PEI	0 (0)	403,080 (0.8)	528,920 (0.5)
NS	0 (0)	1,149,194 (2.5)	1,655,819 (1.6)
NB	0 (0)	1,311,672 (2.9)	5,044,014 (4.8)
Que.	19,556 (0.4)	2,203,864 (4.8)	6,442,967 (6.1)
Ont.	2,156,752 (52.0)	7,283,237 (16.0)	11,823,186 (11.3)
Man.	162,501 (3.9)	5,133,767 (11.3)	9,851,671 (9.4)
Sask.	999,691 (24.1)	16,298,839 (35.9)	28,928,235 (27.6)
Alta.	786,527 (19.0)	10,728,949 (23.6)	31,101,582 (29.7)
BC	21,057 (0.5)	948,557 (2.1)	9,321,910 (8.9)
CANADA	4,146,084	45,463,010	104,808,285

*Percentages are provided in parentheses and refer to the per cent of the total for Canada as found in the bottom row.
Source: Lands Directorate, Environment Canada, 1982, *Agricultural Land Use Change in Canada: Processes and Consequences*, Land Use in Canada Series No. 21 (Ottawa: Supply and Services), January, p. 4

considered other classification schemes, such as one for climate, in order to obtain better information about the *value* of agricultural production as opposed to only productive capacity. The Agroclimatic Resource Index (ACRI) uses number of frost-free days (concurrent days that temperature is above 0°C) divided by 60 (the growing season is about 60 days at the northern edge of crop production, while it is 180 days in the warmest cropping regions), with the resulting number multiplied by a moisture correction factor.[1] ACRI values greater than 2.0 are found in southern Ontario and Quebec. Examples of ACRI values (weighted by hectares of census farms) are 1.82 for Prince Edward Island, 1.70 for New Brunswick, 2.44 for Ontario, 1.44 for Saskatchewan, 1.50 for Alberta, and 1.35 for B.C.

The Canada Land Use Monitoring Program was initiated in 1977 by the Lands Directorate of Environment Canada to better monitor changing land use in Canada. That system is numerically hierarchical, similar to the Standard Industrial Code for Canadian economic activities. The major classes identified are land cover, land activity, land ownership/tenure, and land quality (land cover and land activity classes were established as of 1981). The specifically defined divisions under these main classes are inventoried using air photo analysis and overlay procedures.

Future changes in land classification can be expected to employ Geographic Information System (GIS) models that enable a larger number of factors to be taken into account in classifying land. GIS has the potential to improve land classification beyond what has been done to date. For example, CLI and ACRI classifications can be combined using GIS methods. Further, *ecoclimatic provinces* have also been used for classifying lands (Chapter 9), and biological scientists speak of *biogeoclimatic zones*.

In Canada, land-use conversion has occurred in two zones. The most obvious is the core zone known as the *urban shadow*. Much concern over rural-to-urban land conversion has centred on the fact that much of the land is of high capability for agriculture and forestry (more than 60 per cent in CLI classes 1 to 3). The second zone is the outer, usually northern, agricultural fringe; this is termed the *agriculture-forest interface*. However, it also includes conversion of unimproved land, such as wetlands and forests, in existing agricultural areas. It is estimated that 8.7 million ha of classes 3 and 4 soils are available in the region lying north of the Canadian Great Plains, with another 3.6 million ha of similarly classified land available in the northern clay belt of Ontario and Quebec and 2 million ha available in the Atlantic provinces. There are also a potential 18 million ha of grazing land available.

Urbanization of Rural Land
As a result of urban growth, agricultural land has been developed for residential, commercial, and industrial purposes. Between 1966 and

1986, land-use change was monitored in Canada's 70 urban-centred regions (UCRs) – each region having a population exceeding 25,000. During this period, 301,440 ha of rural land were developed – an area three times the size of Canada's largest city, Toronto. Approximately 58 per cent of the land that was converted had a high capability for agricultural production (classes 1-3). The trend towards development of rural land with high agricultural capability did not slow down in the period between census years 1981 and 1986.

Urbanization of rural land occurs as a result of urban uses – construction of buildings and urban infrastructure – and the isolation of small areas, which are no longer economically viable, in alternative uses. Between 1981 and 1986, 55,210 ha of land were urbanized. Ontario accounted for the largest loss in rural land, with its 26 UCRs accounting for 37 per cent of converted land; Alberta's 5 UCRs accounted for 25 per cent of converted land, while UCRs in British Columbia and Quebec accounted for 24 per cent. Thirty per cent of the land converted to urban uses between 1981 and 1986 had been productively used in agriculture in 1981, whereas 11 per cent had previously been in agriculture but was already abandoned by 1981 as a result of urban encroachment. Since southern Ontario accounts for about 51 per cent of Canada's class 1 agricultural land, development of agricultural land in that province is important with respect to Canada's future ability to produce agricultural commodities.

Canada's urban regions tend to be located in areas where the productive capacity of land in agriculture is also highest. However, there is the possibility of substituting agricultural land in one region for that in another. For example, if an acre of land is lost to urban development in the Fraser Valley of southwestern British Columbia (or southern Ontario), it may be possible to grow these crops in another region, such as southern Alberta or the Peace River region of BC (or northern Ontario). While substitutability is possible to some extent (e.g., forages and grains grown in the Fraser Valley can be grown in northeastern BC), other crops cannot be grown in those regions (e.g., certain fruits grown in southern Ontario cannot be grown in northern Ontario). The main factor is climate and, thus, the ACRI needs to be used for making the comparison. The loss of agricultural land to urbanization is put into perspective in Table 12.2; in particular, the ability to substitute for land lost to urbanization is noted. Not taken into account is the potential to increase agricultural intensity (e.g., produce more fruit on less land than previously) as less land is available and agricultural output prices rise.

Table 12.2. **Replacement of converted agricultural land with land of similar soil quality and ACRI value of 1.0 by province, 1981-6**

Province	No. of UCRs	Converted Class 1-3 land (ha)	% of total converted land	Provincial ACRI value	Replacement land required (ha)
BC	7	1,244	18.4	1.4	2,514
Alta.	5	6,761	49.6	1.6	10,769
Sask.	4	1,368	61.9	1.4	1,922
Man.	2	1,925	79.2	1.9	3,633
Ont.	26	17,081	82.6	2.4	42,572
Que.	19	3,671	58.6	2.0	8,930
NB	3	373	26.3	1.7	638
NS	2	321	27.6	1.7	545
PEI	1	13	38.2	1.8	23
Nfld.	1	1	0.2	1.2	1
Canada	70	32,758	59.3	-	71,547

Source: Warren, Kerr and Turner (1989)

Table 12.3. **Increase in area, population growth, and rate of conversion of rural land for UCRs, by population class, 1966-86**

Population class	Area increase (%)	Population increase (%)	Rate of land conversion (ha/1,000 pop.)
25,000 - 50,000	16.4	6.2	196
50,001 - 100,000	12.5	5.3	175
100,001 - 250,000	13.4	9.9	101
250,001 - 500,000	14.8	14.2	78
> 500,000	42.9	64.6	50
70 UCRs	41.0	33.0	74

Source: Warren, Kerr, and Turner (1989)

While loss and replacement of productive agricultural land, as is indicated in Table 12.2, provides one indicator of efficiency with respect to urbanization, another indicator is the amount of land converted per 1,000 increase in population. This data is provided in Table 12.3 by population size class for UCRs over a 20-year period. Larger cities convert land more efficiently than do smaller ones. The reason has to do with the cost of housing, which tends to be higher in large, urban areas with high population densities.

If Canada wishes to maintain its productive agricultural land base, development of agricultural land will be one of the issues to be addressed, although it is unlikely to be resolved. Related to this are problems of transportation and population density in urban areas and friction along the urban/rural faultline. For example, ignored in the foregoing analysis is the growing number of dispersed country residential lots and the tracts of farmland that are no longer productive because they are held in an idle state by speculators in anticipation of urban development.

Preservation of Rural Land

The concept of quasi-option value applies to the development of agricultural land as well as to the conversion of unimproved land to cropland. If the current and future returns from the decision to preserve agricultural land (i.e., to continue farming) are uncertain, then, in general, it is not correct to replace the uncertain returns by their expected values in calculating the present value of the decision to preserve the land. By using expected values in calculating the net present value of preserving land, the value of the preservation decision is underestimated. (This value is to be compared with the expected present value of returns from developing the land.) The difference between the value obtained by using expected values and the true value under uncertainty is the quasi-option value – the loss of options that an irreversible decision entails.

As noted in Chapter 8, quasi-option values apply to irreversible decisions. A decision to drain and cultivate a wetland may be irreversible (Chapter 13). Likewise, urban development on agricultural land is irreversible from a practical standpoint, because it would be difficult to remove the urban structures (e.g., buildings, pavement) and convert the land back to agriculture. Of course, there are different degrees of irreversibility. Once a farmer plants his/her field to wheat, the decision is irreversible in the sense that it may be too late in the season to once again cultivate the field and plant canola; but canola can be planted next year. In comparison, cutting down a grove of oaks or filling in a wetland area is a decision that is irreversible. Thus, irreversibility can be considered a change in land use that significantly reduces the choices available for a substantial period into the future.

The reason expected values cannot be employed in the case of uncertainty is that more information about the state of the world becomes available. As time passes, the decisionmaker gets more and better information about the costs and benefits of maintaining the land in its present, reversible state. Thus, if the decisionmaker has to choose between developing land and not developing land, he/she can obtain additional information about present and future returns by delaying development and having some uncertainty resolved. That is, it is important to recognize the problem's decision and information structure through time. In evaluating cropping rotations, for example, information about the effect of last period's climate and cropping decisions on the current state of the system become available. This information can then be used to make better current and future decisions – decisions that yield greater returns. As noted earlier, the conclusion is that the discounted net benefits of development need to exceed the present value of the net benefits of preservation by a 'substantial' amount before development should proceed.

Government intervention to preserve agricultural lands is justified on the grounds that farmland preservation is a public good externality (viz., protection against future uncertainty, maintaining agricultural potential, ecological values, and open space). The amount of farmland preserved will be less than socially desirable if left to private markets. Preservation of farmland usually results in conflict at the urban/rural fringe. Farms located near urban centres are characterized by what is sometimes referred to as the *impermanence syndrome*. This refers to the loss in agricultural productivity that occurs because farm operators in the urban/rural fringe are unwilling to make needed investments (e.g., in buildings and equipment) in order to maintain or enhance productivity. The area affected by the 'syndrome' depends upon distance from the urban centre and government policies regarding agricultural land. In this section, we focus on government policies to preserve agricultural land.

Governments usually employ one of four farmland preservation policies: (1) taxation, (2) right-to-farm legislation, (3) zoning, and (4) acquisition of development rights. It has been shown that various tax policies designed to preserve farmland actually have the opposite effect; they increase the area affected by the impermanence syndrome and provide incentives that encourage urban sprawl. One reason is that the tax policies raise housing prices, encouraging commuters to drive farther in their search for affordable housing.

Right-to-farm legislation is designed to protect farmers against nuisance complaints from nearby residents. Many governments, including most U.S. states and provinces in Canada, have implemented such laws. However, right-to-farm laws fail to preserve farmland because (1) their purpose is not specifically designed to stop farmland conversion, (2) they may not apply to succeeding owners of the land, and (3) they do not protect farmers against nuisance suits brought about as a result of changes in agronomic practices, no matter how insignificant such changes may be.

Agricultural zoning is often considered an effective means of preserving farmland and is used in many countries. British Columbia, for example, has implemented an Agricultural Land Reserve using zoning. Zoning is likely to fail because farmers are discouraged from making investments in their operations in order to raise farm incomes – in other words, impermanence syndrome. Since farming is less profitable as a result and because someone will eventually be willing to pay more for the land for residential use than it is worth in the now less profitable agricultural activity, farmers are encouraged to sell their land (in the smallest parcels permitted by the ordinance). Zoning also leads to public pressure for variances, especially where population growth continues and the authority has not taken steps to increase densities in residential areas. Zoning encourages rent seeking that results in the eventual demise of the regional plan.

Finally, development rights to farmland can be acquired either by instituting a private market for development rights (i.e., a system of TDRs) or public purchase of rights. A system of transferable development rights will not work if rights are allocated to farmers without taking into account distance from the urban centre, because farmers least likely to be affected by development sell their rights, while those nearest urban areas reduce farm investment and hold onto development rights (the impermanence syndrome). While public purchase of development rights provides farmers with money to make investments for increasing agricultural productivity (thereby avoiding the impermanence syndrome), there are several problems with this approach. These are:

(1) The costs of purchasing development rights can be prohibitive.
(2) Conflicts along the urban/rural fringe will continue: farmers will be plagued by vandalism and urban residents will complain about farm noise and smell. Right-to-farm legislation will be required, but the problems associated with such laws remain.
(3) Population pressures will not be alleviated by preserving farmland.

Again, urban residents will eventually purchase the farm as a principle residence, either leasing the land to a bona fide farmer or leaving it in an unused state, thereby encouraging urban sprawl.

(4) Population pressure may also result in the eventual sale of development rights by the government authority that initially purchased those rights.

Some researchers have argued that social purchase of development rights coupled with advanced planning (a blueprint development plan for a region) is the best means for preserving farmland, increasing farm productivity, and eliminating speculative values. However, empirical evidence suggests that there is cause for pessimism concerning farmland preservation. Since 1983, residents of New Jersey have twice voted decisively in favour of preserving farmland; yet 100,000 ac (11.8 per cent of total farmland) have been lost since 1983. The reason is that the relation between the regulatory system and its effects and the decision to leave agriculture is poorly understood by the general public and law-makers. Environmental legislation and zoning ordinances created by local legislative bodies that are not representative of farming interests have had an adverse effect on farmland conversion. It appears, therefore, that preservation of agricultural land will require (1) a change in attitude towards and greater understanding of agricultural activities, (2) greater incentives to expand onto the poorest or least productive agricultural lands, and (3) a recognition that greater urban population densities are needed. In this regard, urban transportation policies are also important, as was discussed in the previous chapter.

British Columbia implemented an Agricultural Land Reserve (ALR) in 1973 in an effort to preserve agricultural land. No compensation was provided to those landowners who may have experienced a wipeout. In some regions, where urban pressure exists, farmers are having a difficult time as technology advances. Not only is it difficult to move equipment between fields, but field sizes are too small to achieve economies of scale in some instances. Conflicts along the urban/rural faultline exacerbate the problem of maintaining viable farming operations. Finally, there is pressure from both farmers and urban citizens to develop the land, either for urban uses or for golf courses. The farmers benefit financially, thereby receiving compensation for their earlier wipeout, and urbanites gain from retention of open space, reduction in farm smells, and recreational opportunities (low green fees).

Although the ALR appears to be preserving agricultural land (e.g., Table 12.2), the process for obtaining variances (i.e., removing property from the ALR) is political. A property-owner can appeal to the Agricultural Land Commission but, failing that, can also appeal directly to the provincial cabinet's Environment Land Use Committee. The latter operates without public hearings and can override any ruling made by the Agricultural Land Commission. Further, members of the commission are appointed by the minister of Agriculture and Fisheries, who is also a member of cabinet. Hence, there is the perception that, if one wields sufficient power, a variance can be obtained. Urban pressures in both the Okanagan and Lower Fraser Valley are likely to result in intense future lobbying to remove lands from the ALR.

Effects of Government Agricultural Programs on Land Use
Government agricultural programs have been in existence since the mid- to late 1800s. Early programs consisted primarily of research and extension (providing advice to farmers), followed by farm credit policies, implicit irrigation subsidies, voluntary soil conservation programs, and, at least in Canada, pooling of grain receipts in order to spread risks. Stabilization programs also evolved to cushion farmers from the vagaries in agricultural prices. Since the Second World War, however, programs increasingly contained production subsidies. These subsidies reached unprecedented levels during the 1980s as a result of conflict between American and European farm programs. In Europe and elsewhere, the primary aim is to prevent the wholesale movement of the rural population to the cities – to keep families on the farm. Unintended adverse effects on land use and the environment are a consequence of agricultural subsidies in all countries that provided them. In this section, agricultural programs in the prairie region of western Canada are examined, although some programs apply to other regions as well. The objective is to demonstrate how the many agricultural programs reinforce each other in their adverse effects on land use and the environment.

In Canada's Census of Agriculture, farmland is classified as either improved or unimproved. Improved land is land that is, or has recently been, cultivated and is either growing crops or is fallow. Unimproved land includes woodland, areas of native pasture or hay land that had not been cultivated, brush pasture, grazing and waste land, sloughs, marsh, rocky land, and so on. Unimproved land provides important breeding grounds for waterfowl as well as habitat for wildlife and forage and shelter for domestic livestock. A plot of the ratio of unimproved land to total farmland in western Canada over the period 1951-86 is provided in Figure 12.1. It is clear that farmers have steadily been bring-

Figure 12.1

Ratio of unimproved to total farmland, western Canada, census years

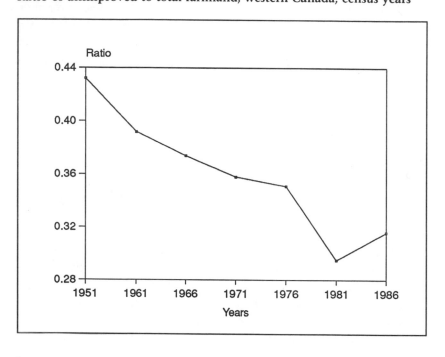

ing unimproved land into production over the period 1951-76, but after 1976 the rate at which unimproved land was converted to improved land increased.

Federal government payments to agricultural producers in western Canada increased from $0.5 billion in the 1982-3 crop year to $3.6 billion in 1987-8, although they fell to $2.2 billion in 1989-90. Saskatchewan received the greatest subsidies of the three prairie provinces; recent estimates indicate that, over a five-year period during the mid- to late 1980s, farmers in the province received an average annual payment exceeding $40 per cultivated acre. On average, each farmer in Saskatchewan received approximately $16,000 per year over the five-year period 1985-9. The rapid rise of government transfers to agricultural producers is illustrated in Figure 12.2.

The effect of government programs on the conversion of unimproved land can be seen in Figure 12.3. Beginning with 1,200 ac (about 500 ha) of unimproved land, the figure indicates how much land a farmer might convert under three levels of government subsidy (high, intermediate, and low) and with no government support payments. In the cases of

Figure 12.2

Net direct government payments to prairie farmers, 1971-90

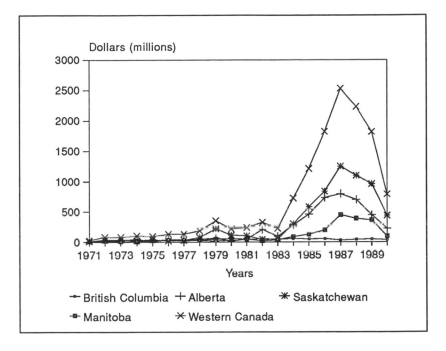

low government support and no support, substantially fewer acres of unimproved land are converted to crop production. The remaining unimproved lands are used for domestic grazing or simply left unused. These lands act as a buffer for soil erosion, habitat for wildlife, and waste receptor for pollution from agronomic activities.

One reason for increases in environmental degradation on agricultural lands in Canada (viz., soil erosion, loss of wildlife habitat) was the rapid rise in grain prices during the 1970s, which encouraged farmers to sell off livestock herds and bring pasture land into grain production. In addition, and particularly during the 1980s, government policies encouraged farmers to drain wetlands and bring unimproved land into production. The impact of specific government policies are discussed below.

The Feed Freight Assistance Program and the Crow Rate are subsidies that lower transportation costs; this effectively raises the farm-gate price of grain on the Prairies, thereby causing a shift in production from livestock towards grain. Again, this encourages cultivation of marginal lands and land degradation. In 1983, the Western Grain Transportation Act (WGTA) was passed, replacing the Crow Rate. The WGTA required

Figure 12.3

Effect of government programs on conversion of unimproved land

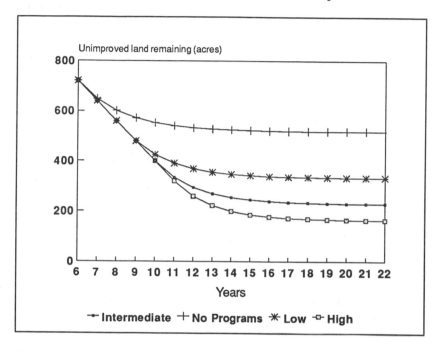

the federal government to provide a transport rate subsidy directly to the railways as opposed to the earlier Crow Rate method of simply instituting a fixed statutory rate. Thus, the WGTA continued to distort resource use by subsidizing western Canadian grain transport rates. Payments to either the railways or to the producers (if based on an improved acreage or current output basis) will continue to distort resource usage on the Prairies. Only if the Crow payment is made to farmers as a lump sum not tied to improved acreage or output will there be no distorting effect on land use.

The Canadian Wheat Board is a compulsory export marketing agency for wheat, oats, and barley grown on the Prairies. Its quota policy is based on cultivated land area and, thereby, encourages the cultivation of unimproved land and excessive tillage summerfallow. Aside from causing excessive soil erosion, tillage summerfallow increases soil salinity and reduces the availability of nesting cover for migrating waterfowl. Tillage summerfallow rather than chemical summerfallow is normally used because it is less expensive. As an alternative, chemical summer-fallow reduces erosion and salinity problems but may harm populations of invertebrates and aquatic plants and result in the poisoning of young mammals and birds.

The Western Grain Stabilization Act (WGSA) of 1976 was a program, the intent of which was to stabilize net income but the consequence of which was to provide income support. The WGSA discouraged farmers from maintaining lands in their natural state (or as pasture) in three important ways. First, WGSA effectively raised the price of grain received by producers, since the program was not actuarially sound; producers gained from WGSA over the length of time that the program was in existence (1976-90). Second, program payments were related to past output: the higher one's output, the greater the payment received from WGSA. Producers were encouraged to increase output over time, thereby causing them to use too many agri-chemicals, particularly nitrogen fertilizer. Finally, WGSA encouraged farmers to grow only those grain crops covered under the program and not to raise cattle. The Special Canadian Grains Program of 1986-91 was also used to subsidize prairie grain producers for depressed world grain prices, and its environmental effects were similar to WGSA.

In 1991, the Special Canadian Grains Program and WGSA were replaced by the Gross Revenue Insurance Plan (GRIP) and the Net Income Stabilization Account (NISA).[2] The NISA acts as a safety net to prevent a farmer's income from falling below his/her five-year average returns after costs (or below $10,000 taxable income). This policy appears to be somewhat decoupled from the production decisions of farmers, because it is paid on a lump-sum basis as opposed to a production or acreage basis. Thus, NISA may not have a distorting effect on resource use. GRIP is basically designed to provide subsidies to farmers. Under the GRIP program, farmers are assured a target revenue per acre based upon the individual producer's past production and defined target prices for the grains or oilseeds grown. The program and payment method may encourage crop choices, input decisions, and land use in a manner that maximizes GRIP benefits but is detrimental to the environment (i.e., planting of grains or oilseeds instead of forage or pasture on marginal land). While Agriculture Canada has argued that 'the program promotes environmental sustainability because it does not encourage production of one commodity over another' (Agriculture Canada, Communications Branch 1991) the large subsidies to be provided under GRIP and the fact that forage and pasture land are not eligible crops under the program may actually encourage the cultivation of marginal lands and land degradation.

The Crop Insurance Act offers financial protection against crop loss caused by uncontrollable natural hazards but militates against the environment in several ways. First, it encourages crop specialization and discourages livestock (an activity more compatible with the environment) by reducing the risks of relying on a single farming activity such as grain growing. Further, along with other programs, such as the Canadian Wheat Board quota system, crop insurance encourages farmers to plant unimproved and other marginal lands with eligible crops. Farmers are encouraged to plant these lands because the yields on marginal lands may be significantly below the recent yield history for the eligible crops in the area, allowing the farmer to receive crop insurance benefits on this land. The effective coverage for this marginal land brought into production may be at 100 per cent or more of the particular field's capability to produce a crop. Although this yield effect declines as more marginal land is brought into production in the region, it does not completely disappear.

Fuel rebates and tax incentives have encouraged the use of large machinery, thereby making field obstacles (viz., potholes and brush cover) nuisances to be eliminated. Large machinery also results in soil compaction, encourages farming of ever-larger fields, and discourages development of shelter belts. Fuel rebates are paid on the basis of amount used, thereby encouraging excessive use of energy resources (and release of CO_2) while discouraging research into alternative energy sources for agriculture.

Fertilizer rebates have contributed to greater fertilizer use. This economic incentive causes farmers to disregard the deterioration of the soil's natural fertility; the natural fertility of the soil may have declined 30 to 50 per cent, with the natural nitrogen-supplying capacity of the soil likely affected. Excessive concentrations of nitrates now affect many ground and surface waters. Chemical rebates and government programs that provide subsidies on a production level basis encourage the use of agri-chemicals. Agri-chemicals contribute to the problem of water pollution by leaching into groundwater and by contaminating the surface waters, thereby affecting both water availability and its quality.

Farm improvement grants have encouraged the draining of wetlands and the clearing of brush. Federal mortgage interest rebate programs, such as the Farm Purchase Program, were targeted towards the purchase of cropland, thus exacerbating the decline of livestock operations and the conversion of unimproved land to annual crop production.

The government programs discussed above have encouraged the

cultivation of marginal lands and farming agricultural land from 'fence row to fence row.' By encouraging environmentally unsound practices, these programs contribute to the problem of water and wind erosion of soil. Water erosion from agricultural lands contributes to the pollution of surface waters and groundwater. Specifically, water erosion affects the users of water recreation sites, navigation channels, water storage facilities, commercial fishing sites, water conveyance facilities (i.e., drainage ditches for flood control and irrigation canals), power plants, and water treatment facilities. Costs from water erosion result from an increase in sediment concentrations in water, which must be treated through the building of larger sedimentation basins, the addition of chemical coagulants, and the more frequent cleaning of filters.

Wind erosion of the soil from agricultural lands can result in damage to buildings, clogging of equipment, increased maintenance of roads and drains, and increased domestic cleaning and maintenance costs. Chemicals attached to the soil particles and simply greater dust in the air may also have an effect on health.

Government subsidies contribute to land degradation, encouraging farmers to 'mine' the soil, use more chemical fertilizers than they otherwise would, and plant crops on marginal lands. The programs have tended to focus on technical- and production-oriented aspects of farming, suggesting to the farm population that technical progress would be used to offset erosion damage caused by adverse farming techniques and reliance on monoculture. In addition to their land degradation costs, agricultural subsidies in the developed world are detrimental in their impact upon both the livelihoods and land use of farmers in low-income countries. By reducing the prices these farmers receive for their own products, rich-country subsidies encourage farmers to sacrifice their own environments (lands) in order simply to produce enough to survive. Thus, agricultural subsidies are like a two-edged sword, causing land degradation in both the country providing subsidies and in developing countries as well.

Although the case of western Canada was considered in some detail, the effects of government programs in other countries, mainly the U.S. and the European Community (EC), have been similar – government agricultural subsidies have resulted in unanticipated environmental degradation. In response to this adverse effect of government programs on land use, some countries have moved to implement stricter control over agricultural operations, including instituting environmental compliance provisions that require farmers to meet certain environmental standards in exchange for subsidy payments. The issue of social control over agricultural operations and environmental compliance are discussed in the next section.

Intervention Mechanisms to Preserve and Conserve Rural Land

Preventing environmental degradation from farming operations may require government intervention because the landowner is unable to capture all of the environmental benefits. For example, benefits of maintaining wildlife habitat on private agricultural lands accrue to hunters, photographers, and others who do not contribute to the costs of preserving habitat. Since the social benefits of habitat preservation are greater than are the private benefits, landowners will not provide socially optimal levels of wildlife habitat without appropriate incentives. This is the classic case of externality that constitutes an argument for government intervention. However, before the government intervenes, it is necessary to first determine whether or not intervention does, indeed, lead to greater economic efficiency and, second, to determine what form such intervention should take. The second of these is an institutional problem and is addressed in this section. Five policy instruments are considered.

Regulation

Land-use planning or regulation of private land uses generally requires the establishment of an 'Official Plan' and, perhaps, the designation of 'Environmental Protection Areas.' This can be accomplished either by direct regulations (e.g., 1,000 kg of trash per ha must be left on fields, or this land must be left uncultivated) or zoning (e.g., tillage summerfallow is not permitted in this region). The objective is to design performance standards to which land uses must conform; in practice, regulations are used to limit agricultural activities or uses on land so that these are compatible with soil conservation, wildland preservation, and other environmental objectives. However, regulations provide little or no incentive to reduce adverse agricultural activities beyond what is specified in the regulations.

With respect to achieving environmental objectives, regulations or standards are inefficient when compared to taxes or other charges. However, from a practical standpoint, the informational requirements for determining appropriate charges may be onerous. For example, costs of soil conservation practices need to be known, and that is difficult when there are thousands of producers and a large array of conservation strategies. Thus, the case for regulation is a strong one, and this may be why it has been used extensively in the U.S., both in agriculture and in other sectors.

Zoning, on the other hand, may be difficult to implement from a political standpoint. The main objection to zoning is that it creates inequities, because farmers' abilities to earn income (i.e., their land values) are affected by zoning ordinances. Where feasible, a system of transferable development rights can be used to mitigate the income-distributional consequences of zoning. Landowners are given development rights or credits based on the difference between the best alternative use of land, in terms of value, and the restricted use of land. These rights can then be sold to those with insufficient rights to farm fields that do not fall under environmental restrictions. One problem with this approach is identifying those agricultural regions that would have to purchase development rights.

Purchase of Property Rights
The idea underlying this approach to preservation is that society, through the government, purchases certain property rights pertaining to agricultural lands. This can be accomplished in one of several ways.
(1) The land can be purchased and subsequently sold back to the original owner or another producer, minus certain rights that contribute to land degradation. Another possibility is to sell back only parts of the purchased land, retaining ecologically sensitive areas or areas that are most susceptible to degradation. The latter option requires that the land be subdivided and that may not be permitted.
(2) Another possibility is to purchase agricultural lands and then lease only certain areas back to farmers. Use restrictions can be placed upon the lease to prevent farming practices that degrade the land; areas in need of protection can be excluded from the lease agreement.
(3) It is also possible for a public agency to purchase *conservation easements* on land that are subsequently binding on all future owners. In essence, society purchases certain development rights to the land. Examples of this include purchase of: the right to cultivate land more than two times per year; the right to use a particular agronomic practice, such as tillage summerfallow; and the right to drain sloughs and/or to burn associated uplands. Purchase of development rights was successfully used in King County (which encompasses Seattle, Washington) in order to preserve agricultural land, although

this turned out to be very expensive. In Canada, there has been no experience with purchase of conservation easements, and laws will likely need to be modified to permit this.

Financial Incentives: Fines, Charges, and Program Incentives
Financial incentives can be an effective method for achieving environmental protection goals, even on agricultural land. Penalties or fines can be assessed for activities that cause harm to the environment. For example, fines could be levied on farmers who illegally drain sloughs and burn associated uplands or on producers who do not have sufficient trash cover on fields during certain times of the year, thereby increasing the potential for soil erosion over what it might otherwise be. Charges or taxes can be imposed to reflect the external damages from erosion. The problems with fines and charges are that (1) they may not be politically acceptable, (2) enforcement may be lax (based on past experience), and (3) they imply a reassignment of property rights away from agricultural producers.

Alternatively, charges or taxes can be levied on fuel and agri-chemicals. By increasing the price of fuel, farmers are discouraged from cultivating marginal fields, while higher chemical prices mitigate the adverse effects that chemical use has on populations of invertebrates and aquatic plants as well as on waterfowl (especially young). However, taxes on chemicals also make chemical fallow and reduced tillage systems less attractive for reducing soil erosion. Taxes on fertilizers reduce their use, thereby alleviating pollution of surface and groundwater by phosphates and nitrates. Again, this alternative may not be politically acceptable, as it increases costs to farmers.

Incentive programs can also be used to encourage soil conservation or the preservation of wildlands. One approach is for agricultural producers to enter into long-term agreements with government in order to idle specified parcels of land or to restrict land use in environmentally sensitive areas. The Conservation Reserve Program (CRP) of the U.S. Food Security Act (1985) and its successor, the Food, Agriculture, Conservation and Trade Act (1990), employs this approach in order to take marginal, environmentally sensitive land out of production. The 1985 act called for the enrolment of 45 million acres, but concerns by the public about agricultural pollution increased the amount of land eligible for the CRP to 70 million acres. Initially, lands in the lowest soil capability classes plus those with a soil-loss tolerance rate of '3-T' were eligible (Chapter 10), but this was changed in 1987 to include all lands with a high potential for degradation. Eligible lands were identified in each region, and competitive bids were designed to keep program costs down. However, since the U.S. Department of Agriculture established an upper limit on accepted bids, bids in subsequent rounds converged on the cap, thereby undermining the cost-saving potential of the bid system. In addition, the CRP affected enrolment in the Acreage Reduction Program (discussed below).

An example of a program similar to CRP is Saskatchewan's 1984 Permanent Cover Program (PCP), which provides financial incentives to farmers to take cropland out of production. The land removed from production is to be planted to trees or forages – permanent cover. The program is managed by the Prairie Farm Rehabilitation Administration (PFRA) under the authority of a 5-year Canada-Saskatchewan Economic and Regional Development Agreement. In 1989, the PCP was extended for an additional three years under the $54 million Canada-Saskatchewan Agreement on Soil Conservation. The purpose of the PCP is to reduce soil deterioration on high-risk lands presently under cultivation. While CLI class 5 and 6 lands are eligible for the PCP, PFRA will determine eligibility of land in other classes.[3] Producers enter into 10- or 20-year agreements to 'seed' land to permanent cover and maintain it. Farmers receive $20/ac to offset the costs of establishing permanent cover (in addition to an annual payment). Initially, a bidding procedure was employed, but, subsequently, payments were fixed. Given low program payments, economists have criticized the program for encouraging enrolment of land that might not have been cropped in any case. If that critique is valid, the PCP simply becomes another mechanism used to transfer income to farmers.

Soil and water conservation agreements between the federal government and the other provinces have also been signed, but each agreement is somewhat different, depending upon the nature of soil deterioration, cropping practices, and financing arrangements between different levels of government. Canadian government policies employ two means for achieving soil conservation goals: financial incentives or subsidies (such as under PCP) and voluntary compliance via awareness programs. One concern with the use of subsidies to mitigate land degradation is that these lower the private opportunity cost of land degradation by reducing the costs of repair. Since the government subsidizes activities to reduce the adverse effects of soil deterioration, producers are provided with an incentive to adopt practices that are relatively more conducive to land degradation.

Cross Compliance

Unlike the aforementioned policies, cross or conservation compliance explicitly recognizes that government subsidies are needed to enable farmers to keep pace with the standard of living enjoyed by the rest of society – the so-called 'farm problem.' It also recognizes that, in many cases, environmental programs simply offset incentives provided under other farm programs. There are two alternative approaches to cross compliance: (1) program payments are provided only if certain conservation standards are attained (the 'red ticket approach'), or (2) program benefits increase as farmers meet or exceed specified (and increasingly higher) conservation thresholds (the 'green ticket approach'). In essence, farmers are required to implement certain conservation practices in order to be eligible for subsidies from applicable present or future government agricultural programs.

The U.S. is the only country that has implemented cross compliance using a number of different approaches (in addition to the CRP). Under the 'Swampbuster' and 'Sodbuster' provisions of the Food Security Act (1985), farmers become ineligible for agricultural program subsidies if they destroy wetlands (including swamps) or cultivate land that has not previously been producing annual crops. It does not aim to prevent land degradation by producers not eligible for farm subsidies. The Acreage Reduction Program (ARP) requires that farmers retire or 'set-aside' land (and seed it with grasses to prevent erosion) each year in order to remain eligible for price supports and deficiency payments. The amount set aside each year depends upon the perceived over-supply of various crops. The main objectives of the ARP have been to reduce supplies and, thereby, program payments rather than to reduce land deterioration. However, the ARP has had little impact on supply due to 'slippage' – the potential supply effects are dampened by farmers idling their least-productive but not necessarily most-erosive lands. Thus, the main effect of the set-aside program has been budget reduction for the United States government.

Finally, there are the conservation compliance provisions that require those farming highly erodible lands to file by 1990, and implement by 1995, an acceptable farm conservation plan in order to remain eligible for agricultural subsidies. The emphasis of conservation compliance is enhanced management. Examples of conservation plans include retaining a certain level of trash on fields during the winter months to retard soil erosion, contour ploughing, grassed waterways to reduce water erosion, planting trees to mitigate wind erosion, and flexcropping to reduce tillage fallow or to include conservation practices (viz., green manure) in management strategies that maximize returns and minimize risk. Conservation plans differ among regions and crop types. However, many problems with conservation compliance have already been identified. Examples of problems include: enforcement of trash levels may give rise to conflicts because local committees of farmers determine whether or not other farmers (their neighbours) are complying with the conservation plan; implementation of flexcropping requires knowledgeable management personnel; and certain aspects of conservation compliance could lead to adverse income-distributional consequences.

The major difficulties of cross compliance are those of identifying appropriate conservation strategies and enforcement. Canada has no conservation compliance provisions in its farm subsidy programs, although there is information about erosion rates on some lands (however, it has a physical bias and is incomplete). In Canada, unless economic information is incorporated, it will be difficult to identify and implement cross compliance strategies that are not doomed to fail. In particular, it is necessary to identify lands that are subject to the most serious degradation problems (provide information on erosion rates for each parcel of land), determine the on-farm costs of erosion (i.e., estimate damage functions), and calculate the off-farm costs of erosion. Otherwise, the benefits of cross compliance could turn out to be lower than the costs.

Education and Moral Suasion

Education and awareness programs can be used to make agricultural producers more sensitive to the environmental impacts of their operations. In some cases, it is then possible to persuade farmers to enter into programs to conserve soil or maintain wildlife habitat either voluntarily or at lower cost than before. For example, some Saskatchewan farmers were persuaded to continuous crop or rely on chemical as opposed to tillage summerfallow, even though this has resulted in lower net returns and higher risks. However, Canadian economists have argued that education and moral suasion have limited usefulness unless accompanied by adequate economic incentives. Nonetheless, Canadian agricultural policies emphasize education and voluntary compliance.

Discussion

The focus of this chapter is on agricultural land use and how it is affected by government actions. Land use is affected by government agricultural programs, including land use in the main agricultural areas, the agriculture-forest interface, and the urban shadow. It is government programs, particularly subsidy programs, that have made a pronounced impact on agricultural land use. Any attempt to resolve environmental problems in agriculture will have to deal with the existence and adverse impacts of agricultural programs. Not all government programs have a negative impact on land use, however. Financial incentives and awareness programs have been directed at improved soil conservation and the preservation of wildlife habitat (Chapter 13).

As noted in Chapter 10, Canadian agricultural programs operate as though the major problem of soil degradation is its on-farm as opposed to its off-farm component. As a result, education and voluntary compliance play a prominent role in Canadian programs. Further, direct financial incentives subsidize farmers for implementing reduced tillage, planting windrows, or taking land out of production. However, the experiences of the United States and Australia indicate that education, voluntary compliance, and financial incentives alone are insufficient, and there seems little reason to suggest that the Canadian experience will be different.

Environmental or land degradation in agriculture are part of the larger issue of sustainable development. In terms of sustainable agriculture, as with other resources, knowledge about the biophysical attributes of land, including climate, are important, and this is considered in terms of land classification and geographic information systems. Such knowledge is important for economic analysis. Before decisions about land preservation, land use, agricultural and other programs, implementation of soil conservation and management plans, and multiple use can be made, it is important to know something about the benefits and costs of preserving unimproved lands, the economics of soil erosion, and multiple-use aspects (eg., value of land in nonagricultural uses). This requires combining knowledge of biophysical attributes with economic parameters. However, the degree of knowledge required depends upon the extent to which governments want to exercise control over private land use. The less control to be exercised, the less knowledge that is required. It is clear, however, that income policies directed at farmers, but not at their land-use decisions, do affect land use in an adverse manner. This, in turn, leads to other policies that attempt to correct these unintended effects. It is the unintended and unanticipated effects of government policies that are so troublesome. Inadequate knowledge of both agro-ecology and economics in the development of policies is a principal concern – a concern that this chapter seeks to address. Additional topics of a similar nature are discussed in Chapters 9, 10, 13, and 16 on global climatic change, soil erosion, wetlands, and multiple use, respectively.

13

Control over Water in Agriculture: Economics of Irrigation and Wetlands Preservation

In many regions of the world, water is a limiting factor in agricultural production. It was noted in the previous chapter that a two-year, wheat-tillage summerfallow rotation is often used in dryland cropping regions in temperate zones in order to conserve moisture from one year to the next and, thereby, to reduce the on-farm risk of crop production. An alternative to dryland cultivation is to employ irrigation. Irrigation was discussed in chapters 5 (project analysis) and 6 (input-output analysis) in the context of economic efficiency and community stability, but, in this chapter, the discussion focuses on water use in the arid regions of western Canada and the U.S.

Preservation of wilderness was discussed in Chapter 12. In this chapter, preservation of wetlands on the northern Great Plains of America is examined. Wetlands are important in the current context, because government agricultural programs have contributed to their demise and because they produce ducks, which have value to hunters, and provide scenic amenities and biological diversity. They also provide habitat for bird species that may become endangered. Since wetlands furnish benefits to individuals who do not make decisions about their use, this is an example of (ownership) externality (Chapter 4). Wetlands are also important to the agricultural ecology of dryland cropping regions, with their disappearance possibly signalling a reduction in the potential level of sustainable development.

The reason for considering irrigation and wetlands conservation is that they illustrate the importance of markets and prices in bringing about sustainable development and the impact of government management and control on land use. In arid regions of western Canada and the U.S., failure to balance market supply and demand for water, especially in agriculture (which accounts for 80 per cent of the world's water use), has resulted in water shortages and pressure to develop and divert northern rivers. The environmental costs of diversions could be high. Rather than internalizing impacts on the environment, current water-pricing policies do the opposite by encouraging waste. Likewise, government policies provide incentives that cause farmers to destroy wildlife habitat through the depletion of wetlands and the excessive use of chemicals. Economists have urged removal of distorting subsidies and implementation of prices that cause agricultural producers to be more cognizant of the damages they impose on the environment (Chapters 4 and 9). The economics of irrigation and wetlands are considered in the next sections.

Irrigation and Water Use
It is clear that irrigation projects affect land use, as is known by anyone who has flown over or driven through regions where irrigated agriculture is prevalent. Irrigation projects are popular in most countries because the benefits of such projects accrue to a small number of individuals, while costs are widely dispersed. As a result, the beneficiaries of water resource development projects are able to influence politicians, who not only cater to these special interests but also view the results provided by irrigation projects – the 'make-the-desert-bloom' syndrome that is most visible in areas characterized by a high degree of irrigated agriculture. Engineers are interested in large construction projects that require the building of dams for interbasin transfers, hydro-power generation, and irrigation, and they often lobby on behalf of those that ultimately gain the most in terms of enhanced property values. However, irrigation projects are generally uneconomic, and, given current grain prices, there is likely no need for interbasin transfers. It is not that there is a water shortage, but rather, water resources are inefficiently allocated.

In this section, we briefly examine the background to irrigation development in the U.S. and Canada. Then we focus on the economics of irrigation and the effects of government subsidies on land use. We also consider the possibility of future interbasin water transfers in order to alleviate real or perceived water shortages.

Irrigation and Water Development in the United States
The western half of North America – that area west of the hundredth meridian – is generally quite arid, with most of the region receiving less than 700 mm (about 28 in.) of precipitation annually and large areas

receiving much less. Many settlers were enticed into the region by false promises: in the U.S., the belief that 'rain follows the plough' was promulgated. The promises seemed real during the twenty years of settlement prior to 1886, but then came the harsh winter of 1886, followed by the drought of 1888-92. The number of farm families in the 17 western states fell from about a million to 400,000. Many of the survivors in the most arid regions farmed along river valleys and constructed irrigation works. By the early 1890s, there were some 3.5 million ac (1.4 million ha) of private irrigation in the west. However, the rugged terrain and deep valleys limited the economic feasibility of investments in irrigation by private groups and individuals, even where subsidies from state governments were made available. Only federal intervention could bring about the massive investment required to develop water resources on a large scale. Under President Theodore Roosevelt, the National Reclamation Act was passed in 1902. This initiated federal involvement (through the Bureau of Reclamation) in the building and management of irrigation projects in the arid west and the draining of water from swampy land in other areas (mainly in the southeast U.S.).

Initially, the Reclamation Act limited water subsidies to 160 ac, but in 1926 this was increased to 320 ac (for a husband and wife), although a farmer could claim subsidies on leased land. In 1982, eligibility was increased to 960 ac, but this included owned plus leased land. Initially, the subsidy amounted to the interest on capital or construction costs with payback to occur over ten years, but it soon became apparent that farmers would not be able to bear even that burden. Eventually, the payback period was increased to fifty years. However, while all costs (including operating, maintenance, and replacement costs plus costs of installing irrigation works and underground drainage to prevent salinization) had to be covered in principle, it appears that even these costs were not all being borne by the agricultural producer. This issue is discussed further later in this chapter.

Between 1902 and 1930, the federal government of the United States constructed some 50 dams, while it constructed about 1,000 dams between 1930 and 1980, mainly in the western U.S. Since 1980, no additional dams have been built, primarily due to the need for environmental impact statements. The environmental costs of dam construction have never been fully taken into account. Not only do dams adversely affect scenic landscapes (e.g., Grand Canyon), but they are responsible for the loss of wildlife habitat. Dams on the Columbia River have reduced the historic salmon run by some 80 per cent (from 10 to 16 million adult fish per year to about 2.5 million currently), with about half of the watershed's historic spawning grounds effectively and irreversibly blocked by the Grand Coulee Dam (which is too high to permit construction of fish ladders). The salmon run on the Sacramento River has been reduced to a mere trickle, while riparian habitat for many species has been irreversibly lost or significantly reduced throughout much of the west. A major factor causing a turn-about in attitude towards irrigation development was the result of publicity surrounding deformities and death among waterfowl at California's Kesterson National Wildlife Refuge during the early 1980s, which was caused by selenium from farmers' fields.

While we are only interested in examining surface waters, it should be noted that groundwater is also important in irrigation. The problem here is that such water is treated as an open access resource: whatever is pumped by one farmer is no longer available for another, and, hence, farmers use more water than they would otherwise. This, then, increases the demand for surface water.

Total irrigated acreage in the 17 western states increased from 17.2 million ac in 1939 to 30.8 million ac in 1959 and reached a peak of 43.6 million ac in 1978. The proportion of total irrigated acreage accounted for by the Bureau of Reclamation increased from 18 per cent in 1939 to 26 per cent currently, with a peak area of 10.6 million ac in 1982. The bureau accounts for 53 per cent of irrigated area in Arizona, 40 per cent in California, 17 per cent in Montana, and 8 per cent in Utah. Table 13.1 provides an indication of the importance of water use in irrigation and, thus, an indicator of the extent to which land use is affected. Irrigation constitutes well over 80 per cent of all water use in the western states.

Table 13.1. Average offstream water uses in selected western states (%)

State/Item	California	Nevada	Colorado	Washington
Irrigation	83	90	85	81
Public water supply	11	5	4	7
Industry	6	5	7	11
Rural water supply	<1	<1	2	1

Source: Reisner and Bates (1990:28-9)

In addition to low prices, institutional and historical factors often resulted in inefficient water use in the western U.S. In all seventeen western states, two doctrines have characterized the allocation of water among users. The first is the first appropriation doctrine of 'first in time, first in use'; an appropriative water right becomes vested when a person intentionally diverts water and applies it to some 'beneficial use.' The term 'beneficial use' is ambiguous and, in practice, means any productive use. The second doctrine is that of 'use it or lose it'; water rights can be lost if they are not used for several years. These doctrines have resulted in inefficient use of water, leading to the practice of 'water ranching' in order to prevent the loss of rights. Water ranching refers to irrigation for the purpose of maintaining water rights rather than crop production for profit, although crops are still sold.

Markets for water rights are poorly developed. While the Colorado River Compact has allocated water from the Colorado River to individual states and Native people on the basis of the expropriation doctrine, the amount of water has been over-allocated (since measurement of water flow took place during the wet years mentioned above), and, until 1982, states had been able to prevent interstate transfers of water rights. The law is not clear as to whether or not water provided by the Bureau of Reclamation may be transferred from one user to another (even if the 960-acre provision is met). While Native appropriative rights are not subject to the 'use it or lose it' doctrine, because they fall under federal and not state jurisdiction, the federal government has in place obstacles that make it difficult, but not impossible, for Native tribes to transfer (i.e., sell or rent) water rights. For the most part, creation of markets for water transfers are determined at the state level. Markets appear most developed in Colorado, where permanent water rights have sold for as much as $6,000 per acre-foot (acf).[1] Development of water markets in California has been slow, likely due to the vast amounts of federal water (12 million acf) tied up in delivery contracts that restrict or prohibit water transfer. Development of institutions to get around these obstacles are already beginning to take shape.

As a result of six years of drought, the state of California's groundwater resources are now accounting for about one-half of water use, compared to, previously, a third. There is concern that fish habitat in the Sacramento River delta may be destroyed, requiring the allocation of water towards the environment; some 800,000 acf has been targeted for that purpose, but it is unclear where this water is to come from.

There is no set price for water. Farmers pay around $10/acf; some farmers pay as little as $2.50/acf under contracts reached during the

1950s, while current contracts are around $35/acf. Cities pay from $50 to over $200 per acf. A federal water bill proposed in 1992 is supposed to make provision for the required 800,000 acf for environmental purposes and, at the same time, enable farmers in the Central Valley Project to sell water to the cities. Farmers might pay $20 per acf for water that they sell for $100/acf; after municipal water charges levied by the Central Valley Project and transportation costs, urban residents will pay $200 per acf. While one-year contracts of this nature had been permitted by the bureau in the past, the new legislation ushers in long-term transfers, but it also reduces water rights contracts from 40 down to 25 years. Given that farmers regard farming as a way of life and have a distrust of the cities, it may be difficult to get their cooperation in both passing the legislation and making it work.

Finally, elaborate and expensive means for diverting water from northern rivers, many of which are in Canada, have been proposed, and, as demand for water continues to increase in the southwest, there will be increasing pressure to implement such diversions. Such mega-projects will generally have an adverse impact upon the environment, and this may prevent their adoption in the short to medium term but, likely, not in the long term. Water efficiency and a reduction in the high demands for water by agriculture can come about by implementing prices for water. This is the best means for solving the 'water shortage' in the arid western part of the continent and bringing about efficient water use.

Irrigation and Water Development in Western Canada

In 1859, the explorer John Palliser identified a triangular area of about 260,000 sq. km, consisting mainly of southern Alberta and southern Saskatchewan (roughly the grassland continental prairie, PCg, in Figure 13.1), to be infertile and unfit for agricultural settlement because of its aridity. (Precipitation is less than 400 mm annually.) Henry Hind had provided a similar report in 1857; he described the southern Prairies as too dry and infertile for farming. Lack of precipitation and organic matter in the soil are evidence of this. In 1872, a botanist, John Macoun, explored the region and reported that the region was well-suited for crop production; but 1872 was a wet year, as indicated above. Acting on Macoun's advice, the government actively recruited immigrants from eastern Europe with exaggerated claims of the land's productivity. Under the Dominion Lands (Homestead) Act of 1872, settlers were provided with a quarter section of land for a $10 registration fee.

The land was unsuited for crop production, and the size of a homestead was too small to permit ranching. Thus began government participation in prairie agriculture.

In 1886, the federal government set up the first in a series of Dominion Experimental Farms in Brandon, Manitoba. The practice of summerfallowing to conserve moisture (enabling farmers to use two years of moisture to grow one crop) was developed several years later at the experimental farm at Indian Head, Saskatchewan. As noted in Chapter 10, summerfallow contributed to soil erosion, which was a particular problem in dry years such as 1910, 1914, and 1917-19. The wet years of the 1920s produced bumper crops and temporarily solved the problem of soil erosion. However, droughts returned in 1929, and these continued, along with low prices and insect infestations (grasshoppers) through most of the 1930s. In response to the drought, the federal government passed the Prairie Farm Rehabilitation Act in 1935, thereby creating the Prairie Farm Rehabilitation Administration (PFRA). PFRA approached the task by encouraging research, development, the adoption of new farming methods, and water conservation. The latter led to the construction of dams for the purpose of irrigation and other uses.

Between 1939 and 1979, thirty dams were built in the southern portions of Alberta, Saskatchewan, and Manitoba, primarily for irrigation purposes and, to a lesser extent, for provision of water supply, flood control, and hydro-power generation. Unlike the U.S., where dam construction was effectively halted, several major dam projects have been built since 1980 (e.g., Three Rivers Dam on the Oldman River in Alberta and the Rafferty-Alameda Project in Saskatchewan). However, it is likely that major dam construction may be difficult in the future because of federal environmental assessment reviews (Chapter 16).

Agriculture constitutes the largest use of water on the Canadian Prairies, accounting for some two-thirds of consumptive use. Irrigation is particularly important in the drier, southwestern region of the Prairies – the region known as the 'Palliser triangle.' The South Saskatchewan River Basin is the most important basin in western Canada in terms of consumptive use, with irrigation accounting for three-quarters of its use; in dry years, when irrigation use is high and river flows are reduced, about 96 per cent of water consumption in the basin is for agriculture. Agricultural use in the South Saskatchewan basin can be expected to increase as more land is brought under irrigation in Alberta and Saskatchewan (Table 13.2). As is indicated in Table 13.2, irrigation acreage expanded by more than 20 per cent in the early 1980s, particularly in Saskatchewan, where it expanded by approximately 50 per cent. Alberta has the greatest amount of acreage currently under irrigation, and this is expected to almost double with the completion of the Three Rivers Dam on the Oldman River in 1992.

Table 13.2. **Irrigated area in western Canada, 1980 and 1985**

Province	Irrigated area (hectares)	
	1980[a]	1985[b]
Manitoba	6,935	9,732
		(40.3)[c]
Saskatchewan	55,913	83,931
		(50.1)
Alberta	393,969	466,281
		(18.4)
British Columbia	100,475	117,811
		(17.3)
TOTAL	557,292	677,755
		(21.6)

[a]Statistics Canada, *Census of Agriculture 1981*, Cat. #96-901, Table 20
[b]Statistics Canada, *Census of Agriculture 1986*, Cat. #96-112, Table 11
[c]per cent change provided in parentheses

Economics of Irrigation Agriculture

With notable exceptions, irrigation does not occur unless subsidies are provided to agricultural producers. In both Canada and the United States, there are important misunderstandings about such subsidies. Foremost among these is the notion that the beneficiaries receive the full amount of the subsidy, namely, the full difference between the taxpayer costs and what the farmer actually receives as a subsidy. This is far from being the case. In the San Joaquin Valley of California, farmers pay $20/acf for irrigation water that is worth $50/acf but costs the Bureau of Reclamation $300/acf to deliver. Thus, the cost of providing a subsidy to farmers is about ten times greater than the actual amount of the subsidy – a very inefficient means of transferring income to agricultural producers. Studies are not available for Canada, but it would not be surprising to find a similar relationship between costs and benefits as is reported for the San Joaquin Valley.

Economists have almost unanimously demonstrated that the economic benefits to irrigation are marginal or negative. In eastern Washington, the latest cost-benefit analyses of irrigation projects indicate that the most optimistic benefit-cost ratio is 0.78, even when secondary benefits are *appropriately* taken into account.[2] However, so-called secondary benefits are not appropriately taken into account. Too often the increase in economic activity associated with an irrigation project is taken as a benefit and is included in the cost-benefit analysis. As noted in Chapter 6, this is inappropriate, since spending the money in some other way or simply providing citizens with an equivalent reduction in their taxes could generate the same or even larger increase in economic activity. The current author is aware of cases, on both sides of the border, in which irrigation projects have been justified by including the estimated change in economic activity as if it were a benefit (as the latter is defined in chapters 3 and 5). Where a large portion of the project costs are paid for by the federal government, it might be possible to exclude those costs in calculating the benefit-cost ratio. Excluding costs paid for by a higher level of government is only valid if these funds would be unavailable to the province (region) under any other circumstances, and then only if efficiency calculations are based on a regional and not a national point of view.

In Canada, one argument along these lines that has been used in support of irrigation projects is that irrigated hay and grain stimulates a livestock sector. For example, Saskatchewan points to the livestock sector in southern Alberta to justify expansion of irrigation in that province, but expansion of the Alberta sector occurred as a result of livestock subsidies and not irrigation. Why would higher hay and/or feed grain yields (as a result of irrigation) bring about a livestock industry that would not exist when yields are lower? After all, the feed requirements could simply be produced on a larger area. The answer is clear: development of a livestock sector is not dependent on irrigation. Likewise, the development of a potato-processing sector is not the inevitable outcome of an irrigation project that permits potato production. Economists have specifically identified 'forward-linked' markets as an inappropriate justification for irrigation projects.

It is important that each project or program be considered on its own merits. Thus, if irrigation works are already in place, it may not make economic sense to restrict subsidies to a certain farm size if, by so doing, farms are prevented from achieving scale economies. Likewise, decisions to install irrigation works on a farm should be made solely on the basis of the on-farm costs and benefits, not on the basis of the costs of bringing the water to the farm, *if the irrigation canals that bring water to the farm are already in place.* Any costs that have already been incurred should be ignored – bygones are bygones.

This reasoning can be extended to larger development projects. Before considering a series of dams on a watershed, a cost-benefit analysis needs to be conducted. However, construction of individual dams and irrigation works also needs to be evaluated in isolation. This prevents the use of 'cash register' dams. To meet the evaluation criteria established by the Flood Control Act (1936), the Bureau of Reclamation evaluated irrigation projects as part of a parcel that relied upon revenues from the sale of electricity ('cash registers') to subsidize irrigation. The irrigation dam and irrigation works need to be evaluated on their own, without reliance on subsidies from other components in the project.

Another problem particularly prevalent in cooler regions is that low-valued crops are grown under irrigation. In western Canada, for example, over 70 per cent of irrigated acres are sown to grains and hay, with a small proportion sown to speciality crops (sugar beets, potatoes, etc.). There are limits to where speciality crops can be grown. Heat units may be adequate for growing sugar beets in southern Alberta and Manitoba, for example, but not in Saskatchewan; even so, sugar beet acreage has not increased, because cheap sugar is available from abroad. Further, irrigating subsidized agricultural products (such as sugar beets, wheat, cotton, rice, and so on) makes no economic sense; it implies that farmers are provided with a double subsidy – an irrigation subsidy and a crop production subsidy.

Problems such as those identified above are not unique to North America. In many parts of the world, large-scale irrigation projects (requiring large dam construction) are undertaken, despite questionable economic efficiency benefits. Where public investment in such projects is required, farmers are usually provided with subsidies to build irrigation works, and water is priced below market rates, if at all. This results in excessive water use, inappropriate irrigation works (e.g., sprinklers rather than drip), and watering at the hottest time of day. Loss of wildlife habitat and subsequent loss of biodiversity often accompany large-scale water development projects, and these costs are not usually taken into account in evaluating such projects. Further, irrigated agriculture results in land degradation by increasing soil salinity. Historically, wherever irrigation was practised, agriculture was eventually abandoned because the soil became saline. Salinity occurs because the water table rises during periods of watering, and salts are deposited when it recedes. Optimal timing of irrigation and flushing of soils might be used to reduce salinization. But water-pricing policies and management expertise in many countries do not provide much hope on this score.

In conclusion, the best hope for appropriate allocation of resources is to rely on sound economic principles and careful cost-benefit analysis in the development of water resources. Subsidies to construct large irrigation works should be avoided, whether these subsidies are from the federal government to a region or from developed to low-income countries. Finally, given the scarcity of water in many regions of the world, the best hope for its conservation is to establish water markets and price the resource at its true economic value.

Preservation of Wetlands in Interior North America

Background
Migratory waterfowl constitute an important recreational resource, having value both in consumptive use (hunting) and non-consumptive use (bird watching, existence value). In a major study of migratory waterfowl and wetlands some twenty years ago, Judd Hammack and Gardner Brown concluded that duck numbers and ponds in North America are well below economically optimal levels. Social welfare could be substantially enhanced by increasing wetlands areas and waterfowl numbers. Since their study, wetland areas have actually declined and, consequently, so have waterfowl numbers.

The North American Waterfowl Management Plan (NAWMP) was formally initiated in 1986, with the goal of restoring North American waterfowl numbers to their mid-1970s' level. This joint venture between Canada and the U.S. calls for an outlay of $U.S. 1 billion over 15 years, with the U.S. paying 75 per cent of program costs. One objective of NAWMP is to encourage agricultural producers to set aside agricultural land in order to permit the establishment of potholes for waterfowl habitat – that is, to maintain potholes and native uplands for nesting cover as opposed to putting them into crop production. Pilot projects under NAWMP were established in each of Canada's prairie provinces; since 1989, these have come under the umbrella of the Prairie Habitat Joint Venture, which is a component of NAWMP, and whose members constitute the Canadian implementing agencies. For example, the Prairie Pothole Project in the Rural Municipality (RM) of Antler in southeastern

Saskatchewan (Figure 13.1) sought to evaluate financial and program incentives designed to preserve and enhance waterfowl habitat on private land. The focus of the Prairie Pothole Project has been primarily biological (monitoring duck populations and broods and determining wetland cover), with economic factors being largely overlooked.

Figure 13.1

Wetlands of western Canada

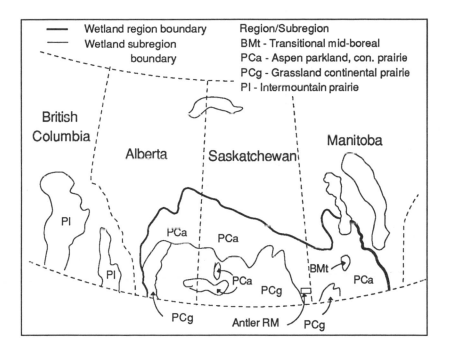

The Saskatchewan project and the pilot projects in Alberta and Manitoba are considered by NAWMP to have been a huge success. The strategies tested in the pilot projects are used to design land-management programs for the preservation of wetlands. In this section, we examine both the biological and economic components of managing land for habitat conservation. While the management techniques adopted by the Prairie Habitat Joint Venture are worthwhile from a narrow point of view, we indicate that there are more efficient means for preserving waterfowl habitat on private agricultural lands.

Biological Aspects of Wetlands Conservation
Migratory waterfowl generally winter in the southern parts of the conti-

nental U.S., but major breeding grounds are found in Canada. One of the most important breeding grounds for the Central and Mississippi flyways is the pothole country of southern Alberta, Saskatchewan, and Manitoba (Figure 13.1). Although also a breeding ground for the Pacific Flyway, California's Central Valley and the McKenzie River delta in northern Canada are more important. The prairie pothole region of Canada accounts for between 25 and 60 per cent (25 and 30 per cent in the last decade) of North American breeding population, but it also supports other waterfowl and birds. The wetlands in the region function as breeding, staging, and moulting habitats for numerous species of waterfowl, wading birds, colonial nesting birds, and shorebirds. Rare, threatened, and endangered bird species, such as migrating Whooping Cranes, Piping Plovers, the White Pelican, the Caspian Tern, and the Trumpeter Swan, utilize prairie wetland regions. Wetlands also provide habitat for Arctic-nesting geese and other shoreline birds (that migrate to the Arctic) when they stop in the prairie pothole region for extended periods to fatten during spring migration.

Not all wetland areas have the same capacity to produce and sustain wildlife; not all wetlands can support migratory waterfowl. The following classification of prairie wetlands is useful for evaluating their biological importance.[3]

(1) *Wet meadows* are covered by surface water for only a few weeks in the spring or for a few days after heavy rains. These occur in a transition zone around deeper ponds or in field depressions. Seepage and evapotranspiration are rapid, and that is why these wetlands are ephemeral.

(2) *Shallow marshes* form as marginal bands about lakes or as inner bands of the wet meadow type. These wetland types are usually saturated with water or are seasonally flooded, having 0-30 cm of water until the middle of summer. Coarse grasses, sedges of intermediate height, water-tolerant herbs, and some floating plants characterize the vegetation in these wetland types, which, by late summer, are covered with vegetation.

(3) *Deep marshes* are covered with surface water until late summer or fall, usually retaining 1-30 cm of water. This wetland type constitutes semi-permanent ponds and the bands about permanent ponds or lakes. Reeds, rushes, tall grasses, and water plants (floating leaf and submergent species) are common.

(4) *Intermittent or transitional open water* is a wetland type, characterized by open water, that may persist for several years, alternating with

shallow marshes during dry years. Plants that characterize permanent open water are missing, because there are drawdowns during dry periods.

(5) *Permanent or shallow open water* characterizes wetlands that are stable, occupy the central or deepest position of a basin, and have water depths of 20 cm or more in September.

Alternatively, five wetland types can be identified as follows: ephemeral, temporary, seasonal, semi-permanent, and permanent. This classification scheme is similar to that above, except that categories 3 and 4 correspond to the semi-permanent category, wet meadows correspond to the temporary category, and shallow marshes correspond to the seasonal category. Ephemeral wetlands are even more short-lived than are wet meadows and may not even be considered wetlands by some scientists. Finally, *fens* are wetlands characterized by vegetation that occurs where groundwater saturates the soil throughout the growing season. These areas cannot be cultivated but can be used as forage for cattle. Fens might appropriately be classified as shallow marshes.

It is the wet meadows and shallow marshes – the temporary and seasonal wetlands – that are most important from the point of view of migrating birds and most species of waterfowl (except diving ducks), because these wetlands supply marsh and aquatic birds with food in the early spring. The proportional use of these wetlands by breeding waterfowl is greatest, because rapid warming of shallow wetlands in the spring results in the early development of invertebrate populations. Researchers found that, although accounting for less than 60 per cent of wetlands area in the Dakotas, these types of wetlands could account for more than 80 per cent of broods. Further, although generally dry during mid- to late summer, these regions may fill with fall rains, providing important temporary habitat for fall migrant dabbling ducks. It is clear, therefore, that temporary wetlands located in bands around more permanent ponds or in singular low-lying basins in the prairie pothole region are important for North American duck production.

Temporary and seasonal wetlands (wet meadows and shallow marshes) are most affected by agricultural operations. Agricultural damage occurs as a result of both mechanical disturbance at the margin and cultivation or drainage of the entire basin. Marginal disturbance by clearing, burning, and cultivation results in the disappearance of natural woody or meadow vegetation and leads to increased erosion and infilling of the wetland basin. Cultivation of the entire wetland area could destroy the organic seal, thereby causing the area to drain more rapidly when reflooded. Drainage and consolidation of sloughs and larger wetland areas alter the ecology of the region, make it difficult for plant and animal species to reproduce, and ruin its biological diversity. It also results in a less diverse and less visually appealing landscape. Agricultural disturbance of temporary wetlands results in a deterioration of marsh-edge vegetation, which is an essential component of waterfowl habitat, while heavy machinery and use of herbicides and pesticides reduces the populations of invertebrates and aquatic plants, which are important to waterfowl and other bird and animal species.

Although damage to wetland areas does not need to be permanent, a substantial degree of agricultural activity in and around potholes results in the irreversible loss of wetlands. In Canada, agricultural reclamation is the main cause of wetlands decline in the prairie pothole region. Studies of the decline in wetlands in the prairie pothole region have focused on wetland losses in specific study sites over a variety of time periods. Extrapolation of regional estimates suggests that the permanent loss of wetlands over the period of pre-settlement to 1982 vary from between 13 and 70 per cent. It also appears that about one-quarter of the wetland areas that existed in the early 1960s were lost by the early 1980s.

A 1988 survey of landowners in Antler RM in southeastern Saskatchewan indicated that approximately 58 per cent of all the land that respondents considered to be feasible for draining or clearing in 1986 was subsequently drained or cleared; this land was considered to be good waterfowl habitat by the farmers themselves. Respondents also indicated that 5.9 per cent of their *cultivated* land had been in potholes within the previous ten years. It is not known whether these results are representative of the prairie pothole region as a whole, but it does appear that these trends are the direct result of government incentive programs (Chapter 12).

That there has been a loss of wetlands and a decline in related waterfowl numbers in southern Saskatchewan is evident from July pond counts and duck numbers (Figure 13.2). While agricultural development on wildlands can be blamed for the loss of waterfowl habitat, there is evidence to suggest that climatic trends are a major determinant of available habitat and that agricultural development on ephemeral wetlands during periods of drought is contributing to overall habitat decline. Since temporary wetlands are important for migratory waterfowl, particularly mallards and northern pintail (which nest early in the spring), July pond counts are subtracted from May pond counts for the period 1955-88 in order to provide an indication of the trend of tempor-

Figure 13.2

Duck numbers and pond counts, southern Saskatchewan, 1955-88

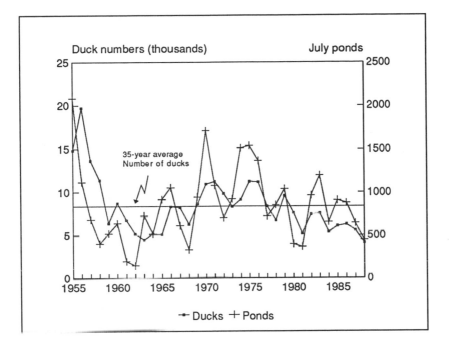

ary wetlands. Temporary wetlands appear to have declined over the period, but, more importantly, they fluctuate widely as a result of drought. Temporary ponds are highly correlated with the Palmer Drought Index (PDI) for Saskatchewan (Figure 13.3). Therefore, investigation of trends in wetlands and waterfowl numbers must take climate into account. Such an investigation will, in turn, have an implication for policies designed to promote waterfowl habitat on private lands.

Economics of Wetlands Preservation on Private Agricultural Land

Government agricultural programs affect variables that impact on farmers' decisions to develop wetland areas. The stock of wetlands on a farm is influenced by government policies that affect (1) crop revenue (e.g., price supports), (2) the cost of converting wetlands to agricultural production (improvement subsidies and tax write-offs), and (3) factor input costs (e.g., quicker depreciation that encourages use of larger equipment, thus enabling cultivation closer to ponds, and input rebates). In many cases, wetlands provide positive benefits to farmers.

Figure 13.3

Temporary ponds and drought, southern Saskatchewan, 1955-91

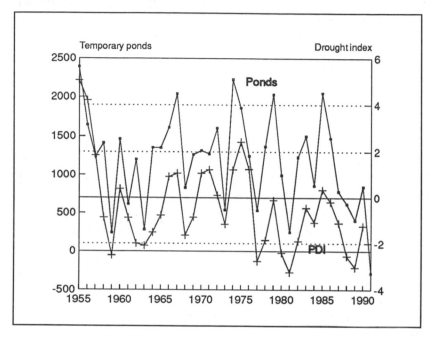

For example, wetlands and their associated uplands and brush might provide water and shelter for livestock or reduce erosion by wind, since they act as a shelterbelt. Wetlands could be useful during years of drought and might provide private benefits from hunting. All told, these private benefits might have a positive value to farmers, but, clearly, the private value, say K, takes into account only private benefits, since extra-market values or external benefits are ignored by the landowner. For some farmers, the value of wetlands could well be zero, in which case farmers will maintain some wetlands and associated uplands as long as land quality is sufficiently low or conversion costs sufficiently high.

The effect of government programs and extra-market benefits can be analyzed with the aid of Figure 13.4. All axes measure positive values. The abscissa in panel (a) represents cultivated land of decreasing quality. Marginal benefits of converting unimproved land fall as more marginal land is brought under cultivation. This is indicated by the declining marginal benefit of crop production curve labelled MB_C. Marginal benefit functions are translated into marginal cost curves in panel (d) via panels (b) and (c). (By way of symmetry, the figure illustrates what is meant by opportunity cost, with subscripts C and W referring to cultivated and wetland, respectively.) Thus, MB_C becomes MC_W, where MB_C is comprised of the crop revenues minus production costs, minus an annualized cost of bringing unimproved land or wetlands into crop production. For convenience, the marginal private benefit of retaining land as wetlands is assumed to be constant and equal to K. It is equal to the marginal opportunity cost of cultivating or cropping the land (MC_C).

With no government programs and assuming land in wetlands has a private value of K, C_0 amount of land is cultivated and W_0 is left unimproved or in wetlands and associated uplands. If there are no private benefits to retaining wetlands ($MB_W = K = 0$), the amount of land that is cultivated is determined by the intersection of MB_C and the horizontal axis; likewise, the amount in wetlands is determined by the intersection of MC_W and the abscissa.

Government programs affect revenues, production costs, and conversion costs in ways discussed above. The effect of government programs that favour crop production, either through direct subsidies or through rebates or tax write-offs that lower factor costs, is to shift the marginal benefit curve for crop production to MB'_C in panel (a) or lower the marginal cost of wetlands to MC'_W in panel (d). The amount of land in crop production will be greater than it would be in the absence of government programs, C_1 rather than C_0, while wetlands area will be lower, W_0 compared to W_1.

What about the divergence between social and private costs in the maintenance of waterfowl habitat? It may well be the case that society values wetlands more highly than does the farmer. Suppose, in Figure 13.4, that S represents the value of wetlands to the farmer plus their value to hunters, environmentalists, neighbouring farmers, and others in society (the off-farm benefits); the marginal benefits to others are given by $S - K$, which is assumed to be constant. In this case, society would wish to maintain an amount W_S of wetlands and only have C_S amount of the farmer's land in crop production. To encourage the farmer to take into account the off-farm benefits of retaining wetlands, it is necessary for the authority to provide him/her with a subsidy of amount $S - K$ to get him/her to preserve the desired amount of wetlands. It is clear that, when farmers are subsidized to produce crops or bring uncultivated land into crop production, the amount of the subsidy will need to be greater. The reason is that the subsidy to preserve wetlands will also have to offset any payments that provide an opposing incentive.

Figure 13.4

Effects of government programs on farm-level land use

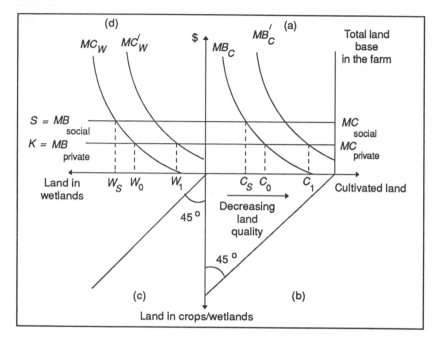

Farmers could be encouraged to preserve wetlands even if government support payments continue to favour development of land for crop production through environmental compliance, as is discussed in Chapter 12. Further, it might be possible to get decisionmakers to take into account the off-farm benefits of wetlands preservation through institutional arrangements that permit farmers to collect revenues from nonagricultural users (e.g., duck hunters), although this still ignores preservation values (which are discussed in Chapter 7).

Economics of Wetlands Preservation: A Case Study
As an example of a wetlands preservation project, the Prairie Pothole Project in Antler RM in southeastern Saskatchewan (Figure 13.1) is briefly examined. The project was started in 1986. Baseline waterfowl population and wetland densities for 1987 were completed for both the 312-square-mile Antler RM – the study area – and the 120-square-mile Walpole RM adjacent to it on the north: the control. According to the biologists attached to the project, the purpose of the baseline evaluation was to determine if a significant difference could be detected in water-

fowl population response between the project and the control areas in regard to cumulative effects of treatments during the five-year study. In the project area, management practices were expected to contribute to duck population gains that would exceed those influenced by favourable habitat, as was found in the control area. Also, wetlands in the control should show greater decline than do those in the study region, while populations in the control and project areas should indicate different responses to habitat trends due to habitat enhancement treatments.[4] There should have been an overall increase in duck populations due to raised recruitment rates and subsequent homing of surviving ducks, *provided that adequate water was available to hold breeding pairs.*

Duck population data for 1987 and two subsequent years are provided in Table 13.3.[5] Each brood consists of a 'successful' pair, with an average of five ducklings. The data indicate a dramatic decline in duck populations in southeastern Saskatchewan from 1987-9. The decline has been slightly greater in the project or study area (93.3 to 93.4 per cent decline) than in the control (90.8 to 92.1 per cent decline), although the difference cannot be considered significant.

Table 13.3. **Waterfowl population densities, southeastern Saskatchewan, 1987-9**

	Pairs		Broods	
Year	Control	Study	Control	Study
	Total ducks/square mile			
1987	253.8	186.4	26.7	19.4
1988	137.4	58.3	31.4	9.9
1989	23.3	12.3	2.1	1.3

There are a number of possible factors that affected the evaluation results:
(1) The duration of the study (1986-90) was deemed too short to permit evaluation of waterfowl trends. Since the years 1986 and 1987 were required to establish treatments, their effects were not operative until 1988, leaving only three years for evaluation.
(2) A drought cycle that started in 1986-7 persisted, leading to no increments in duck populations.
(3) The project was unable to lease sufficient uplands for habitat preservation to counter the rate of loss due to clearing and draining of land.

(4) Ducks may simply have migrated to more productive wetlands despite efforts at enhancement – Antler and Walpole RMs are a very small part of duck breeding habitat.

With regard to the first factor, little can be said, except that a short time frame will not enable one to work through the impacts of the remaining factors; it prevented researchers from identifying the effects of habitat preservation on waterfowl populations during an upturn in populations as opposed to the downturn observed in Table 13.3.

Evidence from both Canada and the U.S. indicates that it is not sufficient to use moral suasion to convince farmers to voluntarily protect wildlife habitat. Migratory and other birds have extra-market or nonmarket value as a result of hunting and viewing. Hunting values for a recent Alberta study are provided in Table 13.4; these values provide some indication of nonmarket values. Since benefits of wetlands preservation accrue to hunters, one possible means for preserving habitat is to permit farmers to charge individuals for hunting on private lands. In Oregon, this has been done to get some farmers to preserve more wetlands than they might have otherwise, while hunting-lease arrangements are widely used in Texas and other states as a wildlife/wilderness management tool.

Not taken into account in the analysis are scenic values (diverse landscape), environmental benefits (e.g., reduced wind erosion), benefits from viewing and photographing wildlife, and preservation values. That is, wetlands have value to non-hunters because they provide scenic amenities and ecological diversity, although these values may be difficult to measure (Chapter 7). Some studies suggest that preservation values for wild game may be four times as great as is their value for hunting. Thus, if the value of migratory waterfowl for hunting is assumed to be between $14.18/bird and $25.39/bird, preservation plus non-consumptive use values range from $56.72/bird and $101.56/bird, for a total value of $70 and $130/bird. This implies that waterfowl habitat may be quite valuable (although it is still necessary to convert bird values into habitat or land values); the major problem is to modify farmers' land-use decisions to take these values into account.

For migratory waterfowl, the divergence between private and social values cannot be adequately taken into account by relying on things such as moral suasion to get farmers to preserve wetlands. Rather, it is necessary to use economic incentives to convince farmers to take into account the effect of their agronomic practices on wildlife habitat. Some methods for doing so were discussed previously (Chapter 11), and they are briefly reviewed later in this chapter. However, it is important to recognize that wetlands loss is attributable, at least in part, to government agricultural policies that have encouraged agricultural producers to cultivate such areas. Not only are output subsidies based on the amount of land under cultivation, but tax laws have encouraged farmers to use larger machinery than needed, thus enabling them to cultivate closer to ponds and also making ponds a nuisance (and, thus, something to be eliminated). In addition, government agricultural policies have enabled farmers to focus on a single enterprise; farmers with livestock need wetlands and the shelter of trees and shrubs, but farmers producing only grains do not.[6] Further, input subsidies often encourage excessive use of chemicals that are harmful to wildlife, particularly young birds and the insects they feed on.

Table 13.4. **Annual extra-market values of game birds in Alberta[a]**

Item	Upland birds	Migratory birds
Number of hunting days/person[b]	6.84	7.95
Average number of birds bagged[b]	15.02	12.11
Value of a hunting day[c]		
Alberta residents	$21.60	
Non-residents	$38.68	
Value per bird[d]		
Alberta residents	$ 9.84	$14.18
Non-residents	$17.61	$25.39

[a]excludes preservation values.
[b]Phillips et al. (1989:17)
[c]Prins, Adamowicz, and Phillips (1990:19)
[d]calculation

Discussion

Water is an important resource in arid regions. In the interior of North America (and elsewhere), it is important both for irrigation and the production of waterfowl and other wildlife. Unfortunately, in both cases, markets are not clearly defined, and this results in a misallocation of resources. In the case of irrigation, it is possible to establish markets for water that will allocate the resource in an efficient manner. Pricing will prevent land degradation and political pressure to find additional sources of water supply. In the case of wetlands, lack of markets for hunting, viewing, and preservation, plus government subsidies that encourage crop production on marginal lands, have caused wetland areas to decline below a level that would be considered socially desirable. The problem is that landowners are unable to capture the extra-market benefits of preserving waterfowl and other wildlife habitat.

One policy is to provide subsidies to encourage farmers to retain wetlands. There is evidence to suggest that payments to agricultural producers to maintain wetlands are an effective method for preserving them, but only if such payments are adequate and cover the farmers' opportunity costs for keeping land out of agricultural production. While agricultural production subsidies are an important contributing factor to the loss of wetlands (Chapter 12), incentive payments provided under NAWMP simply substitute for these subsidies. The Canadian experience indicates that payments offered farmers have been inadequate; indeed, payments were sometimes provided for preserving wetlands and associated uplands (i.e., nesting areas) that would likely not have been brought into production in any event, because agricultural operations on these lands would have been difficult or impossible.

Sodbuster and swampbuster provisions are alternative means for maintaining wetlands and associated uplands in the Canadian prairie provinces. Such provisions would make farmers ineligible for agricultural subsidies if they brought wetlands into production and/or farmed upland areas. However, before such provisions could be enacted, it would be necessary to identify all areas that would qualify, and this may not be feasible from a political point of view. Geographic information system models might be helpful in constructing the needed data bases.

Canada has no definitive wetlands policy, and it does not require landowners to obtain permits to dredge or fill in wetlands (as is required by the 404 Permit Program of the U.S. Federal Clean Water Act). While Canadian law prevents farmers from draining sloughs, except for the purpose of consolidating sloughs on a single field, these regulations are not enforced.

Additional mechanisms for preserving wetland areas include purchase of land or development rights by environmental groups or government. Under the Small Wetlands Acquisition Program of the U.S. Fish and Wildlife Service, wetland easements were purchased from cooperating farmers. However, the program met with political opposition, because the existence of preserved wetland areas began to limit water diversion projects at both the local and state level. The Small Wetlands Acquisition Program has since been abandoned. Canada has no experience with this kind of policy, and current laws may inhibit employing this option. It is clear, however, that current policies in Canada make only a half-hearted attempt to protect critical waterfowl habitat and other ecologically important areas in the country's agricultural regions.

Drought is a problem for wetlands preservation. An important policy consideration is that it may be possible to provide incentives for wetlands preservation during the drought cycle only. If that is the case, substantial sums of money can be saved by appropriate policy design.

While NAWMP-funded research in the pothole region of western Canada has focused primarily on biological aspects of habitat preservation (identifying suitable wetlands areas, monitoring populations, etc.) and communications (viz., public relations and education), economics has been all but ignored. While economics may not be important to many biologists, it would seem that economics would be a major concern to those environmentalists and taxpayers who contribute to NAWMP. Given the scarcity of environmental dollars, it is necessary to ensure that the greatest potential increase in waterfowl populations be obtained at the least cost. This is far from the situation in Canada, where NAWMP funds simply offset incentives provided under other agricultural programs, and where no thought has been given to the development of optimal policies and institutions for preserving waterfowl habitat. It would seem that these issues would be foremost in the minds of environmentalists, who contribute their financial resources and time in the attempt to preserve wildlife habitat.

Part Five:
Economics of Public Land Management

Introduction to Part Five

A high degree of public ownership of forest and rangelands characterizes much of North America, especially the more arid western half of the continent and the North. Different institutions have evolved in Canada and the U.S. concerning the management of public forest and rangelands, with the most important of these likely being the different roles of the federal government in the respective countries. In the U.S., the federal government controls much of the public land through the Bureau of Land Management (BLM) and the U.S. Forest Service; in Canada, the constitution has vested ownership primarily with the provinces. However, there remain commonalities. For example, multiple use and sustainable yield were embodied in U.S. legislation during the 1960s and 1970s, as they were in Canada. Grazing fees on public lands in Canada are based on the BLM's fees, despite the controversy that has surrounded the setting of fees in the United States.

Canada's population is much smaller than that of the United States. Along with differences in the Canadian political system and a lesser degree of federal ownership of public lands, this has affected the extent to which multiple use and other aspects of land management have been implemented. The U.S. has pursued multiple-use management much more vigorously than has Canada. This is a result of differences in legislation, the political structure, the role of the courts, and, more important, greater population pressure on the land resource.

Chapter 14 reviews forest economics and forestland use and management. Alternative harvest ages for timber are described and compared. Harvest or rotation age depends upon the objectives of the decision-maker and whether there is to be one cut or many. A strategy to maximize sustainable yield results in a rotation age that is different from the rotation age based on maximization of discounted net returns from timber production. Both of these will differ from the cutting age obtained when all forest values, including nonmarket values, are maximized. One purpose of Chapter 14 is to indicate to the reader the basis of the various harvest decisions and how these differ from one another.

The purpose of Chapter 15 is to introduce readers to range economics and management. This is done by providing a background to biophysical aspects of range management and economic issues pertaining to the use of range. Included in Chapter 15 is a discussion of public grazing fees and the coevolutionary nature of private and public roles with respect to public range in the U.S.

The concepts developed in chapters 14 and 15 are utilized to study trade-offs in the use of public forest and rangelands, which are the focus in Chapter 16. Chapter 16 begins with a brief history of institutional change and public land management in both Canada and the United States. The main problem that all public land agencies face is the requirement that lands be allocated in a way that maximizes their social value; that is, decision-making must take into account multiple and conflicting land uses. The extent to which this mandate is satisfied, or even considered, in agency decision-making varies according to both the legislative guidelines and the constituency affected by such decisions. Thus, for example, British Columbia's Forest Service has tended to manage land primarily for its timber value, although this single-use focus is changing as recreationists, environmentalists, and other groups become more vocal in pointing out alternative uses and their values. Consequently, the public is seeking to hold decisionmakers more accountable to multiple-use mandates. In this regard, the courts in the U.S. have been active in the interpretation of multiple-use legislation and its enforcement – often to a degree not anticipated by Congress.

The perspective throughout Part Five is clearly an economic one. The focus is on economic tools that are used to manage public lands and to analyze land-use conflicts. But the discussion will also consider biophysical aspects of resource use and the institutions that have evolved.

14

Economics and Management of Public Forestlands

Forests cover approximately one-third of the earth's land area. They are an important source of income and employment because of the wood products they provide, but they also contribute a natural bounty, the value of which is difficult to measure. Forests are an important carbon sink, perform a weather regulation function, absorb pollutants, provide recreational and scenic amenities, contribute wildlife habitats, protect watersheds, and so on. Therefore, management of forestlands for both commercial timber production and the other amenities they provide is significant to the overall welfare of society. While production of, and trade in, wood products is vital to many economies, the emphasis in this chapter is on timber production on public lands. Although aspects of multiple use are considered, discussion of its economics is delayed until Chapter 16.

The focus is primarily on policies and management of public lands and on forest economics. The chapter begins with background on forestlands at both the international and North American level. This is followed by an examination of cutting ages for different objectives, using an example illustration. The rotation age that maximizes net worth (Faustmann rotation) is compared with the rotation that generates maximum sustainable timber yield. If forests have standing value, the Faustmann rotation age changes; where non-timber values of the forest are related to the amount of timber on a site, the optimal rotation age will need to be modified if society's economic welfare is to be maximized. One purpose of this chapter is to indicate how non-timber values affect harvest decisions.

Background to Forestlands and Land-Use Conflicts

Forests cover 4.3 billion ha or one-third of the world's land area, although 40 per cent of the earth's land is capable of growing trees. Of the forested area, 2.9 billion ha, or 68 per cent, is considered productive forestland, defined as land capable of growing merchantable stands of timber within a reasonable period of time (Table 14.1). It is estimated that the standing volume of timber on productive forestlands amounts to 310 billion cubic metres (m^3). Canada's forests account for about 10 per cent of the world's forested land and 8 per cent of its productive forestland; the United States accounts for about 7 per cent of total forested land and the same proportion of productive forestland. Only Russia has greater forest resources (Table 14.1).

Table 14.1. **World forest resources**

Country/Region	Total forestland (million ha)	Productive forestland (million ha)	Timber volume (billion m^3)
Canada	453	244	23.2
United States	296	210	23.6
South & Central America	988	740	97.0
Africa	744	236	25.0
Europe	159	137	12.0
USSR	929	792	85.9
Asia-Oceania	767	585	44.0
WORLD	4,336	2,942	310.7

Source: Forestry Canada (1990)

The U.S. is the largest producer of softwood lumber and wood products in the world, followed by Russia and Canada, as is indicated in Table 14.2. In terms of production and value, softwoods are more important than hardwoods. The main reason is that softwood forests, located primarily in the northern hemisphere, are more homogeneous than are hardwood forests, which are the main forest type in tropical regions. Lack of species uniformity makes it difficult to use trees in the pulping process, so that tropical forests are used primarily for lumber and veneers. Once tropical forests are harvested, they generally revert to agriculture (see section on deforestation below), although they can be replanted to faster growing species. In the wet tropics, hardwood species, with rotation ages of 5-10 years, can be planted; in the dry tropics, fast-growing softwood species can be planted. These species can be used for pulp production.

Table 14.2. Timber production and exports by country, selected statistics, 1988

Country	Industrial softwood roundwood production (million m³)[a]	Wood product exports ($US billions)[b]
Canada	162.7	17.4
United States	322.2	10.7
Sweden	42.6	7.4
Finland	38.1	8.2
USSR	270.8	3.0
Japan	19.1	net importer
WORLD	1,146.1	85.0

[a]Forestry Canada (1990)
[b]Nemetz (1992:30-1)

Canada is the world's foremost exporter of wood products, followed by the United States and the Scandinavian countries (Table 14.2). Although not included in Table 14.2, Germany and France rank ahead of the ex-Soviet Union in terms of wood product exports. Compared to other timber-producing regions in the world, Canada and Russia are likely at a disadvantage because of climate (particularly in the interior regions of these countries); to a lesser degree, the same might be true of the Scandinavian countries. Canada and Russia currently rely on harvests of virgin timber or timber that has regenerated on its own, while the Scandinavians are banking on past and continued plantings of fast-growing species. Average mean annual growth per hectare in Scandinavia averages more than three times that of British Columbia, for example. Rotation ages in the U.S. are much shorter than are those in Canada, and total annual growth greatly exceeds that in the latter country, particularly in the U.S. South, where plantation forests dominate (Table 14.3). Timber shortfalls have been forecast for the U.S. Pacific Northwest and South and, particularly, for Canada, where lack of plantings and reductions in the availability of virgin forests are the main reasons for the anticipated downfall. Globally, these shortfalls will likely be covered by production of radiata pine from Chile and New Zealand. But unless adequate investments are made in planting and silviculture, countries such as Canada will decline in importance in terms of world timber production. Unfortunately, reforestation and silvicultural investments on many sites are often uneconomic, and it may well be that forests in these regions provide non-timber benefits

Table 14.3. Estimated fibre availability, major North American forest regions, 1989-90

Forest region	Commercial forestland (million ha)	Rotation age[a] (years)	Annual growth in region[b] (million m³/yr)	Apparent annual growth[b] (m³/ha /yr)	% growth[b]
Ont./Que.	77.2	137.0	76	1.0	10.0
BC	24.8	72.5	80	3.2	10.5
U.S. Pacific	21.6	57.4	93	4.3	12.2
U.S. South	66.4	18.4	270	4.1	35.4
U.S. North	62.4	36.3	157	2.5	20.5
U.S. West	30.8	56.3	87	2.8	11.4
Total (average)	283.3	(53.3)	763	(2.7)	100.0

Source: BC Forest Resources Commission (1991)
[a]softwoods only
[b]softwoods and hardwoods combined

to society that exceed their commercial timber value (as is argued later in this chapter).

In the remainder of this section, we ponder a particular problem of sustainability, namely, deforestation. Then, the role of public forestlands and the determination of the allowable annual cut (and its importance as a tool of government) are considered. Finally, the economics of reforestation are examined.

Environmental Concerns and Sustainable Development: Deforestation

Many parts of the globe experience unsustainable forest removal and associated deforestation as a result of a combination of domestic and international demands for wood products (including fuel wood) and conversion to agricultural and ranch land. Brazil experienced the largest areal decrease in forestlands of any country during the 1980s, with removals of forestland averaging 3.65 million ha per year throughout the decade. Among other countries that experience a large absolute loss in forest area, deforestation in India amounted to 1.5 million ha/year; Columbia, 890,000 ha/year; Myanmar, 677,000 ha/year; Mexico, 615,000 ha/year; Zaire, 588,000 ha/year; and Côte d'Ivoire, 510,000 ha/year. But this says nothing about rates of loss, which were only 0.4 per cent per year for Brazil, for example. Annual deforestation in the United States and Canada amounted to 159,000 and 55,000 ha, respectively, during the 1980s. Globally, an average of 15.5 million ha or 0.4 per cent of forestland was deforested annually. Selected national rates of deforestation during the decade of the 1980s for those countries that experienced high annual rates are provided in Table 14.4. These indicate that the highest rates of deforestation are found in low-income countries. In contrast, the U.S. and Canada had annual deforestation rates of less than one-tenth of one per cent.

Table 14.4. **Selected national rates of deforestation for countries with high annual rates during the 1980s (per cent per year)**

Country	Deforestation rate	Country	Deforestation rate
Côte d'Ivoire	5.2	Nigeria	2.7
Nepal	4.0	Nicaragua	2.7
Haiti	3.8	Thailand	2.5
Madagascar	3.5	Mali	2.4
Sri Lanka	3.5	Liberia	2.3
Mauritius	3.3	Honduras	2.3
El Salvador	3.2	India	2.3
Jamaica	3.0	Myanmar	2.1
Burundi	2.7	Guatemala	2.0
World average	0.4		

Source: Nemetz (1992:7)

Reasons for deforestation differ among countries. Loss of forestlands in Brazil resulted because government policies promoted unsustainable land-use practices. In particular, in order to raise foreign exchange, the government provided incentives to deforest large areas in order to establish cattle ranches for export of beef. These incentives took the form of subsidized credit, tax concessions, tenure arrangements that encouraged deforestation of large tracts of land as a means to establish ownership rights, and investment in public infrastructure that encouraged access. Forests were not used for productive purposes in most cases but were razed through burning.

In many low-income countries, governments have provided private logging contractors *timber concessions*, with a view to collecting the rents from harvesting trees in wilderness areas. Empirical studies indicate that, for the most part, governments have not been successful in collecting all of the timber rents, thereby encouraging rent-seeking behaviour which resulted in timber booms. To forestall risks of contract renegotiation or revision, and sometimes because of contractual obligations imposed by government, concessionaires quickly entered the forest, employing large-scale, land-degrading forest practices. Further, royalties and other revenue schemes often encouraged *high grading* (or taking the most valuable species and the best trees), but extensive forest areas were disturbed in the process. Because the timber contractors had provided access to wilderness areas that were rarely penetrated by agricultural settlers, migrants followed the loggers, finishing the task of clearing the land and converting it to agricultural use.

Thus, deforestation has come about through a variety of ill-devised government policies that have now resulted in land that is simply more valuable when used for agriculture. Property rights to the forest resource are not clearly specified. The timber contractors have no property right to future harvests, so they have no interest in what happens to a site once the trees are removed. Agricultural settlers have no incentive to invest in crop activities that do not yield a harvest in the same season. In addition, timber production is often a lower-valued use of land than is agriculture. That forestry is a lower-valued land use is reinforced by restrictions on purchase of tropical timber by developed countries. Restrictions on the purchase of tropical timber lead to greater and not less deforestation, since such restrictions lower the value of land in timber production.

About 1 per cent of tropical forests are sustainably managed. Of the major tropical timber producers, Indonesia and Malaysia together account for 80 per cent of output (Table 14.5). However, as noted above, attempts to ban tropical wood products only make the land more attractive with respect to agriculture. Rather than implementing outright bans, developed countries need to devise incentives that encourage landowners (whether public or private) in low-income countries to practise sustainable management of forestlands.

In Canada, deforestation has occurred primarily as a result of timber harvest and inadequate replanting, but there is no alternative use that

Table 14.5. **Tropical forestry: Deforestation in major timber-producing countries**

Country	1990 forested area	1981-90 average annual deforestation	
	('000s ha)	('000s ha)	(per cent)
Indonesia	108,600	1,315	1.21
Malaysia	18,400	255	1.39
Philippines	6,500	110	1.69

Source: *Economist*, 14 November 1992, p. 40. See also Repetto and Gillis (1988).

would suggest permanent loss of forestland. Reforestation has simply not kept pace, because private companies have little incentive to plant trees on public land without guarantees over future benefits; alternative tenure arrangements may be required to accomplish this (Chapter 16). On the other hand, governments have appeared unwilling to make the needed investments in public lands, although that appears to be changing. For example, between 1985 and 1990, the federal and provincial governments eliminated 301,000 ha of denuded forestlands in British Columbia, with another 437,000 ha scheduled for elimination by the year 2000. Although replanting is occurring in much of Canada, most of the land would normally re-establish trees on its own, although the establishment of commercial as opposed to early successional or 'weed' species might take a long time. Further, trees planted today will not be available for harvest for another 80-100 years.

But there is also evidence to indicate that government policies are inadvertently contributing to deforestation in Canada. A study of old-growth timber in the Stein River Valley in British Columbia suggests that it is only profitable for forest companies to harvest timber in the region because of the tax benefits they receive. Without these, the company would lose money harvesting the trees. Governments interested in protecting wilderness areas must not only look to forest policies but must also consider the effects of the large number of other government policies (e.g., tax incentives) that affect what decisionmakers do on forestlands.

The U.S. Forest Service has long been criticized for subsidizing logging activities on public land. It is estimated that taxpayers contribute $100 million annually to subsidize timber harvest on Forest Service lands. However, public forestlands are managed for multiple use, and it is possible that, by harvesting trees, other benefits become available. If the sum of the commercial timber plus external benefits are taken together, then the costs incurred by the U.S. Forest Service are more than covered; society is better off as a result of *below-cost timber sales*. One example would be a case in which timber harvest enhances stream flow from snow melt, thereby making more water available for irrigation. Road construction and maintenance are costs incurred by the Forest Service. However, loggers are not the only beneficiaries, since the roads constructed by the Forest Service also provide access for recreationists. Thus, the externality argument is used to justify below-cost timber sales; this is examined in more detail in Chapter 16.

Public Ownership of Forestlands

Ownership of forestlands influences the management of a country's timber and non-timber resources. The extent of public ownership for selected countries (and some regions) is provided in Table 14.6. Except for the ex-Soviet Union, Canada has the highest degree of public ownership of any country or region in the world. The extent of public ownership may be important, but only if it results in a higher or lower level of social welfare than private ownership. Welfare is related both to the performance of the wood products industry and to the management of forestlands for non-timber values. Industry performance should not be influenced by ownership if tenures on public forestland give companies rights similar to those they would obtain under private land ownership. That is, industry should have the same incentives to invest in silviculture under public as under private ownership (i.e., receive the same benefits from such investments), and public ownership should not result in higher uncertainty for the forest companies. Such a state could be accomplished through appropriate tenure arrangements, which are discussed in more detail in Chapter 16.

Table 14.6. **Public forestland ownership in selected countries, 1990**

Country	Productive forestland area (millions ha)	Per cent of forestland that is public
Finland	20	24
Great Britain	21	40
Japan	25	43
Sweden	24	26
New Zealand	1	46
USSR	672	100
United States	210	28
- Oregon & Washington	17	56
- 12 southern states	66	10
Canada	244	91
- BC	51	96
- Alberta	25	96
- Ontario	38	85
- Quebec	55	88
- NB	6	51

Source: BC Forest Resources Commission (1991:36) and Forestry Canada (1990)

In the U.S., private companies have not been granted long-term tenures over public forestlands. Rather, standing timber or stumpage is sold to the highest bidder. The public agency is responsible for silvicultural investments and reforestation. In Canada, long-term tenures over certain forestlands have been granted forest companies, while other lands are managed directly by the government. Governments in Canada have, historically, altered property rights to public lands, thereby creating uncertainty (Chapter 16). But the same has occurred in the U.S. Northwest, where changes in the availability of public timber have resulted in community instability. Therefore, it is not clear whether the Canadian or American system of public land management leads to better industry performance or enhanced social welfare. It is clear, however, that plantation forests in the U.S. South and Scandinavia have generated higher yields and shorter rotation ages than is the case in Canada and regions in the U.S. where public ownership is high. Further research into forest tenures is required in order to establish the links between ownership, performance, and social welfare. Tenure is also important with respect to public rangelands, as is indicated in Chapter 15.

Timber Harvests and the Allowable Annual Cut

The *allowable annual cut* or AAC is related to sustainable development. The AAC is defined as the volume of timber, consistent with sustained yield, that may be cut each year from a forest management unit. As is indicated in the next section, the AAC should equal the mean annual increment in the growth of the trees in the management unit. However, the AAC is determined by government fiat, because yield and inventory data are unreliable. It is determined by such factors as: (1) the rate of timber production that can be sustained on a given land base; (2) the age of the trees; (3) the growth rate of the forest that regenerates after logging; (4) the technology of wood processing; (5) the need to protect other forest values; and (6) the production capacity and fibre requirements of the timber processing industries. It is clear that determination of the AAC is partly political. Protecting forestlands from logging reduces the AAC; harvests reduce the AAC, but planting higher yielding species increases the AAC. Government incentives, the tax system, tenure arrangements, and so on all impact on the allowable annual cut.

The AAC for each of Canada's provinces is provided in Table 14.7, as are the average harvest levels for the years 1982-6 and the 1986 harvest levels. British Columbia accounts for 43 per cent of Canada's total AAC and between 48 and 50 per cent of the country's timber harvest. Examination of historic AACs on public lands in BC indicates the somewhat erratic nature of its determination. The AAC increased from 1971 to

1973, when it peaked at 102.1 million m³; subsequently, it declined to between 77.0 and 79.1 million m³ for the period 1974-6, rising to over 105.0 million m³ during 1978-9, and then falling to 66.0-75.0 million m³ thereafter. Current government policy is to reduce the AAC by 10 per cent to appease environmental groups.

In 1987, roundwood output in BC reached a peak of 91 million m³, much greater than the AAC of 75 million m³. Current pulp mill capacity exceeds the available fibre supply. A recent study indicates that, due to the fibre shortage, pulp mills on the Coast will operate at only 70 per cent of capacity, while those in the northern Interior will operate at about 80 per cent of capacity. By setting the AAC at 82.5 million m³, a fibre shortage would be averted. This increase could be achieved through more intensive forestry; indeed, the current AAC could be achieved on a much smaller land base if the land were managed more intensively and if faster-growing species were planted. The reduction in the AAC proposed by the government would only add to pulp mill excess capacity and result in the decline of forest-dependent communities.

Table 14.7. **Allowable annual cut and harvest levels by province for softwoods**

Province	AAC	Average harvest (1982-6)	1986 harvest
BC	74.7	71.3	77.5
Alta	15.1	7.6	9.4
Sask.	3.6	2.5	3.1
Man.	2.6	1.3	1.6
Ont.	28.4	20.4	23.5
Que.	35.7	30.3	33.1
NB	8.1	6.6	7.6
NS	3.5	3.0	3.3
PEI	0.3	0.2	0.2
Nfld.	3.0	2.5	2.4
CANADA	175.0	145.7	161.9

Source: Runyon (1991:24)

Economics of Reforestation

Foresters are generally concerned that new forests be established on clearcut forestlands as soon as possible. They are also in favour of intensive silviculture to enhance tree growth and quality. The economist does not take reforestation and intensive silviculture for granted. Rather, the economist argues that it is necessary to establish the profitability of such investments. Unfortunately, economic research suggests that the net returns from reforestation and intensive silviculture in many parts of Canada and much of the northern U.S. are negative. Where reforestation and intensive silviculture are not economically viable if based solely on commercial timber values, this is the result of two factors. First, benefits occur far in the future, while costs are incurred early on. Even at low rates of discount (say 4 per cent), many investments in silviculture (including reforestation) yield negative returns. Second, the benefits of reforestation and silviculture are incremental. That is, most stands that have been denuded as a result of fire, disease, or harvest will often re-establish a growing stand of trees on their own. Silviculture results in incremental growth and, perhaps, an increase in timber quality and value. Again, benefits of silviculture often accrue in the distant future, and this makes these activities uneconomic. However, there are notable exceptions, and each investment in reforestation or silviculture must be judged on its own merit. The exceptions occur where faster-growing species are planted, and intensive forestry is practised on lands best suited for commercial timber production.

Two arguments have been used to justify reforestation where it is not otherwise viable. One is that reforestation is a cost of harvest and, there-fore, should be treated as such. Although this is a legitimate argument from the point of view of a private forest company that is constrained by a law requiring it to regenerate harvested lands, it is, nonetheless, a social cost that must be evaluated in terms of the benefits provided (in the same way that any other public investment should be evaluated). Another argument is that reforestation results in an increase in the AAC, and that the *allowable cut effect* has a positive and immediate benefit that is to be attributed to investments in reforestation. The fallacy in this argument is that any action raising the AAC (including a simple executive decision to increase it) can then be justified on the basis of the benefits from cutting timber faster. The timber cut as a result of a higher AAC cannot be used to justify investments on unrelated forestlands. The benefits of investments in reforestation and silviculture are only the value of the enhanced future timber yields.

It is possible to justify investments in reforestation and intensive silviculture in the aforementioned situations on the basis of their exter-nal or nonmarket benefits, however. For example, studies indicate that reforestation of denuded lands may be justified on the basis of carbon sequestration benefits alone. Silviculture may be economically feasible because it also promotes wildlife habitat, which has value to society; or silviculture might enhance the watershed function of forestlands. It is on the basis of both the commercial timber and the nonmarket values that investments in forestry can and should be justified.

Economics and Forestland Use

Harvesting of timber by clearcutting a stand has an obvious and immediate impact upon land use. Selective harvesting also has an impact on land use, but it is not nearly as dramatic as is clearcutting, nor does it have the same visual impact. The age at which trees are harvested is an important factor in determining how forestlands are used. Depending on the decisionmaker's objectives, there are a number of different criteria that are used to determine the age of harvest. These are examined in this section, and a hypothetical illustration is used to demonstrate the effect of different harvesting strategies.

Maximizing Sustainable Yield

Maximum sustainable yield (MSY) is used by biologists to determine optimal harvest ages for timber. As implied by its name, the objective is to find the forest rotation age that leads to the maximum possible annual output that can be maintained in perpetuity. The allowable annual cut is based on the MSY concept. The annual allowable cut is the amount of timber that can be harvested each and every year without diminishing the amount that can be harvested in any future year. It is simply the net increase in timber volume in a region or district that results from tree growth – the *mean annual increment*. The AAC will increase if slower-growing, mature trees are harvested and replaced by faster-growing, young trees. This is the *allowable cut effect*. If there is much mature or over-mature timber, harvesting such timber and reforesting the site will increase the AAC. But the increase in the AAC resulting from reforestation should *not* be counted as an immediate benefit of reforestation, as was discussed above.

The MSY rotation age is found by setting the rate of growth of timber, which is a function of age (t), equal to the inverse of the forest's age, and solving for t. Denote the rate of growth in timber over time as $v(t)$. The rate of change of any variable is given by the change in that variable during the time period divided by the average of the variable at the beginning and end of the time period. Thus, the rate of change in timber volume or its rate of growth over the discrete time interval $t = 0$ to $t = 1$ is

$$\frac{v(1) - v(0)}{1/2 \ [v(0) + v(1)]}.$$

The instantaneous rate of change is given by the change in the variable at that moment in time (i.e., the first derivative) divided by its value at that time:

$$\frac{v'(t)}{v(t)}. \tag{14.1}$$

Then the MSY rotation age is determined by finding the age for which

$$\frac{v'(t)}{v(t)} = \frac{1}{t}. \tag{14.2}$$

As an illustration, suppose the following function describes the growth in the yield of commercial timber for a stand of spruce trees:

$$v(t) = 0.25 \ t^2 \ e^{-0.02t}, \tag{14.3}$$

where v is timber volume measured in m^3. Hypothetical commercial

Figure 14.1

Comparison of MSY, single harvest and Faustmann ages for r = 4%

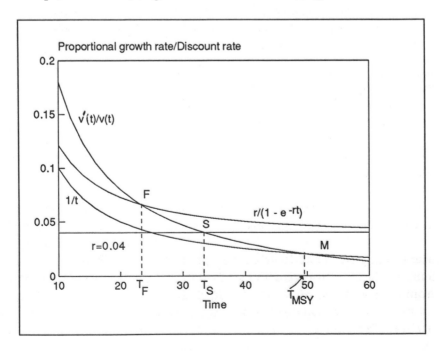

timber yields and values at different ages are provided in Table 14.8, while a plot of the growth rate, $v'(t)/v(t)$, is provided in Figure 14.1. Also included in Figure 14.1 is a plot of 1/age or $1/t$. The MSY rotation age is determined by the intersection of the two functions; this occurs at point M in the figure or for rotation age T_{MSY}.

Table 14.8. Commercial timber growth and value, and amenity values, for a hypothetical stand of spruce trees

Age	Timber volume[a] (m³)	Value of timber ($/ha)[b]	Rate of growth[c]	Amenity values[d] ($/ha)	Rate of change in amenity value
4	3.69	184.62	0.48	0.47	0.24
8	13.63	681.72	0.23	0.90	0.11
12	28.32	1,415.93	0.15	1.28	0.07
16	46.47	2,323.68	0.11	1.62	0.05
20	67.03	3,351.60	0.08	1.92	0.04
24	89.10	4,455.24	0.06	2.19	0.03
28	111.96	5,597.85	0.05	2.42	0.02
32	134.99	6,749.34	0.04	2.62	0.02
36	157.71	7,885.39	0.04	2.80	0.01
40	179.73	8,986.58	0.03	2.95	0.01
44	200.75	10,037.75	0.03	3.08	0.01
48	220.55	11,027.32	0.02	3.18	0.01
52	238.94	11,946.77	0.02	3.27	0.01
56	255.80	12,790.17	0.02	3.34	0.00
60	271.07	13,553.74	0.01	3.40	0.00

[a]Equation (14.3)
[b]assumes net price of $50/m³
[c]Equation (14.1)
[d]Equation (14.8)

For plantation forests and under an MSY rotation, the AAC is equal to the MSY. The same is not true for forests that consist of mature, over-mature, and young stands of trees. In that case, the AAC and MSY are subject to vagaries of harvesting and planting. However, if one's desire is to maximize the welfare of society, the MSY rotation may not be the one on which to base decisions.

Maximizing Net Benefits from a Single Cut

Suppose the objective of forest operations is to maximize the net benefit from a one-time harvest of the forest; that is, the discounted value of future harvests (or *soil expectation* of the land) is not considered in the decision. For simplicity, it is assumed that the cost of harvest is zero.[1]

The economic decision concerning when to harvest is quite simple. Timber should be held uncut as long as the value of the timber is increasing at a rate greater than the rate of return on alternative investments (i.e., the discount rate). When the rate of tree growth is falling, the trees should be harvested the moment the rate of growth in value equals the discount rate. The owner of the woodlot simply keeps his or her investment tied up in the forest stand unless more can be earned by liquidating the investment (cutting the timber) and investing the funds from its sale at the alternative rate of return – the interest or discount rate. The harvest age is determined by solving for t in

$$\frac{v'(t)}{v(t)} = r, \tag{14.4}$$

where r is the (instantaneous) rate of discount.

It should be noted that the decision to harvest is independent of price, as can be seen by multiplying both the numerator and denominator in equations (14.1) and (14.4) by price. However, price is important in the decision for one reason: if price is too low, so that the net revenue from harvesting a stand of trees is negative, then the trees will not be harvested regardless of their rate of growth. The cost of harvesting trees can be incorporated in the decision by modifying equation (14.4) as follows:

$$\frac{P\,v'(t)}{P\,v(t)\,-\,c} = r, \tag{14.5}$$

where P is output price and c is the cost of harvesting the stand.[2] In Figure 14.1, the age at which to harvest trees is given by T_S (where S denotes single harvest).

The Faustmann Rotation Age

What is not taken into account in the single-harvest solution is the possibility that, once timber is harvested, a new stand of trees can be generated on the land. The second growth can be harvested at a later date. Regeneration can be hastened through reforestation and silviculture. By taking into account the potential of the land to grow another stand of trees, the harvest period is actually shortened. The reason is that, by cutting trees sooner, it also makes available a second and third harvest sooner than would otherwise have been the case. The optimal rotation age can be found mathematically by finding the rotation age t^* that maximizes the present value formula

$$P\ v(t)e^{-rt} + P\ v(t)e^{-2rt} + \ ... \ = \frac{P\ v(t)e^{-rt}}{(1-e^{-rt})}, \qquad (14.6)$$

where $P\ v(t)$ is the value (prime x volume) of timber growing on the site at time t, and r is the rate of discount, as before. Maximizing present value (by setting the first derivative of equation (14.6) to zero) gives

$$\frac{v'(t)}{v(t)} = \frac{r}{1 - e^{-rt}}. \qquad (14.7)$$

Compared to the cutting rule in equation (14.4), the fact that the denominator on the right-hand side of (14.7) is less than one but greater than zero has the same effect as does increasing the discount rate in (14.4). An increase in the discount rate would cause one to harvest sooner.

The Faustmann harvest or rotation age (T_F) is indicated in Figure 14.1. It is given by the intersection of the timber growth curve and the 'modified' discount formula, or point F in Figure 14.1.

Including Externalities or Nonmarket Values: The Hartman Rotation Age

The Faustmann rotation considers only the value of a forest in production of commercial timber. Excluded from the calculation are extramarket benefits of standing trees. Standing trees have value to society in addition to commercial timber value; these values are derived from scenic amenities, watershed functions, sequestration of carbon, absorption of other pollutants, habitat for wildlife, and so on. If nonmarket values are related to the number of trees or timber volume growing in the forest, then (if society is to maximize its welfare from managing the forest) the Faustmann rotation age needs to be modified to take these values into account. The Hartman rotation age (T_H) is based on the maximization of external or amenity values.

Two things must be remembered. First, not all external benefits of the forest are related to the volume of timber or number of trees growing on a site. Where external benefits are not correlated with growth, it is not possible to determine directly the optimal harvest age that would take external values into account. Other methods will be required, some of which are discussed in Chapter 16. Second, unlike commercial timber benefits (which accrue at the time the forest is harvested), nonmarket benefits accrue in each period and must be counted at that time.

Assume that amenity values for a stand of spruce increase with age according to the function

$$a(t) = 0.125 \; t^2 \; e^{-0.0132t}, \tag{14.8}$$

where $a(t)$ is measured in dollars per hectare. Selected amenity or external values and their rate of change are provided in Table 14.8. Since amenity values accrue annually rather than when the trees are harvested (as is the case for commercial timber values), the Hartman rotation age is found by solving the following equation for t:[3]

$$\frac{a'(t)}{a(t)} = \frac{r \; e^{-rt}}{1 - e^{-rt}}. \tag{14.9}$$

The Faustmann and Hartman rotation ages are compared in Figure 14.2. The Hartman rotation age is longer than the Faustmann age, but only if amenity values increase with stand age; if they decline with age, the Hartman rotation is shorter. When decisions are based on maximizing both commercial timber benefits and external values, the rotation age falls somewhere between the Hartman and Faustmann ages. How-

Figure 14.2

Comparison of Hartman and Faustmann rotation ages for r = 4%

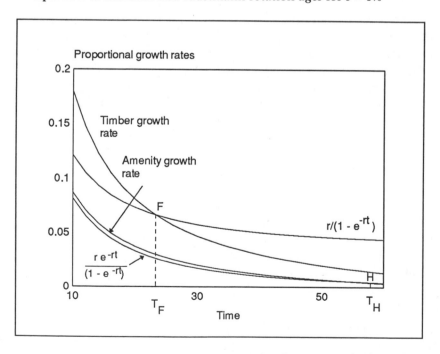

ever, for some forests, the external benefits (which would include preservation value) might be so great that it would not be economically feasible to harvest the forest. Thus, in contrast to the Faustmann model, the age of the inherited stocks may matter. If the age of the timber exceeds the Hartman age, it may be preferable to delay harvest or simply never harvest. The existing flow of amenity values associated with 'over mature' forests may be sufficient to justify their preservation, especially if such forestlands are relatively scarce and highly valued. With commercial timber value alone, the optimal strategy is to cut the trees as soon as possible when their age exceeds the Faustmann age.

Discussion

The topics covered in this chapter are only a small component of the many issues and problems with which forest economists deal. The focus here was rather narrow; we examined the impact of forestry on land use, and even that topic received only cursory treatment. However, the purposes of the discussion were to indicate that forestlands provide multiple resources, and that proper management of public forestlands requires that both timber and non-timber values be taken into account in decision-making. This topic is addressed further in Chapter 16, where we also examine the historical development of policy relating to public forestlands and how institutions evolved in the U.S. and Canada. A second purpose of the discussion in this chapter was to examine the role of government in affecting sustainable forestland use decisions. It turns out that in many cases, the unintended and unanticipated consequences of government policies (and not just forestry policies but also policies that affect forestry indirectly) have been to aggravate forestland degradation. Solving the dilemma of sustainable development in forestry will require better knowledge of the links between the ecological and social systems, as is noted in Chapter 8.

15
Economics and Public Rangeland Management

Rangelands are any lands suitable for grazing or browsing by livestock and wildlife. They include natural grasslands, savannahs, shrublands, wet meadows, forestlands, and lands revegetated naturally or artificially in order to provide forage cover that is managed like native vegetation, if at all. Range resources refer to the vegetation, including forage, used by livestock and wildlife. Rangelands are an important natural resource in many areas of the world, including Canada and the United States, but they are often neglected because of their low profile with the public. This is particularly true in regions such as British Columbia and Washington, where issues related to timber harvest take centre stage. This is less true in arid regions of the western U.S. and the Sahel, where range resources are important for the livelihoods or very survival of the people living in the region.

Given the extent of public ownership of rangelands in Canada and the western U.S., the focus of this chapter is on public rangelands. Public rangelands are important, because the clientele served by the public range manager is not confined to a single user. In British Columbia, for example, the beneficiaries of public rangeland management are identified as including the beef-ranching industry, commercial horse operators, sheep producers, hunters, guides and outfitters, consumptive and non-consumptive wildlife enthusiasts, recreationists, timber companies, trappers, and Aboriginal peoples. Given the diversity of these interest groups, it is only natural that conflicts concerning management should arise. Resolving conflicts in a way that maximizes the social benefits received from the range resource is the principle task of range economics and management.

In this chapter, we provide a background to biological and economic issues related to range management and an introduction to potential rangeland conflicts. Rather than focus on ranch management, the objective is to indicate the economic role of public range in the production of domestic livestock and, with it, a discussion of grazing fees. The chapter provides background to a more in-depth discussion of multiple use in Chapter 16.

Background to Rangeland Resources

The bioeconomic unit of measurement describing use of rangeland resources is the animal unit month, or AUM. An AUM is the amount of feed or range services required to maintain a 1,000-lb. (450-kg) cow or its equivalent for a period of one month. Since it is based on metabolic weight, the AUM serves as a conversion factor of forage requirements across herbivorous species. Cattle equivalents are used to measure the forage requirements of other animals; for example, forage required by a sheep is equivalent to 0.2-0.25 AUMs (i.e., forage requirements of five sheep are the same as those of one cow). The general formula for converting the forage requirements of other animals is

$$W^{3/4}/AU^{3/4},$$

where W is the weight (in lbs.) of the animal in question and AU refers to the basic animal unit, namely, a 1,000-lb. cow.

When converting wildlife forage (wildlife AUM) requirements to livestock AUM equivalents, it is necessary to keep in mind that the conversion formula assumes similar foraging habits, which may not be the case. Some animals are grazers and some are browsers, while others are mixed feeders. Nutrient requirements and comparison of AUMs cannot truly be represented by the foregoing equation; not only do feeding requirements and habits vary by species, for example, but according to the breed of cattle. This makes it difficult to evaluate use of rangeland by wildlife in AUM equivalents, which is a particular problem for the construction of trade-offs between domestic livestock and wildlife.

Research indicates that, on average, the feed requirements for one AUM equal about 300 kg (660 lbs.) of available forage. A rough rule of thumb for determining the amount of grazing to permit on grasslands is to estimate the total forage yield, allow a 45 per cent carry-over to avoid damage to the range, and divide the remaining forage by the requirements of one AUM. It is not clear, however, if this rule holds for forest range (e.g., clearcuts).

In this section, technical aspects of range resources are discussed, primarily because the complexity of the ecosystem has implications concerning the types of models that economists use. The focus is on the interactions between vegetation growth and grazing, although the discussion begins by considering investments in range improvements. Additional discussion is found in Chapter 16.

Investments in Range Improvements

There are a number of management practices that can enhance the productivity of rangelands. Seeding of forest clearcuts to forages is one possibility. Although native forage is available on clearcuts, there are benefits to seeding domestic species. In addition to such benefits as erosion control, increased soil fertility, and mitigation against weed invasion, seeding of domestic species increases productivity of the range for cattle. Studies of burn sites, for example, found that yields on seeded sites were 3,400 kg/ha compared to 1,300 kg/ha on sites left to regenerate on their own; undisturbed sites yielded about 500 kg/ha. However, there is little information concerning the biophysical aspects of seeding clearcuts (i.e., yields, competition among between and tree seedlings, fate and persistence of seeded forages, rate of recolonization of native plants, etc.), let alone economic feasibility.

On forestlands that have not been denuded, management to improve forage for livestock consists of tree thinning and prescribed burning. While thinning is not economically feasible (due to the expense of slash removal), the same is likely true for prescribed burning. However, there is little or no economic information about either of these management activities.

Finally, there have been economic studies that examine the feasibility of cultivating open range and seeding domestic forage. These studies are the result, primarily, of efforts in the United States to restore range that had previously been overgrazed. Investments in range improvements via ploughing and seeding, provision of inputs (water, fencing), and prescribed burning or chemical spraying to eliminate unproductive species have occurred, primarily, as a result of political factors. Although congressional appropriations in the U.S. for range improvements require a cost-benefit analysis, in practice, this has not always been the case. Ex post analysis of investments in range improvements in Oregon, for example, found that such investments were only marginally feasible. However, the rangelands chosen for improvement were considered to be less productive than were alternative sites; that is, the public decisionmaker had not chosen the most profitable sites for seeding.

In summary, investments in range improvements can enhance the productivity of both forest and open rangelands. These investments include prescribed burning, seeding (with or without seedbed preparation), and physical structure (e.g., fencing). Along with herd management (location and duration of grazing), range investments can increase the output of the livestock sector. Although studies of the biophysical interactions of these management techniques are ongoing, too little attention is given to their economic aspects. Economic analysis of rangeland investments indicate that some yield net benefits to society, but that others result in losses. It is important to identify range investments that are efficient, weeding out projects that are unable to cover society's costs.

Forage/Cattle/Wildlife Interaction: Range Condition and Production Functions

The interactions among vegetation (forage), domestic livestock, and wildlife are important in the context of range management; they are also important considerations in economic models of multiple use of public rangelands (Chapter 16).

Systems Modelling

The integration of all possible interactions in a systems model of rangelands and their management rarely occurs in practice, primarily due to difficulties in modelling them. Nonetheless, simple models may be useful as an aid to policymakers. A possible systems model is provided in Figure 15.1. The model is, essentially, composed of three modules identified by rectangular boxes. Exogenous factors or management decisions are enclosed by an oval.

In Figure 15.1, biophysical factors, such as weather and elevation, are instrumental in determining the types of vegetation (species and competition) and their quantity and quality, that is, the *range condition* (defined below). Range condition is affected by grazing and human intervention (viz., range investments). In order to simulate the herbivory, it is necessary to identify the various herbivores that use the range, the plants they eat, the amounts eaten, the interactions among herbivores, and so on. Based on this information, population growth over time for cattle, elk, and other animals are constructed. Population growth minus harvests have a feedback effect on future vegetation and range condition, as do range investment, stocking decisions, and exogenous biophysical factors.

Figure 15.1

Systems model of rangeland use

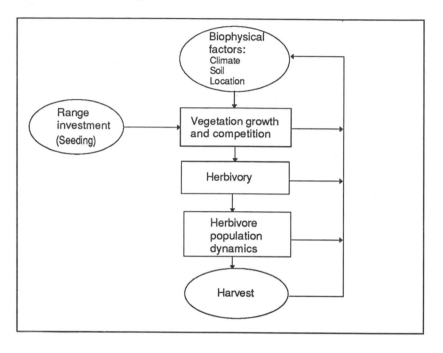

Production Relations
Utilization of the range by cattle is a function of the relative palatability
and availability of forage. The presence of slash from logging operations
significantly lowers utilization, for example, although slash helps to
control erosion. The mix of domestic and native forages, and the types
of domestic forages that are seeded, affect utilization.

Range condition is an appraisal that depends on how much the current vegetation deviates from its potential on the range site (Figure
15.2). The term 'potential' usually refers to the climax community, so
that range condition refers to the extent to which the present plant
community still represents the climax vegetation. The term *range condition trend* refers to the direction of change in forage composition and
productivity on a range site, normally in response to grazing. Competition from native herbs and shrubs leads to a downward trend in range
condition (unrelated to livestock utilization), while grazing may result
in an upward or downward trend in range condition.

Figure 15.2

Qualitative basis for determining range condition

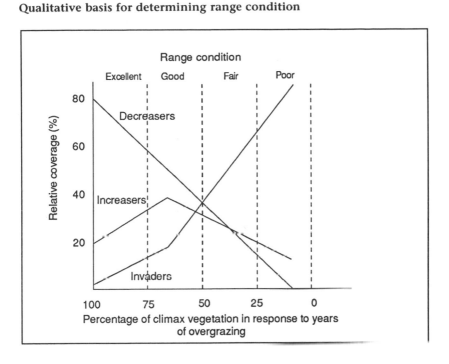

With some exceptions, climax grasses are preferred livestock forage and are known as *decreasers*. Somewhat lower quality plants are known as *increasers*, because their proportion within the plant community expands with grazing. Management needs to balance the decreasers and increasers so that the range remains as productive and useful for forage as possible. Finally, *invaders* are unwanted or weed species that become more prevalent with long periods of excessive grazing pressure. The decreasers and increasers are grasses that are palatable to herbivores (although palatability varies from one species to the next), while invaders are not eaten. In British Columbia, knapweed is a particularly problematic invader of rangelands.

The relation between decreasers, increasers, and invaders provides a quantitative measure of range condition, as is illustrated in Figure 15.2. As the range is grazed, the more palatable decreasers begin to decline, but increasers are able to expand their cover. However, as the availability of decreasers declines and increasers are utilized to a larger extent, increasers also begin to decline, thereby permitting invaders to overtake the range. Range condition declines from excellent into classes of good, fair, or poor as the percentage of climax or preferred species decreases. The categories excellent, good, fair, and poor are also referred to, respectively, as climax and late, mid-, and early successional.

Overgrazing is the main cause of depletion of the range resource. In 1986, 18 per cent of the U.S. Bureau of Land Management's rangeland was considered to be in poor condition, while 35 per cent was in good or excellent condition; 20 per cent of U.S. Forest Service rangeland was thought to be in an unsatisfactory management state.

Production functions for a range are indicated in Figure 15.3. Rather than constituting a 'single-line' frontier, as is typical in production economics theory, the range production function (depicting range condition and trend) is a thick curve. The upper line (A) represents conditions where forage plants are vigorous, while the lower line (B) represents the average lowest yield recorded for the range condition – low-vigour forage plants. Vigour is affected not only by weather but also by grazing and range investments (e.g., burning and fertilization). If vigour is related, primarily, to the stocking rate, then one can consider the upper line to represent the case where the stocking rate permits the range to recover, while the lower line represents excessive grazing pressure. In the former case, it is possible (perhaps with other investment) to improve the range, while, in the latter case, range condition trend is negative. This is indicated by the directional arrows on lines A and B in Figure 15.3.

With data from Texas, utilization and carrying capacity of the range are also illustrated in Figure 15.3. Domestic cattle and antelope are assumed to graze on the range in question. Since each animal prefers a different species of plant, utilization and carrying capacity for cattle and antelope vary with range condition, as is indicated at the bottom of the diagram. The bottom rows in the diagram provide some information regarding the trade-off between domestic and wildlife grazing – information that is important in deciding optimal multiple use of rangelands, as is discussed in the next chapter.

Dynamic modelling is needed to analyze the interaction among vegetation, domestic cattle, and wildlife grazing and the effect of stocking rate or harvest decisions on the dynamics of the system. The effect of stocking rates on animal growth might be modelled using information similar to that in Table 15.1.

Since questions concerning 'will it pay' cannot be separated from

Figure 15.3

Production functions for vegetation and herbivores for hypothetical 100-hectare range in Texas

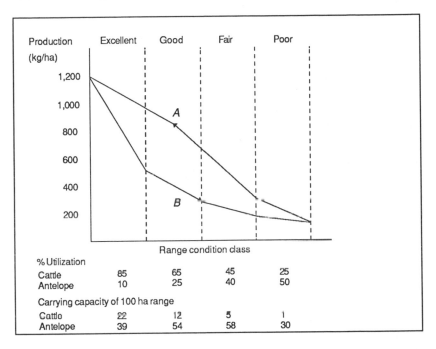

those dealing with 'will it work,' it is clear that the economic consequences of range management decisions cannot be separated from the biophysical consequences. Biophysical constraints constitute the production function of economics – the trade-off function among competing land uses. Therefore, range economics cannot be practised without input from biologists, and biologists cannot make efficient management decisions without input from economists.

Table 15.1. **Stocking rate and effect on livestock growth**

Stocking rate	Cows		Calves	
(ha/AUM)	(kg/head/yr)	(kg/ha/yr)	(kg/head/yr)	(kg/ha/yr)
4.0	16.8	1.12	88.0	5.71
1.2	13.2	1.12	81.7	6.95
0.8	-1.8	-0.11	76.2	8.96

Source: Nordstrom (1984:68)

Range Economics: Grazing on Public Lands

It is clear that ranchers cannot be permitted to graze domestic livestock on public land without some mechanism for allocating the range resource. Historically, over-grazing by domestic animals (especially sheep) resulted in rangeland degradation in the western U.S. The reason was that the range was an *open-access* resource. Ranchers had no stake in conserving or improving the range, because they did not own the resource and would, therefore, not be the sole beneficiaries of any efforts on their part to preserve it. Rangeland degradation currently occurs in the Sahel, because property arrangements permit individual farmers to obtain the benefits from planting annual crops but discourage investments, such as seeding forages or planting trees, that yield benefits over a longer period. Benefits of long-term investments would be captured by others. It is because individuals are unable to reap all the future benefits of investments that rangeland degradation often occurs, and that public intervention is required. (This is also a reason for deforestation, as is noted in Chapter 14.)

Open access and lack of investment in range resources do not, by themselves, warrant public ownership of the resource. The problem of open access can be solved simply by providing tenure to the range, but this does not need to be accompanied by ownership, since there are legitimate externality reasons for public ownership of the resource. These reasons concern other values of the range that cannot be captured by a private owner. For example, when farmers are not permitted to trap or hunt wildlife in order to reduce grazing pressure, there is no incentive to maintain the range. In addition, rangelands have non-trivial option and existence values. As is noted in earlier chapters, recreation, hunting, and preservation values are generally not captured by the private resource owner, and these range benefits are not taken into account in private investment decisions concerning public range. These factors have resulted in public ownership of rangelands in much of the western U.S. and in some regions of Canada.

Cattle operators can be divided into four categories: cow-calf, cow-yearling, background, and finishing. Cow-calf and cow-yearling operators have a substantial investment in a cow herd, which generally includes one bull for every twenty cows. Bulls are replaced every three years, although some ranchers lease bulls to avoid the costs of winter feed and to provide greater flexibility in breeding. Approximately 80 per cent of the cows give birth to calves which are born in the early spring. In the fall, 15 per cent of the herd is generally culled, and calves are sold, except for those to be used as replacement heifers. (For genetic reasons, replacement steers are always purchased.) A cow-yearling operator will keep the calves somewhat longer, selling them the following year as short or long yearlings, depending upon whether they are sold in the spring or fall, respectively. Background operators have no investment in a cow herd but purchase calves in the fall for sale the following year. Finishing occurs in beef lots.

In remote, arid regions of western North America, cow-calf and cow-yearling operations dominate. These activities are also those which rely most upon range resources. Depending upon location and climate, cattle feeding can be divided into six periods per year, two of which occur during the winter: (1) early spring, (2) early summer, (3) summer, (4) fall, (5) winter, and (6) calving. The year can also be divided into monthly feeding periods (or feeding periods that differ from the above), but, practically speaking, these are a function of when calves are born and the availability of range and pasture lands (i.e., climatic conditions). In northern areas, public range is not available during the winter and calving seasons, so at those times cattle graze on private pastures found at low elevations or utilize private feed stocks.

The rancher has to make decisions concerning the allocation of privately owned improved and unimproved lands subject to the availability of public range or community pastures. Tenure requirements may also make the rancher responsible for allocation decisions on public range, subject to any constraints imposed by the public agency.[1] In Canada, ranchers are given either grazing licences, which provide some guarantee regarding long-term use of the range, or grazing permits, which are renewable but subject to periodic review. In the U.S., grazing rights take the form of permits, which appear to be an inviolable property right (see discussion later in chapter).

Administered Prices and Domestic Grazing on Public Range

Grazing rights on public rangelands and the fees charged to ranchers are not determined in the marketplace; public grazing fees are an example of administered prices. In Canada and the United States, public agencies determine both the amount of domestic livestock that can be grazed and the amount that needs to be paid in order to graze them; in Canada, public agencies might also determine to whom grazing rights are given (grazing licences), while in the U.S., grazing permits are bought and sold by individuals. The government agency responsible for rangeland management also makes decisions concerning range improvements, although ranchers themselves will often make improvements on public lands.

Figure 15.4

Benefits of grazing on public rangeland

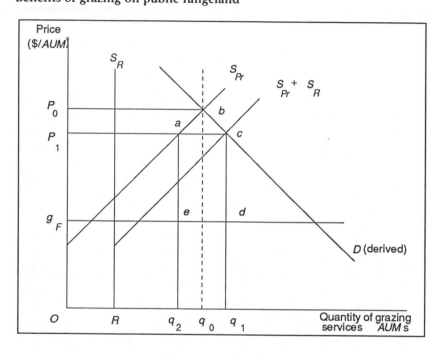

The effect of grazing on public rangelands and the impact of administered prices (grazing fees) is illustrated in Figure 15.4. In the figure, the derived demand for range and pasture services is assumed to have the usual negative slope. Although final output price (price of beef) is a parameter to the individual beef producer, it is likely that some of the inputs into production will have finite supply elasticities, thereby giving rise to the negative slope for derived demand.

The supply of private foraging services (S_{Pr}) is upward sloping, because sources of supply can be ordered according to their basic unit costs: unimproved land (with little alternative use) owned by the farmer, pasture land rented from other private owners, and improved land on the farmer's own property that can be used for hay or grain production. The supply of public rangeland (S_R) is determined by public agency fiat and, therefore, is assumed to be totally inelastic at the number of AUMs of public grazing made available by the government agency (amount OR).

Given that there is a public supply of rangeland services (measured in AUMs) of amount q_2q_1 ($= OR$), the supply of grazing services is given by $S_{Pr} + S_R$, and the net amount of grazing services resulting from public provision of rangeland is given by q_0q_1, with the actual amount depending on the elasticities of supply and demand. If N is the increase in total range and pasture consumption as a proportion of the amount of public range made available ($N = q_0q_1/q_1q_2$), then $N = Ed/(Es + Ed)$, where Es is the elasticity of supply and Ed is the elasticity of demand. The benefits of grazing on public rangeland are the results of two effects. (1) There is an increase in the benefits accruing to cattle producers, because the price of private range/pasture services has fallen from P_0 to P_1. This increase in benefits is measured by the area under the demand function, namely, q_0bcq_1. (2) An amount q_2q_0 of range/pasture services is released for use in its best alternative. In the current situation, there is a shift of grazing from own pasture land to public range. The freed pasture land can be used to produce hay or other crops (e.g., barley) that can be fed to the cattle during the winter months. This benefit is measured by the area q_2abq_0.

The private users of the public range (i.e., cattle ranchers) pay a grazing fee (g_f) that is administered and likely below the market price. There are several reasons why the grazing fee might be below the market price: (1) the agency does not know what impact provision of public range has on market prices (i.e., P_1 versus P_0); (2) the opportunity costs of providing public range are negligible – a result of normal forest harvesting and administrative activities; and (3) the administered price structure is an institutional arrangement that has bestowed historic property rights upon cattle ranchers. These historic rights or benefits are capitalized in ranch values, and withdrawal of them, now or in the future, may require some form of compensation. Compensation is required because current owners paid for the grazing rights when they purchased the ranch.

In terms of Figure 15.4, ranchers pay a price of P_1 for Oq_2 AUMs of grazing services and g_f for the remaining q_2q_1 AUMs. Thus, the net benefits to cattle ranchers from public grazing are given by area $eabcd$, which consists of a subsidy equal to the rectangle $acde$ plus an efficiency gain equal to triangle abc. The efficiency gain may be quite large if ranchers are able to increase herd size and, thereby, achieve economies of scale that are not possible without publicly provided range services.

Whenever cattle are shifted from private pasture to public range during the spring, summer, and fall grazing periods, a constraint on cattle numbers is relaxed. Private pasture can now be used to produce hay, forages, or other feed that can be used in the winter months. Thus, an increase in grazing on public range will make private lands more productive and ranchers better off. These benefits are capitalized in ranch values or grazing permits (generally attached to ranches). The capitalized value of these grazing permits is given by area (*abc* + *eacd*) divided by the private discount rate (with the discount rate including an allowance for risk). In a 1986 study, the U.S. departments of Agriculture and the Interior estimated that the value of public land grazing permits was between a low of \$30/AUM in Idaho and a high of \$140/AUM in Nebraska. These estimates represent the capitalized value of the two areas identified in Figure 15.4, as derived from the bond formula, $V = B/r$, where r is the discount rate (Chapter 5). Assuming a discount rate of 5 per cent ($r = 0.05$), the areas average to between \$1.50 and \$7.00 per AUM. If a higher discount rate is employed (e.g., to account for the risk that grazing rights might be lost at some future date), then the value of grazing is greater (e.g., \$3-\$10 at a 10 per cent rate).

There remains the question of whether or not ranchers receive a subsidy; this question concerns the size of rectangle *eacd* or, put another way, the nearness of the grazing fee g_f to the price P_1. The costs to taxpayers are equal to the amount spent by the public agency in providing grazing services minus revenues from grazing fees, where revenues equal g_f times *OR*. Suppose that public agency costs are covered by a grazing fee g_f that is strictly less than P_1. Is there still a subsidy to ranchers? Since the public grazing fee could be set at P_1 without changing the amount of forage services demanded by ranchers (i.e., the number of AUMs utilized), the public agency does not collect the rent to which it, as the owner of the range, is entitled. Hence, the low grazing fee (g_f) constitutes a subsidy to ranchers even if the fee covers all agency costs. This does not constitute an argument to raise grazing fees, however, because proprietary property rights and political factors also need to be taken into account in setting fees.

Often the public agency is faced with decisions regarding *marginal* changes in animal units of grazing on public rangeland. Perhaps the decision is whether or not to make a particular range improvement or whether or not to reduce domestic grazing so that more is available for wildlife. Since changes are marginal, the total benefits of an increase (costs of a reduction) in public grazing can be approximated by the market price P_1 of an AUM of grazing times the number of AUMs made available by the program (decision). Again, the net private benefit of (loss due to) such a decision is given by the change in AUMs times the difference between the market price and g_f. However, if the changes in the availability of public range are *non-marginal*, then an analysis similar to that in Figure 15.4 is required. For example, *OR* might be considered the change (increase or decrease) in public range services rather than the total forage available from public rangelands.

The difficulty in the foregoing analysis is that of determining the costs of providing public range, since these are not incurred by the private operators but by the public agency that administers the range. These non-private costs are difficult to measure and may even be negligible in cases where excess capacity exists or where the public range was previously poorly managed. The costs of providing grazing services on public lands consist of two components. First, there are administration costs, transaction costs, and outlays for range improvements. These costs are measurable. The second, and more difficult, component of costs involves alternative uses of the range, including wildlife grazing. A reduction in wildlife numbers implies a reduction in the welfare of hunters as well as of preservationists, sightseers, and so on. If the range is to be managed in a way that maximizes the total welfare of society, and not just that of one group, it needs to be managed for multiple use. Multiple use is considered in Chapter 16.

Finally, there is the problem of setting grazing fees. Efficient fees can be determined by means of auctions or bids. While actual grazing rights may be worth more than is indicated by current charges and may depend on range condition, access distance, and so on, auctions may not be practical due to questions of equity and political acceptability. There may be local monopsony that militates against an efficient use of auctions – an example is the preferred behaviour of established herds. Appropriate fee setting is a difficult and politically dangerous task, but the best way to move towards economic efficiency is to charge variable fees, depending upon, for example, regional climatic and productivity factors, season of use, distance to access, species of livestock, and, perhaps, breed of animals. However, this requires a level of knowledge that is beyond the reach of the public agencies and is simply too expensive to obtain. An example of fees that reward ranchers for providing forage for wildlife is provided in the next chapter.

Politics, Economics and Grazing on Public Range

In the United States, environmental groups have lobbied to abolish livestock grazing on public lands; their slogan has been 'Cattle Free by

'93.' In response to pressure from environmentalists, the Synar-Atkins-Darden Bill was introduced in the House of Representatives by the three Democrats after whom it is named. This bill proposes to quadruple the grazing fee from $1.97/AUM in 1992 to $8.70/AUM by 1995. Whether or not this will be possible, without at the same time eliminating or dramatically reducing grazing on public lands (which is likely the ultimate purpose of the bill), depends on the difference between P_1 and g_f. The environmentalists argue that the difference (and subsidy) is large (but certainly less than the subsidy received by grain producers). Others have argued that there is no subsidy whatsoever.

Ranchers lease about 270 million ac (110 million ha) or 80 per cent of the western public lands administered by the federal Bureau of Land Management (BLM), the U.S. Forest Service, and the National Park Service. Areas are divided into 31,000 grazing allotments, varying in size from 40 ac (15 ha) to over a million acres (more than 400,000 ha). Proponents of the Synar-Atkins-Darden Bill argue that the cattle produced on these lands represent just 2 per cent of U.S. production. However, as is indicated by BLM publications, the 11 western states account for 19 per cent of the U.S.'s beef cattle and half its sheep; about half of these cattle and sheep rely on seasonal BLM and Forest Service range.

Environmentalists have also argued that rangeland is in a poor and declining ecological state, and that this is the result of grazing by domestic livestock. They suggest that some 68 per cent of inventoried BLM rangelands are in an 'unsatisfactory' condition; in total, 36 per cent of public rangelands are in a state of 'extreme depletion,' with another 47 per cent 'severely depleted.' A survey by the U.S. Government Accounting Office indicated that more than half of the areas surrounding Colorado's streams and rivers were in 'poor' condition, while 80 per cent of rangelands in Idaho were in some state of degradation. According to the BLM, however, the public range is in better condition now than it has been at any time this century; 87 per cent of the range is in stable or improving condition. Wildlife populations on public lands have increased dramatically as a result of improvements in public range: between 1960 and 1988, antelope on public lands increased by 112 per cent, bighorn sheep by 435 per cent, deer by 30 per cent, elk by 782 per cent, and moose by 476 per cent. This is the result of better management and complementarity between cattle and wildlife under certain management regimes (Chapter 16). The goal of BLM's 'Range as Our Vision' program is to have 40 per cent of its rangelands in the 'highest ecological condition' by 2009, the seventy-fifth anniversary of the Taylor

Grazing Act (1934); its 'Riparian-Wetlands Initiative' hopes to see 75 per cent of its riparian areas in 'sound condition' by 1997.

It would appear that the conflict between environmentalists and ranchers will be difficult to resolve. The slogan 'Cattle Free by '93' is an indication of how entrenched positions are and certainly affords a reason to be dubious about the possibility of conflict resolution – but there are two other reasons as well. First, eastern livestock producers, or their representatives, will align themselves with environmentalists, because a reduction in forage availability in the western U.S. will result in a reduction of cattle numbers and higher prices. This is a form of rent seeking. Second, environmentalists are generally unfamiliar with range ecology and management. The quality of public range is improving as a result of government regulations and ranchers' compliance with multiple-use requirements. Ranchers increase the value of public range by bringing water and salt for livestock (which also increases living conditions for wildlife), building fences, and constructing access roads, and they monitor use of natural resources by recreationists in remote regions (where policing by public agencies is difficult). Further, wild horses and burros, which are protected by legislation, cause more damage to the range than do cattle.

Given that ranchers provide services to the public agencies for which they are not compensated, what constitutes a fair grazing fee? Are ranchers really paid a subsidy? Two issues need to be considered: the grazing fee/subsidy debate and whether or not grazing permits constitute a property right. These are considered in turn.

Is the Grazing Fee a Subsidy?

Grazing fees on public rangelands and forestlands in the U.S. were first levied in 1906. The first unified BLM-Forest Service grazing fee structure was implemented in 1969; it derived from the 1966 Western Livestock Grazing Survey. (The U.S. fee structure is also important to Canada, because grazing fees on public lands in Canada are often equivalent to U.S. fees.) The 1966 survey found the weighted average of costs (weighted over cattle and sheep) to be $0.55 per AUM higher on public as opposed to on private lands. The average private land grazing rental rate, with all services provided by the lessee, was found to be $1.79/AUM. The federal grazing fee was then set equal to the private rate minus the cost difference, or $1.23/AUM. Referring back to Figure 15.4, P_1 can represent either the private rate of $1.79 or the 'adjusted' fee of $1.23, depending on whether or not the respective supply and derived demand curves include services. The Public Rangelands Improvement Act (1978) established the present fee structure, again using a cost equalization formula. The formula requires that, in the interests of efficiency and equity, the total costs of using forage should be the same for those both with and without public grazing permits; fees are adjusted annually, using a formula indexed to market prices of beef cattle, production costs, and forage rental rates, with a floor fee of $1.35/AUM.

The cost equalization formula appears to rule out a grazing subsidy; that is, the current fee structure does not provide ranchers with a subsidy. However, given that the private rental rate and cost differentials are calculated over eleven states, a uniform fee is likely to confer a substantial subsidy on some users of public range, while proving to be a hardship for others. The 1991 grazing fee was $1.97/AUM.

The next question to ask is whether or not a subsidy even exists if the revenues from fees exceed the costs of providing public range services. But the opposite is generally true: the costs to public agencies of managing range resources and providing support services to the livestock sector exceed grazing fee receipts. For example, in British Columbia, the costs of managing the resource are approximately $6.0 million/year, but, based on a grazing fee of $1.75/AUM and almost 1 million AUMs of grazing on public lands, revenues amount to about $1.75 million, or 30 per cent of costs. Even if the grazing fee were increased to $2.30/AUM, only 38.5 per cent of costs would be recovered. In 1988, out of $19 million spent on administering its grazing program, the U.S. Forest Service recouped $8.7 million from grazing fees; in 1990, the BLM recovered all of its grazing program expenditures from grazing fees.[2] In comparison, these agencies recover only about 1 per cent of their expenditures on recreation through user fees. Further, the Forest Service sells much of its timber below cost, because timber harvests provide other benefits, such as enhanced stream flow and access for recreationists. However, these joint products are rarely sold at market prices, mainly because markets do not exist or user fees are not levied.

The size of any subsidy depends on the actual market value of an AUM of grazing on similar quality land and the efficiency of providing public services to the livestock producers. Basing charges on management costs is inappropriate from an economic standpoint, since costs do not reflect values or opportunity costs. (If they did, any project that covered its costs could be justified, even if land was considered more valuable for some other use.) Even if ranchers receive a subsidy, it is unlikely to be of the same order of magnitude as that received by other agricultural producers, either as a direct payment from government or as an in-kind payment (e.g., subsidized water for irrigation), or other users of the same range-lands.

Further, as is noted above, ranchers argue that they provide services to the public agencies that are not taken into account. In addition, wild animals, such as elk, often forage on private pasture (their behaviour indicates a preference for range that has previously been grazed by cattle) or on feedstocks (alongside cattle) during the winter. This imposes an external cost on the rancher, since he or she is unable to capture the benefits associated with the maintenance of the elk. Compensatory payments from hunters or the government to ranchers may be required in this case. Cattle are sometimes lost due to predation, although this seems to be a minor problem that can be resolved with restitution payments.

In addition to the external costs that ranchers might bear, there is the additional problem that public range services are not the same as private ones, even if the cost differences noted above are taken into account. Private lands tend to be of higher quality; in arid regions, 14 ac (5¾ ha) or more are needed in order to produce sufficient forage to support an animal for one month, while about one-tenth of the same private land is required to service one AUM. Animals are easier to care for on private land and operating costs are often lower than on public land. This is illustrated in Table 15.2, which compares operating costs on private and public range. These data do not provide evidence of a subsidy. However, as before, the calculations are indicative of a particular situation and would tend to vary greatly from one region to another.

Grazing Permits
Grazing of domestic livestock on public forestland has taken place in the U.S. since 1896. As early as 1905, the Forest Service considered grazing permits to be privileges, not rights. That position continues in Forest Service regulations and has been confirmed in the Taylor Grazing Act of 1934. (See Chapter 16 for a history of the evolution of public land management.) The U.S. administration has consistently argued that a federal grazing permit does not constitute a partial and attenuated property right, so no compensation is required if the permit is revoked or its terms and conditions changed; that is, no taking occurs. Thus, in establishing grazing fees, the amortized cost of acquiring permits should not enter into the calculations. However, various states and the U.S.

Table 15.2. Comparison of operating costs per AUM in the U.S. for 1990: Private vs. public range

Operation	Federal grazing permit	Private leases
Lost animals	$1.82	$1.12
Association fees	0.27	0
Veterinary	0.45	0.53
Moving livestock	1.11	1.16
Herding within operation	1.86	0.77
Salt and feed	2.32	3.09
Travel to and from operation	1.49	1.19
Water (production items)	0.27	0.20
Horse	0.50	0.31
Fence maintenance	0.89	0.92
Water maintenance	0.69	0.55
Development depreciation	0.37	0.10
Other	0.44	0.47
Totals	$2.48	$10.41
Federal grazing fee (1990)	1.81	0
Private forage value -includes lesee's overhead and risk	0	4.35
Total operating cost per AUM	$14.29	$14.79
Capitalized cost of grazing permit	3.25	0
TOTAL COSTS	$17.54	$14.79

Source: data from Darwin Nielson as quoted by Obermiller (1992a)

Internal Revenue Service recognize permit value and tax it either as possessory interest or as the value of the leasehold estate. The courts have upheld the view that a grazing permit is a taxable lease, not a non-taxable licence. This establishes the grazing permit as a property right; if it is revoked or otherwise changed, compensation must be provided under the takings clause of the U.S. Constitution (Chapter 17). Range economists favour this interpretation because it establishes perpetual grazing rights, and these provide economic incentives for the sustained management of range vegetation.

There are three reasons why grazing permits have value. First, given that grazing fees are determined over a large area and are based on average costs determined from rancher surveys, there are, undoubtedly, going to be some allotments in which the value of grazing on public land exceeds that which the rancher would be able to pay (as determined by the derived demand for forage). There will be cases in which area *eacd* (in Figure 15.4) is non-zero. However, there may be other instances in which it is zero, and even in which part of area *abc* is captured by the public authority. Unless the authority is willing to make calculations on a case by case basis, it is unlikely that it can avoid rent capture by some ranchers. Second, the grazing permit's value also represents the capitalized value of the efficiency gain, as is given by area *abc* in Figure 15.4. Third, ranchers have made private investments on public range, and the grazing permit's value may simply reflect those improvements.

The main factor favouring retention of grazing on public lands might be community viability. Economics has a number of roles to play in this debate. Regional development models, such as input-output models, can be used to determine the extent of income redistributional impacts from changes in the mix of uses on the public range. It can give some indication of the expected changes in employment and, thereby, the hardships that those living in communities dependent on ranching might face. Economics can help determine the values of rangeland with respect to alternative uses, particularly recreation and hunting. Finally, economics is needed in order to investigate the trade-offs among alternative demands on public range resources and to suggest what mix of uses might lead to the greatest societal benefits. These topics are explored further in Chapter 16.

Discussion

Both harvesting timber and stocking range with domestic cattle or sheep have profound effects upon land use. While issues concerning the clearcutting of public forestlands are generally controversial and, thus, brought to the attention of the public, damage to public rangelands from domestic livestock are also important in terms of their impact upon wildlife. But deterioration of rangelands is not as apparent and often does not command the same degree of media attention as does timber harvest. What is common in both instances is the role of amenity or external values. Too little effort is directed towards the measurement of these values, because (1) they are difficult to measure and (2) the public do not even perceive these as having economic value. That these values are important is easy to demonstrate. For example, as is argued in Chapter 14, reforestation of denuded public forestlands is often uneconomic if based solely on commercial timber values, but when nonmarket or external values are taken into account, it may be possible to justify such investments. The same is true for rangeland investments.

In the next chapter, land-use trade-offs are examined. The trade-off is usually between an activity such as timber or livestock production and recreation or preservation. Timber is valued in markets, but recreation and preservation values need to be measured using the techniques discussed in Chapter 7. Further, given that biological data are often lacking, production functions (or trade-off functions) are difficult to construct.

16
Management of Public Lands for Multiple Use

Managing public lands for multiple use is mandated in both Canada and the United States. If proper attention is paid to economics, such management could result in maximum benefits to society; if not, resources could be wasted and the land degraded. Society is better off if land is managed in a way that takes into account all of its uses, including those that do not have commercial value.

In addition to recreational use and watershed functions, forestlands also produce wildlife, domestic grazing services, and timber, but little is known about the extent to which one use (e.g., domestic grazing) interferes with another (e.g., timber production); such information would be contained in the trade-off or transformation function. Although it is generally possible to measure land values in uses such as logging and livestock grazing, value in other activities is either not measurable in the marketplace or measurable only with great difficulty. A recent survey of U.S. Forest Service foresters found that they considered domestic grazing to contribute 10 per cent of the total value associated with multiple use of forestlands, timber to contribute 15 per cent, water value 25 per cent, recreation 25 per cent, and wildlife 25 per cent. The U.S. Forest Service itself estimates that the potential annual value of national forests is $3.4 billion; recreation is most important, accounting for 41 per cent of this value, followed by timber (27 per cent), minerals (17 per cent), fish and wildlife (12 per cent), water (2 per cent), and domestic grazing (1 per cent). By receipts, the annual value of the national forests total $1.1 billion, with timber accounting for 82 per cent of receipts, minerals for 14 per cent, recreation for 3 per cent, and grazing for 1 per cent; other potential sources of value contribute nothing to receipts. It is clear, therefore, that multiple use is an important consideration in valuing and managing public lands.

Until recently, the presumption in Canada had been that timber production was by far the most valuable use of public forestlands and that only minor adjustments in the timber-harvesting plan were required in order to serve wildlife, outdoor recreation, wilderness, fisheries, and water supply demands. This premise in favour of timber values resulted in unnecessary conflict among competing users and led to the inefficient use of land resources. Currently, government policies and institutions are in a state of flux, as efforts to incorporate multiple uses into public land management are being implemented. However, the multiple-use mandate for public lands in Canada does not have the full force of law, as it does in the U.S.

One can identify three steps for managing public lands in such a way that, in the long run, net benefits will be maximized.

(1) It is important to determine the maximum net benefit of land in each use, on a sustainable basis, separate from interference by any other use.

(2) It is necessary to identify conflicts among different uses and their economic significance – the trade-off function.

(3) Finally, combinations of uses must be examined in an iterative fashion, so that the mix of uses that maximizes the net benefits of the land can be identified. To the extent possible, *alternative uses are accommodated to the point where the marginal benefit of each use equals the marginal cost imposed upon other uses*. This is the economic efficiency criterion of multiple use.

Economic efficiency is only one of several criteria that can be used to evaluate multiple use for policy-making. Three other criteria are (1) income distribution, (2) fairness, and (3) political acceptability. In the current context, the income distribution criterion refers, primarily, to local economic impacts: management decisions pertaining to public land use have an impact on regional incomes that cannot be ignored. Such issues are often analyzed through the use of input-output analysis. Fairness refers to such things as historic property rights (e.g., access to range forage by domestic cattle or hunting access to public lands), and political acceptability refers to society's concern with sustainable development (e.g., maintenance of land productivity), acceptability of land-use policies, and so on. Operational practicality should also be included with political acceptability. This refers to the feasibility of making decisions regarding multiple use in the field; regional managers often rely on rules of thumb and intuition when making decisions, and such decisions are often the 'right' ones, in light of the constraints faced by local decisionmakers. Each of the aforementioned criteria will be discussed in this chapter. But first we briefly examine how the management of public forest and rangelands has evolved.

Background to Public Land Management in North America

It is useful to briefly consider the history of public land management because it provides useful insights for economists and a background to existing institutional structures. Management of public lands in North America began in the United States as a result of land acquisitions. In 1782, the original states gave their western lands (from the Ohio River to the Mississippi River) to the federal government. The Louisiana Purchase of 1803 for $15 million gave the U.S. rights to the area drained by the Mississippi River, while Florida was acquired from Spain in 1819 for $7 million. The Texas rebellion against Mexico (1836) led to its annexation to the U.S. in 1848, with subsequent cession of lands outside its current boundaries to the federal government in 1850. The U.S. government gained the territories of New Mexico, Colorado, Arizona, Nevada, Utah, and California as a result of the 1848 war with Mexico and the Gadsen Purchase in 1853. A compromise with Britain over disputed western territory in 1846 established the 49th parallel as the international boundary between Canada and the U.S., while Alaska was obtained from Russia in 1867 for about $7 million.

Britain controlled the remainder (northern part, except Alaska) of the continent. Canada was established by the British North America (BNA) Act in 1867, with British Columbia added to the Confederation in 1872. (Alberta and Saskatchewan were carved out of Canadian territory in 1905, while Newfoundland joined Confederation in 1949.) The BNA Act granted control over public land to the provinces, with federal control confined principally to the Yukon and Northwest Territories. However, the federal government maintained control over land use in a number of ways.

Since much of the land in both countries was not yet settled, governments were involved in the disposal of 'public' lands, particularly agricultural land. (In Canada, where provincial governments were established, they took over this responsibility from the federal government.) Both countries employed the rectangular cadastral survey method that was used in the U.S. to survey public lands at the suggestion of President Thomas Jefferson (1801-9).[1] Each country granted lands to railway companies to get them to build railways; the land could be sold or given to settlers so that rail traffic could be built up. In addition, homestead acts were used to encourage settlement by providing individuals with land for farms; settlers were sold a quarter section of land (160 ac) at a very low price, with the proviso that they must establish a homestead and farm the land. While 160 ac were adequate for those locating in moist climates, they were too little to encourage ranching or farming in the arid regions of the west.

United States

Reservation of land began in the United States in the latter part of the 1800s, because the eastern establishment was concerned about the potential loss of wildlands in the west. As a result, Yellowstone National Park was established in 1872. In 1891, the Forest Reserve Act or Creative Act was passed, and, with it, land management became a task for public foresters. The act gave the president authority to withdraw public domain lands and put them into a wildland reservation, even if these lands had commercially valuable timber growing on them. Although Congress never intended to create forest reserves, 40 million ac (16 million ha) were reserved by 1897. However, there was no provision in law for the management of this land. This was provided by the Organic Act of 1897, which superseded the Creative Act and was interpreted to provide authority for rehabilitating degraded forest and rangelands; it introduced active management of public lands. As a result, managers of public lands became somewhat schizophrenic, not quite knowing whether they were managing public wilderness or timber stands.

An important event in the evolution of institutional arrangements for managing public lands in the U.S. (which also had an effect upon Canada) occurred in 1898, when a disgruntled Gifford Pinchot went from the General Land Office (GLO), which was established in 1812 and managed all lands in the public domain, to head up the small Division of Forestry in the U.S. Department of Agriculture. In 1905, his friend, President Theodore Roosevelt (1901-9), created the U.S. National Forest System and made the Division of Forestry into the Forest Service, assigning it responsibility for managing the forest reserve lands. The GLO had managed the forests from 1891 to 1905. As a result of Roosevelt's friendship with Pinchot and the latter's unhappiness with the way his career at the GLO had been progressing, the U.S. ended up with two large and bureaucratic agencies to manage its public lands. Whether this has resulted in better management or not is a question open to debate.

During his presidency, Roosevelt reserved vast amounts of public lands, increasing the forest reserve almost to its current level. The Weeks

Act of 1911 permitted the federal government to purchase private lands for reservation in the public domain under the guise of soil and water conservation. This enabled the federal government to establish forest reserves in the eastern states, where there were few National Forests.

The Taylor Grazing Act of 1934 was a watershed piece of legislation for two reasons. First, it marked an end to both acquisition and disposal of further federal lands. The U.S. public land base was fixed and has remained about the same ever since. About half of the remaining unappropriated and unreserved public lands in the forty-eight contiguous states was placed in a grazing reserve, with the rest being included two years later. Second, it put a stop to the grazing commons and its deleterious effects – that is, overgrazing on public lands (especially by sheep). A Division of Grazing (Grazing Service) was set up in the Department of the Interior, as opposed to in the GLO. By 1936, the Grazing Service looked after 142 million ac of public land, but political pressure on Congress by ranchers resulted in its becoming ineffectual. In 1946, the Grazing Service was amalgamated with the GLO to become the Bureau of Land Management (BLM). Currently, the federal government owns some 738 million acres of land, with 188 million acres under Forest Service management and 398 million acres under the BLM.

Ever since the 1940s, U.S. foresters have debated their role: was forestry part of multiple resource management or was it to be confined to trees? The appropriate role of foresters has profound implications for the type of training that a forester should receive. During the 1950s, outdoor recreation became an increasingly important use of public lands, and there was increasing concern about preservation of wildlands and roadless wilderness areas. The broader view of forestry was advanced with the Multiple Use and Sustained Yield (MUSY) Act of 1960, which explicitly recognized the importance of public wildland management. It gave the legislative foundation for multiple-use management, which had always been practised by the Forest Service. The Classification and Multiple Use Act of 1964 did the same for the BLM.

Despite MUSY, the conflict intensified between those interested in the production of a larger volume of natural resource commodities from public lands and increasingly militant outdoor recreationists and preservationists. Knowledge of resource matters among the public also increased. As a result of rising public pressure, Congress passed a number of pieces of legislation to appease various interests, but this resulted in a greater role for the courts – something that was neither anticipated nor desired by Congress.

The Wilderness Act (1964) sought to set aside wilderness areas. In 1967, John Krutilla (an economist with Resources for the Future) argued that 10 million acres of land should be preserved as wilderness; when Congress passed the Wilderness Act, it implicitly agreed to a set-aside of about 15 million acres. However, by 1972, more than 105 million acres were under consideration for wilderness designation.

As a result of court cases and the fact that Congress was unhappy with the annual budget presentations of the Forest Service, it passed the Forest and Rangeland Resources Planning Act (RPA) in 1974. But it turned out that the Forest Service was ill-prepared for analyses and report writing. Additional manpower and budget for intensifying management became available, but, while an objective of RPA was to balance supply and demand, it consisted of little more than an inventory process. Resource availability was known, but there was no provision for such things as jointness in supply. The 1974 RPA was amended extensively in 1976, with a piece of legislation known as the National Forest Management Act (NFMA). This act replaced the Creative Act and sought to introduce more economic considerations into the 1974 act. A similar planning act was passed for the BLM in 1976, namely, the Federal Land Policy and Management Act (FLPMA).

During this period, other acts impacting on public land management were the National Environmental Policy Act (1970), which required environmental impact statements, and the Endangered Species Act (1973). As a result of court decisions, environmental impact statements are now required for almost all activities related to public land management and the environment. However, the environmental statements have become so complicated (e.g., filled with many meaningless figures) that they are useless as a decision tool.

The National Forest Management Act (1976), the Federal Land Policy and Management Act (1976), and the Public Rangeland Improvement Act (1978) have mandated that management of public lands in the U.S. must satisfy both a sustained yield and a multiple-use mandate. (For example, U.S. Forest Service planning regulation 36CFR219 pursuant to the National Forest Management Act requires that wildlife species in a national forest be maintained at viable population levels.) A number of court cases have reinforced the multiple-use mandate in the legislation. In the legislation, sustained yield implies that annual consumption by *all* users be no greater than annual growth, as determined by government fiat. In effect, multiple-use management of public lands has been interpreted as a trade-off that does not give timber interests, recreational activities, domestic livestock, or wildlife an exalted status over other uses.

There are problems with this legislation, however. The main problem is that the courts have become so involved in interpretation, that rulings are clearly against what Congress originally intended. Further, considerable confusion, frustration, and cynicism have been generated by conflicts between centralized planning and control (mandated by the Endangered Species Act and RPA) and decentralized land management planning (mandated by NFMA and FLPMA). These problems will need to be resolved in the future if the U.S. is to maximize the welfare of its citizens from the management of its public land resources.

Canada

Public land management in Canada has evolved differently than it has in the U.S., although there are similarities. As noted, disposal of agricultural lands relied upon homestead acts, as it had in the U.S. But differences arose for two reasons. First, Canadian settlement occurred much later than did settlement south of the border, and even now there is less population pressure on, or demand for, Canadian wilderness areas. There are large forest areas that remain unexploited and inaccessible, although that is likely to change in the future (viz., development of pulp mills in northern Saskatchewan and Alberta in the late 1980s and early 1990s).

Second, and perhaps more important, political institutions in Canada differ from those in the U.S. Ownership and administration of public or Crown lands mostly falls under the jurisdiction of individual provinces. Each province is responsible for determining its own criteria for managing public lands. Resource development projects are often undertaken with the consent, and even urging, of a provincial government, and development subsidies are sometimes involved. As a result of the British North America Act (1867), natural resources are owned by the provinces, and they jealously guard their right to develop these resources, although with subsidies from, and without benefits to, the federal government. Even environmentalists are unwilling to recommend transfer of resource *ownership* to the federal government, although they do want to retain the ability to appeal to a higher authority than the province.

Constitution and Federal/Provincial Jurisdiction

The federal government exercises some authority over the environmental impacts of public land-use decisions through one of a number of mechanisms. Since land resource projects (e.g., reforestation, construction of dams) often rely on some federal funding, the federal government is able to require some standard with respect to their impact on the environment. As well, the federal government is responsible for (1) transboundary movement of resource products (control over exports of pulp, electricity, uranium, etc.), (2) fisheries, (3) migratory species, and (4) navigation and shipping. Finally, the federal government can invoke its *declaratory power* in matters dealing with the environment, although this power is rarely exercised and is used primarily in cases of emergencies. It would seem, therefore, that the federal government can have a large say in land-use decisions. While the federal government may lack a jurisdictional basis for intervention in agricultural and forest practices that are ecologically objectionable, its powers to offer and withdraw financing give it wide powers to exercise control over the environmental impacts of these practices as well as those of resource development and other land-use projects. For example, there is nothing to prevent the federal government from implementing cross-compliance provisions for agricultural subsidies (Chapter 12).

On the basis of the federal cabinet's Environmental Assessment Review Process Guidelines Order of 1973, an environmental review is required for all resource development projects. Although the review process was criticized because it lacked a statutory basis and appeared to represent the voice of the federal government's ecological conscience, it was given the force of law by the Federal Court of Canada (which was created in 1971 to adjudicate disputes involving federal law), a judgment that was confirmed in 1992 by the Supreme Court of Canada in the decision concerning the Oldman River in southern Alberta. In mid-1992, the guidelines were replaced by the Canadian Environmental Assessment Act. This act (as its predecessor) requires only that projects be delayed until an environmental review is completed, but there is no means to enforce compliance with the findings. However, a negative environmental statement results in adverse publicity that could halt a project.

In 1988, the Supreme Court invoked the Peace, Order, and Good Government (POGG) provision of the constitution in a case involving marine pollution by a forest company in provincial waters. There is no reason why the POGG provision cannot be used in the future in other cases dealing with the environment, resource development, and public or private land use. This introduces an added degree of uncertainty in decisions concerning resource use.

Federal intervention in resource development and land-use decisions can be justified on one or more of the grounds indicated above. In some cases, the federal government has assigned its jurisdictional powers to the provinces, but it is not clear that this would forestall federal intervention in provincial decisions concerning environment and resources without changes in the Constitution. Recent federal proposals (1991) to change the Constitution appear to offer greater control over certain aspects of resource development to the provinces, perhaps including environmental impacts, in an effort to streamline federal government services. The areas for increased provincial responsibility include wildlife conservation and protection, and soil and water conservation, while forestry, mining, and recreation are to be given over exclusively to provincial responsibility. The federal government has not proposed to grant exclusive responsibility to provinces for agriculture, likely because no province would be willing to forgo federal aid to agriculture. With regard to the declaratory power and POGG provisions, the federal government has offered to transfer to the provinces authority for non-national matters not specifically assigned to the federal government under the Constitution or by virtue of Supreme Court decisions. Perhaps this is in recognition of the fact that external effects of provincial decisions on other parts of Canada may not be that great, and, therefore, that a provincial government may be at least as capable of achieving an optimal solution to environmental conflict as is the federal government.

Provincial Land Control: The Case of BC
Public management and decisions over land use occur at the provincial level, so it is at that level that land-use management will be examined. A brief history of forestland use in British Columbia is provided, because it is the most important forest products producing province in Canada and it has more diversity of wildlife species than has any other province. British Columbia accounts for 70 per cent of native breeding bird species, 72 per cent of the terrestrial mammal species, 49 per cent of the amphibian species, and 41 per cent of Canada's reptile species. Of the province's bird species, 77 per cent are forest dwelling; for mammals, 81 per cent are forest dwelling. About a quarter of forest-dwelling wildlife species may be dependent on mature and/or old-growth forests. BC's forestlands are also important for maintaining forms of biodiversity. Since about 94 per cent of BC's forestlands are publicly owned, policies regarding these public lands are important for both the province and Canada.

Early disposals of public lands in BC granted freehold ownership to the buyer, including all timber rights. However, by 1865, land ordinances became popular, introducing the principle that individuals or companies could acquire rights to timber without purchasing land. This arrangement enabled the provincial government to access revenues over a long period of time without losing control over land, while loggers were primarily interested in the timber and not ownership of land. The Land Act of 1884 anticipated the Taylor Grazing Act in the U.S. by fifty years, in that it formalized the land ordinances and made additional sales of forestlands difficult.

During the 1800s, the government permitted timber harvests on public lands through a number of timber and pulp lease or licence arrangements. Initially, such tenures were not associated with charges, because the government was interested in development; but that changed in 1888, when charges for public timber were implemented. To encourage economic development, a system of export permits was brought into effect in 1901, followed in 1906 by a law that required timber cut on public lands to be processed in BC. This amounted to a ban on log exports from public lands, although the ban was effectively circumvented by exports of 'cants' (squared logs).

In 1907, concerned that it had given away too much of the timber resource, the government suspended further issue of cutting rights and placed all unallocated forestlands in reserve. Existing leases at the time subsequently became known as 'old temporary tenures.' While no such tenures were ever issued again, legally, the old licences and levies remained until 1978, when they were changed to timber licences (see below). In 1910, the first royal commission into forestry (chaired by F.J. Fulton) recommended that all unalienated forestlands be placed in a forest reserve (as was done in the U.S. in 1891) and that a Ministry of Forests be established. Gifford Pinchot was approached by the provincial government for advice and consultation, with the result that a provincial Forest Service was established in 1912 (by the Forest Act), along the lines of the U.S. Forest Service. The Forest Act of 1912 defined what was meant by 'forest reserves' and introduced the timber sale licence (TSL), which was the primary form of forest tenure (except for the old temporary tenures) between 1912 and 1947.

The problem with these timber sale licences was that they were short term (3-5 years), providing the holder with the right to harvest a certain area. They provided no incentives for management of forestlands, investments in silviculture, or management for more than one use. As an institutional device, timber sale licences did not (and do not) promote sustainable development in forestry, with this task left to the Forestry Service.

In 1945, the second forestry commission, the Sloan Commission, recommended adoption of a formal sustained yield policy. As a result, the Forest Act was amended in 1947 and two types of management units were established – a private and a public one. In the first case, companies were given Forest Management Licences – that is, long-term tenures of twenty-one years – in order to encourage them to invest in basic and intensive silviculture. While the old temporary tenures were renewable annually in most cases until the timber was harvested, the Forest Management Licences were made perpetual over the period 1947-58, but, in 1958, they were converted into renewable, twenty-one-year tenures and redesignated Tree Farm Licences (TFLs). Management plans were to be submitted every five years for approval, the tenure holder was required to operate a mill, and the holder was responsible for reforestation. In the second case, Public Sustained Yield Units (PSYUs), later to be renamed Timber Supply Areas (TSAs), were managed by the government and were designed initially to provide timber to smaller operators. The smaller operators do not have the resources to manage the forests and make investments in silviculture. As part of the sustained yield policy, an annual allowable cut was determined for each PSYU based on productivity estimates. In 1967, the Timber Sale Harvesting Licence (TSHL) was introduced, and TSLs were amalgamated with TSHLs to increase the licence term from 3-5 to 10 years. Further, the TSHLs were volume based rather than area based, but they shifted some timber management responsibilities onto the holder. By 1976, TSHLs accounted for some 30 per cent of BC's annual harvest.

In 1956, a third royal commission, also chaired by Gordon Sloan, reiterated the sustained yield policy. However, sustained yield referred only to commercial timber, not to other forest uses.

During the 1960s, pulpwood harvesting area agreements were introduced to encourage pulp production in the Interior of BC. The agreements required the user to construct a pulp mill and to purchase residual wood chips from sawmills located in the Interior.

Professor Peter Pearse was the sole commissioner of the fourth royal commission, which released its report in 1976. While reiterating the concept of public ownership of forestlands, Pearse recommended that the old temporary tenures be eliminated and that the 21-year TFLs be made 'evergreen.' This meant that TFLs would become 25-year tenures, with renegotiation of a new 25-year term occurring every 10 years; this enabled the tenure holder to have a secure timber supply for 15 years if the licence was not renewed. Pearse also recommended that the volume-based TSHLs be replaced by area-based forest licences and that competition be increased by issuing more timber sale licences. The commissioner's report was also concerned about integrated resource management (e.g., recommending that the Forest Service be amalgamated with Fish and Wildlife), that economic criteria be incorporated in utilization standards, that greater competition and efficiency be encouraged in the processing sectors, and that more public investment in forests take place. Consequently, in 1978, the Ministry of Forests Act (1978), a new Forest Act, and the Range Act (1978) were passed. These require that public lands be managed for multiple use. To 1992, economic issues regarding multiple-use management of public land resources have received inadequate attention, and the courts have played no role in the interpretation and enforcement of multiple-use legislation.

In 1992, the New Democratic government of BC proposed amendments to the Forest Act to allow for more careful planning – planning that would balance the timber harvest and recreational and environmental benefits from the forest resource – although it remains unclear as to what this implies. In addition to proposals to re-evaluate the annual allowable cut every five years, the government proposed doubling (from 6 per cent to 12 per cent of public land) the area set aside for parks and wilderness.

While there now appears to be greater interest in non-timber benefits of public lands in BC, the history of public land use and management in the province has focused on tenure arrangements for harvest of timber. The arguments over tenure continue and are important with respect to multiple use. Canada's forest products compete in international markets, primarily with products from the Scandinavian countries (Sweden and Finland), the U.S. South, and the U.S. Pacific Northwest (Chapter 14). Compared to BC, ownership of forestlands in each of these regions is much less dominated by the state. Further, there is evidence that the forest industry and log and timber markets in BC are less efficient than are those of its competitors. For example, stumpage charges in the U.S. Pacific Northwest, which has the highest degree of public ownership outside of Canada, are about four times as high as those in BC. It would appear, therefore, that the provincial government is not collecting the resource rents to which it is entitled as the resource owner. Further, since stumpage prices will almost always be lower and output higher with administered as opposed to competitive prices, the rate of harvest in BC may be higher than it should be if society's welfare from timber harvest is to be maximized.

One solution to the problem is for the public to divest itself of ownership of much of the forestlands. Certain wilderness areas that society wishes to safeguard can be identified and retained in the public domain. Additional forestlands might be placed in a forest reserve as a precaution against unforeseen circumstances and, perhaps, to act as a counterbalance against production of timber from private lands (e.g., to stabilize economic swings). The amount of land kept in the public domain might constitute 30-50 per cent of current holdings, with the remaining lands privatized. The public lands retained for wilderness should be managed for biodiversity, watershed and wildlife values, roadless recreation, and so on. The forest reserves should be managed for multiple use. Private owners should be allowed to manage their lands to capture (through fees or charges) not only benefits from timber harvest but also values associated with range and recreation (e.g., hiking, fishing, camping, and other access by the public).

Economic Efficiency and Multiple Use

Prior to the 1920s, much of the southern Rocky Mountain Trench in Canada was covered with forests. As a result of intensive logging at lower elevations (to supply a growing prairie economy) and subsequent fires during and shortly after the decade, large rangeland areas became available for domestic and wildlife grazing. As a result, populations of whitetail and mule deer, elk, and bighorn sheep reached their peaks in the East Kootenay region of BC during the 1950s. During the next thirty years, wildlife populations declined, partly as a result of overharvesting, but also because forage availability declined.

Public land resources in the East Kootenays experience constraints that arise from multiple use. Forest succession and ingrowth, combined with fire suppression, have reduced the range, thereby exacerbating conflicts for forages between domestic cattle and wildlife. In the East Kootenays, there remains conflict (1) between those who wish to increase cattle numbers and those who desire increased use of the range by wildlife; (2) between those advocating the land be used for timber production and those favouring range; and (3) between the aforementioned groups and those who would promote some form of residential or suburban development. To a greater or lesser degree, similar conflicts among commercial timber, wildlife, ranching, and other interests characterize public land conflicts in all regions of the world. In this section, the examples focus primarily on conflicts between domestic and wildlife grazing and between timber production and grazing, because these have been an object of study by economists. However, the economic techniques described can be used to evaluate other land-use trade-offs as well. We begin by examining the biophysical aspects of the conflict between timber production and livestock grazing.

Grazing/Timber Production Conflict on Public Land

Multiple use of forestlands for timber production and grazing has the potential to enhance the allocative or economic efficiency of land use. However, a major area of disagreement concerns the effect of grazing on conifer regeneration in transitory range, such as clearcuts and burns, as well as loss of forage production and summer grazing areas due to single-purpose logging and silvicultural practices. In this section, the conflict between grazing and timber production is examined, primarily from a biological perspective. The purpose is to illustrate the difficulty of finding a production possibility frontier, that is, a transformation or trade-off function between uses.

In addition to recreational use and watershed functions, forestlands are used for wildlife and domestic grazing and timber production, although it is not clear to what extent one use (domestic grazing) interferes with the other (timber production). Forest rangeland can be considered to be either herb and shrub dominated (early successional forest) or tree dominated (late successional or climax forest). Forage production declines in going from the former to the latter, with perhaps the most decline in forage occurring when overstory cover reaches 20-30 per cent. As is indicated in Table 16.1, the grazing productivity of forest range is substantially lower than is that of clearcuts. Nonetheless, forage productivity on forestlands is substantially higher, perhaps ten times higher, than it is on open range.

The primary use of clearcut forestland is commercial timber production. Although such land may be used for cattle, there is conflict between range and forest users over possible damage to tree seedlings by cattle. Research indicates that the potential for damage and the actual costs of such damage depend on whether or not the clearcut is seeded to domestic grasses, whether or not tree seedlings are planted, the tree species, the stocking rate, the presence of wildlife (e.g., big game, rodents), and so on. The evidence indicates that, with appropriate management, the damage to tree seedlings from domestic livestock is minimal. The damage that does occur is the result, primarily, of repeated trampling, and this occurs as a result of overgrazing or simply where cattle congregate. One strategy, therefore, is to employ appropriate management tactics to reduce damage (e.g., fencing, location of salt and water, slash removal). Another suggestion is to prevent grazing until trees reach 2-3 m in height, but this reduces the economic viability of seeding clearcuts for domestic cattle or sheep.

Table 16.1. Grazing productivity on forest vs. clearcut land

Range type	Location	Stocking (ha/AUM)	Average daily gains (kg)	Class of animal
Clearcut	BC	0.73	0.64	calves
			0.13	cows
Forest	BC	1.94	0.79	yearling steers
Clearcut	Oregon	0.66	0.74	yearling steers
Forest	Oregon	1.21	0.48	yearling steers

Source: Nordstrom (1984:68)

Trampling by domestic livestock is a problem, but damage from other causes, such as browsing by game animals and rodent damage, may be greater. Further, domestic grazing can help in establishing a seedbed for tree seedlings and conifer release (where natural regeneration is relied upon) and can be used as a method of natural and random thinning. Therefore, it is possible that domestic grazing on clearcuts aids forest reproduction.

Although studies have focused on the interactions between forage, trees, and livestock, there is little information about the economic aspects of these multiple-use interactions. Nor are costs and benefits of various management strategies calculated or compared across alternative management regimes. For example, it may be that economic losses to loggers, resulting because cattle increase the time required to establish a second-growth forest, are more than compensated for by gains to livestock producers. Further, as is indicated below, it is difficult to calculate production functions (trade-offs) for alternative uses of land and ecological resources.

Transformation Functions for Alternative Land Uses
Various land uses can be considered outputs produced by the land resource. Alternative land uses are (1) competitive, (2) complementary, (3) supplementary, and (4) antagonistic. Competitive and complementary land uses can be discussed with the aid of Figure 16.1. Competitive

products are those for which an increase in utilization of the land for one use results in a decrease in output from another use. When products are complementary in their use of the land, this implies that an increase in utilization by one use actually increases the amount of product available from the other use.

Figure 16.1

Complementary and competitive land uses

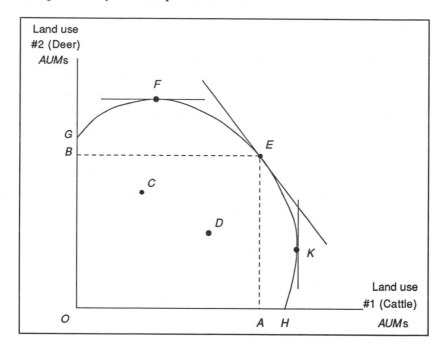

In Figure 16.1, suppose that rangeland can be used by cattle (use #1) or by deer (use #2). If the rangeland is utilized only by domestic animals, the number of animal unit months (AUMs) of grazing that can be supported is given by *OH*. If the land is utilized only by deer, then the *carrying capacity* of the range is *OG*. When cattle are introduced onto a range that is currently used only by deer, there may be an increase in the number of deer that can be supported by the range. By grazing cattle, more winter range becomes available for deer, because cattle prefer grasses and forbs that compete with shrubs and other plants preferred by a browser. By grazing cattle, the shrubs grow better, providing more forage for deer. Likewise, if the range is currently used by cattle, introducing deer will increase the carrying capacity of the range for cattle. In both cases, there is complementarity in land uses that is illustrated by the segments *GF* and *HK̂* in Figure 16.1. At moderate stocking levels, and with proper management, the interaction between deer and cattle can be mutually beneficial. (As another example of complementary land uses, sheep are sometimes grazed in reforested areas in order to reduce competition for trees. The sheep will eat the plants that compete with trees in the early stages of growth.)

At higher stocking levels, complementarity often gives way to competition. Competitive use implies that there is substitution between the products available from the land, and this substitution can be either constant or increasing. The case of *increasing marginal rates of substitution* is indicated by the concave-to-the-origin curvilinear segment *FK* in Figure 16.1. This indicates that, as more cattle graze on the land, the number of deer that are displaced increases – deer are supplanted at an ever-increasing rate. A *constant rate of substitution* implies that the rate at which deer are dislodged by cattle is the same, regardless of the number of cattle that graze on the range, up to the carrying capacity of the range for cattle (see Figure 16.2).

Figure 16.2

Constant rate of substitution between land uses

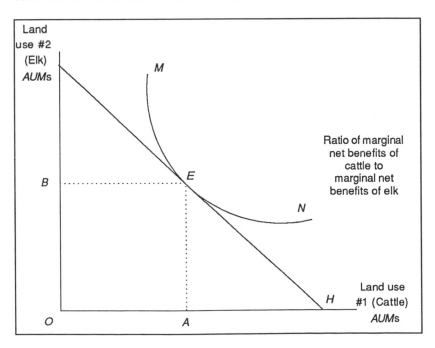

A constant rate of substitution is frequently postulated for the interaction between elk and cattle. The reasons are twofold. First, the most common range conflict studied in western North America is between elk and cattle. Given a paucity of information about the actual shape of the biological trade-off function, researchers have found it convenient to express forage requirements of one species as a fixed proportion of those of another. For elk, the trade-off in BC, for example, has been between 0.33 and 0.625 AUM per elk; with the best estimates of the trade-off appearing to be 0.33 AUM/elk in the summer and 0.43 AUM/elk in the winter. (While somewhat suggestive of a non-linear trade-off function, linearity remains the workable assumption.) Second, there is evidence to suggest that elk and cattle do have similar foraging habitats, which permits a linear trade-off or transformation function, as is illustrated in Figure 16.2.

The case of supplementary outputs is a special case of complementarity, in which the output from one use is unaffected by the other use. Rather than an upward slope on the production possibility function, the trade-off function is horizontal, as is indicated by the straight line segments GF and HK in Figure 16.3. Suppose that use #2 refers to sheep. The segment GF is horizontal (and HK is vertical), because the two types of livestock (cattle and sheep) prefer different plant species. At sufficiently low numbers of cattle, there is no competition for forages between sheep and cattle; nor does grazing of plants preferred by sheep increase availability of plants preferred by cattle. However, as the number of cattle increases, they begin to compete with the sheep for the same plants. Once again, the shape of the curved segment FK indicates an increasing marginal rate of substitution between competing uses of the range.

Given positive values (prices) for the land uses discussed above, and assuming that multiple uses are indeed possible for the land, the optimal or best economic use of the land will be determined where a line with slope determined by the ratio of the prices of the alternative uses $(= -P_1/P_2)$ is tangent to the trade-off function. (Prices are on a per AUM basis.) This is illustrated by point E in figures 16.1 and 16.3. In Figure 16.1, optimal multiple use of the range implies that OA AUMs are allocated to domestic (cattle) grazing and OB AUMs are allocated to deer. Likewise, in Figure 16.3, OA AUMs are allocated to sheep and OB AUMs to cattle. Although it is difficult to determine the price of an AUM for domestic cattle (and sheep) (Chapter 15), the major difficulty in this analysis is determining AUM values in wildlife production. It is in these instances that the valuation methods discussed in Chapter 7 need to be employed.

Figure 16.3

Supplementary land uses

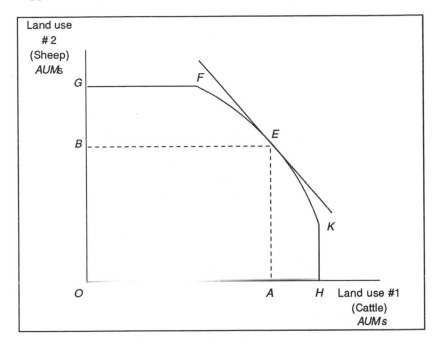

Figure 16.2 illustrates the case in which simply finding market values for an AUM in cattle and elk will lead to the exclusion of one of the two uses of the range – unless the ratio of the prices happens to equal the biological ratio of AUMs of cattle per elk. The use of price ratios is an approximation of the correct procedure, which is to find the marginal net benefit functions for wildlife and for domestic use of the range. That is, it is necessary to determine how the net benefit to cattle ranchers changes as one more AUM is provided to cattle versus the change in the net benefit to society (hunters and nonconsumptive users) when that AUM is made available to wildlife. As more and more of the resource becomes available for any of the uses, the value of that use declines relative to that of the other uses at an increasing rate, thereby giving rise to a non-linear marginal value function, as is indicated in Figure 16.2. (The ratio of the marginal net benefits will have the form indicated by the curve *MEN* in Figure 16.2.) There is, however, greater difficulty in

determining this relationship than there is in determining the simpler, constant price ratio.

The foregoing analysis can be extended either to cases of commercial timber production versus livestock, timber production versus wildlife grazing, snowmobiling versus cross-country skiing, heli-skiing versus snowmobiling, hunting versus hiking, and so on or to the case of three or more possible uses of the land. (In the case of more than two land uses, the dimensions of the diagrams simply need to be increased, which makes visual but not mathematical conceptualization of the problem more difficult.) For commercial timber production and cattle grazing, it is necessary to determine the shape of the biological transformation function (how much is timber production reduced as more cattle are grazed on commercial forestland) in addition to the (shadow) values of each of the uses. Where there are conflicts (or harmony) between recreational uses, it will be necessary to ask recreationists, professional guides, outfitters, and so on about how one use interferes with (e.g., hunting activity reduces backpacking) or complements (e.g., snowmobiles create trails for cross-country skiers) another. It is necessary to determine by how much one activity will be reduced (or increased) as the level of another activity is changed.

The preceding discussion assumes that public and private resource allocation decisions are efficient, enabling the economy to attain the production possibility frontier. However, resource allocation decisions often result in production at an interior point, such as C or D in Figure 16.1. It is necessary to improve the efficiency of public institutions so that public lands can be managed to make more outputs of all kinds available, thus allowing land-use decisions involving trade-offs to occur along, not inside, the production possibility frontier.

Finally, an antagonistic relationship between land uses results when the trade-off function is convex to the origin, as is shown in Figure 16.4. Such a situation occurs if, for example, domestic cattle and buffalo are susceptible to the same disease, and one of the species becomes infected. In Figure 16.4, an economically optimal mix of land uses occurs at one of the corners (either point X or Y in the figure). This implies incompatible land uses, with single use constituting the best outcome.

Determining Optimal Use: Applications to Rangelands

There have been only a few attempts to determine optimal multiple use of public lands. Public lands have four major economic use values:

Figure 16.4

Economically incompatible (antagonistic) land uses

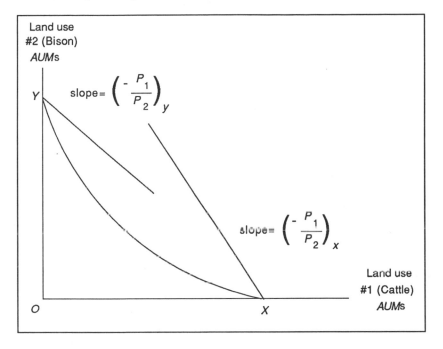

commercial timber production, water runoff, domestic grazing, and recreation. It is often easiest to interpret the latter as related to wildlife grazing and habitat, with economic value accruing as a result of hunting. Two uses – wildlife (hunting services) and water runoff – are not traded in the marketplace. Given the difficulty of analyzing all four uses, one study focused only on the trade-off between hunting values and domestic grazing of cattle in Arizona. The rangeland manager is interested in determining (1) the permitted level of cattle grazing, (2) the level at which game species should be encouraged, and (3) the level of public access for hunting.

The Arizona study was, in the first instance, an attempt to estimate the average rather than the marginal trade-off between land uses. The researchers determined the loss in consumer plus producer surpluses from the elimination of beef production on all public range in Arizona. The change in consumer surplus was determined by the area under the national retail demand curve for beef, resulting from a reduction in Arizona output. Producer surplus was taken as the value of a cattle ranch in Arizona and determined by the sale price of such ranches. Likewise, the researchers assumed a reduction in all elk hunting activity in Arizona, since this is the land use that is most competitive with cattle. The area under the demand curve for elk hunting was taken as the loss to hunters (hence society) from using rangeland solely for the purpose of cattle production. No complementarity between uses was assumed. The authors concluded that beef production in Arizona had a social worth that is five times greater than is that of hunting. They argued that hunters had been able to protect their rights, because they have great economic potential for political activity.

The main shortcoming of the Arizona study was that it considered an 'all-or-nothing' scenario and did not permit more than one use of rangeland in Arizona. This shortcoming was later addressed by postulating a biological trade-off function with the linear form

$$Q_C = \alpha - \beta \, Q_E,$$

where Q_C is the size of the cattle herd, Q_E is the size of the elk herd, and α and β are positive constants. The capacity of the rangeland under investigation is given by α for cattle and α/β for elk, or points H and G, respectively, in Figure 16.2. In the central plateau of Arizona, 32 ac are required to support one animal unit, while 170 ac are required to support one AU in the deserts of the southwestern part of the state; thus, to support a 700-cattle operation in the central plateau requires about 22,400 ac (9,068 ha) of rangeland. The Arizona researchers set $\beta = 0.5$; the carrying capacity for the range is half as many animal units of cattle as of elk.

In order to find an optimal for multiple use that does not result in a corner solution (choose one of the two uses), it is necessary to derive marginal net benefit functions for both cattle and elk. To avoid a corner solution, it is not possible to have fixed prices for elk and cattle. The marginal net benefit function for public range in cattle production was found from market data, while the marginal net benefit function for public range in elk production was determined from information about hunters' willingness-to-pay function for elk hunting. Hunters' WTP for elk was related to hunting success (or elk population size); this enabled the researchers to use number of hunting permits issued as a management variable. Adjustments were made for the probability of success as a function of the number of hunting permits issued. Finally, the optimal numbers of cattle and elk to allow on a given size of range was found by solving the following mathematical programming problem:

$$\text{Maximize } NB_C(Q_C) + NB_E(Q_E)$$
$$\{Q_C \ Q_E\}$$

$$\text{subject to } Q_C = \alpha - \beta \ Q_E$$
$$Q_C, Q_E > 0,$$

where $NB_C(Q_C)$ is the net benefit function for cattle as a function of the number of cattle, and $NB_E(Q_E)$ is the net benefit function for elk as a function of the number of elk.

Upon applying their model, the researchers concluded that the marginal elk is much more valuable than is the marginal beef animal, indicating that cattle and elk numbers are far from an economically efficient equilibrium (e.g., as is given by point E in Figure 16.2). In particular, the evidence indicated that fewer cattle should be permitted on the range, thus encouraging greater elk numbers. This conclusion differed remarkably from the earlier one, thereby illustrating how average analysis can result in misleading conclusions for public land management.

Discussion

Although the foregoing presents a correct procedure for analyzing multiple use on public lands, there are some inherent difficulties with such an approach.

(1) Cooperation is required among economists, wildlife biologists, and plant scientists in order to determine the transformation function between various biological land uses. For example, the carrying capacity of the rangeland in multiple uses needs to be determined. Cooperation among social scientists may be required to determine the trade-offs among different recreational uses. These are the production relations discussed earlier.

(2) It is necessary to determine wildlife values, both for hunting and other recreational uses. In this regard, it is necessary to estimate the relationship between wildlife numbers and hunting success and between willingness-to-pay and success. It is also important to relate nonconsumptive uses of wildlife to wildlife numbers. Likewise, it is necessary to find out the values of other nonmarket uses and how these values are affected by changes in the level or quality of the recreational activity. If these tasks cannot be accomplished, the economist's claim of assisting management is hollow.

(3) Effects on recreation at alternative sites from changes in the opportunities at one site are generally ignored, although recent research has suggested methods of accounting for interaction among alterna-

tive recreational sites. Models need to take into account site characteristics and alternative sites.

(4) Finally, the analysis presented here is static, and this is somewhat disconcerting, since biological relations are dynamic. Dynamic optimizing procedures are available and should be employed, although their discussion is beyond the scope of this text (see references and suggested readings).

Income Distribution and Multiple Use

Issues of income distribution are often the preoccupation of politicians. Consider, for example, the effect of lobbying by environmental groups in British Columbia to protect old-growth and wilderness areas. The government is in the process of doubling the area of the province to be protected for ecological and wilderness purposes and, as a consequence, is reducing the annual cut by about 10 per cent province-wide (although effects in some regions will be greater than in others). An important cost of preservation is the net value of the lost timber, which, if harvested, would contribute to society's overall welfare. The social welfare loss (or real economic cost) shows up as job search costs, retraining costs, higher government administration costs, and higher prices to consumers for forest products. It also shows up as negative environmental effects – this being the result of using non-wood substitutes or increasing harvests in areas (such as the tropics) with more fragile ecosystems. On the other hand, there are benefits to preservation, such as those that accrue from maintaining biodiversity, recreational opportunities, existence value, and so on. But it may be the regional development and income distributional impacts that are most important.

Major public land issues in the western U.S. have been associated with attempts by the BLM and the U.S. Forest Service to increase grazing fees or to reduce the numbers of cattle grazed on public lands. The reasons have to do with agency revenues, the fact that grazing fees are below market value (although it remains to be determined by how much), and with carrying capacity. (Biologists have suggested that overgrazing is taking place, but others dispute this, because they feel that public agencies need to invest resources in range improvements.) Either an increase in grazing fees or a reduction in grazing allotments on public lands will result in a welfare loss to ranchers. An increase in fees will reduce ranch values and will result in a transfer of income from private ranchers to public agencies. Such a loss is considered to be a violation of ranchers' inalienable property rights to the public range (see Chapter

15). In addition, there is a loss in economic activity in the regions that are impacted by reduced grazing or higher grazing fees. At the centre are questions regarding compensation to ranchers (see next section) and the viability of resource-dependent communities.

Similar issues are raised with respect to logging (timber harvesting) both in Canada and in the United States. A reduction in the allowable annual cut or removal of old-growth from future logging results in an outcry not only from the timber companies but also from individuals and communities whose economic lives are tied to logging and other timber operations. These individuals and communities are concerned about the effects that the use of land for non-logging purposes (e.g., preservation or recreational use) will have on their ability to earn a living, or, in the case of communities, their long-term viability. In some sense, these individuals and communities have an inalienable property right to continue harvesting trees on public lands.

Historically, the method for analyzing the regional economic development impacts of changes in land use has been via primary-data, local input-output models (Chapter 6). In a multiple-use context, regional I-O models can be used to determine the impacts on a local community of changes in the allocation of range resources, logging activity, tourism, and hunting, which may occur as a result of public decisions concerning the optimal use of public lands. While such models can aid in identifying the income distributional consequences of public planning, it is left to the decisionmaker to determine how, or if, these are to be mitigated.

Fairness and Political Acceptability

An important aspect of public land management concerns historical property rights. While historical rights to publicly owned resources, such as rangelands and timber, appear to be well established in the United States, they are less obvious in Canada. However, there is implicit recognition of historical property rights when, for example, federal funds for agricultural programs include contributions to improve public range resources in BC. Further, any subsidy component related to public provision of forage is capitalized in ranch values, and attempts to dramatically depart from previous policies (e.g., by large increases in grazing fees) will result in unanticipated and, perhaps, unfair losses to ranchers. Based on criteria of both fairness and political feasibility, it is unlikely that government decisionmakers would restrict ranchers' access to public range or even reduce the number of AUMs available to them (either through regulation or substantial increases in grazing fees). However, there may be circumstances in which it is necessary to restrict domestic grazing on public range for reasons of economic efficiency (e.g., grazing by elk has greater social value than grazing by domestic livestock).

Likewise, individuals living in resource-dependent communities perceive that they have a property right to continued harvesting of timber from public lands. The government implicitly recognizes this property right when it makes land-use decisions that favour timber interests; where a large number of jobs depend on logging operations, it may not be politically feasible to restrict harvests.

Whenever public land-use decisions result in a reduction in domestic grazing or timber harvests, it may be necessary to compensate or otherwise help those individuals who lose their jobs and those communities whose tax base is eroded. The question that needs to be addressed is not whether compensation should take place but, rather, how compensation should occur (see also Chapter 17). In some cases, it is possible to use economic incentives to address income distributional issues. In Chapter 8, transferable development rights were suggested as one method of mitigating against the adverse income redistributional effects of zoning. In other situations, it is not possible to use economic incentives. For example, if a reduction in access to timber for logging saves a stand of old-growth timber but causes a sawmill in a remote town to close down, the compensation may simply take the form of payments from a state or provincial government to local government and/or individuals. But even in these circumstances, it may be possible to get environmentalists to help pay some of these costs. Indeed, it is economically efficient to get non-users to pay the costs, because it causes them to place a more realistic value on preservation or the alternative use of the resource.

Difficulties in making transfer payments can be illustrated by the example of ranching and access to public rangeland. An approach that can be used when access to range is restricted is to simply pay ranchers according to the AUMs of grazing that are lost. This poses a difficulty associated with the evaluation of such losses, but this is not an insurmountable measurement problem (although it is a problem that could have political ramifications). The greatest difficulty is that some compensation schemes may not be politically acceptable either to the ranchers or to the public at large (as represented by the government). Further, compensation is not economically efficient, since it does not lead to the best land use.

One approach to resolving the rangeland conflict between multiple use and historic property rights, and yet obtain a solution that is economically efficient, is to charge ranchers a higher fee for grazing, while, at the same time, providing compensation based on the amount of forage left behind or not used. This is referred to as an *offsetting grazing fee*. The reason for increasing grazing fees is that they might not reflect the true opportunity cost of grazing. The current system of grazing fees results in inefficient allocation of the range between cattle and other uses (primarily big game). Further, grazing fees do not now take into account differences in range productivity, and that is both inefficient and unfair. An increase in grazing fees and/or a change in the structure of fees will increase efficiency of land use, but it will also take away implicit rights that ranchers currently enjoy. This is the reason that fee increases have been resisted – they are politically not feasible.

One mechanism for making higher grazing fees more acceptable is to compensate ranchers according to the amount of forage that is left unused on the public range. An offsetting fee structure (in which producers are paid for unused grazing) can improve land-use efficiency, since it takes into account other uses of the range. For such a system to work, range utilization by cattle and wildlife, and range productivity, will need to be determined and monitored by biologists. Although there are practical difficulties implementing an offsetting fee system, it is possible to overcome them. Further, it is likely to result in an efficient, effective, and fair allocation of the range resource among competing users.

The major limitation of an offsetting fee system is that it does not address the issue of grazing by wildlife. The fee structure can and should be extended to include wildlife grazing. Commercial timber values on clearcut land could also be taken into account by, for example, compensating ranchers in a way that encourages them to prevent trampling damage to tree seedlings or that encourages them to graze sheep to control fireweed (which competes with tree seedlings). In these cases, greater information about the bioeconomics of the system than is currently available will likely be required.

Finally, wherever they can be identified and assessed, fees need to be assessed for non-grazing services received by environmentalists and recreationists. This will help to allocate public forestlands in an economically efficient manner among multiple users.

The offsetting fee system recognizes issues of economic efficiency, fairness (equity), and political acceptability. It is fair because the grazing fee and payment for unused forage could be set in a way that leaves the welfare of ranchers unchanged; their historical property right is protected, and ranch values remain unaffected. (It would not necessarily result in an efficient allocation of the range, however.) It would also seem that an offsetting fee structure is politically acceptable, both for the foregoing reason and for the fact that users of the range pay according to its actual grazing value. However, it is still necessary to determine the origin of the funds needed to pay ranchers for leaving behind forage.

A mechanism for charging hunters, recreationists, and environmentalists according to the value they place on the land in an alternative use needs to be determined. This can be done via increased hunting fees, which are somehow related to the probability of hunter success (i.e., wildlife numbers), hiking tolls, and so on. Where environmental groups, recreationists, hunters, and other users of scarce resources are not charged for their use of the natural resource, distortions in land use occur. These distortions contribute to a lower level of general welfare for all members in society.

Discussion

Geographic information systems provide an excellent method for visualizing conflicts among land uses. These conflicts might even be viewed in dollar terms, where data are available. For example, if a GIS model of a watershed is constructed, it might include timber harvest, preservation of certain wildlife habitat, recreation, and hunting and fishing. Areas where potential conflicts are likely to be greatest can be identified; but without knowledge of the value of alternative uses, it is not possible to determine which use or mix of uses is most efficient. Where use can be translated into dollar terms, it may be possible to make economically efficient decisions. However, it is unlikely that the data necessary for determining the values of land involved in uses that are not traded in markets (e.g., recreation, hunting, preservation) will be available. Values might be determined using methods considered in Chapter 7, but that may be asking too much. Shadow prices for nonmarket uses can be obtained from constrained optimization models, such as a linear programming model, but this implies that the land-use conflict can be resolved with such a methodology. This, too, is unlikely.

What types of models should be used? Probably the best approach is to use a combination of GIS and constrained optimization (mathematical programming) models. The former enable decisionmakers to visualize the problem in ways that are not possible with other tools of analysis; the latter permit the decisionmaker to examine the trade-offs in value terms, which is not possible with GIS. Future research needs to focus on more than one methodology, plus such research needs to combine the talents of experts in a number of different fields.

What economic instruments can be brought to bear on the problem of multiple use? In principle, the optimal solution is to charge users at the margin according to the costs that their use imposes on other uses. For practical reasons this will not be possible. First, information about many non-timber uses (such as preservation and watershed values) are simply not available, and current techniques for valuing them are suspect (as is noted in Chapter 7). Second, even if all marginal values were available, the administrative costs of determining and regulating an optimal mix of uses may be prohibitive. Therefore, it makes sense, as a second-best solution, to zone areas according to their most valuable use. Some regions will be zoned exclusively for timber production, others for wildlife habitat, and still others for recreation. Where secondary uses do not interfere with the dominant use (i.e., where complementarities exist), such secondary uses should be permitted. Again, economics, GIS, and mathematical programming models are useful for determining which areas to zone for which uses.

Part Six:
Conclusions

Introduction to Part Six

Although a variety of topics related to land use and sustainable development have been considered in the preceding chapters, there remains unfinished work. Society's attitude towards sustainable development, the role of government, morality, and so on depends upon the prevailing premise or philosophy that underlies the way people think – that is, where they are coming from. The Dutch philosopher Herman Dooyeweerd (1979) refers to this as the religious foundation to which the society, as a whole, subscribes at the time. It has also been referred to as the prevailing or dominant world-view. It would be presumptuous for a book such as this to tackle the subject of what constitutes a world-view and how such a view affects distribution of resources, economic policy, and so on. One would think, however, that such knowledge would be important to the decision-making process, particularly in a democratic society, where a minority of the people may hold a view radically different from the dominant one.

As a consequence, the book concludes with a chapter on ethics and land resource economics. The objective of Chapter 17 is not to resolve ethical issues related to the topics discussed in the foregoing chapters but, rather, to raise the issue and to get the reader to think about issues from an ethical point of view. In particular, the reader needs to determine whether or not the subject of economics has anything to contribute to the study of land resources and sustainable development. Does economics provide a perspective that agrees with or is opposed to the reader's world-view?

In addition to discussing the contribution of various religious viewpoints to the study of environmental ethics, ethical issues relating to takings (expropriation and eminent domain), cost-benefit analysis, ecosystem irreversibility, intergenerational equity, and advocacy are examined. Probably the most important and controversial contribution of the chapter is the author's advocacy for greater use of economics in determining the way in which sustainable development is pursued.

17
Ethics and Land Resource Economics

The prevailing ethical, religious, or philosophical foundation determines how individuals collectively decide upon, or at least give tacit consent to, public policy pertaining to the topics discussed in the preceding chapters. In this chapter, these foundations are explored by considering several seemingly divergent topics relating to what might loosely be described as 'ethics.' In particular, stances relating to collective action, religious views about environment, the ethical viability of cost-benefit analysis, and advocacy are examined. In the next section, 'takings' of private property rights by the state are briefly discussed. Since takings relate to justice, three alternative views of social justice are described; these views will affect policy design regarding environment and land use. Issues relating to the ethics of cost-benefit analysis as a tool of policy are also examined. An important aspect of land and ecosystem management, and of stewardship, concerns intergenerational transfers of human, human-made, and natural resource capital, which, in turn, is related to the choice of a discount rate. Religion and environmental ethics are intertwined; thus, religious viewpoints on environment are examined. Finally, given the recent advocacy role adopted by some scientists, advocacy and science are also discussed.

Three 'Isms' of Social Justice
The U.S. Constitution is based on John Locke's principle concerning the inviolability of private property rights. It includes an eminent domain or 'takings clause,' which states: 'nor shall private property be taken for public use, without just compensation' (Amendment V to the Constitution of the United States, November 1791). Exceptions to just compensation occur under provisions of the state's police power (no compensation provided) and in-kind compensation (e.g., an owner is

prevented from erecting signs on his/her property, compensated by the fact that other owners are also prevented from doing so). The police power cannot be used to justify takings without compensation, except in a few circumstances. The police power of the state is often used to justify correcting externality, but this is not required, given existing common law (such as trespass law), and Ronald Coase would undoubtedly consider state intervention to be unacceptable in most cases because institutions (such as common law) already exist to correct for it. Likewise, in-kind compensation is limited to a few situations. Notwithstanding the intellectual case in favour of just compensation (Epstein 1985), the state has 'taken' away private property rights on a large scale.

In Canada, the concept of private property is similar to that in the United States, but private property is not explicitly protected in the Constitution (although constitutional proposals during 1992 included a clause pertaining to private property). Expropriation of private property (*condemnation* of property for public purpose) is permitted with or without compensation, and such laws vary from one province to another. The peace, order, and good government provision of the current Constitution can be used by the federal government to 'take' private property from individuals without compensation. This is the police power mentioned above.

It is on the basis of the police power provisions that governments, for example, have taken income from one group of individuals and transferred it to another. There are different stances that can be adopted with respect to government intervention. Here, three stances regarding social justice and the role of government are examined. These stances are important with respect to deciding upon policies relating to land use and sustainable development.

Libertarianism
Libertarianism originates with classical liberal philosophy, and its more recent proponents have included Freidrich von Hayek, Milton Friedman, Robert Nozick, and the populist writer Ayn Rand. Central to the libertarian approach to justice is a set of inviolable Lockean rights concerning one's entitlement to be free from the interference of others. A person's rights or entitlements are natural and negative. They are natural because they existed prior to the state and, therefore, set limits within which the state can justifiably act. They are negative because they prohibit interference by external agents.

Nozick focuses on the conditions that enable one to obtain and transfer entitlements under libertarian justice. He posits three principles of justice with respect to the holding of entitlements.

(1) The principle of justice in the acquisition of holdings is Lockean in the sense that an individual can obtain the entitlement to a previously unowned thing by mixing his/her labour with it, subject to the proviso that others who no longer have the liberty to use this thing are not made worse off. This is Nozick's interpretation of Locke's statement 'enough and as good left in common for others,' which he refers to as the Lockean proviso. Nozick adds that if others are made worse off, then compensation must be provided.

(2) The principle of justice in the transfer of holdings permits the transfer of entitlements to others by means of voluntary exchange, gift, and so on. A distribution is just if it comes from another just distribution by legitimate means. An individual can only gain entitlement to something through the principle of justice in acquisition or the principle of justice in transfer. An individual's rights can only be restricted for the good of all if he or she consents to the restriction.

(3) Since past injustice may have shaped the current distribution of holdings, a principle for rectifying injustice with respect to holdings is also required.

Under the assumption of perfect competition and ruling out interdependent utility and various forms of market failure, the market can be considered a morally free zone. Morality does not apply to market interaction under the conditions for perfect competition. Of course, the entire world is not a market, nor would there be an absence of morals even if the conditions for a morally free market are met. (This is not to suggest that people do not have strong views about what is and is not fair and acceptable economic behaviour.) But libertarians defend the unregulated market as a matter of principle; they envisage the market as a means for obtaining and preserving freedom. While there will always be inequalities that appear unjust or disappointments that appear unmerited, the reaction of individuals is quite different if the reasons are due to impersonal market forces as opposed to someone's choice.

Libertarian justice has been criticized for a number of reasons. It prevents a legislator from doing what, to the utilitarian, is good: a utilitarian legislator might tax the rich in order to give aid to the poor, but a libertarian legislator would not. Indeed, any tax and transfer scheme is shunned by the libertarian because it infringes upon one's rights. The libertarian would not provide aid to the poor, because he or she is only concerned about their *rights*, or entitlements, nothing else. The implication for project evaluation is that evaluation is restricted to those situations where the government raises the required funds for a program through borrowing or tariffs on the users, but no one can be coerced into bearing any program cost (e.g., through involuntary taxes). Only programs that satisfy the Pareto criterion (that at least one person gain and no one is made worse off) are acceptable. This is in keeping with the 'takings clause'.

Finally, there is the view that the individual's moral obligations to society restrict what he/she can and cannot do. From a legal point of view, the individual does not have an absolute right to do as he/she wishes with her/his property, because the rights of others could be violated. But this is a misinterpretation of the classical liberal position. It is true that libertarians reject any attempt to create material equality among different people, as such an ideal of justice will inevitably lead to the destruction of what Hayek calls the 'Rule of Law' – the fundamental and unshakeable laws governing relations among free people. Contrary to common perception, this does not imply that libertarians are opposed to certain minimal standards of education, health, and material well-being. Hayek, for example, accepts things such as universal health care and sign posts on roads because these create a 'suitable framework for the beneficial working of competition' (Hayek 1944:39), despite the fact that some need to be coerced into paying for these. Libertarians are opposed to an extended role for government in the economy, as, more often than not, such a role leads to monopoly, rent-seeking, and market failure.

Utilitarianism
Jeremy Bentham is considered to be the father of economic utilitarianism, although utilitarian philosophy already existed in the writings of Hutcheson, Priestley, and Locke. According to utilitarianism, the rightness or wrongness of actions is determined by the goodness or badness of their consequences – not just for the actor but for all those affected. Utilitarians consider maximization of social utility to be the basic criterion of morality, with social utility defined either as the sum, or the arithmetic mean, of the utility levels of all individuals in the society. The utilitarian seeks to maximize social welfare, with social welfare being defined as a strictly increasing function (usually additive) of individual utilities. It does not allow for a value judgment concerning

the relative worth of one individual vis à vis another, as it is generally accepted that all individuals be counted equally.

Not everyone adheres to utilitarian philosophy, as is evident from the writings of Bertrand Russell, John Rawls, and others. There are arguments against utilitarian philosophy, several of which follow.

(1) First, one needs to determine if each person does indeed pursue his/her own happiness and, next, whether or not general happiness is a right end of human action. But happiness itself can be interpreted in two ways, one of which is a truism and the other of which is false. It is a truism if it can be said that pleasures are what I desire. It is false if it means that I desire something because of the pleasure it will bring me. Thus, food is desired because a person is hungry, but pleasure is secondary to this desire and, necessarily, follows it.

(2) The ethical part of the utilitarian doctrine states that good desires and actions are those that increase the general happiness. All that is required is that the effect of actions and desires be such that it increases general happiness, although actual intentions may be quite different. It would seem that a philosophy of ethics should be concerned with intentions as much as, or more than, effect.

(3) Finally, the social optimum arrived at when one has determined the social utility function does not necessarily coincide with the optimal equilibrium one would obtain via the operation of a perfectly competitive market. Different initial endowments result in different competitive market equilibria, but there is only one social optimum. Once the social maximum is determined, it may be necessary to redistribute initial endowments in order to attain that optimum under a perfectly competitive market. The utilitarian is, therefore, led to reject the outcome of perfect competition. But it is not the market mechanism that is at fault; rather, it is the initial distribution of endowments that is rejected.

Although utilitarianism provides a foundation for cost-benefit analysis, it is not accepted by many. By implicitly invoking a potential, if not an actual, compensation test (e.g., in summing consumer and producer surpluses), cost-benefit analysis becomes a handy tool for circumventing the straitjacket of the strict Pareto principle. Each person in society is assigned a weight (say, 1.0 for each person) in the summing of welfare effects.

Contractarianism

Contractarian justice is offered as an alternative to utilitarian justice.

Under contract theory, an individual is willing to accept constraints upon his/her actions, because, if everyone accepts these constraints, all can benefit. This is unlike utilitarianism, wherein individual rights may be constrained because the sum total of individual welfares, however this total is arrived at, is greater in the presence than in the absence of constraints. Whereas coercion may be acceptable to the utilitarian, only enforcement of the socially determined contract is acceptable to the contractarian.

Immanuel Kant used the concepts of the 'original position' and the 'veil of ignorance' to derive principles of morality. To make decisions, an individual must cast him/herself into a hypothetical situation, in which he/she does not know his/her position in life (original position) nor his/her intellectual abilities, inheritance, and so on (veil of ignorance). The decisions arrived at will then be morally correct, since the decisionmaker does not know a priori if he or she is a benefactor or beneficiary.

John Rawls uses these concepts to derive a set of social institutions that would guarantee certain rights. He argues that two principles of justice *for institutions* will be chosen in the original position.

First Principle
> Each person is to have an equal right to the most extensive system of equal basic liberties compatible with a similar system of liberty for all.

Second Principle
> Social and economic inequalities are to be arranged so that they are both:
> (a) to the greatest benefit of the least advantaged, consistent with the just savings principle, and
> (b) attached to offices and positions open to all under combinations of fair equality of opportunity. (1971:60)[1]

The principles are to be ranked in lexicographical order, with liberty receiving the highest priority. The second of these principles of justice is what Rawls calls the *Difference Principle*. Given that the First Principle is satisfied, any adjustment in the position of the original liberties (entitlements) must work to the advantage of the least fortunate group in society.

The difference principle suggests that my actions affect the liberty others derive from their holdings, thereby implying a need for interpersonal comparisons of some sort or some form of utilitarianism. Further, this concern with the welfare of the worst-off group has been interpreted to be essentially a 'maxi-min' criterion – maximize the welfare of the minimum (worst-off) group in society. Thus, utilitarians object to contractarianism, because, they argue, the maxi-min criterion itself is a form of utilitarianism; only the weighting scheme has changed. In cost-benefit analysis, this simply implies assigning a weight of 1 to the net benefits of the worst-off group and of 0 to all others. Of course, the set of individuals in the worst-off category may change through time (and cost-benefit calculations involve time). Rawls permits gains in the other categories as long as those in the worst-off group can expect to be made relatively better-off.

Libertarians object to Rawls's two principles of justice, because they restrict liberty without prior consent, and because Rawlsian justice is confined to distribution only. Thus, the difference principle might be appropriate if manna from heaven is provided only if a just system of distributing the manna were agreed upon. However, because it ignores the production side, Rawls's view is not realistic. As Rawls's colleague, Robert Nozick, argues:

> The situation is not one of something's getting made, and there being an open question of who is to get it. Things come into the world already attached to people having entitlements over them. From the point of view of the historical entitlement conception of justice in holdings, those who start afresh to complete 'to each according to his _____' treat objects as if they appeared from nowhere, out of nothing. (Nozick 1974:160)

In the contractarian framework, this objection can be resolved by cooperation; however, cooperation in the Rawlsian model is with respect to distribution only, with the potential increase in production offered by cooperation totally ignored. David Gauthier proposes a contractual theory of justice based on cooperation. He begins with an initial bargaining position that is determined by Nozick's principle of justice in the holding of entitlements. Only Gauthier adds to Nozick's interpretation of the Lockean proviso the requirement that one cannot worsen the situation of another person, except to avoid worsening one's own situation through interaction with that person. The initial bargaining position could also be considered the non-cooperative outcome that would prevail under ideal markets, given Locke-Nozick-Gauthier rights.

The initial position may not be a coercive one. Then, by cooperating, it is possible to increase the physical quantity of goods and services available to the individuals, which is referred to as the cooperative surplus. Hence, it is also possible to increase at least one person's utility without, at the same time, reducing someone else's utility by cooperating.

In the initial bargaining situation, a bargainer can lay claim to a point represented by a utility level equal to the maximum amount of the cooperative surplus that he/she could possibly get by cooperating. Since everyone makes the same claim and there is not enough surplus to satisfy every claim, the initial claim vector lies outside the set of cooperative outcomes; hence, it is necessary for concessions to be made: the rational cooperative strategy is determined by a bargain among the cooperators, in which each advances his or her maximal claim and then offers a concession no greater in relative magnitude than the minimum of the maximum concession. It is a moral principle because each person agrees to constrain his/her utility-maximizing behaviour in order to allow the cooperative solution to be implemented. This results in classification of Gauthier's 'cooperative bargain' as a contractarian theory of justice, unlike other bargaining solutions in economics.

Ethics, Valuation, and Cost-Benefit Analysis

In this section, the focus is on cost-benefit analysis and questions concerning the validity of attaching dollar values to nature. Consider biological diversity or biodiversity. Ecologists have accorded either first-principle or preeminent value status to species or the preservation of biodiversity; consequently, they reject anthropocentric valuation. But biocentrism is itself a value judgment based on human valuation of wants and desires. Further, by according biodiversity preeminent status, its value to humans is immaterial or even irrelevant. Preservation of species simply becomes an ethical constraint on human behaviour (much like any other), but this does not imply that human values have not been considered (they have) or that anthropocentric valuation is not acceptable.

In general, economists reject the argument that biodiversity should be preserved at all costs because species have intrinsic value – that humans are duty-bound to preserve all species. The duty-based approach does not survive critical scrutiny when one assumes that there are at least two moral goods, namely, preserving biodiversity and enhancing the life prospects of the world's worst-off people. Which takes preeminent status? It is clear that the claims of humans must trump those of non-humans. While humans should make some sacrifices for biodiversity, these cannot be unlimited.

A similar line of argument has been pursued by some Christian writers, who correctly indicate that species have more than an anthropocentric value. As argued later in this chapter, the Christian view is that humans are in a position of stewardship and, therefore, have a responsibility to prevent species from going extinct. Stewardship is abrogated as a result of greed, a vice that is somehow, mysteriously and implicitly, attributed to the economic way of thinking. What is conveniently forgotten about the Christian view is that it points to sin as the root cause of irresponsible behaviour towards creation. More important, sin prevents the realization of effective policies for achieving a harmonious relationship between humans and the environment. Along with humanity's fall into sin, the creation also became 'polluted.' Thus, while Christianity states that humans have an obligation to preserve creation, it also points to our inability to achieve that which is desired. This, then, provides a case for the imposition of constraints on human behaviour by the public authority.

Philosophical approaches to decision-making concerning biodiversity are essentially limited to utilitarianism, social contract theory, libertarianism, and intuition. Those who adhere to a 'person in community' or subsidiary principle would reject libertarian philosophy, because it places onerous limits on public control over private decisions. Libertarians are likely to be receptive to cost-benefit analysis, but with restrictions on what can be done to reduce the welfare of some in order to enhance the total welfare. Intuition, on the other hand, is simply too vague and inconsistent to be politically accepted, although intuition probably plays a larger role in decision-making than is admitted. That leaves the utilitarian and contractarian philosophies. The former is the foundation upon which cost-benefit analysis is based.

As is indicated above, a contractarian case for preserving biodiversity relies upon thought experiments. In some experiments, the possibility that one is 'born' non-human is accepted. Preservation of all species relies upon the notion that one has a chance of being 'born' into a non-human species that might become extinct. Therefore, similar to the Rawlsian principle that gives priority to the least-off individuals in society (but subject to the principle of liberty), it is concluded that extinguishing any species is wrong. The argument falters on the same grounds as mentioned above – the claims of humans must have priority over those of non-humans. While equality between humans and non-humans might be acceptable to some, it cannot be the foundation upon which to base a society. Another problem with this approach is that it is based on a religious presupposition (that differences between humans and non-humans are only biological) that has no more right to priority claim than does some alternative presupposition.

Modification of the contractarian argument to permit only the satisfaction of human preferences leads to the possible inclusion of the safe minimum standard of conservation as a component of a just constitution. The cost-benefit approach emerges as a second-best result; a plausible contractarian solution is to maximize net benefits (to satisfy preferences) subject to a safe minimum standard of conservation as a constraint (because participants in the 'veil of ignorance' process would insist on it).

Criticisms of Cost-Benefit Analysis

Cost-benefit analysis has been criticized by ecologists and others for a number of reasons. The reasons and a defence are provided below.

(1) Cost-benefit analysis is assumed to have a utilitarian foundation and, consequently, is only a means for operationalizing the rule of the greatest good for the greatest number. Some contractarians reject utilitarian approaches to policy analysis as a matter of principle. However, cost-benefit analysis is not necessarily utilitarian. Although it seeks to maximize the net benefits to society of a particular action, regardless of the distribution of welfare (adverse distributions are assumed to be rectifiable), cost-benefit analysis simply points out the costs and benefits of achieving objectives. Even a contractarian should agree to pursue particular goals at least cost.[2] Outside of these foundational issues, the cost-benefit method has merit in deciding upon nature and biodiversity. Values to be included in cost-benefit calculations are solicited either directly from individuals as their willingness to pay (in the case of amenity and existence values) or indirectly from expenditures (for items that can be traced through market transactions). Direct responses are aggregated with values determined from market transactions in order to obtain welfare measures; valuation is anonymous. If biodiversity can be valued using the tools of economics, then aggregation of individual preferences in this way ensures that everyone in society is counted and that each person is treated equally – these are the fundamental assumptions underlying cost-benefit analysis.

(2) Preferences are myopic; individuals are more interested in immediate gratification than they are in future consequences. But binding behaviour (to take into account future consequences) is both rational and consistent with utilitarianism. That is, individuals are willing to constrain their behaviour to avoid possibly unpleasant consequences later on. A logical approach, then, is to make decisions about preserving biodiversity on the basis of cost-benefit analysis, constrained by the safe minimum standard of conservation.

(3) Humans do not understand the technical complexity of ecosystems, thereby precluding the use in cost-benefit analysis of values solicited from individuals via, for example, contingent valuation procedures. (This view also suggests that beavers, termites, ants, and other 'engineering' species somehow know better than humans how to change and manipulate their environment to their immediate advantage.) There is no reason to believe that values obtained anonymously from individuals (either using contingent values or market data) will be more or less misleading than opinions voiced at public hearings. To argue to the contrary is to say that the general public has less technical competence than members of special interest groups – environmentalists, loggers, citizens of resource dependent communities, Native people, unionized sawmill workers, and so on.

(4) There remains the argument that valuation of amenity functions and preservation is not possible. Admittedly, this is a controversial issue (Chapter 7), although it is likely no less problematic than that of determining how many species or subspecies are actually in existence and how many are being lost each year. Optimistic writers believe that measurement is possible and that it will improve over time. Impartial observers simply insist that, while it is difficult to assign values to things like clean water and standing forests, this is no excuse – such measures need to be developed.

(5) Retaining biodiversity involves concern for future generations (bequest values). The argument of some non-economists is that any positive discount rate results in exploitation of the earth's resources and atmosphere to the detriment of future generations. The cost-benefit approach discounts future costs and benefits, and this creates a bias in favour of current consumption. It is implicitly assumed that the market rate of discount is somehow unfair in distributing resources among generations, and that one can correct the market rate to obtain a fairer distribution. This view provides justification for government interven-

tion to impose the 'correct' discount rate, perhaps even a zero rate of discount (one that would treat a dollar in the distant future the same as a dollar today). This issue is discussed further below.

Intergenerational Ethics and Discounting
The problem of land use and intergenerational equity involves more than simply adopting the 'correct' number for the social discount rate. Indeed, the debate about intergenerational equity should not even be about the discount rate. Society must make an explicit decision concerning the amount of income that it feels each future generation should be permitted. This implies that decisions have to be made about the level of knowledge (human capital), the amount of physical (human-made) capital, and the stock of environmental resources to leave future generations. Once such decisions are made, the discount rate is also determined. Distributing income across generations and determining the amounts of each of the three types of capital to bequeath future generations are ethical questions upon which it will be difficult to reach agreement.

It is inconsistent to use a low discount rate on investments in environmental resources (e.g., those that mitigate land or atmospheric degradation), while the return on other capital investments is high. Faced with the choice between investments to improve the environment and capital investments, the efficient policy may be to invest heavily in the high-return options and use the proceeds to improve the environment in the future. While this may not be very appealing if there are unforeseen irreversibilities, it should be noted that investments in human and physical capital result in greater resilience on the part of an economy to cope with the adverse impacts of environmental degradation; the latter investments make more sense than do uncertain and low-return investments with respect to averting the consequences of some forms of degradation.[3]

As noted, concern for intergenerational equity is an argument frequently used to justify government intervention in order to regulate economic activities that are thought to be harmful to the biosphere. In some cases, such action is necessary, but in others the costs of intervention may exceed the environmental damage caused or may lead to additional costs imposed upon the environment. Given international posturing by scientists and bureaucrats, it is clear that an expanded role for government is being called for in such areas as acid rain, global warming, species preservation, and so on. It is argued that intervention is required to prevent current activities from endangering the ability of future generations to meet their needs. The implication is that we are either ill-informed about the relationship between our consumption and the environment, or that we do not properly value future prosperity.

Five objections to immediate action by the state can be raised. First, there is evidence that individuals are willing to incur personal costs to help others when they recognize a definite need, but they are unwilling to incur such costs to achieve a *distant and uncertain* public benefit. Individuals are concerned with future generations, but only when they perceive that they can really help them, which is unlikely to be the case for global warming, say, since it is not clear that future generations will be worse off on account of warming. Indeed, as argued in Chapter 9, the wise thing to do, both from an economic and an ethical standpoint, may be to rely on adaptation, not avoidance.

Second, public action (e.g., expenditures to preserve species or carbon taxes to reduce greenhouse gas emissions) is not costless; it will make the current generation poorer, and poorer people pass on less wealth to future generations. Even if the government transfers wealth to future generation via enhanced environmental amenities, there remains the efficiency question. If current generations pay $2 for every $1 transferred, this is surely inefficient, and it may be in the interests of future generations to receive wealth in the form of human and physical capital as opposed to environmental amenities.

Third, future generations are represented, to some extent, by those who are currently alive. Certainly those of high school and university age will experience the loss of environmental services, and they are represented in today's decisions about the future.

Fourth, one logical implication of the intergenerational equity argument is that the current generation does not appropriately value future prosperity. But this is a value judgement based upon the views of those advocating state intervention. It might well be that the majority of individuals would be unwilling to make the sacrifices necessary to ensure that a future society, one that has a greater endowment of technology, also has more environmental options.

Fifth, experience indicates that it would be a grave error to place the task of maintaining or enhancing the welfare of future generations in the hands of the state. One characteristic appears to be common to all countries that have embarked on state-run programs to enhance the welfare of future citizens: they have mortgaged the future in order to pay for programs that can best be described as failures. Too often politicians and bureaucrats have been more than willing to jeopardize the welfare of future generations in order to enhance their own chances of staying in power.

Choices concerning the protection of natural resources and, consequently, the amount of such resources made available to future generations depends upon society's ethical stand regarding the environment. Stewardship of our natural heritage, whether global, national, or regional, depends on environmental ethics, and ethics, in turn, is influenced by religion. Hence, we now examine religious stands concerning the environment.

Religion and Environmental Ethics

In Genesis 1:28, humans are commanded by God to 'be fruitful and increase in number; fill the earth and subdue it. Rule over the fish of the sea and the birds of the air and over every living creature that moves on the ground.' Many have used this passage from the Bible to argue that the Judeo-Christian religion is largely responsible for the environmental degradation that has taken place in the past 250 years. But there are two serious flaws with this view.

First and foremost, the view that the Bible commands humans to subdue the earth, *and* that this is the root cause of environmental degradation, is a distortion of what the Bible really teaches. Only by ignoring the remainder of the Old Testament, as well as the New Testament and the writings of Christians throughout the ages, can such a view possibly be considered, because it is clear, beginning in Genesis, that nature was created by God and that He interacts with it to achieve a purpose – a teleological or linear as opposed to cyclical view of history is presented. God is not to be found in nature; indeed, to worship nature as if He is found there is idolatry. Humans are commanded not to satisfy their selfish desires but to be responsible co-workers with God in working out His purpose. It is clear from the writings of the prophets that, while humans are placed in a superior position, nature will have dominion over humans in exacting God's punishment when people misbehave or sin (e.g., Isaiah 34-5). Thus, the dominion of humans over creation (nature) is contingent upon their moral fitness.

Further, to attribute environmental degradation to the aforementioned biblical command ignores environmental degradation in regions that do not adhere to the creationist view of Genesis. In India and Nepal, for example, centuries of deforestation, overgrazing (goats are as effective as bulldozers in destroying the land), and soil erosion have resulted in untold land devastation. Likewise, environmental degradation has characterized the self-declared atheistic countries that subscribe to Marxist philosophy. Degradation of the Aral Sea in the former USSR is a prime example. Both India and China produce ozone-depleting CFCs, and, by 2050, China is projected to have greater emissions of carbon dioxide than all of the OECD countries put together. Archaeological and anthropological evidence indicates that nomadic tribes in North America camped at one spot until it was trashed, before moving on to another one. The environment was safe only as long as the population remained small. During land settlement negotiations over the first phase of the massive James Bay Hydro Project in northern Québec, the Cree Indians argued that it would be impossible to place a value on land – it was part of their heritage and religion and, thus, priceless. Upon being awarded the land, however, they promptly turned around and sold it.

In contrast to Hebrew thought, the Greeks viewed plant and animal life as existing only for the sake of humans. Nature was viewed, by the Greeks, as something evil from which the good human soul sought to escape. Marx also viewed nature as an instrument to fulfil human needs – an instrument that could be mastered by human technology. He paid little attention to the exploitation of nature, only to the exploitation of people.

Christianity, Judaism, and Islam are all based upon the Hebrew or biblical view of stewardship, not the view presented by Aristotle. Medieval writers sought to marry Greek and Christian thought, but this was not possible. The scientific world-view that arose in the seventeenth century was more influenced by Greek than by Hebrew thinking. It is the world-view that began with Francis Bacon, René Descartes, Isaac Newton, John Locke, and others; it dominates today's modern society, not Judeo-Christian or Islamic thought. This does not, however, imply that the current, non-Christian world-view is solely responsible for environmental degradation. What about other religious traditions?

Eastern religions disagree on many points, but there is strong agreement among Hindus, Buddhists, and Jains regarding the relationship between humans and nature. Humans and animals (and, in the Jainist case, even rocks, trees, plants, air, and water) are composed of the same spiritual and non-spiritual elements, with no radical break between the human and the non-human. (Of the three, the Jainist view is most radical and is the root of today's 'deep ecology' movement.) There is inherent respect for nature because of the notions of rebirth and the law of *karma*. The law of karma (memory traces) holds that humans have

free will that can be used to either subdue evil memory urges or reinforce them. One's ability to deal with memory urges will determine the
level of existence attained in one's next life, which may be as an animal.
Consequently, there is respect for nature on two grounds: first, one
could become a part of nature; and, second, the endless cycle of birth,
death, and rebirth results in a karmic responsibility towards not only
the individual but the cosmos. In some ways the karmic view is similar
to the Greek view that nature is evil, because it is something individuals
want to avoid falling into in a next life.

While not adhering to karma theory, Taoism requires surrender to the
natural world in order to overcome disharmony. Taoism respects nature
and requires humans to adjust to its demands.

The similarity between the eastern religions and the Native American
religion is that both view nature as having spiritual qualities. While
animals may be killed when needed, apologetic prayers need to be
offered to the animal's spirit. There is a need for humans to live in
harmony with nature, with the environment.

Another view of nature arose out of a response to industrialization and
modern society and is found in the Romantic Movement in literature
and philosophy. The 'noble savage,' the need to 'get back to nature,' and
the view that nature is a source of inspiration, vitality, and renewal (or
healing) are part of this. These views inspired the founding of the Sierra
Club in 1892 and the 'green movements' of modern time (with herbal
medicines, natural foods, back-to-nature communes, etc.).

Finally, evolutionary theory challenges the separation of humankind
and nature. This is because biological evolution assumes that humans
and nature share a common evolutionary history – that they have the
same origins. Therefore, a respect for nature is required because there
is nothing to prevent new life forms, superior, perhaps, to our own,
from evolving, and, by destroying ecosystems, we may prevent their
development; indeed, we may prevent our own development to a
superior life form through our thoughtless degradation of the biosphere.
On the other hand, given that evolution is based on competition and
the survival of species best able to appropriate the greatest amount of
resources for reproduction, humans may simply be ensuring their survival by eliminating competing species and creating a technological and
sterile environment. Coevolutionary development (Chapter 8) is a product of the evolutionary point of view.

While most societies (an exception being Marxist ones) adhere to
religious systems that proclaim harmony between humankind and

nature and the need to prevent environmental degradation, all are characterized by actions that are contrary to the religious presuppositions upon which they are founded. A distinguishing feature among the various religions is their position regarding the spirituality of nature. In Eastern, Native American, and many modern forms of humanist religions ('new age,' Romanticism, etc.), nature is assigned spiritual or mythical attributes and becomes an object of worship. In Judeo-Christian and Islamic traditions, God is separate from nature and humans are judged for their stewardship of God's creation; the individual is accountable to God as well as to the living for his/her actions towards the environment. A biblical view of nature indicates that it has intrinsic value because God derives pleasure from nature, it declares His glory and it serves His purpose – a purpose that humans are to share and work towards. Of course, nature also has value to humans, but it is subordinate to its intrinsic value. Intrinsic value is also assigned to nature by other religions, but only because it has spiritual value, namely, that of individuals caught in the endless cycle of birth, death, and rebirth.

Economics takes the pragmatic view that nature does not have value outside of its value to human beings. Economics is neither a philosophical nor a religious system; rather, it is a social science that is best suited to practical judgments concerning public policy. When it comes to environmental degradation, it seeks to determine whether or not the costs of maintaining certain environmental standards are worth the benefits, as measured in utility or dollar values (anthropogenic values). Assigning values to nature has nothing to do with morality or ethics; it is no different from classifying plant and animal species. Ultimately, it is what is done with nature that constitutes ethics. The advantage of economic analysis is not only that economics seeks to take into account all values (including nonmarket values), but that it leads to the identification of costs or benefits that are often ignored or simply not recognized because they are not immediately obvious. While there is much about economic theory (and its foundations) that is questionable from an ethical perspective, this does not imply that economics has nothing to offer to the environmental debate. Just because the intrinsic values of nature are not explicitly included in project evaluation, for example, does not mean that these are unimportant. Rather, economics asks individuals to identify explicitly why the course of action advocated by economic analysis (perhaps one that leads to somewhat greater environmental degradation) is not suitable. Economic analysis requires that individuals state their value judgments up front, and it points out the utility or dollar value of the costs that one might impose upon society by adhering to a particular viewpoint.

Science and Advocacy

In their review of the 1990 report of the Intergovernmental Panel On Climate Change (IPCC), several highly regarded scientists found that the scientific evidence to support an enhanced greenhouse effect is not presently available.

> Scientists *cannot* at this time make the definitive statement: Yes we have now seen an enhanced greenhouse effect ... Until science understands better the reasons for past climatic episodes, *it is not possible to attribute a specific proportion of the recent* (small) *warming to the increase of greenhouse gases.* (Smith, Lindzen, and Evans 1991:ii, 49) (emphasis in original)

Interestingly, upon examining the same report (and evidence), other scientists concluded that the scientific community is united over 'what the likely future climate will be if no action is taken to reduce greenhouse gas emissions' (Bruce 1991:89); this stance clearly implies that there is, indeed, an enhanced greenhouse effect and that the threat is sufficiently great to warrant immediate action through state intervention. What could account for the diverging opinions (for that is what they are) between these two groups of scientists over the climatic future *and* the urgency of government action?

The risk assessment literature provides useful insights for answering this question. Risk assessment is based on perception and judgments. 'Whatever role judgment plays, its products should be treated with caution. Research not only demonstrates that judgment is fallible, but it also shows that the degree of fallibility is often surprisingly great and that faulty beliefs may be held with great confidence' (Sturdy et al. 1980:332). Scientists often draw conclusions from their research that may not hold beyond the narrow confines of a particular problem, while the special dynamics of groups might result in lack of scientific vigilance along with a scientifically unfounded condemnation of those not concurring with the group consensus regarding the 'facts.'

In addition to the problem of taking results from the specific or narrow to the broader case (where they may not hold), there are other reasons why professional judgment may not be totally reliable with respect to the proper assessment of risks. Reality and theory are not the same, nor is it true that the system being simulated always represents the actual situation in all its complexity. Scientists focus on the known and knowable, while downplaying the uncertain. The focus is usually on the deterministic, and scientifically based statements often imply that there is little or no uncertainty, when uncertainty may actually be very high. There is also the temptation to make statements about the whole based upon investigations of the parts – a common fallacy in all science.

When a scientist makes policy statements, there is often a failure to define the limits of one's professional competence. This leads to a failure to recognize the validity of other points of view or the findings of others. The approach/view/findings of one group of scientists becomes the centrepiece of the problem. (This makes it difficult to separate the parts from the whole.) Every profession has certain ethical values that are inculcated into those practising that profession. These generally include a desire to protect society, thereby leading scientists to make policy prescriptions that they believe follow logically from their research findings but may lead to results opposite to those expected. Related to this is the professional's own values and his/her own agenda (e.g., concern about research funding, politics, etc.). Thus, for example, many scientists are involved in environmental politics; they only accept positions or research that fit with their views, while denigrating those that have contrary views.

The problem of scientific evidence and advocacy can be summarized by the following quote from J. Sturdy and his collaborators (1980:343):

> The problem of validity of scientific information has two facets: (1) the internal resolution of conflicts within the scientific community as to what constitutes valid information, and (2) the perception of the public and policy makers as to the validity of scientific information. The internal problem stems from the fact that the degree of conclusiveness required by the traditional scientific method cannot accommodate the demands of policy making in a complex and rapidly changing environment. Scientists are asked to provide information before it is subjected to a rigorous, time-consuming systems of checks ... [and are] requested to interpret their results in policy terms.

Conclusion

Economics is a social science that provides but one approach to the study of land use and sustainable development. It is an important approach because it addresses the utility and monetary aspects of topics that are often discussed in emotional terms. Economics does not have all the answers, nor do economists qua economists insist that they do. However, it would be a grave error to ignore economic considerations when deciding how society's human, human-made, and natural resources are to be used. A failure to adequately value land resources, whether traded in markets or not, could lead to their depletion; this was demonstrated to be the case for timber and range resources in low-income countries. Likewise, overvaluing ecosystem resources leads to inefficiency and a society that is poorer than it would otherwise be. Such a society has a lower capacity to invest in means for reducing reliance on natural resource wealth and may, indeed, place a greater demand on natural resources in the future than would otherwise be the case.

One purpose of this book is to sound a warning bell concerning government intervention in the economy for protection of the earth's natural resources. Externality constitutes the prime theoretical basis for government intervention, but the existence of externality is not, by itself, sufficient to warrant public action. Indeed, if there is anything to be learned from the history of state intervention it is this: governments are unable to decide what is best for society and, more often than not, they choose courses of action that are as likely to degrade natural resources than if intervention had never occurred. Further, governments need to please a large number of different constituents, and this leads to contradictory policies; an example of the latter is a policy to reduce CO_2 emissions at the same time that subsidies and tax breaks are provided to interests seeking to develop a coal mine. Government deficits are a good indicator of how governments really value future generations and, thus, the value they place on the preservation of ecosystems.

As demonstrated throughout the book, economics does concern itself with land and ecosystem resources, and the possibility that important natural amenities can be lost forever. Economics has a tool kit for thinking about and analyzing problems of sustainability and irreversibility, but it is not a panacea. It provides information about the instruments that can be used to achieve sustainable development, but it also focuses attention on the (opportunity) costs and limits of what is possible. Perhaps it is for these reasons that economics is often called the 'dismal science' – it puts a damper on the visions of the optimists. If nothing else, the reader should be aware that decisions about sustainable development and the use of natural resources involve tradeoffs. Perhaps more than ever before, it is necessary to allocate scarce resources among competing demands, which is a task well suited to economic analysis.

Notes

Chapter 2: The Concept of Rent

1 Henri Gossens also argued for a single tax, but his book appeared one year after that of George (1880 versus 1879), although it is unlikely that these economists were aware of each other's writings.
2 This might mean that soil is depleted (eroded) at the same rate as it is replaced, or that soil is rebuilt by the intermixing of the layers below the humus and green manuring (adding humus).

Chapter 3: The Theory of Welfare Measurement

1 Equivalent number of arrows on lines denote that the lines are parallel.
2 This occurs when an increase or decrease in income has no effect upon purchases of the good or service in question.
3 Ignored in this discussion is that interventions in one market have effects in other markets that must be taken into account when measuring welfare.
4 The term 'public good' is defined in the next chapter.

Chapter 4: Property Rights, Market Failure, Externality

1 Pareto optimal or Pareto efficient means that it is not possible to make one person better off (produce more of one good) without, at the same time, making someone else worse off (produce less of some other good).

Chapter 5: Social Cost-Benefit Analysis

1 The literature on project appraisal is profuse, and it would be inappropriate to document all of it here. It should be noted that some of the literature originates with the World Bank, with particular focus on project evaluation in developing countries (Dreze and Stern 1987; Gittinger 1982; Dasgupta et al. 1972).
2 The theoretical foundations of B-C analysis have been well documented by Harberger (1972), Boadway (1974), Just et al. (1982), and Boadway and Bruce (1984), among others.
3 This is the well-known bond formula: $V = B/r$, where V is the value of the bond (present value of benefits), B is the annual return, and r is the interest

(discount) rate. An increase in *r* will decrease *V*, while reductions in *r* will increase *V* because future *B* are worth more today.

4 One method is to employ Monte Carlo simulation, constructing probability distributions about uncertain costs and benefits and about the discount rate (e.g., a uniform distribution over rates from 0 to 15 per cent). Then NPV and B/C information can be presented in terms of both an expected value and a variance about the average.

Chapter 7: Valuing Nonmarket Benefits

1 The problem of aggregating over individuals is usually ignored. This problem can be overcome by assuming a representative individual and multiplying the result by all persons in society.

Chapter 10: Economics of Soil Conservation

1 Given the unprofitability of farming in some regions of the world, there is a need to take this land out of production. The Palliser Triangle region in the southwestern Great Plains of Canada is an example of land that should never have been cultivated to begin with. How does one remove such marginal lands from cultivation? This question concerns socioeconomic issues beyond the scope of this book.

2 This assumption is realistic when there is sufficient topsoil available, but is less realistic when topsoil depth declines to more critical levels.

Chapter 11: Efficiency and Equity in Land-Use Planning

1 Sweden has a gasoline sales tax of 133 per cent and an automobile sales tax of 41 per cent, compared to gasoline and automobile sales taxes of 41 and 5 per cent, respectively, in the U.S. Yet the average number of kilometres driven per person is higher in Sweden than it is in the U.S. (8,000 versus 7,700). Comparisons for other countries also indicates how little impact taxes appear to have on automobile use.

Chapter 12: Land Preservation and Conservation

1 For the coastal region of British Columbia, rather than frost-free days, number of days above 5°C is used.

2 GRIP was designed from the ground up by farmers, provinces, and the federal government working together. The problem was that the committee that designed the new agricultural program consisted of 19 farmers and 14 provincial and federal representatives. Such representation was bound to favour farmers.

3 CLI class 5 and 6 lands were defined as suitable for forages but not for crop production. It is clear that farm programs have created distortions leading to their cultivation, and this now needs to be corrected.

Chapter 13: Control over Water in Agriculture

1 An acre-foot of water is the amount of water required to cover one acre to a

depth of one foot and is equal to 1,233 cubic metres of water.

2 Cost-benefit analyses in Canada often fail to take into account the opportunity cost of water. Water used in irrigation is unavailable (except for some runoff) for driving electrical turbines. Even when the opportunity cost of water is ignored, benefit-cost ratios tend to be less than 1.0.

3 Systems used to classify wetlands are based on hydrology and moisture requirements of hydrophytes. Where wetland vegetation is disturbed by agricultural practices, for example, it becomes difficult to categorize the wetlands.

4 Project treatments consisted of (1) licence agreements for wetlands (minimum of 15 a of water with an equal or greater amount of uplands); (2) lease agreements on good quality agricultural lands that are then enclosed with a predator fence and seeded to dense nesting cover; (3) hayfield agreements; and (4) nesting baskets.

5 Data for 1990 were not yet available in 1992.

6 Cattle can also lead to increased mortality of waterfowl nesting in uplands and decreased nesting success. With high cattle densities, fencing may be required to keep cattle away from waterfowl habitat.

Chapter 14: Economics and Management of Public Forestlands

1 An assumption with similar implications is that costs are a linear function of the amount harvested. Then each m^3 of timber costs the same to harvest, regardless of the amount harvested. This simply says that the marginal cost is constant and can, therefore, be subtracted from price to obtain a net price.

2 Price is now important, unless the conditions of the previous footnote hold.

3 Equation 14.9 is obtained by maximizing the present value of the flow of amenity services that occur annually and depend on the volume of timber growing on the site. If amenity services depend on the change in timber volume (as is the case for carbon uptake benefits), then 14.9 is no longer appropriate.

Chapter 15: Economics and Public Rangeland Management

1 One problem of tenure concerns grazing on clearcuts, where herds must be moved from one spot to the next. In this case, existing ranchers are preferred over new entrants because herd behaviour has been established, making it easier to move herds and satisfy public agency regulations.

2 These data suggest that the BC government either spends too much on its grazing program or that its grazing fees are too low.

Chapter 16: Management of Public Lands for Multiple Use

1 The survey method was to divide land into one mile by one mile rectangles. Such a rectangle was called a section and comprised 640 ac. A township consisted of 36 sections, of which one was generally assigned to

public purpose (e.g., schools). Sections were, in turn, divided into quarters of 160 ac.

Chapter 17: Ethics and Land Resource Economics

1 A further statement of the two principles occurs in Rawls (1971:250).
2 Consider the following illustration. A family is starving in the wilderness and happens upon a locked cabin with food in it. Contractarians (and others) would readily agree that they have a moral right to the food. However, access to it should be gained at least cost (e.g., breaking a window) and not burning down the cabin. A contractarian arrives at this result using principles of cost-benefit analysis.
3 An illustrative example may be helpful. The cost of averting global warming is high (Chapter 9), but research in the Netherlands indicates that it is possible to defend against sea-level rise by injecting sulphuric acid (an industrial pollutant) into the calcium carbonate (chalk) beds underlying most coastal regions. The chalk reacts with sulphuric acid to form gypsum which has twice the volume of the original rock, thereby raising the land a metre or more. Money used in this research yields a higher return than if it were invested in averting climatic change.

References and Suggested Readings

Chapter 1: Introduction

Barlowe, Raleigh. 1986. *Land Resource Economics*. 4th edition. Englewood Cliffs, NJ: Prentice Hall

Bromley, Daniel W. 1989. *Economic Interests and Institutions: The Conceptual Foundations of Public Policy*. New York: Basil Blackwell

Castle, Emery N., Maurice M. Kelso, Joe B. Stevens, and Herbert H. Stoevener. 1981. 'Natural Resource Economics, 1946-75.' In *A Survey of Agricultural Economics Literature, Volume 3: Economics of Welfare, Rural Development and Natural Resources in Agriculture 1940s to 1970s*, edited by Lee R. Martin. Minneapolis: University of Minnesota Press

Daly, H.E. 1977. *Steady-State Economics: The Economics of Biophysical Equilibrium and Moral Growth*. San Francisco: W.H. Freeman

— . (ed.). 1980. *Economics, Ecology, Ethics: Essays toward a Steady-State Economy*. San Francisco: W.H. Freeman

Georgescu-Roegen, Nicholas. 1971. *The Entropy Law and the Economic Process*. Cambridge, MA: Harvard University Press

Mirowski, Philip. 1988. *Against Mechanism: Protecting Economics from Science*. Totowa, NJ: Rowan and Littlefield

— . 1989. *More Heat than Light*. New York: Cambridge University Press

Richardson, Nigel. 1989. *Land Use Planning and Sustainable Development in Canada*. Ottawa: Minister of Supply and Services, Canada

Salter, Leonard A. Jr. 1967. *A Critical Review of Research in Land Economics*. Madison: University of Wisconsin Press

Samuels, Warren (ed.). 1979. *The Economy as a System of Power*. New Brunswick, NJ: Transaction Books

Tool, Marc. 1987a. *Evolutionary Economics I: Foundations of Institutional Thought*. Special edition of the *Journal of Economic Issues* 21(September)

— . 1987b. *Evolutionary Economics II: Institutional Theory and Policy*. Special edition of the *Journal of Economic Issues* 21(December)

Chapter 2: The Concept of Rent

Anderson, F.J. 1985. *Natural Resources in Canada*. Toronto: Methuen. Chapter 5

Barlowe, Raleigh. 1986. *Land Resource Economics*. 4th edition. Englewood Cliffs, NJ: Prentice-Hall. Chapters 6 and 9

Friedman, Milton. 1962. *Price Theory.* Chicago: Aldine

Gaffney, M.M. 1965. 'Soil Depletion and Land Rent.' *Natural Resources Journal* 4(January):537-57

Larmour, Peter. 1979. *The Concept of Rent in 19th Century Economic Thought: Ricardo, Mill, Marx, Walras, and Marshall.* Resources Paper No. 36. Vancouver: Department of Economics, University of British Columbia. May. 45 pp.

Pearse, Peter H. 1990. *An Introduction to Forestry Economics.* Vancouver: UBC Press. Chapter 5

van Kooten, G.C. and W.H. Furtan. 1987. 'A Review of Issues Pertaining to Soil Deterioration in Canada.' *Canadian Journal of Agricultural Economics* 35(March):33-54

Chapter 3: The Theory of Welfare Measurement

Boadway, Robin W. and Neil Bruce. 1984. *Welfare Economics.* New York: Basil Blackwell. Chapter 7

Freeman, A. Myrick III. 1979a. *The Benefits of Environmental Improvement. Theory and Practice.* Baltimore: Johns Hopkins University Press. Chapter 3

— . 1979b. 'Approaches to Measuring Public Goods Demands.' *American Journal of Agricultural Economics* 61(December):915-20

— . 1985. 'Methods for Assessing the Benefits of Environmental Programs.' Chapter 6 in *Handbook of Natural Resource and Energy Economics, Vol I,* edited by A.V. Kneese and J.L. Sweeney. Amsterdam: North-Holland

Johansson, Per-Olov. 1991. *An Introduction to Modern Welfare Economics.* Cambridge: Cambridge University Press

Just, Richard E., Darrell L. Hueth and Andrew Schmitz. 1982. *Applied Welfare Economics and Public Policy.* Englewood Cliffs, NJ: Prentice-Hall

Maler, Karl-Goran. 1985. 'Welfare Economics and the Environment.' Chapter 1 in *Handbook of Natural Resource and Energy Economics, Vol. I,* edited by A.V. Kneese and J.L. Sweeney. Amsterdam: North-Holland

Mishan, Ezra J. 1981. *Introduction to Normative Economics.* New York: Oxford University Press

Randall, Alan. 1982. 'Economic Surplus Concepts and Their Use in Benefit-Cost Analysis.' *Review of Marketing and Agricultural Economics* 50(August):135-63

Willig, R. 1976. 'Consumer's Surplus without Apology.' *American Economic Review* 66(September):589-97

Chapter 4: Property Rights, Market Failure, Externality

Bator, Francis M. 1958. 'The Anatomy of Market Failure.' *Quarterly Journal of Economics* 72(August):351-79

Baumol, William J. and Wallace E. Oates. 1988. *The Theory of Environmental Policy.* 2nd edition. Cambridge: Cambridge University Press

Bohm, Peter and Clifford S. Russell. 1985. 'Comparative Analysis of Alternative Policy Instruments.' Chapter 10 in *Handbook of Natural Resource and Energy Economics, Vol. I,* edited by Allen V. Kneese and James L. Sweeney. Amsterdam: North-Holland

Buchanan, James M. and William C. Stubblebine. 1962. 'Externality.' *Economica* 29(November):371-84

Coase, Ronald. 1960. 'The Problem of Social Cost.' *Journal of Law and Economics* 3(October):1-44

Cropper, Maureen L. and Wallace E. Oates. 1992. 'Environmental Economics: A Survey.' *Journal of Economic Literature* 30(June):675-740

Hartwick, John M. and Nancy D. Olewiler. 1986. *The Economics of Natural Resource Use.* New York: Harper & Row. Chapters 12, 13, and 14

Hecht, Neil. 1965. 'From Sesin to Sit-in: Evolving Property Concepts.' *Boston University Law Review* 45:435-66

Johansson, Per-Olov. 1987. *The Economic Theory and Measurement of Environmental Benefits.* Cambridge: Cambridge University Press

Mishan, Ezra J. 1974. 'What is the Optimal Level of Pollution?' *Journal of Political Economy* 82(December):1, 287-99

Pearce, David W. and R. Kerry Turner. 1990. *Economics of Natural Resources and the Environment.* Baltimore: Johns Hopkins University Press

Pigou, A.C. 1946. *The Economics of Welfare.* 4th edition. London: Macmillan

Randall, Alan. 1981. *Resource Economics: An Economic Approach to Natural Resource and Environmental Policy.* New York: Wiley

Turvey, Ralph. 1963. 'On Divergences between Social Cost and Private Cost.' *Economica* 30(August):309-13

Part Two: Introduction

Pearse, P.H., F. Bertrand, and J.W. MacLaren. 1985. *Currents of Change: Final Report. Inquiry on Federal Water Policy.* Ottawa: Minister of Supply and Services Canada

Chapter 5: Social Cost-Benefit Analysis

Arrow, K.J. 1951. *Social Choice and Individual Values.* New Haven: Yale University Press

Bentkover, Judith D. 1986. 'The Role of Benefits Assessment in Public Policy Development.' Chapter 1 in *Benefits Assessment: The State of the Art,* edited by Judith D. Bentkover, Vincent T. Covello, and Jeryl Mumpower. Dordrecht: D. Reidel

Boadway, R.W. 1974. 'The Welfare Foundations of Cost-Benefit Analysis.' *Economic Journal* 84:426-39

Boadway, R.W. and N. Bruce. 1984. *Welfare Economics.* New York: Basil Blackwell

Brown, Gordon L. 1990. 'Assessment of Crop Losses from Ozone using Biomonitor Plants and Risk Estimates by Experts.' Unpublished PhD dissertation. Vancouver: University of British Columbia

Dasgupta, Partha, Stephen Marglin, and Amartya K. Sen. 1972. *Guidelines for Project Evaluation.* New York: United Nations International Development Organization

Deason, J.P. 1982. 'Water Resources Planning in the New Principles and Guidelines.' In *Multi-Objective Analysis in Water Research,* edited by Y.Y. Haimes and D.J. Allee. New York: American Society of Civil Engineers. 37-45

Diewert, W.E. 1983. 'Cost-Benefit Analysis and Project Evaluation.' *Journal of Public Economics* 22(December):265-302

Dreze, J. and N. Stern. 1987. 'The Theory of Cost-Benefit Analysis.' Chapter 14 in *Handbook of Public Economics,* edited by A.J. Auerbach and M. Feldstein. Amsterdam: North Holland

Eckstein, Otto. 1958. *Water Resource Development: The Economics of Project Evaluation.* Cambridge: Harvard University Press

Gittinger, J.P. 1982. *Economic Analysis of Agricultural Projects.* 2nd edition. Baltimore: Johns Hopkins University Press

Grigg, Neil S. 1985. *Water Resources Planning.* Montreal: McGraw-Hill

Hamilton, Joel R. and Richard L. Gardner. 1986. 'Value Added and Secondary Benefits in Regional Project Evaluation: Irrigation Development in the Snake River Basin.' *The Annals of Regional Science* 20(March):1-11

Harberger, Arnold C. 1972. *Project Evaluation. Collected Papers.* Chicago: University of Chicago Press

— . 1978. 'On the Use of Distributional Weights in Social Cost-Benefit Analysis.' *Journal of Political Economy* 86 (April):S87-S120

Just, Richard E., Darrell L. Hueth and Andrew Schmitz. 1982. *Applied Welfare Economics and Public Policy.* Englewood Cliffs, NJ: Prentice-Hall

Maass, A. 1966. 'Benefit-Cost Analysis: Its Relevance to Public Investment Decisions.' In *Water Research,* edited by A.V. Kneese and S.C. Smith. Baltimore: Johns Hopkins Press

McKean, R.N. 1958. *Efficiency in Government through Systems Analysis.* New York: Wiley

McKee, Michael and Edwin G. West. 1981. 'The Theory of Second Best: A Solution in Search of a Problem.' *Economic Inquiry* 19(July):436-48

Marglin, Stephen A. 1967. *Public Investment Criteria: Benefit-Cost Analysis for Planned Economic Growth.* Cambridge, MA: MIT

Mishan, E.J. 1971. *Cost-Benefit Analysis.* London: George Allen and Unwin

— . 1982. 'The New Controversy about the Rationale of Economic Evaluation.' *Journal of Economic Issues* 16 (March):29-47

Pearce, D.W. 1971. *Cost-Benefit Analysis.* London: Macmillan

Pierce, D.W. and C.A. Nash. 1981. *The Social Appraisal of Projects.* London: Macmillan

Prairie Farm Rehabilitation Administration and Saskatchewan Water Corporation. 1985. *Saskatchewan Irrigation Project Appraisal Study.* Regina, SK. October

Prest, A.R. and R. Turvey. 1974. 'Cost-Benefit Analysis: A Survey.' In *Readings in Natural Resource Economics,* edited by John E. Reynolds, J. Margin Redfern, and Robert N. Shulstad. New York: MSS Information Corporation. 145-71

Reisner, Marc. 1986. *Cadillac Desert.* New York: Penguin

Roberts, T.L. and J.W.B. Stewart. 1987. 'Update of Residual Fertilizer Phosphorous in Western Canadian Soils.' Saskatchewan Institute of Pedology Publication No. R523. Saskatoon: University of Saskatchewan. July

Sassone, Peter G. and William A. Schaffer. 1978. *Cost-Benefit Analysis: A Handbook.* New York: Academic Press

Self, P. 1972. *Econocrats and the Policy Process.* London: Macmillan

Smith, V. Kerry. 1986. 'A Conceptual Overview of the Foundations of Benefit-Cost Analysis.' Chapter 2 in *Benefits Assessment: The State of the Art,.* edited by Judith D. Bentkover, Vincent T. Covello, and Jeryl Mumpower. Dordrecht: D. Reidel

Squire, Lyn and Herman G. Van Der Tak. 1975. *Economic Analysis of Projects.* Baltimore: John Hopkins University Press (A World Bank Research Publication)

Stabler, Jack C., G.C. Van Kooten, and Neil Meyer. 'Methodological Issues in Appraisal of Regional Resource Development Projects.' *Annals of Regional Science* 22(July 1988):13-25

Treasury Board Secretariat (Planning Branch). 1976. *Benefit-Cost Analysis Guide.* Ottawa: Canadian Government Publishing Centre

United States Inter-Agency Committee on Water Resources. 1958. *Proposed Practices for Economic Analysis of River Basin Projects.* Report to the Inter-Agency Committee on Evaluation Standards, rev. ed. (The Green Book)

— . 1962. *Policies, Standards and Procedures in the Formulation, Evaluation, and Review of Plans for Use and Development of Water and Related Land Resources.* Senate Document No. 97, 87th Congress, Second Session

United States Inter-Agency River Basin Committee (Sub-Committee on Costs and Budgets). 1950. *Proposed Practices for Economic Analysis of River Basin Projects* (The Green Book) Washington, DC

United States Water Resources Council. 1973. 'Water and Related Land Resources: Establishment of Principles and Standards for Planning.' *Federal Register* 38(December 10):24778-869

— . 1979. 'Principles and Standards for Planning Water and Related Land Resources.' *Federal Register* 44(242):72878-976

— . 1983. 'Economic and Environmental Principles and Guidelines for Water and Related Land Resources Implementation Studies.' Washington, DC. Mimeograph. 10 March. 137 pp.

Chapter 6: Input-Output Models

Adelman, Irma and Sherman Robinson. 1986. 'U.S. Agriculture in a General Equilibrium Framework: Analysis with a Social Accounting Matrix.' *American Journal of Agricultural Economics* 68(December):1,196-207

Bromley, D.W., G.E. Blanch, and H.H. Stoevener. 1968. *Effects of Selected Changes in Federal Land Use on a Rural Economy.* Agricultural Experiment Station Bulletin 604. Corvallis: Oregon State University

Chenery, Hollis B. and Paul G. Clark. 1959. *Interindustry Economics.* New York: Wiley

Davis, H. Craig. 1990. *Regional Economic Impact Analysis and Project Evaluation.* Vancouver: UBC Press

Forsund, Finn R. 1985. 'Input-Output Models, National Economic Models, and the Environment.' Chapter 8 in *Handbook of Natural Resource and Energy Economics, Vol I,* edited by A.V. Kneese and J.L. Sweeney. Amsterdam: North-Holland

Hamilton, J.R., N.K. Whittlesey, M.H. Robison, and J.Ellis. 1991. 'Economic Impacts, Value Added, and Benefits in Regional Project Analysis.' *American Journal of Agricultural Economics* 73(May):334-44

Harberger, Arnold C. 1972. *Project Evaluation.* Chicago: University of Chicago Press

Miernyk, William H. 1965. *The Elements of Input-Output Analysis.* New York: Random House

Miller, Ronald E. and Peter D. Blair. 1985. *Input-Output Analysis: Foundations and Extensions*. Englewood Cliffs, NJ: Prentice-Hall

Statistics Canada. 1969. *The Input-Output Structure of the Canadian Economy 1961, Vol. 1,* Bureau of Statistics, Catalogue No. 15-501, Ottawa. August

Yan, Chiou-Shuang. 1969. *Introduction to Input-Output Economics.* New York: Holt, Rinehart, and Winston

Chapter 7: Valuing Nonmarket Benefits

Anonymous. 1992. '"Ask a Silly Question ... "': Contingent Valuation of Natural Resource Damages.' *Harvard Law Review* 105(June):1,981-2,000

Clawson, Marion. 1959. *Measuring the Demand for and Value of Outdoor Recreation.* RFF Reprint #10. Washington: Resources for the Future

Bishop, Richard C. and Thomas A. Heberlein. 1990. 'The Contingent Valuation Method.' Chapter 6 in *Economic Valuation of Natural Resources: Issues, Theory and Application,* edited by Rebecca L. Johnson and Gary V. Johnson. Boulder: Westview. 81-104

Bowes, Michael D. and John V. Krutilla. 1989. *Multiple-Use Management: The Economics of Public Forestlands.* Washington: Resources for the Future

Brown, Thomas C. and Terry C. Daniel. 1986. 'Predicting Scenic Beauty of Timber Stands.' *Forest Science* 32:471-87

Crocker, Thomas D. 1985. 'On the Value of the Condition of a Forest Stock.' *Land Economics* 61(August):244-55

Cummings, Ronald G., David S. Brookshire, and William D. Schulze (eds.). 1986. *Valuing Environmental Goods: An Assessment of the Contingent Valuation Method.* Totowa, NJ: Rowman and Allanheld

Eberle, W. David and F. Gregory Hayden. 1991. 'Critique of Contingent Valuation and Travel Cost Methods for Valuing Natural Resources and Ecosystems.' *Journal of Economic Issues* 25(September):649-87

Edwards, J.A., K.C. Gibbs, L.J. Guedry, and H.H. Stoevener. 1976. *The Demand for Non-Unique Outdoor Recreational Services: Methodological Issues.* Corvallis: Oregon Agricultural Experiment Station Technical Bulletin. May

Freeman, A. Myrick III. 1979. *The Benefits of Environmental Improvement.* Baltimore: Johns Hopkins University Press

Greenley, Douglas A., Richard G. Walsh, and Robert A. Young. 1981. 'Option Value: Empirical Evidence from a Case Study of Recreation and Water Quality.' *The Quarterly Journal of Economics* 96(November):657-72

Gunton, Thomas, John Richards, Nancy Knight, et al. 1986. *Stein River Watershed Resource Evaluation.* Natural Resources Management Program Research Report No. 5. Burnaby: Simon Fraser University. July. 69 pp.

Kahneman, D. and J.L. Knetsch. 1992a. 'Valuing Public Goods: The Purchase of Moral Satisfaction.' *Journal of Environmental Economics and Management* 22:57-70

— . 1992b. 'Contingent Valuation and the Value of Public Goods: Reply.' *Journal of Environmental Economics and Management* 22:90-4

McKillop, William. 1992. 'Use of Contingent Valuation in Northern Spotted Owl Studies: A Critque.' *Journal of Forestry* 90(August):36-7

Mitchell, R.C. and R.T. Carson. 1989. *Using Surveys to Value Public Goods: The*

Contingent Valuation Method. Washington, DC: Resources for the Future

Pearse, Peter H. 1990. *An Introduction to Forestry Economics.* Vancouver: UBC Press. Chapter 4

Phillips, W.E., W.L. Adamowicz, J. Asafu-Adjaye, and P.C. Boxall. 1989. 'An Economic Assessment of the Value of Wildlife Resources to Alberta.' Department of Rural Economy Project Report No. 89-04. Edmonton: University of Alberta

Randall, Alan, J.P. Hoehn, and D. Brookshire. 1983. 'Contingent Valuation Surveys for Evaluating Environmental Assets.' *Natural Resources Journal* 23:637

Sinden, J.A. and A.C. Warrell. 1979. *Unpriced Values: Decisions without Market Prices.* New York: Wiley

Smith, V.K. 1992. 'Arbitrary Values, Good Causes, and Premature Verdicts.' *Journal of Environmental Economics and Management* 22:71-89

— . 1990. 'Can We Measure the Economic Value of Environmental Amenities?' *Southern Journal of Economics* 56(April):865-78

Thrice, A.H. and S.E. Wood. 1958. 'Measurement of Recreation Benefits.' *Land Economics* 34(August):195-207

Walsh, R.G., J.B. Loomis, and R.A. Gillman. 1984. 'Valuing Option, Existence, and Bequest Demands for Wilderness.' *Land Economics* 60(February):14-29

Wilman, Elizabeth A. 1988. 'Modeling Recreation Demands for Public Land Management.' In *Environmental Resources and Applied Welfare Economics,* edited by V.K. Smith. Washington, DC: Resources for the Future. 165-90

Part Three: Introduction

Meadows, Donella H., Dennis L. Meadows, Jorgen Randers, and William W. Behrens III. 1972. *The Limits to Growth.* New York: Universe

Schumacher, E.F. 1973. *Small is Beautiful.* New York: Harper & Row

World Commission on Environment and Development. 1987. *Our Common Future.* New York: Oxford University Press.

Chapter 8: Conservation, Sustainable Development, and Preservation

Anderson, F.J. 1985. *Natural Resources in Canada.* Toronto: Methuen. Chapter 4

Anonymous. 1992. 'Sharing. A Survey of the Global Environment.' *Economist* 30 May

Barbier, E.B., A. Markandya, and D.W. Pearce. 1990. 'Sustainable Agricultural Development and Project Appraisal.' *European Review of Agricultural Economics* 17:181-96

Barnett, Harold J. and Chandler Morse. 1963. *Scarcity and Growth.* Baltimore: Johns Hopkins University Press

Batie, Sandra S. 1989. 'Sustainable Development: Challenges to the Profession of Agricultural Economics.' *American Journal of Agricultural Economics* 71(December):1,083-101

— . 1990. 'Agricultural Policy and Environmental Goals: Conflict or Compatibility?' *Journal of Economic Issues* 24(June):565-73

Berkes, Fikret (ed.). 1989. *Common Property Resources. Ecology and Community-Based Sustainable Development.* London: Bellhaven

Bishop, Richard C. 1978. 'Endangered Species and Uncertainty: The Economics of a Safe Minimum Standard' *American Journal of Agricultural Economics* 60(February):10-18

Brundtland, Gro H. (Chair, World Commission on Environment and Development). 1987. *Our Common Future.* Oxford: Oxford University Press

Bunce, Arthur. 1942. *The Economics of Soil Conservation.* Ames: Iowa State College Press

Buttel, F.H. and M.E. Gertler. 1982. 'Agricultural Structure, Agricultural Policy, and Environmental Quality: Some Observations on the Context of Agricultural Research in North America.' *Agriculture and Environment* 7:101-19

Ciriacy-Wantrup, S.V. 1968. *Resource Conservation. Economics and Policies.* 3rd ed. Berkeley: University of California, Agricultural Experiment Station (original 1952)

Fisher, Anthony C. 1988. 'Key Aspects of Species Extinction: Habitat Loss and Overexploitation.' In *Environmental Resources and Applied Welfare Economics,* edited by V.K. Smith. Washington: Resources for the Future. 59-69

Fisher, Anthony C. and John V. Krutilla. 1985. 'Economics of Nature Preservation.' Chapter 4 in *Handbook of Natural Resource and Energy Economics, Vol. I,* edited by Allen V. Kneese and James L. Sweeney. Amsterdam: North-Holland

Hileman, B. 1990. 'Alternative Agriculture.' *Chemical and Engineering News* 68 (March):26-40

Lutz, E. and M. Young. 1990. 'Agricultural Policies in Industrial Countries and Their Environmental Impacts: Applicability to and Comparisons with Developing Nations.' Environment Working Paper No. 25. Washington: The World Bank. February

Madden, P. 1988. 'Low-Input/Sustainable Agricultural Research and Education — Challenges to the Agricultural Economics Profession.' *American Journal of Agricultural Economics* 70(December):1,166-72

Maurice, Charles and Charles W. Smithson. 1984. *The Doomsday Myth.* Stanford, CA: Hoover Institution

Meadows, Donella H., Dennis L. Meadows, Jorgen Randers, and William W. Behrens III. 1972. *The Limits to Growth.* New York: Universe

Norgaard, Richard B. 1984. 'Coevolutionary Development Potential.' *Land Economics* 60(May):160-73

— . 1985. 'Environmental Economics: An Evolutionary Critique and a Plea for Pluralism.' *Journal of Environmental Economics and Management* 12:382-94

Pezzey, J. 1989. 'Economic Analysis of Sustainable Growth and Sustainable Development.' Environment Department Working Paper No. 15. Washington: The World Bank, March

Prigogine, I. and I. Stengers. 1984. *Order Out of Chaos: Man's New Dialogue With Nature.* Toronto: Bantam

Scott, A. 1973. *Natural Resources. The Economics of Conservation.* Toronto: McClelland and Stewart. (Originally published in 1955.)

Scott, A. and P.H. Pearse. 1989. *Natural Resources in a High-Tech Economy: Scarcity versus Resourcefulness.* Forest Economics and Policy Analysis Research Unit Working Paper 117. Vancouver: UBC

Uimonen, Peter. 1992. 'Trade Policies and the Environment.' *Finance & Development.* (June):26-7

Chapter 9: Economics of Global Climatic Change

Adams, R.M. 1989. 'Global Climate Change and Agriculture: An Economic Perspective.' *American Journal of Agricultural Economics* 7(December):1,272-9

Arthur, L.M., V.J. Fields and F. Abizadeh. 1987. *Socio-Economic Assessment of the Implication of Climate Change for Agriculture in the Prairie Provinces: Phase III.* Report presented to the Atmospheric Environment Service. Winnipeg: Deparatment of Agricultural Economics, University of Manitoba. March

Canadian Wildlife Service. 1989. *Ecoclimatic Regions of Canada.* Ottawa: Supply and Services

Chapman, D. and T. Drennen. 1990. 'Equity and Effectiveness of Possible CO_2 Treaty Proposals.' *Contemporary Policy Issues* 8(July):16-28

Coward, Harold and Thomas Hurka (eds.). 1993. *Ethics and the Greenhouse Effect.* Waterloo: Wilfrid Laurier University Press

Crosson, P. 1989. 'Climatic Change and Mid-Latitudes Agriculture: Perspectives on Consequences and Policy Responses.' *Climatic Change* 11:51-73

Dudek, D.J. and A. LeBlanc. 1990. 'Offsetting New CO_2 Emissions: A Rational First Greenhouse Policy Step.' *Contemporary Policy Issues* 8(July):29-42

Grubb, M. 1989. *The Greenhouse Effect: Negotiating Targets.* Dartmouth: The Royal Institute of International Affairs.

— . 1990. *Energy Policies and the Greenhouse Effect, Vol. 1. Policy Appraisal.* Dartmouth: The Royal Institute of International Affairs

Hanson, K., G.A. Maul and T.R. Karl. 1989. 'Are Atmospheric Greenhouse Effects Apparent in Climatic Record of the Contiguous U.S. (1895-1987)?' *Geophysical Research Letters* 16:49-52.

Jackson, I. 1990. *Global Warming: Implications for Canadian Policy.* Ottawa: Institute for Research on Public Policy. September

Jaques, A.P. 1990. *National Inventory of Sources and Emissions of Carbon Dioxide.* Report EPS 5/AP/2. Ottawa: Environment Canada. May

Jones, P.D. and T.M.L. Wigley. 1990. 'Global Warming Trends.' *Scientific American* 263(August):84-91.

Kates, R.W., J.H. Ausubel, and M. Berberian (eds.). 1985. *Climate Impact Assessment: Studies of the Interaction of Climate and Society.* SCOPE 27. (Scientific Committee on Problems of the Environment, International Council of Scientific Unions.) Chichester, UK: Wiley

Kellogg, W.W. 1987. 'Mankind's Impact on Climate: The Evolution of Awareness.' *Climatic Change* 9:113-36

Kimball, B.A. 1983. 'Carbon Dioxide and Agricultural Yield: An Assemblage and Analysis of 430 Prior Observations.' *Agronomy Journal* 75(September-October):779-88

Kokoski, M.F. and V.K. Smith. 1987. 'A General Equilibrium Analysis of Partial-Equilibrium Welfare Measures: The Case of Climate Change.' *American Economic Review* 77(June):331-41

Kronberg, B.I. and W.S. Fyfe. 1992. 'Forest-Climate Interactions: Implications for Tropical and Boreal Forests.' Chapter 2 in *Emerging Issues in Forest Policy,* edited by P.N. Nemetz. Vancouver: UBC Press

Lave, L.B. 1982. 'Mitigating Strategies for Carbon Dioxide Problems.' *American Economic Review* 72(May):257-61

— . 1991. 'Formulating Greenhouse Policies in a Sea of Uncertainty.' *The Energy Journal* 12:9-21

Manne, A.S. and R.G. Richels. 1990. 'CO2 Emission Limits: An Economic Cost Analysis for the USA.' *The Energy Journal* 11(April):51-74

— . 1991. 'Global CO2 Emission Reductions – The Impacts of Rising Energy Costs.' *The Energy Journal* 12:87-108

Mooney, S. and L.M. Arthur. 1990. 'Impacts of 2 x CO2 on Manitoba Agriculture.' *Canadian Journal of Agricultural Economics* 38(December):685-94

Nordhaus, W.D. 1990. 'Global Warming: Slowing the Greenhouse Express.' Chapter 6 in *Setting National Priorities. Policy for the Nineties,* edited by H.J. Aaron. Washington: Brookings Institution

— . 1991. 'The Cost of Slowing Climate Change: A Survey.' *The Energy Journal* 12:37-66

Parry, M.L., T.R. Carter, and N.T. Konijn (eds.). 1987. *The Impact of Climatic Variations on Agriculture, Vol. 1. Assessments in Cool Temperate and Cold Regions.* Dordrecht: Reidel

Pollard, D.F.W. 1991. 'Forestry in British Columbia: Planning for Future Climate Today.' *Forestry Chronicle* 67(August):336-41

Rizzo, B. and E. Wiken. 1992. 'Assessing the Sensitivity of Canada's Ecosystems to Climatic Change.' *Climatic Change* 21:37-55

Rosenberg, N.J., W.E. Easterling III, P.R. Crosson, and J. Darmstadter (eds.). 1989. *Greenhouse Warming: Abatement and Adaptation.* Washington, DC: Resources for the Future

Rosenzweig, C. 1989. 'Global Climate Change: Predictions and Observations.' *American Journal of Agricultural Economics* 7(December):1,265-71

Schneider, S.H. 1989. 'The Changing Climate.' *Scientific American* 261(September):70-9

Smith, V.K. 1981. 'CO2, Climate, and Statistical Inference: A Note on Asking the Right Questions.' *Journal of Environmental Economics and Management* 8:391-4

Spencer, R.W. and J.R. Christy. 1990. 'Precise Monitoring of Global Temperature Trends from Satellites.' *Science* 247(March):1,558-62

Tobey, James, John Reilly, and Sally Kane. 1992. 'Economic Implications of Global Climate Change for World Agriculture.' *Journal of Agricultural and Resource Economics* 17(July):195-204

van Kooten, G.C. and L.M. Arthur. 1989. 'Assessing Economic Benefits of Climate Change on Canada's Boreal Forest.' *Canadian Journal of Forest Research* 19(April):463-70

van Kooten, G.C., L.M. Arthur, and W.R. Wilson. 1993. 'Potential to Sequester Carbon in Canadian Forests: Economic Considerations.' *Canadian Public Policy* 18(August):127-38

van Kooten, G.C., W.A. Thompson, and I. Vertinsky. 1992. 'Economics of Reforestation in British Columbia when Benefits of CO2 Reduction are Taken into Account.' Chapter 12 in *Forestry and the Environment: Economic Perspectives,* edited by W.A. White, W. Adamowicz, and W. Phillips. Wallingford, UK: CAB International

Whalley, John and Randall Wigle. 1991. 'Cutting CO2 Emissions: The Effects of Alternative Policy Approaches.' *The Energy Journal* 12:109-24

White, Robert M. 1990. 'The Great Climate Debate.' *Scientific American* 263(July):36-43

Williams, R.H. 1990. 'Low-Cost Strategies for Coping with CO_2 Emission Limits.' *The Energy Journal* 11:35-59

Wong, R.K.W., M. English, F.D. Barlow, L.Cheng, and K.R. Tremaine. 1989. *Towards a Strategy for Adapting to Climate Change in Alberta.* Edmonton: Alberta Research Council. 79 pp.

Chapter 10: Economics of Soil Conservation

Anderson, J.R. and J. Thampapillai. 1990. *Soil Conservation in Developing Countries: Project and Policy Intervention.* Policy & Research Series 8. Washington: World Bank

Barrett, Scott. 1991. 'Optimal Soil Conservation and the Reform of Agricultural Pricing Policies.' *Journal of Development Economics* 36(October):167-87

Bunce, Arthur. 1942. *The Economics of Soil Conservation.* Ames: Iowa State College Press

Burt, O.R. and M.S. Stauber. 1988. 'Dryland Cropping Decision Theory with Application to Saline Seep Control.' *Journal of Production Agriculture* 2:47-57

Butala, Sharon. 1990. 'Field of Broken Dreams.' *West* (An insert to the *Globe and Mail*) (June):30-9

Clark, E.H., J.A. Haverkamp, and W. Chapman. 1985. *Eroding Soils: The Off-Farm Impacts.* Washington: The Conservation Foundation

Conrad, Jon M. and Colin W. Clark. 1987. *Natural Resource Economics. Notes and Problems.* Cambridge: Cambridge Univ. Press

Crosson, P.R. and N.J. Rosenberg. 1989. 'Strategies for Agriculture.' *Scientific American* 261(3 September):128 35

Crosson, P.R. and A.T. Stout. 1983. *Productivity Effects of Cropland Erosion in the United States.* Washington, DC: Resources for the Future

Dickson, E.J. and G. Fox. 1989. *The Costs and Benefits of Erosion Control on Cropland in Southwestern Ontario.* Guelph: Department of Agriculture Economics and Business, University of Guelph

Dumanski, J., D.R. Coote, G. Luchiuk, and C. Lok. 1986. 'Soil Conservation in Canada.' *Journal of Soil and Water Conservation* (July/August):204-10

Fairbairn, Garry L. 1984. *Will the Bounty End? The Uncertain Future of Canada's Food Supply.* Saskatoon: Western Producer Prairie Books

Federal-Provincial Agriculture Committee on Environmental Sustainability (G. Leblond, Chairman). 1990. *Growing Together.* Ottawa: Supply and Services

Fox, G., A. Adamowicz, G. Debailleul, and P. Thomassin. 1990. *Agriculture and the Environment: Economic Dimensions of Sustainable Agriculture.* CAEFMS Occasional Publication No. 1. Guelph: Department of Agricultural Economics and Business. November. 45 pp.

Froster, Lynn, Chris P. Bardos, and Douglas D. Southgate. 1987. 'Soil Erosion and Water Conservation and Treatment Costs.' *Journal of Soil and Water Conservation* 42(5) 340-52

Huszar, Paul C. and Steven L. Piper. 1986. 'Estimating the Off-Site Costs of Wind Erosion in New Mexico.' *Journal of Soil and Water Conservation* 41: 414-16

Jefferson, R.W. and R.N. Boisvert. 1989. *A Guide to Using the General Algebraic Modelling System (GAMS) for Applications in Agricultural Economics*. Bulletin A.E. Res. 89-17. Ithaca, NY: Cornell University Agricultural Experiment Station

Lerohl, M.L. 1991. 'The Sustainability of Selected Prairie Crop Rotations.' *Canadian Journal of Agricultural Economics* 39(December):667-76

McConnell, K. 1983. 'An Economic Model of Soil Conservation.' *American Journal of Agricultural Economics* 65(February):83-9

Prairie Farm Rehabilitation Administration. 1983. *Land Degradation and Soil Conservation Issues on the Canadian Prairies*. Ottawa: Supply and Services

Rennie, D.A. 1989. 'Managing Soil Conservation: Sustainable Agriculture on the Prairies.' *AgriScience* (December):8-9

Rennie, D.A. and E. de Jong. 1989. 'Innovation Acres: Maintaining Productivity and Soil Quality.' *AgriScience* (December):5-6

Science Council of Canada. 1986. *A Growing Concern: Soil Degradation in Canada*. Ottawa: Science Council of Canada. September

Sparrow H.O. 1984. *Soil at Risk*. Report of the Standing Senate Committee on Agriculture, Fisheries and Forestry. Ottawa: Supply and Services

Thiessen, Shirley and G.C. van Kooten. 1991. 'Estimating Economic Damages from Wind Erosion from Draw Down of a Reservoir in the Interior of British Columbia.' Vancouver: Department of Agricultural Economics, University of BC, mimeograph

van Kooten, G.C. 1991. 'Improving Policy Instruments for Sustainable Agriculture.' *Canadian Journal of Agricultural Economics* 39(December):655-64

van Kooten, G.C. and W.H. Furtan. 1987. 'A Review of Issues Pertaining to Soil Degradation in Canada.' *Canadian Journal of Agricultural Economics* 35(March):33-54

van Kooten, G.C., Ward P. Weisensel, and Duangdao Chinthammit. 1990. 'Valuing Tradeoffs between Net Returns and Stewardship Practices: The Case of Soil Conservation in Saskatchewan.' *American Journal of Agricultural Economics* 72(February):104-13

van Kooten, G.C., Ward P. Weisensel, and E. de Jong. 1989. 'The Costs of Soil Erosion in Saskatchewan.' *Canadian Journal of Agricultural Economics* 37(March):63-75

Walker, David J. and Douglas L. Young. 1986. 'The Effect of Technical Progress on Erosion Damage and Economic Incentives for Soil Conservation.' *Land Economics* 62(February):83-93

Weisensel, Ward P. 1988. *The Economics of Soil Erosion in Saskatchewan: A Stochastic Dynamic Programming Approach*. Unpublished MSc thesis. Saskatoon: University of Saskatchewan

Weisensel, Ward P. and G.C. van Kooten. 1990. 'Estimation of Soil Erosion Time Paths: The Value of Soil Moisture and Top Soil Depth Information.' *Western Journal of Agricultural Economics* 15(July):63-72

Chapter 11: Efficiency and Equity in Land-Use Planning

Barlowe, Raleigh. 1986. *Land Resource Economics*. 4th edition. Englewood Cliffs, N.J.: Prentice-Hall

Epstein, Richard A. 1985. *Takings. Private Property and the Power of Eminent Domain.* Cambridge: Harvard University Press

Ervin, David E., James B. Fitch, R. Kenneth Godwin, W. Bruce Shepard, and Herbert H. Stoevener. 1977. *Land Use Control: Evaluating Economic and Political Effects.* Cambridge, MS: Ballinger

Hecht, Neil. 1965. 'From Sesin to Sit-in: Evolving Property Concepts.' *Boston University Law Review* 45:435-66

Lindblom, Charles E. 1959. 'The Science of Muddling Through, ' *Public Administration Review* 19:79-88

Lowe, Marcie D. 1989. *The Bicycle: Vehicle for a Small Planet.* Worldwatch Paper 90, September. Washington: World Watch Institute

— . 1990. *Alternatives to the Automobile: Transport for Livable Cities.* Worldwatch Paper 98, October Washington: World Watch Institute

Newman, Peter and Jeffrey Kenworthy. 1989. *Cities and Automobile Dependence: An International Sourcebook.* Aldershot, England: Gower

Sorensen, Donald M. and Herbert H. Stoevener (eds.). 1977. *Economic Issues in Land Use Planning.* Corvallis: Oregon State University, Agricultural Experiment Station Special Report 469. April

Chapter 12: Land Preservation and Conservation

Agriculture Canada, Communications Branch. 1991. 'News Release: Federal Government Announces New Safety Net Program for Farmers.' Ottawa, 11 January

Anderson, J.R. and J. Thampapillai. 1990. *Soil Conservation in Developing Countries: Project and Policy Intervention.* Policy & Research Series 8. Washington: World Bank

Batie, S.S. and A.G. Sappington. 1986. 'Cross-Compliance as a Soil Conservation Strategy: A Case Study.' *American Journal of Agricultural Economics* 68(November):880-5

Buttel, F.H. and M.E. Gertler. 1982. 'Agricultural Structure, Agricultural Policy, and Environmental Quality: Some Observations on the Context of Agricultural Research in North America.' *Agriculture and Environment* 7:101-19

Corbett, Ron (ed.). 1990. *Protecting Our Common Future: Conflict Resolution within the Farming Community.* Ottawa: Canada Mortgage and Housing Corporation

Federal-Provincial Agriculture Committee on Environmental Sustainability (G. Leblond, Chairman). 1990. *Growing Together.* Report to Ministers of Agriculture. June 30. Ottawa

Fox, G., A. Adamowicz, G. Debailleul, and P. Thomassin. 1990. *Agriculture and the Environment: Economic Dimensions of Sustainable Agriculture.* CAEFMS Occasional Publication No. 1. Guelph: Department of Agricultural Economics and Business. November. 45 pp.

Fox, M.F. 1988. 'Canada's Agricultural and Forest Lands: Issues and Policies.' *Canadian Public Policy* 14(September):266-81

Frankena, M.W. and D.T. Scheffman. 1980. *Economic Analysis of Provincial Land Use Policies in Ontario.* Toronto: University of Toronto Press

Girt, J. 1990. *Common Ground. Recommendations for Policy Reform to Integrate*

Wildlife Habitat, Environmental and Agricultural Objectives on the Farm. Ottawa: Wildlife Habitat Canada

Gray, Richard, Ward Weisensel, Ken Rosaasen, Hartley Furtan, and Daryl Kraft. 1991. 'A New Safety Net Program for Canadian Agriculture: GRIP.' *Choices* (3rd Quarter):34-5

Haigis, Bill and Will Young. 1983. *Methods of Preserving Wildlife Habitat.* Land Directorate Working Paper No. 25, Environment Canada (March). Ottawa: Supply and Services

Hodge, Ian. 1984. 'Uncertainty, Irreversibility and the Loss of Agricultural Land.' *Journal of Agricultural Economics* 35(May):191-202

Kennedy, John O.S. 1987. 'Uncertainty, Irreversibility and the Loss of Agricultural Land: A Reconsideration.' *Journal of Agricultural Economics* 38(January):75-80

Kirby, Michael G. and Michael J. Blyth. 1987. 'Economic Aspects of Land Degradation In Australia.' *Australian Journal of Agricultural Economics* 31(August):154-74

Lutz, E. and M. Young. 1990. *Agricultural Policies in Industrial Countries and their Environmental Impacts: Applicability to and Comparisons with Developing Nations.* Environment Working Paper No. 25 Washington: The World Bank

Painter, Kathleen M. and Douglas L. Young. 1990. 'Needed: More Federal Involvement in Water Quality Protection.' *Journal of Soil and Water Conservation* 45(2 March/April):280-2

Soil and Water Conservation Society. 1990. *Implementing the Conservation Title of the Food Security Act, A Field-Oriented Assessment by the Soil and Water Conservation Society.* Ankeny, Iowa

Stonehouse, D. Peter and Martin Bohl. 1990. 'Land Degradation Issues in Canadian Agriculture.' *Canadian Public Policy* 16(December):418-31

United States General Accounting Office. 1983. *Report to the Congress, Agriculture's Soil Conservation Programs Miss Full Potential in the Fight against Soil Erosion.* Comptroller General of United States, Washington, DC

— . 1990. *Farm Programs. Conservation Reserve Program Could Be Less Costly and More Effective.* GAO/RCED-90-13. Report to the Chairman, Committee on Agriculture, Nutrition, and Forestry, United States Senate, Washington, DC

van Kooten, G.C. 1993. 'Bioeconomic Evaluation of Government Programs on Wetlands Conversion.' *Land Economics* 69(February)

Veeman, Terrence S., Wiktor L. Adamowicz, and William E. Phillips. 1989. 'A Canadian Conservation Reserve Program: An Economic Perspective.' Staff Paper No. 89-12. Edmonton: Deptartment of Rural Economy, University of Alberta. 16 pp.

Warren C.L., A. Kerr and A.M. Turner (1989). *Urbanization of Rural Land in Canada, 1981-86.* Environment Canada SOE Fact Sheet No. 89-1. Ottawa: Supply and Services

Williams, G.D.V. 1983. 'Agroclimatic Resource Analyses: An Example using an Index Derived and Applied in Canada.' *Agricultural Meteorology* 28:31-47

Young, Douglas L., David J. Walker, and Paul L. Kanjo. 1991. 'Cost Effectiveness and Equity Aspects of Soil Conservation Programs in a Highly Erodible Region.' *American Journal of Agricultural Economics* 73(November):1,053-62

Chapter 13: Control over Water in Agriculture

Adams, G.D. 1987. *Prairie Pothole Project – Redvers: Baseline Habitat Evaluation.* Saskatoon: Environment Canada, Canadian Wildlife Service.

— . 1988a. 'Wetlands of the Prairies of Canada.' Chapter 5 in *Wetlands of Canada.* Ecological Land Classification Series No. 24, Environment Canada. Ottawa: Supply and Services

— . 1988b. 'Biological Evaluation Plan, 1988-89.' In *Prairie Pothole Project 1987 Annual Report* by R.D. Russell and R.M Howland. Regina: Saskatchewan Parks, Recreation and Culture, 77-90

Duebbert, Harold F. and Anthony M. Frank. 1984. 'Value of Prairie Wetlands to Duck Broods.' *Wildlife Society Bulletin* 12:27-34

Gardner, B. Delworth. In press. 'Irrigation Subsidies: Some Efficiency, Equity and Environmental Implications.' In *Essays in Honor of D. Gale Johnson,* edited by J. Antle and D. Sumner. Chicago: University of Chicago Press

Girt, J. 1990. *Common Ground. Recommendations for Policy Reform to Integrate Wildlife Habitat, Environmental and Agricultural Objectives on the Farm.* Ottawa: Wildlife Habitat Canada

Haigis, Bill and Will Young. 1983. *Methods of Preserving Wildlife Habitat.* Land Directorate Working Paper No. 25, Environment Canada (March). Ottawa: Supply and Services

Hammack, Judd and Gardner M. Brown, Jr. 1974. *Waterfowl and Wetlands: Toward Bioeconomic Analysis.* Baltimore: Johns Hopkins University Press

Hochbaum, G.S. and A.B. Didiuk. 1988. *Prairie Pothole Project: Evaluation of Waterfowl Populations, Production and Habitat Conditions on the Redvers, Saskatchewan Study Area.* Winnipeg: Canadian Wildlife Service, Environment Canada

Kantrud, Harold A. and Robert E. Stewart. 1984. 'Ecological Distribution and Crude Density of Breeding Birds on Prairie Wetlands.' *Journal of Wildlife Management* 48:426-37

Kantrud, Harold A., Gary L. Krapu and G.L. Swanson. 1988. *Use of Frequently Tilled Wetland Basins by Waterfowl and Aquatic Birds in the Dakotas.* Jamestown, ND: Northern Prairie Wildlife Research Center. Mimeograph

Melinchuk, Ross and Ron MacKay. 1986. *Prairie Pothole Project: Phase I. Final Report.* Regina: Wildlife Branch, Saskatchewan Parks and Renewable Resources. February 28

Pearce, David W. and R. Kerry Turner. 1990. *Economics of Natural Resources and the Environment* 5. Baltimore: Johns Hopkins University Press. Chapter 21

Phillips, W.E., W.L. Adamowicz, J. Asafu-Adjaye, and P.C. Boxall. 1989. *An Economic Assessment of the Value of Wildlife Resources in Alberta.* Project Report No. 89-04. Edmonton: Department of Rural Economy. August. 70 pp.

Prairie Farm Rehabilitation Administration. n.d. *Prairie Soil Prairie Water. The PFRA Story.* Regina: PFRA

Prins, R., W. Adamowicz, and W. Phillips. 1990. *Non-Timber Values and Forest Resources. An Annotated Bibliography.* Project Report No. 90-03. Edmonton: Department of Rural Economy. 27 pp.

Reisner, Marc. 1986. *Cadillac Desert.* New York: Penguin

Reisner, Marc and Sarah Bates. 1990. *Overtapped Oasis: Reform or Revolution for Western Water.* Wahington, DC: Island

Rubec, C.D.A., P. Lynch-Stewart, G.M. Wickware, and I. Kessel-Taylor. 1988. 'Wetland Utilization in Canada.' Chapter 10 in *Wetlands of Canada*. Ecological Land Classification Series No. 24, Environment Canada. Ottawa: Supply and Services

Stavins, Robert N. 1990. *The Welfare Economics of Alternative Renewable Resource Strategies. Forested Wetlands and Agricultural Production*. New York: Garland

Stavins, Robert N. and Adam B. Jaffe. 1990. 'Unintended Impacts of Public Investments on Private Decisions: The Depletion of Forested Wetlands.' *American Economic Review* 80(June):337-52

van Kooten, G.C. In Press. 'Preservation of Waterfowl Habitat in Western Canada: Is the North American Waterfowl Management Plan a Success?' *Natural Resources Journal*

— . 1993. 'Bioeconomic Evaluation of Government Agricultural Programs on Wetlands Conversion.' *Land Economics* 69(February)

van Kooten, G.C. and A. Schmitz. 1992. 'Preserving Waterfowl Habitat on the Canadian Prairies: Economic Incentives vs. Moral Suasion.' *American Journal of Agricultural Economics* 74(February):79-89

Chapter 14: Economics and Management of Public Forestlands

Anonymous. 1991. 'The Future of Forests: Tree-lover, Spare the Woodman.' *Economist*, 19-23 June

Binswanger, Hans P. 1989. *Brazilian Policies that Encourage Deforestation in the Amazon*. Environment Deptartment Working Paper No.16. Washington: The World Bank

Bowes, M.D. and J.V. Krutilla. 1989. *Multiple-Use Management: The Economics of Public Forestlands*. Washington: Resources for the Future

British Columbia Forest Resources Commission. 1991. *The Future of Our Forests*. Victoria: Queen's Printer

Brumelle, S.L., J.S. Carley, I.B. Vertinsky, and D.A. Wehrung. 1991. 'Evaluating Silvicultural Investments: A Review in the Canadian Context.' *Forestry Abstracts* 52(September):803-56

Duerr, William A. 1960. *Fundamentals of Forestry Economics*. New York: McGraw-Hill

Forestry Canada. 1990. *Forestry Facts*. Ottawa: Supply and Services

Goodland, Robert. 1991. *Tropical Deforestation: Solutions, Ethics and Religions*. Environment Working Paper No.43. Washington: The World Bank

Gregory, G. Robinson. 1972. *Forest Resource Economics*. New York: Ronald

Gunton, Thomas and John Richards (Supervisors). 1986. *Stein River Watershed Resource Evaluation*. Natural Resources Management Program Research Report No. 5. Burnaby: Simon Fraser University

Lonnstedt, Lars, Garry Merkel, and F.L.C. Reed. 1990. *The Outlook for Wood Fibre Supply in British Columbia: A Modelling Approach*. Forest Economics and Policy Analysis Research Unit Working Paper 153. Vancouver: UBC

Nemetz, Peter N. (ed.). 1992. *Emerging Issues in Forest Policy*. Vancouver: UBC Press

Pearse, Peter H. 1990. *An Introduction to Forestry Economics*. Vancouver: UBC Press. Chapters 5, 9, and 10.

Repetto, Robert. 1988. *The Forest for the Trees?* Washington: World Resources Institute

Repetto, Robert and Malcolm Gillis (eds.). 1988. *Public Policies and the Misuse of Forest Resources.* Cambridge: Cambridge University Press

Runyon, K.L. 1991. *Canada's Timber Supply: Current Status and Outlook.* Forestry Canada Information Report E-X-45. Ottawa: Supply and Services

Chapter 15: Economics and Public Rangeland Management

Bowes, Michael D. and John V. Krutilla. 1989. *Multiple-Use Management: The Economics of Public Forestlands.* Washington: Resources for the Future

Boyd, Ernst. 1991. 'A Model for Successional Change in a Grassland Ecosystem.' *Natural Resource Modeling* 5(Spring):161-89

Burt, O.R. 1971. 'A Dynamic Economic Model of Pasture and Range Investments.' *American Journal of Agricultural Economics* 53(May):197-205

Dyksterhuis, E.J. 1949. 'Condition and Management of Range Land Based on Quantitative Ecology.' *Journal of Range Management* 2(July):104-15

Godfrey, E.B. and C.A. Pope III. 1990. 'The Case for Removing Livestock from Public Rangelands.' In *Current Issues in Rangeland Resource Economics,* edited by F.W. Obermiller. Special Report 852. Corvallis: Oregon State University Extension Service, February. 6-23

Graham, J.D. and D. Borth. 1988. 'An Inventory Approach for Common Use Stock Range Units in British Columbia.' *Canadian Journal of Agricultural Economics* 36(July):279-94

Huffaker, R. and B.D. Gardner. 1987. 'Rancher Stewardship on Public Ranges: A Recent Court Decision.' *Natural Resources Journal* 27:887-98

Huffaker, R.G. and J.E. Wilen. 1989. 'Dynamics of Optimal Stocking in Plant/ Herbivore Systems.' *Natural Resource Modelling* 3/4(Fall):553-75

Martin, W.E. and G.L. Jefferies. 1966. 'Relating Ranch Prices and Grazing Permit Values to Ranch Productivity.' *Journal of Farm Economics* 48:233-42

Nordstrom, L. 1984. *The Ecology and Management of Forest Range in British Columbia: A Review and Analysis.* Land Management Report No. 19. Victoria: Ministry of Forests. November. 91 pp.

Obermiller, F.W. (ed.). 1989. *Current Issues in Rangeland Resource Economics.* Special Report 852. Corvallis: Oregon State University Extension Service. February

Obermiller, F.W. 1992a. *Costs Incurred by Permittees in Grazing Cattle on Public and Private Rangelands and Pastures in Eastern Oregon: 1982 and 1990.* Special Report 903. Corvallis: Oregon State University Extension Service. July. 32 pp.

— . 1992b. 'In Search of Reason: The Federal Grazing (Fee)Debate,' *Congressional Record – Senate.* August 6. S11703-18

Passmore, G. and C. Brown. 1991. 'Analysis of Rangeland Degradation using Stochastic Dynamic Programming.' *Australian Journal of Agricultural Economics* 35(August):131-55

Quigley, T.M. 1989. 'Value Shifts in Multiple Use Products from Rangelands.' *Rangelands* 11(December):275-9

Quigley, T.M. and J.W. Thomas. 1989. 'Range Management and Grazing Fees on the National Forests – A Time of Transition.' *Rangelands* 11(February):28-32

Roberts, N.K. 1963. 'Economic Foundation for Grazing Use Fees on Public Lands.' *Journal of Farm Economics* 45:721-31

Robinson, W.L. and E.G. Bolen. 1989. *Wildlife Ecology and Management.* 2nd edition. New York: Macmillan. Chapter 14

Southgate, D., J. Sanders, and S. Ehui. 1990. 'Resource Degradation in Africa and Latin America: Population Pressure, Policies, and Property Arrangements.' *American Journal of Agricultural Economics* 72(December):1,259-63

Stevens, J.B. and E.B. Godfrey. 1972. 'Use Rates, Resource Flows, and Efficiency of Public Investment in Range Improvements.' *American Journal of Agricultural Economics* 54(November):611-21

Torell, L. Allen and John P. Doll. 1991. 'Public Land Policy and the Value of Grazing Permits.' *Western Journal of Agricultural Economics* 16(July):174-84

Wagstaff, Fred J. (ed.). 1983. *Proceedings – Range Economics and Symposium Workshop.* U.S. Forest Service General Technical Report INT-149. Ogden: Intermountain Forest and Range Experiment Station

Workman, J.P. 1986. *Range Economics.* New York: MacMillan

Chapter 16: Management of Public Lands for Multiple Use

Anonymous. 1991. 'The Future of Forests.' *Economist,* June, 19-23

Bowes, Michael D. and John V. Krutilla. 1989. *Multiple-Use Management: The Economics of Public Forestlands.* Washington: Resources for the Future

Clary, W.P. 1983. 'Interfacing Physical Data and Economics.' In *Proceedings – Range Economics and Symposium Workshop,* compiled by Fred J. Wagstaff. U.S. Forest Service General Technical Report INT-149. Ogden: Intermountain Forest and Range Experiment Station. 115-19

Clawson, Marion. 1983. *The Federal Lands Revisited.* Washington, DC: Resources for the Future

Cory, D.C. and W.E. Martin. 1985. 'Valuing Wildlife for Efficient Multiple Use: Elk versus Cattle.' *Western Journal of Agricultural Economics* 10(December): 282-93

Godfrey, E.B. 1983. 'Economics and Multiple Use Management on Federal Rangelands.' In *Proceedings – Range Economics and Symposium Workshop,* compiled by Fred J. Wagstaff. U.S. Forest Service General Technical Report INT-149. Ogden: Intermountain Forest and Range Experiment Station. 77-81

Huffaker, R.G. and J.E. Wilen. 1989. 'Dynamics of Optimal Stocking in Plant/ Herbivore Systems.' *Natural Resource Modelling* 3/4(Fall):553-75

Huffaker, R.G., J.E. Wilen, and B.D. Gardner. 1989. 'Multiple Use Benefits on Public Rangelands: An Incentive-Based Fee System.' *American Journal of Agricultural Economics* 71(August):670-78

— . 1990. 'A Bioeconomic Livestock/Wild Horse Trade-off Mechanism for Conserving Public Rangeland Vegetation.' *Western Journal of Agricultural Economics* 15(July):73-82

Hyde, William F. and Steven E. Daniels. 1988. 'Balancing Market and Nonmarket Outputs on Public Forest Lands.' In *Environmental Resources and Applied Welfare Economics,* edited by V.K. Smith. Washington: Resources for the Future. 135-61

Lambrecht, Kirk N. 1991. *The Administration of Dominion Lands, 1870-1930.*

Regina: Canadian Plains Research Center, University of Regina

MacDonald, David (Chairperson). 1992. *Environment and the Constitution*. Report of the Standing Committee on Environment. Ottawa: House of Commons Issue No. 30. March

Martin, W.E., J.C. Tinney, and R.L. Gum. 1978. 'A Welfare Economics Analysis of the Potential Competition between Hunting and Cattle Ranching.' *Western Journal of Agricultural Economics* 3(December):87-97

Nemetz, Peter N. (ed.). 1992. *Emerging Issues in Forest Policy*. Vancouver: UBC Press

Nordstrom, L. 1984. *The Ecology and Management of Forest Range in British Columbia: A Review and Analysis*. Land Management Report No. 19. Victoria: Ministry of Forests, November. 91 pp.

Obermiller, F.W. 1982. 'Economic Efficiency vs. Distributive Equity: the Sagebrush Rebellion. ' *Western Journal of Agricultural Economics* 7(1982):253-63

Pearse, Peter H. 1990. *An Introduction to Forestry Economics*. Vancouver: University of British Columbia Press. Chapters 5, 9, and 10

Pitt, M.D. 1982. *East Kootenay Problem Analysis. The Interactions among Grass, Trees, Elk and Cattle*. Victoria: Research Branch, Ministry of Forests. February. 65 pp.

Quigley, T.M. 1989. 'Value Shifts in Multiple Use Products from Rangelands.' *Rangelands* 11:275-9

Standiford, Richard B. and Richard E. Howitt. 1992. 'Solving Empirical Bioeconomic Models: A Rangeland Management Application.' *American Journal of Agricultural Economics* 74(May):421-33

Steinkamp, Eric A. and David R. Betters. 1991. 'Optimal Control Theory Applied to Joint Production of Timber and Forage.' *Natural Resource Modeling* 5 (Spring):147-60

Part Five: Conclusions

Dooyeweerd, H. 1979. *Roots of Western Culture*. Toronto: Wedge Foundation

Chapter 17: Ethics and Land Resource Economics

Arthur, J. and W.H. Shaw. 1978. *Justice and Economic Distribution*. Englewood Cliffs, NJ: Prentice-Hall

Ayer, A.J. 1982. *Philosophy in the Twentieth Century*. New York: Vintage

Barbour, I.G. 1980. *Technology, Environment and Human Values*. New York: Praeger

Block, W., G. Brennan, and K. Elzinga (eds.). 1985. *Morality of the Market. Religious and Economic Perspectives*. Vancouver: Fraser Institute

Bruce, J.P. 1991. 'Myths and Realities of Global Climate Change.' *Ecodecision* 1(1):89-92

Coward, H. and T. Hurka (eds.). 1993. *Ethics and Climate Change: The Greenhouse Effect*. Waterloo: Wilfrid Laurier University Press

Daly, Herman E. and John B. Cobb, Jr. 1989. *For the Common Good*. Boston: Beacon

d'Arge, R.C., W.D. Schulze, and D.S. Brookshire. 1982. 'Carbon Dioxide and Intergenerational Choice.' *American Economic Review* 72(May):251-6

De Witt, Calvin B. (ed.). 1991. *The Environment and the Christian.* Grand Rapids: Baker Book House

Dooyeweerd, H. 1979. *Roots of Western Culture.* Toronto: Wedge Foundation

Ehrenfeld, David. 1988. 'Why Put a Value on Biodiversity?' In *Biodiversity,* edited by E.O. Wilson and F.M. Peter. Washington: National Academy Press. Chapter 24

Elster, Jon. 1979. *Ulysses and the Sirens.* Cambridge: Cambridge University Press

Epstein, Richard A. 1985. *Takings: Private Property and the Power of Eminent Domain.* Cambridge, MA: Harvard University Press

Fischhoff, B., S. Lichtenstein, P. Slovic, S.L. Derby, and R.L. Keeney. 1981. *Acceptable Risk.* Cambridge: Cambridge University Press

Gauthier, D. 1983. 'On the Refutation of Utilitarianism.' In *The Limits of Utilitarianism,* edited by H.B. Miller and W.H. Williams. Minneapolis: University of Minnesota Press

— . 1986. *Morals by Agreement.* Oxford: Oxford University Press

Granberg-Michaelson, Wesley. 1988. *Ecology and Life: Accepting our Environmental Responsibility.* Waco, TX: Word

Hahn, F. and M. Hollis (eds.). 1979. *Philosophy and Economic Theory.* New York: Oxford University Press

Harsanyi, J.C. 1982. 'Morality and the Theory of Rational Behaviour.' In *Utilitarianism and Beyond,* edited by A. Sen and B. Williams. Cambridge: Cambridge University Press. 39-62

Hayek, von F.A. 1944. *The Road to Serfdom.* Chicago: University of Chicago Press

— . 1988. *The Fatal Conceit: The Errors of Socialism.* In *The Collected Works of F.A. Hayek, Vol. 1,* edited by W.W. Bartley III. Chicago: University of Chicago Press

Kneese, Allen V. and William D. Schulze. 1985. 'Ethics and Environmental Economics.' Chapter 5 in *Handbook of Natural Resource and Energy Economics, Vol. I,* edited by Allen V. Kneese and James L. Sweeney. Amsterdam: North-Holland

Norgaard, R.B. 1991. *Sustainability as Intergenerational Equity: The Challenge to Economic Thought and Practice.* Internal Discussion Paper, Asia Regional Series, Report No. IDP97. Washington: World Bank, June. 75 pp

Nozick, R. 1974. *Anarchy, State, and Utopia.* New York: Basic

Page, T. 1988. 'Intergenerational Equity and the Social Discount Rate.' In *Environmental Resources and Applied Welfare Economics,* edited by V.K. Smith. Washington: Resources for the Future. 71-89

Pearce, David W. and R. Kerry Turner. 1990. *Economics of Natural Resources and the Environment.* Baltimore: Johns Hopkins University Press. Chapter 15

Randall, Alan, 1988. 'What Mainstream Economists Have to Say about the Value of Biodiversity.' Chapter 25 in *Biodiversity,* edited by E.O. Wilson and F.M. Peter. Washington: National Academy Press

Rawls, J. 1971. *A Theory of Justice.* Cambridge, MA: Harvard University Press

— . 1982. 'Social Unity and Primary Goods.' In *Utilitarianism and Beyond,* edited by A. Sen and B. Williams. Cambridge: Cambridge University Press. 159-86

Rolston, H. III. 1988. *Environmental Ethics. Duties to and Values in the Natural World.* Philadelphia: Temple University Press

Russell, B. 1979. *History of Western Philosophy.* London: Unwin Paperbacks (original 1946)

Schaeffer, Francis A. 1972. *Genesis in Space and Time.* Downers Grove, IL: Intervarsity Press

Slovic, P., B. Fischhoff, and S. Lichtenstein. 1979. 'Rating the Risk.' *Environment* 21:(3):14-20, 36-9

Smith, M., R.S. Lindzen, and W.F.J. Evans. 1991. 'Assessment of Intergovernmental Panel on Climate Change.' Calgary: Canadian Petroleum Association, Mimeograph (July).

Sturdy, J., P. Nemetz, D. Uyeno, I. Vertinsky, P. Vertinsky, and A. Vining. 1980. 'An Adaptive Information Policy for Management of Chemical Risks in the Environment.' *Journal of Business Administration* 11:319-66

White, L. Jr. 1973. 'The Historical Roots of Our Ecological Crisis.' In *Western Man and Environmental Ethics,* edited by I.G. Barbour. Reading, MA: Addison-Wesley. 18-30

Wolf, Charles Jr. 1988. *Markets or Government: Choosing between Imperfect Alternatives.* Cambridge, MA: MIT

Index

Printed on acid-free paper ∞

Set in Stone by The Typeworks

Printed and bound in Canada by
D.W. Friesen & Sons Ltd.

Copy-editor: Joanne Richardson

Proofreader: Camilla Jenkins